THE BURIED

ALSO BY PETER HESSLER

Strange Stones

Country Driving

Oracle Bones

River Town

Akhenaten and Nefertiti distributing rewards to a faithful official named Huya. This scene appears in Huya's tomb, which dates to the fourteenth century BC. *The faces and names of the royal couple were removed at the command of a subsequent ruler.*

THE BURIED

An Archaeology of the Egyptian Revolution

Peter Hessler

PENGUIN PRESS ◆ NEW YORK ◆ 2019

PENGUIN PRESS
An imprint of Penguin Random House LLC
penguinrandomhouse.com

ISBN 9780525559566 (hardcover)
ISBN 9780525559573 (ebook)

Printed in the United States of America
1 3 5 7 9 10 8 6 4 2

Book design and page ornamentation by Daniel Lagin
Endpaper maps and timelines by Angela Hessler
Illustrations by Meighan Cavanaugh

For Doug Hunt

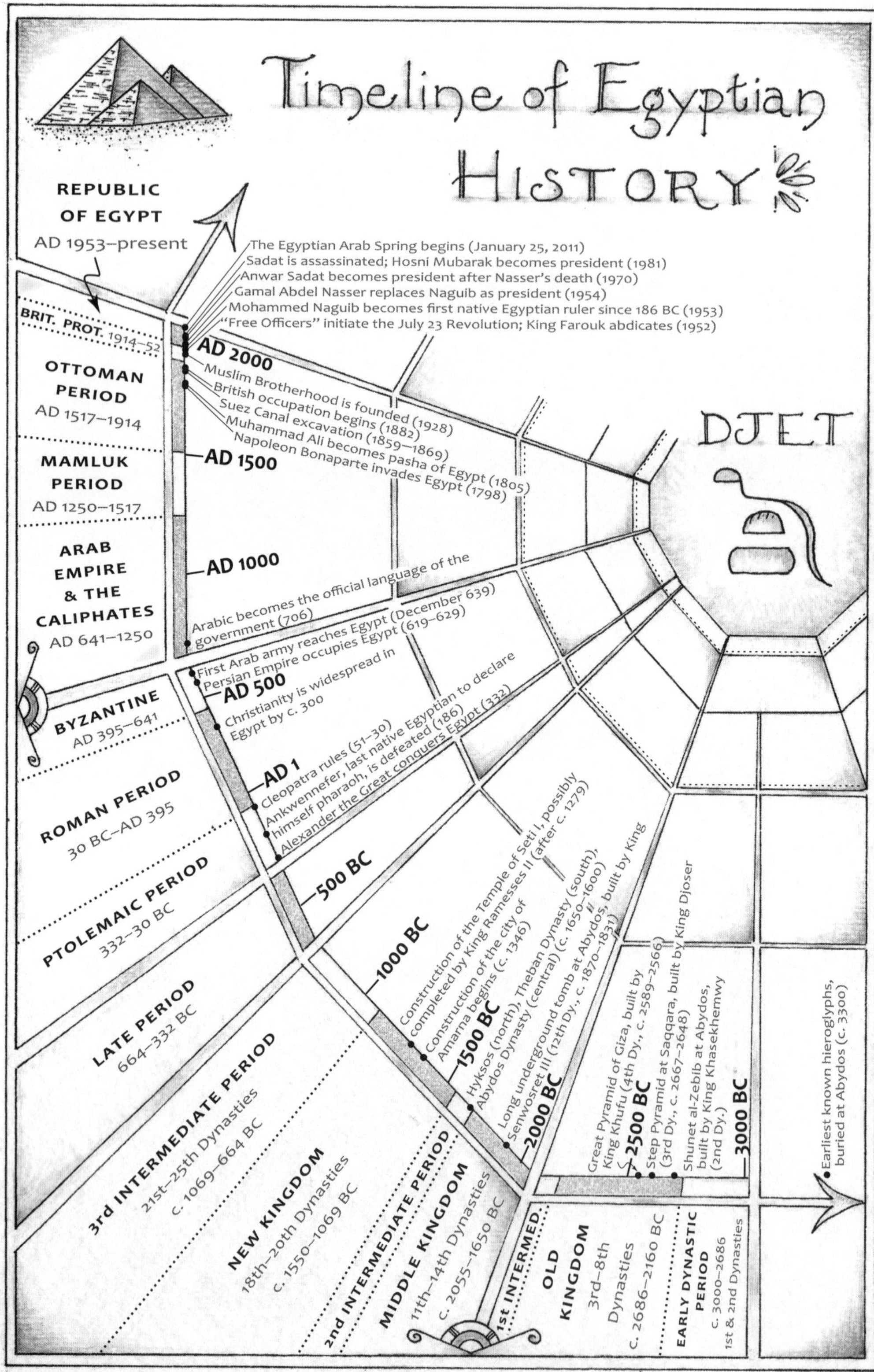

Timeline of Egyptian History
REPUBLIC OF EGYPT
AD 1953–present
The Egyptian Arab Spring begins (January 25, 2011)
Sadat is assassinated; Hosni Mubarak becomes president (1981)
Anwar Sadat becomes president after Nasser's death (1970)
Gamal Abdel Nasser replaces Naguib as president (1954)
Mohammed Naguib becomes first native Egyptian ruler since 186 BC (1953)
"Free Officers" initiate the July 23 Revolution; King Farouk abdicates (1952)
BRIT. PROT. 1914–52
AD 2000
Muslim Brotherhood is founded (1928)
British occupation begins (1882)
Suez Canal excavation (1859–1869)
Muhammad Ali becomes pasha of Egypt (1805)
Napoleon Bonaparte invades Egypt (1798)
OTTOMAN PERIOD
AD 1517–1914
DJET
MAMLUK PERIOD
AD 1250–1517
AD 1500
ARAB EMPIRE & THE CALIPHATES
AD 641–1250
AD 1000
Arabic becomes the official language of the government (706)
First Arab army reaches Egypt (December 639)
Persian Empire occupies Egypt (619–629)
AD 500
Christianity is widespread in Egypt by c. 300
BYZANTINE
AD 395–641
Cleopatra rules (51–30)
AD 1
Ankwennefer, last native Egyptian to declare himself pharaoh, is defeated (186)
Alexander the Great conquers Egypt (332)
ROMAN PERIOD
30 BC–AD 395
PTOLEMAIC PERIOD
332–30 BC
500 BC
LATE PERIOD
664–332 BC
1000 BC
Construction of the Temple of Seti I, possibly completed by King Ramesses II (after c. 1279)
Construction of the city of Amarna begins (c. 1346)
1500 BC
Hyksos (north), Theban Dynasty (south), Abydos Dynasty (central) (c. 1650–1600)
Long underground tomb at Abydos, built by King Senwosret III (12th Dy., c. 1870–1831)
2000 BC
Great Pyramid of Giza, built by King Khufu (4th Dy., c. 2589–2566)
2500 BC
Step Pyramid at Saqqara, built by King Djoser (3rd Dy., c. 2667–2648)
Shunet al-Zebib at Abydos, built by King Khasekhemwy (2nd Dy.)
3000 BC
Earliest known hieroglyphs, buried at Abydos (c. 3300)
3rd INTERMEDIATE PERIOD
21st–25th Dynasties
c. 1069–664 BC
NEW KINGDOM
18th–20th Dynasties
c. 1550–1069 BC
2nd INTERMEDIATE PERIOD
MIDDLE KINGDOM
11th–14th Dynasties
c. 2055–1650 BC
1st INTERMED.
OLD KINGDOM
3rd–8th Dynasties
c. 2686–2160 BC
EARLY DYNASTIC PERIOD
c. 3000–2686
1st & 2nd Dynasties

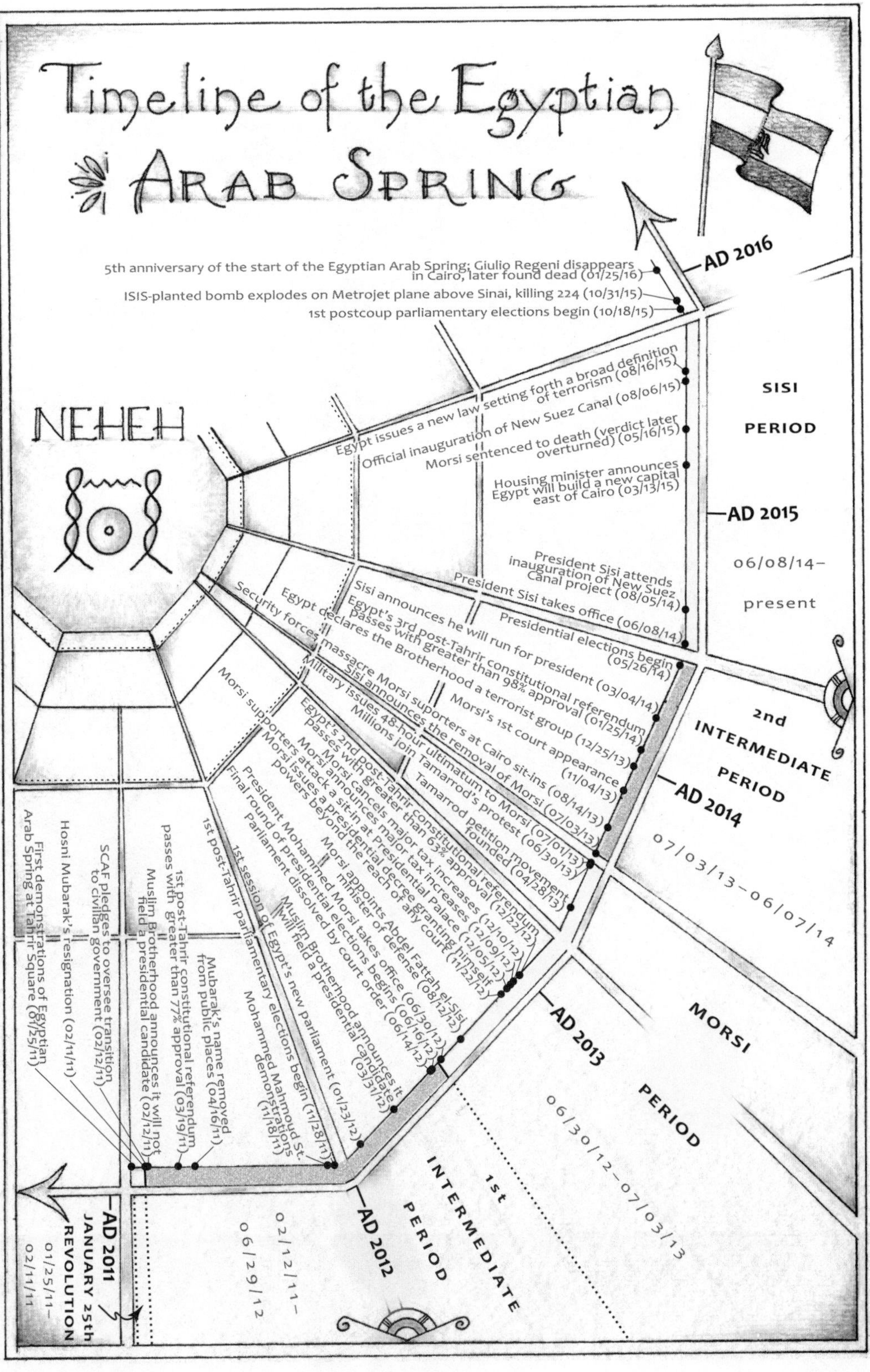

Timeline of the Egyptian
Arab Spring
NEHEH
AD 2016
5th anniversary of the start of the Egyptian Arab Spring; Giulio Regeni disappears in Cairo, later found dead (01/25/16)
ISIS-planted bomb explodes on Metrojet plane above Sinai, killing 224 (10/31/15)
1st postcoup parliamentary elections begin (10/18/15)
Egypt issues a new law setting forth a broad definition of terrorism (08/16/15)
Official inauguration of New Suez Canal (08/06/15)
Morsi sentenced to death (verdict later overturned) (05/16/15)
Housing minister announces Egypt will build a new capital east of Cairo (03/13/15)
SISI PERIOD
AD 2015
06/08/14–present
President Sisi attends inauguration of New Suez Canal project (08/05/14)
President Sisi takes office (06/08/14)
Presidential elections begin (05/26/14)
Sisi announces he will run for president (03/04/14)
Egypt's 3rd post-Tahrir constitutional referendum passes with greater than 98% approval (01/25/14)
Egypt declares the Brotherhood a terrorist group (12/25/13)
Morsi's 1st court appearance (11/04/13)
Security forces massacre Morsi suporters at Cairo sit-ins (08/14/13)
Sisi announces the removal of Morsi (07/03/13)
Military issues 48-hour ultimatum to Morsi (07/01/13)
Millions join Tamarrod's protest (06/30/13)
Tamarrod petition movement founded (04/28/13)
2nd INTERMEDIATE PERIOD
AD 2014
07/03/13–06/07/14
Egypt's 2nd post-Tahrir constitutional referendum passes with greater than 63% approval (12/22/12)
Morsi cancels major tax increases (12/10/12)
Morsi announces major tax increases (12/09/12)
Morsi supporters attack a sit-in at Presidential Palace (12/05/12)
Morsi issues a presidential decree granting himself powers beyond the reach of any court (11/22/12)
Morsi appoints Abdel Fattah el-Sisi minister of defense (08/12/12)
President Mohammed Morsi takes office (06/30/12)
Final round of presidential elections begins (06/16/12)
Parliament dissolved by court order (06/14/12)
Muslim Brotherhood announces it will field a presidential candidate (03/31/12)
1st session of Egypt's new parliament (01/23/12)
1st post-Tahrir parliamentary elections begin (11/28/11)
Mohammed Mahmoud St. demonstrations (11/18/11)
Mubarak's name removed from public places (04/16/11)
1st post-Tahrir constitutional referendum passes with greater than 77% approval (03/19/11)
Muslim Brotherhood announces it will not field a presidential candidate (02/12/11)
SCAF pledges to oversee transition to civilian government (02/12/11)
Hosni Mubarak's resignation (02/11/11)
First demonstrations of Egyptian Arab Spring at Tahrir Square (01/25/11)
MORSI PERIOD
AD 2013
06/30/12–07/03/13
1st INTERMEDIATE PERIOD
AD 2012
02/12/11–06/29/12
AD 2011
JANUARY 25th REVOLUTION
01/25/11–02/11/11

CONTENTS

THE BURIED

Part One

THE PRESIDENT

Worship the king within your bodies,
Be well disposed towards His Majesty in your minds.
Cast dread of him daily,
Create jubilation for him every instant.
. . . .
He sees what is in hearts;
His eyes, they search out every body.

—*The Loyalist Instruction,*
nineteenth century BC

CHAPTER 1

ON JANUARY 25, 2011, ON THE FIRST DAY OF THE EGYPTIAN ARAB SPRING, nothing happened in Abydos. There were no demonstrations, no crowds, and no problems for the police. By that point in the winter excavation season, only one unusual incident had occurred. Earlier that month, a team of archaeologists from Brown University had uncovered a hole that contained two small bronze statues of Osiris, a small stone statue of the god Horus in child form, and exactly three hundred bronze coins.

The archaeologists had been excavating a series of tombs that had been looted thoroughly during antiquity, and they had neither expected nor hoped to find such relics. For Laurel Bestock, who was directing the dig, the immediate reaction was mixed. Along with the thrill of discovery, she felt a wave of nervousness, because now the team had to deal with more intense issues of security and bureaucracy. The local police contacted their superiors, and an official from the Egyptian Ministry of Antiquities arrived. There was a great deal of paperwork to be filled out. Over a period of days, Bestock and the others worked long hours, and they painstakingly cleaned, measured, and photographed each of the coins and statues. Then everything was transported to Sohag, the capital of the region. The artifacts were locked in a wooden box that was placed in the back of a pickup truck and escorted by half a dozen policemen armed with rifles.

The objects themselves weren't especially valuable. None of the statues was taller than ten inches, which made the departing procession—the truck, the police, the guns—slightly comical. The coins dated to the mid-Ptolemaic period, between the third and second centuries BC, which is late by the standards of Egyptology. For the archaeologists, the true value of the discovery was its context, because the relics appeared to have been interred as part of some ancient ritual. But this wasn't what people would talk about in the surrounding villages, where the alchemy of rumor was bound to transform the coins from bronze to gold, and the statues from modest pieces to relics as valuable as Tutankhamun's funerary mask. The worst-case scenario would be for such a discovery to be followed by some breakdown in civil order. But there was no reason to expect that this might occur. President Hosni Mubarak had ruled Egypt for almost thirty years, and protests in the capital rarely affected remote parts of the country.

On January 26, 2011, the second day of the Egyptian Arab Spring, nothing happened in Abydos.

The archaeologists had been working to the west of the local settlements, in an ancient necropolis that villagers refer to as *al-Madfuna:* the Buried. The Buried contains the earliest known royal graves in Egypt, and it's also home to one of the oldest standing mud-brick buildings in the world. This structure dates to around 2660 BC, with nearly forty-foot-high walls that form a massive rectangular enclosure. Nobody is certain of its original purpose. The local Arabic name—*Shunet al-Zebib,* "Storehouse of Raisins"—is another mystery. At various times, people have speculated that it was once a depot for goods or animals. Auguste Mariette, a French archaeologist who worked here in the middle of the nineteenth century, suggested without citing any evidence that the structure had been a "sort of police station." This theory seems to have been a projection of Mariette's concerns about looting, which has been a problem in Abydos for approximately five thousand years.

On January 28, 2011, in Cairo, on the fourth day of the Egyptian Arab Spring, tens of thousands of people gathered in Tahrir Square, and somebody set fire to the nearby headquarters of Mubarak's National Democratic Party.

In Abydos, the team from Brown University had already returned home, and now another group of archaeologists had arrived from the Institute of Fine Arts at New York University. This group was restoring parts of the Shunet al-Zebib, or the Shuna, as the structure is usually called. The NYU team was led by an archaeologist named Matthew Adams. He was forty-eight years old, and he had the well-cooked appearance of any Westerner who has spent a career in the Sahara. His ears and cheeks were red, and the shadow of his shirt line had been permanently burned into his neck and chest—a V-shaped hieroglyph that means "Egyptologist."

Adams's career in Abydos represented an exact parallel with the span of the Mubarak regime. The American first worked in the necropolis in the fall of 1981, as an undergraduate intern. That October, shortly after the archaeological season started, President Anwar Sadat was assassinated during a military parade in Cairo. After the assassination, Mubarak was elevated from vice president to the highest office, and the capital remained stable. Other than an increased police presence, there was no noticeable impact on Abydos. As an intern, Adams was assigned the lowly task of sorting thousands of pieces of ancient pottery. He still recalled the autumn of Sadat's assassination as the most tedious season he ever spent in Egypt.

This experience influenced Adams's response to the early Tahrir protests. When NYU administrators began to talk about evacuating the team, Adams resisted. He knew that looting would be much more likely if the foreigners left the dig house where they resided in the necropolis. But on February 1, 2011, at least 200,000 people gathered on Tahrir. Police were abandoning their posts across the country, and mobs had overrun a number of prisons. At the Wadi al-Natroun Prison, in the desert northwest of Cairo, attackers had freed hundreds of criminals, political prisoners, and Islamists, including a leader of the Muslim Brotherhood named Mohammed Morsi.

After the prison breaks, Adams decided to evacuate. It took three days to arrange a charter plane that would transport the team directly from Luxor to Athens. On the way to the airport, the archaeologists tried to organize a McDonald's run, but one effect of the revolution was that the Luxor franchise had run out of meat.

Within hours of the foreigners' departure, looters appeared in the Buried. The dig house employed private guards, who typically called the authorities if there was a serious problem. But now the police didn't respond. The guards chased off the first thieves, and a few hours later, at two o'clock in the morning, a larger band of men arrived. Their faces were covered by masks and they carried tools for excavation. They confronted the guards, warning them that they would be killed if they didn't abandon the site.

The dig house was managed by Ahmed Ragab. He was nearly forty years old, a calm, capable man who came from Aswan, in the far south. At Egyptian archaeological sites, it's common for foreigners to hire a manager from another part of the country so that he'll be free from local pressures of family and tribe. Ahmed knew that these same pressures also represented his best hope against the looters. Many of them carried guns, but as long as they were from Abydos, they probably wouldn't shoot the unarmed site guards. If outsiders arrived, though, they might not feel the same restraint.

For Ahmed, the fear wasn't so much that artifacts would be stolen. After millennia of looting, and after more than a century of professional archaeology, most easily found objects of value had already been extricated from the necropolis. But looters never understood this, and by digging rapidly in the dark, they were likely to damage underground structures that had yet to be properly studied. Many thieves must have heard about the recently excavated statues and coins, because they targeted the site of those discoveries.

On February 11, a government official appeared on national television and announced that Mubarak had vacated the office of president. Around the same time, outsiders began to arrive in the Buried, and some of them were inspired by the long tradition of magical beliefs in Upper Egypt. One evening, the guards caught and interrogated a young looter who had come from Nagaa Hammadi, a town more than an hour to the south. The young man said that a sheikh in his village had performed a divination and declared that treasure could be found in Abydos. Ahmed tried to contact the police, but they remained unresponsive, so the guards released the looter.

In addition to having management skills, Ahmed was good with a hammer and a saw. He decided there was one last thing he could do to defend the site. At the dig house, he gathered some lumber, nails, and paint, and he went to work.

The ancient Egyptians first divided their land into Upper and Lower, a classification that confuses moderns who orient themselves by the compass rather than by the river. South is up, north is down: the imagination has to be recalibrated in this part of the country.

Even the most basic terms of the landscape are difficult to grasp. In Upper Egypt, the Nile has carved a deep gorge into the North African plateau, and thirty million people make their homes here, more than the combined populations of Lebanon, Jordan, Israel, and Libya. But all of these Upper Egyptians are concentrated into a valley that in many places is less than ten miles wide. This band of green, like an oasis stretched thin, is surrounded by a desert so large that it seems galactic. At Abydos, if you start at the banks of the Nile and head due west, the next river you encounter will be in southern Florida.

The Buried represents the first step into this vast emptiness. It sits on a broad shelf just above the cultivation, where the transition from soil to sand is as abrupt as a border drawn onto a map. There are no villages in the necropolis, and virtually nothing grows there; the expanse of sand and rubble continues for most of a mile to the western wall of the gorge. This cliff rises five hundred feet, and it's broken by a single wadi, or canyon, that winds up to the North African plateau. In ancient times, this wadi was believed to be the entrance to the afterlife: souls followed the canyon to the mysteries of the setting sun.

The first line of kings who unified Egypt built their tombs near the mouth of the wadi. The earliest known written words in Egypt, which date to around 3300 BC, were discovered in these graves. The hieroglyphs were inscribed into labels made of ivory, because in those days elephants still roamed the Egyptian highlands. By the beginning of the First Dynasty, around 3000 BC, kings were already ruling from near present-day Cairo, where it was easier to control both Upper and Lower Egypt. But they returned to construct tombs and carry out rituals in Abydos, which is believed to have been their ancestral homeland. Eventually, the necropolis became a pilgrimage site, with people coming from all over Egypt to participate in a festival to the god Osiris that was held annually for more than a millennium. Ancient Egyptians called this place the Terrace of the Great God. It was isolated but accessible, mysterious but visible, lifeless but animated with the royal and the divine. Matthew Adams describes it as a kind of theater. The Buried is the stage; the cliffs are the backdrop; the villages are the audience. And the first actors to step upon this stage were the kings who defined the essence of political power.

The week that Mubarak was forced from office, Ahmed constructed a large rectangular wooden box in the dig house yard. The box was thirteen feet long and six feet high, with a bottom that was left open except for a series of interior struts. The sides were smooth. Ahmed painted the box a dark blue-black color.

One group of looters was so emboldened that they drove a bulldozer into the Buried. The remains of the last Egyptian royal pyramid are located here, on the southern end of the site, and the bulldozer thieves excavated a ten-foot-deep trench in front of the ruined monument. Another group of looters went to the base of the western cliffs and tunneled straight down for a dozen feet, although they weren't close to any burial. But perhaps some sheikh had told them that they would find treasure beneath the cliffs.

Balyana, the local district center, is about six miles east of Abydos, and Ahmed went there to purchase a rooftop rack of fake police flashers. He installed the lights atop his wooden box, along with a siren. The other guards helped him hoist the box onto his four-wheel drive Daihatsu.

In the dark, the vehicle was a strikingly good imitation of the armored personnel carriers that are ubiquitous at any Egyptian tourist site. Every night, Ahmed and the guards drove the fake APC around the Buried, lights flashing, siren blaring. Soon they began to hear rumors in the village that the police were active again. During daytime, Ahmed hid the wooden APC frame within the walls of the Shuna, thus at last fulfilling Auguste Mariette's theory that the mud-brick structure was a police station.

There were no other proposals for protecting the site. Every evening was the same: drive into the Buried, ring the siren, roll the lights. Leave the fake APC in the Shuna before dawn. After sunset, do it all over again. Months later, many Egyptians who were active in the first wave of the Arab Spring would describe their experiences in similar terms. Nothing seemed to exist but the present: no time for plans, no time for memories. But eventually a sense of order was restored. In Cairo, a council of military officers established a transitional government, and they promised to hold democratic elections for a new parliament and a new president. Tahrir celebrated; the street clashes ended. By late March, real police were patrolling again in Abydos. And once the intensity of the moment passed, time returned to normal, and people thought about what had just occurred and what might happen next.

Ancient Egyptians had words for two different kinds of time: *djet* and *neheh*. These terms cannot be translated into English, and it may be impossible for them to be grasped by the modern mind. In our world, time is a straight line, and one event leads to another; the accumulation of these events, and the actions of the people who matter, are what make history. But for ancient Egyptians, time was not linear, and events—*kheperut*—were suspect. They were oddities, distractions; they interrupted the world's natural order. History did not exist as we would define it. The Egyptians were writing by 3300 BC, and they were still writing in 332 BC, when they were conquered by Alexander the Great, but across those three millennia they never produced anything that would be considered a work of history in the modern sense.

Neheh is the time of cycles. It's associated with the movement of the sun, the passage of the seasons, and the annual flood of the Nile. It repeats; it recurs; it renews. *Djet,* on the other hand, is time without motion. When a king dies, he passes into *djet*, which is the time of the gods. Temples are in *djet,* as are pyramids, mummies, and royal art. The term is sometimes translated as "eternal," but it also describes a state of completion and perfection. Something in *djet* time is finished but not past: it exists forever in the present.

The world that was created by the gods is not permanent. It's an island, in the words of the Egyptologist Erik Hornung, "between nothingness and nothingness." The place where we live will disappear. But ancient Egyptians weren't obsessed with forecasting this future, just as they didn't concern themselves with analyzing and replaying the past. Perhaps when time is nonlinear, it's easier to focus on today. Raymond Johnson, a scholar at the University of Chicago, has written that ancient Egyptians "saw normal time as a circle that described an endlessly repeating present." Johnson believes this to have been a natural response to the southern terrain. In his view, *neheh* was inspired by the cycles of the river valley, while *djet* reflected the desert's timelessness. And the proximity of these radically different landscapes—that abrupt transition from the Buried to the fields—prepared Egyptians to envision time in two parts. Anywhere in Upper Egypt you can walk from eternity to now.

The next time that Matthew Adams returned to Abydos with a team from NYU, nearly two years later, they undertook an archaeology of the revolution. In the necropolis, thieves had excavated more than two hundred large pits, all of which had been hastily filled in by the authorities after order was restored.

Now Adams and his team reopened nearly every hole, measuring and mapping with satellite technology. The team included four excavators, three conservators, two surveyors, two architectural specialists, a photographer, an artist, and two inspectors from the Egyptian Ministry of Antiquities. They hired more than fifty local laborers. A custom-built fifteen-foot-tall stepladder allowed the photographer to shoot the pits from above, as if they were crime scenes. Sometimes a pit contained bullet casings from looters who had fired their weapons into the air, in order to intimidate the guards. Other artifacts were more mundane.

"There are cigarette butts here."

"This is our best find of the day."

"So it's filtered?"

"The filter suggests that it's not one hundred years old."

"This is round. The ancient Egyptians did not build round things like that here."

A circular brick wall had been partially excavated from the sand; such a shape would never have been used for an ancient tomb. Adams knelt to study the bricks, along with a young American archaeologist named Kate Scott. Both wore broad-brimmed hats against the sun, which, at eight o'clock in the morning, was already blazing hot.

"They hacked at the wall top," Scott said. "It's clear that there was a disturbance here and that a structure was affected. But it's not clear what this structure is."

"That's heat-treated brick."

"No question about it. Those are not ancient bricks."

"The looters saw the wall and didn't know what it was," Adams said. "They hacked at it a bit. But in this area they didn't appear to be all that determined."

Adams speculated that the wall might have belonged to a shepherd's hut from the 1950s, or perhaps a field house from an earlier generation of archaeologists. The ignorance of the looters, as well as the randomness of their digging, was another reason why Adams had decided to excavate the pits. In effect, the thieves had created the template for a survey. They had dug in most sections of the necropolis, so by following their tracks, the archaeologists could catch glimpses of underground structures throughout the site. And someday this information could be used to plan future digs. Already the looters' pits had revealed one important discovery: a section of the Buried had been used as a cemetery for elites during the New Kingdom, which began during the sixteenth century BC.

Many of these areas were professionally excavated more than a century ago, during the early age of archaeology. Back then, scholars moved quickly, and they usually focused on retrieving artifacts for museums and private collectors. Records were poor or nonexistent; many details were lost. Nowadays, archaeologists take meticulous photographs and measurements, and they rebury their excavations, because ancient structures are best protected if they remain underground. The archaeologists know that someday in the future another scholar will arrive with better technique or technology, in order to study the things that we failed to understand.

On the great stage of the Buried, the original actors were royal, but since then countless others have played their parts. A single site might have been excavated in succession by ancient looters, nineteenth-century archaeologists, modern looters, and post-Tahrir archaeologists, all of them digging in the same place. People come and go, like the dynasties and the regimes; sand is removed, replaced, and then removed again.

After the police returned to work, Ahmed disassembled the fake APC. He figured that he wouldn't need it again, but something about the project triggered a renewed interest in carpentry. One year, when Matthew Adams arrived at the dig house, he was pleasantly surprised to find two new beds and two new closets, all of them beautifully handmade.

The early experience of the revolution changed Ahmed's routines in other ways. During one of the calmer periods of the Arab Spring, he returned to Balyana, where he visited the appropriate government offices, filled out the necessary paperwork, and was granted permission to purchase and carry a handgun.

CHAPTER 2

IN THE FIRST FALL OF THE ARAB SPRING, I MOVED WITH MY FAMILY TO Cairo. We came in October 2011, during the time of year when the light in the city begins to change. The days were still hot and hazy, but at night there was often a pleasant breeze from the north, where the river empties into the Mediterranean. Over a period of weeks, the breeze slowly washed the summer glare from the sky, and the details of the capital drew into sharper focus. Along the Nile, shadows darkened beneath the bridges, and the river shifted from a dull, molten gray to cooler shades of blue and brown. At sunset even decrepit buildings acquired a golden glow. The views lengthened into winter, until there were moments when I found myself on some elevated place—an upper-story apartment, a highway overpass—and saw clearly the pyramids of the Giza Plateau.

We lived on Ahmed Heshmat Street, in Zamalek, a district on a long, thin island in the Nile. Zamalek has traditionally been home to middle- and upper-class Cairenes, and we rented a sprawling apartment on the ground floor of a building that, like many structures on our street, was beautiful but fading. I guessed that it must have been constructed sometime in the 1920s or 1930s, because the facade was characterized by the vertical lines of the Art Deco style. Out in front, the bars of a wrought-iron fence were shaped like spiderwebs.

The spiderweb motif was repeated throughout the building. Little black webs decorated our front door, and the balconies and porches had webbed railings. Our apartment had a small garden, part of which was enclosed by more wrought-iron webs. When I asked the landlady about the meaning of the spiderwebs, she shrugged and said that she had no idea. She had the same response when I inquired about the building's age. She was Coptic Christian, like a number of Zamalek real-estate owners. Often their families had come into possession of buildings during the chaotic period after Egypt's last revolution, in 1952. Back then, Gamal Abdel Nasser had instituted a number of socialist economic policies, and his government had driven many businesspeople out of the country. The landlady told me that the building had belonged to her family for more than half a century, but she didn't know anything about the original owners.

On the lower floors, few things had been significantly renovated or improved. The elevator seemed to be the same age as the building, and it was accessed through iron spiderweb gates. Behind the gates, rising and falling in the darkness of an open shaft, was an old-fashioned elevator box made of heavy carved wood, like some Byzantine sarcophagus. The gaps in the webbed gates were as large as a person's head, and it was possible to reach through and touch the elevator as it drifted past. Not long after we moved in, a child on an upper floor got his leg caught in the elevator, and the limb was broken so badly that he was evacuated to Europe for treatment.

Safety had never been a high priority in old Cairo neighborhoods, but standards were especially lax during the Arab Spring. Electricity blackouts were common, and every now and then we had a day without running water. But somehow things mostly functioned, although it was hard for a newcomer to grasp the systems at work. Once a month, a man knocked at the door, asked politely to enter, studied the gas meter in the kitchen, and produced a bill to be paid on the spot. Another man appeared periodically to collect a fee for electricity. Neither of these men wore a uniform or showed any form of identification, and they could materialize at any time from early morning to late at night.

The process for garbage removal was even more mysterious. The landlady instructed me to deposit all of our refuse outside the kitchen, where a small door led to a metal fire escape. There was no pickup schedule and no preferred container; I could use bags or boxes, or I could simply toss loose trash outside. Its removal was handled by a man named Sayyid, who was employed neither by the government nor by any private company. When I asked the landlady about the monthly fee, she said that I needed to work it out on my own with Sayyid.

At first, I never saw him. Every day or two, I put a bag of trash on the fire escape, and then it would quickly vanish. After nearly a month of this invisible service, a knock sounded in the kitchen.

"*Salaamu aleikum,*" Sayyid said, after I opened the door. Instead of a handshake, he held out his upper arm so that I could grasp his shirt. "*Mish nadif,*" he explained, smiling. "Not clean." He showed me his hands—they were stained like old leather. The fingers were so thick that they looked as if he were wearing gloves.

He stood barely taller than five feet, with short curly hair and a well-groomed mustache. His shoulders were broad, and when he held out his hands, I noticed that the veins on his forearms bulged like those of a weight lifter. He wore a baggy blue shirt, a huge pair of stained trousers cinched with a belt, and big leather shoes that flapped like those of a clown. Later I would learn that most of his clothes were oversized because they had been harvested from the garbage of bigger men.

Speaking Arabic slowly for my benefit, he explained that he was there to collect the monthly fee. I asked him for the amount.

"It's whatever you want to pay," he said.

"How much do other people pay?"

"Some pay ten pounds," he said. "Some pay one hundred pounds."

"How much should *I* pay?"

"You can pay ten pounds. Or you can pay one hundred pounds."

He wouldn't bargain in the proper sense—those numbers never moved. He dropped them like end lines on a football field, and then he left me with all that empty space. Finally I handed him forty Egyptian pounds, the equivalent of six and a half dollars, and he seemed satisfied. During subsequent conversations with Sayyid, I learned that the Reuters correspondent who lived upstairs paid only thirty a month, which made me feel good about my decision. It seemed logical that a long-form magazine writer would produce more garbage than somebody who worked for a wire service.

After I met Sayyid, I started seeing him everywhere in the neighborhood. He was always on the street in the early mornings, hauling massive canvas sacks of trash, and then around noon he took a break at the H Freedom kiosk that stood on the other side of my garden wall. The kiosk was owned by a serious man with a purple-black prayer bruise, the mark that devout Muslim men sometimes develop from touching their foreheads to the ground during prayer. The kiosk had been there for years, but after the fall of Mubarak the owner renamed it in honor of the revolution. H Freedom was a popular hangout for local men, and when Sayyid sat there, he often called out to passersby. He seemed to know everybody who lived on the street.

One afternoon, he approached me near the kiosk. "You speak Chinese, don't you?" he said.

I told him that I did, although I had no idea how he knew this.

"I've got something that I want you to look at," he said.

"What is it?"

"Not now." He dropped his voice. "It's better to talk about this at night. It has to do with medicine."

I told him I'd be free that evening at eight o'clock.

Like virtually everybody else, I had been surprised by the start of the Arab Spring. Before Egypt, I lived for more than a decade in China, where I met my wife, Leslie Chang, who was also a journalist. We came from very different backgrounds: she was born in New York, the daughter of Chinese immigrants, whereas I had grown up in mid-Missouri. But some similar restlessness had motivated both of us to go abroad, first to Europe and then to Asia. By the time we left China together, in 2007, we had lived almost our entire adult lives overseas.

We made a plan: We would move to rural southwestern Colorado, as a break from urban life, and we hoped to have a child. Then we would go to live in the Middle East. We liked the idea of going to a place that was completely unfamiliar, and both of us wanted to study another rich language. I looked forward to visiting Middle Eastern archaeological sites, because in China, I had always been fascinated by the deep time of such places.

All of it was abstract: the kid, the country. Maybe we'd go to Egypt, or maybe Syria. Maybe a boy, maybe a girl. What difference did it make? When I mentioned moving to Egypt, an editor in New York warned me that the place might seem too sluggish after China. "Nothing changes in Cairo," he said. But I liked the sound of that. I looked forward to studying Arabic at a relaxed pace, in a country where nothing happened.

The first disruption to our plan occurred when one kid turned into two.

In May 2010, Leslie gave birth to identical-twin girls, Ariel and Natasha. They were born prematurely, and we wanted to give them twelve months to grow before moving. We figured that the timing didn't matter; a year in a newborn's life is a rush compared with never-changing Cairo. But when protests broke out on Tahrir, our girls were eight months old, and they were exactly eighteen days older when Mubarak was overthrown.

We delayed and reconsidered. At last, we decided to follow through with the move, but the terms had changed: now I would be writing about a revolution. Before leaving, we enrolled in a two-month intensive Arabic course in the United States. We applied for life insurance but couldn't get it; the company sent a short letter rejecting us on account of "extensive travel." We visited a lawyer and wrote up wills. We moved out of our rental house; we put our possessions in storage; we gave away our car. We didn't ship a thing—whatever we took on the plane was whatever we would have.

The day before departure, we got married. Leslie and I had never bothered with formalities, and we had no desire to organize a wedding. But we had heard that if a foreign couple has different surnames, the Egyptian authorities sometimes make it difficult to acquire joint-residence visas. So we drove to the Ouray County Courthouse, where we were issued a license that noted, in an old-fashioned script, that we *"did join in the Holy Bonds of Matrimony."* I shoved the license into our luggage. The next day, along with our seventeen-month-old twins, we boarded the plane. Neither Leslie nor I had ever been to Egypt.

At eight o'clock sharp, the bell rang. When I opened the door, Sayyid reached into a pocket and produced a small gold box decorated with red calligraphy.

The Chinese text was elegant but evasive. It described the contents of the box as "health protection products" that "promoted development and power." Inside the box, a sheet of pills was accompanied by a page of instructions in English. The words reminded me how sometimes the Chinese are at their most expressive when they use English badly:

2 pills at a time whenever nece necessary
Before fucking make love 20minutes

"Where did you get this?" I asked.

"In the trash," Sayyid said. "From a man who died."

He explained that the man had been elderly, and his sons had thrown away all the possessions they didn't want, including the pills. "Many of these things were *mish kuaissa,*" Sayyid said. "Not good."

I asked what he meant by that.

"Things like this—" He sketched in the air with a thick finger, and then he pointed below his belt. "It's electric. It uses batteries. It's for women. This kind of thing isn't good." But talking about it seemed to make Sayyid happy. He grinned and told me that the elderly man's trash had also contained a large collection of pornographic magazines. He didn't say what he had done with the magazines. I asked where the dead man used to work.

"He was an ambassador."

Sayyid's tone was matter-of-fact, as if this were a job that routinely involved the accumulation of pornography and Chinese sex pills. I wasn't certain that I understood correctly, so I asked him to repeat the word: *safir.* "He was in embassies overseas," Sayyid explained. "He was very rich; he had millions of dollars. He had 4,000,044 dollars in his bank account."

The precision of this figure caught my attention. "How do you know that?" I asked.

"Because it was on letters from the bank."

I made a mental note to tell Leslie to be careful about the things she threw away. Sayyid asked about the Chinese medicine's instructions for use, and in broken Arabic I did my best to translate the part about waiting twenty minutes before fucking make love. He said something about selling the pills, but the way he asked questions made me think that he was more likely to use them himself. I checked the ingredients: *"white ginseng, pilose antler, longspur Epimedium, etc."* The *"etc."* was slightly unsettling—what in the world might be the next logical ingredient in this series? But such medicines are common in China, and I decided there probably wasn't any risk. I had a feeling it wouldn't be the first time Sayyid ingested something he found in the trash.

After that, Sayyid stopped by regularly at night. The next object he brought me was a Kiev brand 35-millimeter camera. The camera had been manufactured in Ukraine during the days of the Soviet Union, and it was as heavy as a hammer; I had never imagined that so much metal could be used to create a photograph. Sayyid wanted to know if it still worked and whether it was worth any money. It had been discarded by an elderly resident who was moving out of his apartment.

Many of Sayyid's best finds came when people moved or died. But he discovered things all the time, because he hand-sorted the garbage, pulling out recyclables and anything else of value. His route wasn't small—it covered four hundred apartments in more than a dozen buildings—but he worked so attentively that he could always identify a resident by his trash. One afternoon, I fed lunch to my daughters, and after cleaning up, I left a full sack of garbage on the fire escape. Less than an hour later there was a knock at the door. When I opened it, Sayyid was holding a baby-sized metal fork. "It was with the rice," he said.

This was one reason why residents tended to be generous with their fees: Sayyid functioned as a kind of neighborhood lost and found. Whenever somebody moved or died, it was understood that the objects in the trash belonged to Sayyid, but otherwise he double-checked with residents if he turned up something suspiciously valuable. He alerted people if something seemed amiss in the neighborhood, and he was a reliable source of local information. Over time, he introduced me to the various figures who were prominent in the neighborhood: a one-eyed doorman, a silver-haired man who ran the government bread stand, a friendly tea deliverer who carried a shiny tray up and down the street.

Some of these individuals served as informal consultants for Sayyid. He was illiterate, like more than a quarter of the Egyptian population, and if he wanted to understand a document, he brought it to the H Freedom kiosk, whose owner could read. If Sayyid became involved in some local dispute, he usually went to the silver-haired man, whose status as the bread distributor put him on good terms with everybody.

As a foreigner, my field of expertise came to encompass imported goods, pharmaceuticals, sex products, and alcohol. If Sayyid found some medicine, I read the instructions and told him what it was intended to treat and how many pills a person should take. For something like the Kiev camera, I went online and gave him a rough estimate of what such a thing might sell for in the United States. Those cameras went for around forty dollars on eBay, although it would have been impossible for Sayyid to command such a fee in Cairo. But he always wanted to know the American price. It seemed to give him pleasure to know that in another place, in another life, he could have sold the object for a significant sum.

Occasionally, a Muslim drinker was driven by guilt to discard his liquor cabinet, and then Sayyid would appear at my door, carrying the bottles discreetly in a black plastic bag. It was my job to evaluate the bottles' resale value. Even a quarter-full jug of whiskey could be sold, because people tended to be shy about entering the few liquor stores that were sprinkled throughout the city. Sayyid was Muslim, and when I first got to know him, he told me that he planned to vote for Muslim Brotherhood candidates in the various post-Tahrir elections. But he had no formal affiliation with the group, and he didn't take the Islamic prohibition on alcohol as seriously as most Egyptian Muslims. When he stopped by my apartment after a hard day's work, he often asked for a cold beer. He was the only guest I ever entertained who carried off his empties, because he knew he'd end up collecting them anyway.

The spiderweb building was just a mile and a half from Tahrir Square, but it felt farther. In Zamalek, the river creates a powerful sense of separation, and there are only half a dozen bridges that connect to the rest of the city. When we lived there, our part of the island didn't have a subway stop or any prominent political ministries. There were no important squares, no major mosques, and no public places that were likely to attract protesters. The revolution was something that happened elsewhere.

By chance, we had arrived during a lull in the upheaval. It had been eight months since Mubarak was forced out of office, and the country had yet to schedule elections for a new president. It was unclear who was leading the Egyptian Arab Spring. There was still no permanent constitution and no legislature, although parliamentary elections were planned for winter. At such a moment, it was easy to ignore the national events, and several weeks passed before I made my first visit to Tahrir.

Most of my neighbors avoided the square entirely. After the political events resumed, I often saw prosperous-looking people sitting in Zamalek coffee shops, watching the revolution on television, as if the images had been beamed in from some distant land. Neighbors told me frankly not to go to Tahrir. In their opinion, it was no place for a foreigner with small children at home.

Sayyid was also a political skeptic. He came from a social class that theoretically should have benefited from a revolution, but he didn't seem to think in such terms. He told cautionary tales about local figures, like the one-eyed doorman on the block. During a demonstration, the doorman became curious and walked to a street near Tahrir, where he decided to climb an overpass in order to get a better vantage point. This was a mistake: when Egyptian police disperse crowds, they usually raise their shotguns and fire into the air. The doorman got hit with bird shot and lost his eye.

"He wasn't even protesting," Sayyid said. "*Mafeesh faida.* There's no purpose. That's why you should stay away from there."

I told him that talking to demonstrators was part of my job, but I promised to be careful.

"*Ba'oolek ay,*" Sayyid said. "Let me tell you something." This Egyptian phrase is a common preface to advice, and during my early months it was often the last thing I understood before somebody embarked on a long-winded explanation. I would smile and nod while the words whizzed past, wondering if I was missing some elusive secret to survival in Cairo. But Sayyid's suggestion was easy to follow. He said, "Don't stand on high places."

CHAPTER 3

IN LATE NOVEMBER, WHEN THE LULL IN THE REVOLUTION ENDED, AND PROtesters returned to Tahrir Square, I walked there from Zamalek almost every day. Following the island's eastern bank, I passed beneath the 6th October Bridge, and then there was a series of small parks and gardens that lined the river. It took about half an hour to reach the Qasr al-Nil Bridge. This bridge had been constructed in the 1930s, under the reign of King Fuad, who had named the structure in honor of his father. After the revolution of 1952, when Nasser and his compatriots overthrew the monarchy, the bridge was given its new title, which means "Palace of the Nile."

Many central Cairo landmarks had been named or renamed after various events of the twentieth century. Even nonpolitical Zamalek was an island of historical dates: the main thoroughfare was 26th July Street, after the day when King Farouk abdicated, and the 15th May Bridge honored the start of the 1948 Arab-Israeli War. The 6th October Bridge celebrated the Egyptian invasion of Sinai, in 1973. In the official view, these were all glorious events, but they had a tendency to begin better than they ended. The Arab-Israeli War turned out to be a disaster for the Arabs; the 1973 military action in Sinai concluded with the Egyptian Third Army surrounded by the Israelis. Eight years later, also on October 6, Sadat was assassinated, largely because of his willingness to negotiate with Israel. I had never lived in a place that commemorated so much history that could be seen as ambivalent at best.

The Qasr al-Nil Bridge spanned a wide section of the Nile, and then its roadway descended directly into Tahrir. Strictly speaking, Tahrir Square wasn't really a square—it was more of a traffic circle with an endless stream of cars revolving around its center. The buildings around the circle were of varied styles, as if they had converged on this space from all directions. The

Mogamma, a large government complex, had a stolid modernist facade, and then some private apartment blocks had columned balconies with French doors. The Egyptian Museum, with its domed roof and vaulted windows, was the rich orange color of an Italian palazzo. There was a Hardee's and a KFC. A mosque called Omar Makram had a graceful minaret and delicate Islamic-style window screens.

After the November protests became violent, the traffic circle shut down, and all the restaurants closed. My walks over the bridge felt like crossing a border: behind me, the banks of the island were lush with trees and flowers; ahead, the high-rise buildings loomed above the square. Even the air changed on the other side of the river. There was dust from protesters throwing rocks and bricks, and the square reeked with the chemical smell of tear gas.

When the protests began, my only experience with the revolution had involved watching the early phase on television in Colorado. The celebratory scenes at the time of Mubarak's resignation had impressed me, and I dressed nicely for my initial visits to Tahrir. I wore pressed trousers and button-front shirts, as if it were a formal occasion, but soon I realized that nobody else dressed this way. There was too much dust, too much chaos; in any case, it was better not to stand out. The first time I went to the square, a pickpocket stole my wallet. I had been caught up in a crowd, pushed along by a mass of people, and I couldn't stop the hand when I felt it enter my pocket. I was lucky—the wallet didn't contain much money—and I learned my lesson. Those were Tahrir rules: Don't wear nice clothes, don't carry a wallet. Don't stand on high places.

The second time I went to Tahrir, I saw a thief who was caught stealing at the Omar Makram Mosque. The crime happened during midday prayers, when most of the men in the mosque were lined up, facing the front. The mosque is situated on the southwestern corner of the square, and on that day the door and windows were open to the roar of the crowd outside. The sound had the rhythm of the ocean: it was constant but ever changing, and periodically it swelled to a crescendo, like a big wave hitting a beach. Every time the sound peaked, I wondered what had happened outside. Perhaps a tear-gas canister had been lobbed into the crowd, or maybe another injured teenager had been carried back from the front lines.

With all the excitement, the thief probably assumed that nobody would pay attention to a cell phone plugged into a charger. He crept over and pocketed the phone while its owner was praying. But an old sheikh with a long white beard happened to be watching from the back. After the prayers were finished, the sheikh whispered a few words to some men nearby, including a college student who had invited me into the mosque. By the time a second round of worshippers had begun to pray aloud—*"Allahu akbar! Allahu akbar!"*—the men had surrounded the thief. I stood behind the group, watching.

They had the thief's back against the prayer-room wall. He gave up the phone without a struggle. When the sheikh asked why he had stolen it, he said that his own phone had been taken earlier in the day.

"Where's your ID?" the college student asked.

The thief claimed he was too young to have a government-issued card. He was very thin, with a sallow, unhealthy complexion, and his clothes were filthy. His left eye was red. The inflammation could have been caused by tear gas, or perhaps somebody had hit him. There were many red-eyed people on the square that day.

"This is *haraam*!" the sheikh said. "Forbidden! Do you understand that? We could call the police and have you arrested."

In truth, no cop was going to approach the Omar Makram Mosque on a day like this, and any justice would have to come from the group of men. The thief's body had gone limp; his arms jerked up like a puppet's when the college student searched his pockets. The student found a lighter, as well as a box of Ventolin, an asthma medication that volunteer doctors were distributing to tear-gas victims. He handed the items to the sheikh, who leaned close and lectured the thief for a long minute. He spoke quietly; nobody in the group had raised his voice throughout the confrontation. When the thief realized that he was being allowed to go, he froze for a moment, as if overwhelmed by relief. Then he walked quickly to the door of the mosque, his head bowed. Without looking back he vanished into the roar of the square.

The specific cause of the violence was hard to identify. Three days earlier, the Muslim Brotherhood had organized a protest against the military officials who were ruling on an interim basis. These officials were known as the Supreme

Council of the Armed Forces, or SCAF, and recently there had been signs that they might try to extend their hold on power. Some people feared that the generals planned to delay the country's first free parliamentary elections, which were scheduled to begin at the end of November.

The Brotherhood's protest was essentially a warning. By gathering peacefully on Tahrir, they reminded SCAF that any attempt to derail the transition to democracy would result in resistance. After a day, the Brothers vacated the square, satisfied that their message had been received. But some liberal activists remained on Tahrir overnight, and the next day they came into conflict with the police. The activists claimed that the cops attacked without provocation; others said that the young people had antagonized the authorities. In any case, the political climate was so volatile that even a minor spat quickly escalated. Once the news went out on social media, young people of all political affiliations flooded onto the square, concerned that their hard-fought victory over Mubarak might be stolen by the military.

By the third day of protests, more than twenty people had been killed. Most had died on Mohammed Mahmoud Street, which begins at the southeastern corner of Tahrir and runs to the Ministry of the Interior. The ministry was the bureaucratic center for the police, and it had become the target of angry protesters. Periodically, groups of young men stormed the ministry wall, armed with sticks and rocks, and cops in riot gear fought back with tear gas, rubber bullets, and bird shot.

On that morning, when I walked to Tahrir, the crowd numbered in the tens of thousands, and there was still no violence on the square itself. But people were skittish. Every now and then, a group would get startled for no apparent reason and begin to run away from the entrance to Mohammed Mahmoud Street, as if the police were coming. It might start with only four or five young men, but the panic was contagious, and soon hundreds would be sprinting across the square—and then the surge would stop as abruptly as it had begun. Like the sounds of the square, there was something ocean-like about this rhythm, and it was mesmerizing to watch the waves of runners start and stop.

During one of these rushes, I noticed a young man standing off to the side with a gentle, heavy-lidded expression. It was rare to see somebody in this crowd who looked so calm. I struck up a conversation in my bad Arabic and then we switched to English. He was a senior at Ain Shams University, studying pharmacology. He told me that he had participated in the protests the previous January and February, and now he had returned to make sure that the dream of democracy wasn't abandoned.

After we talked for a while, the Omar Makram Mosque sounded the call for midday prayers. The student asked if I wanted to accompany him to the mosque, and I told him that I wasn't Muslim.

"It doesn't matter," he said. "Anybody can come."

Of all the buildings and institutions that surrounded the square, only Omar Makram remained fully open to the revolution. Inside the prayer room, volunteer doctors had set up a medical clinic to treat the wounded, and the mosque's bathrooms could be used by anybody. When I entered with the student, I saw dozens of people charging their phones, and others were sleeping around the edges of the prayer room.

After that, when I made my daily journey across the Qasr al-Nil Bridge, I always stopped at Omar Makram. Soon I was spending most of my time on Tahrir at the mosque. The square itself was overwhelming; the scenes of fighting were so chaotic that I couldn't begin to understand what was happening. But inside the mosque there was a sense of order. Certain sheikhs led the prayers, and various young activists served as volunteer doctors, pharmacists, and security guards. They organized a lost-and-found department for any item that turned up on Tahrir. In normal times, the main prayer room was restricted to men, but now the women's entrance had been converted into a small hospital, so women were allowed to pass through the men's section on their way to their own part of the mosque.

It was an easy place to be an outsider. I always introduced myself as an American journalist, and people were happy to talk. Sometimes I filmed the events in the mosque so I could review them later with a translator. Often people made a point of telling me that any mosque is open to nonbelievers, because Islam welcomes all faiths. They were even kind to people who broke the rules, at least in the first few days of the protests. The group of men seemed to treat the cell-phone thief gently because they were in a holy place, but also because they had faith in the revolution outside.

On the fifth day of protests, I saw the dead body of a demonstrator carried into Omar Makram. The funeral began as another wave of sound: first, there was a low rumble outside the mosque, and then it grew into a roar. I was sitting in a corner of the prayer room when suddenly a crowd burst in through the front door. At the head of the crowd, half a dozen men carried an open coffin on their shoulders.

They set the body before the mihrab, the niche at the front of a mosque that marks the direction of Mecca. A small group of women dressed in black had accompanied the men, and one of them was the dead man's mother. She clutched a passport-sized photograph of her son. Some men tried to block her way, shouting that it was *haraam* for women to be there during a funeral. But the mother brandished the photograph—in her hands, this tiny image was as powerful as a cudgel. The men quickly backed down, and the women remained in the prayer room throughout the short service.

One of the men who had accompanied the coffin told me that the dead protester was only twenty-five years old, and he had a college degree in tourism. He had been killed the previous night. When I asked how the protester died, the man silently reached into his pocket and pulled out two empty bullet casings. People who had fought near the Ministry of the Interior sometimes collected such things as evidence that the government had started to use live ammunition.

The young protester was one of more than thirty who had died thus far. Standing before the body, a bearded sheikh told the story of Hamzah, an uncle of the Prophet who had been martyred in a battle with the Meccans, during the rise of Islam in the seventh century AD. Then the sheikh talked about the protests.

"Know that we are counting this man as a martyr in God's paradise!" he said, his voice rising. "We swear to God that this will not be in vain! This blood is good blood! It was spilled for the world of justice! So hear me, people of God! We will demonstrate; we will stay here until we get revenge for the martyrs!"

A man in the crowd joined in: "God, please let us die for our cause! God, please let us die for our cause!"

"Allahu akbar! Allahu akbar!"

And now the men were yelling, and pulling on face masks, and pushing to get outside and back to the fighting. Some of them carried the coffin away. The dead man's mother wailed, and another woman at her side shouted about the cruelty of the police. "*Haraam! Haraam!*" she yelled. "These are lessons in crime!"

"Woman, this is the military system," a man said. "This is what we get from a military regime."

After the coffin was outside, and the wave of sound receded, it became very quiet in the prayer room. Some people in the back had slept through the service. A young volunteer pharmacist named Ahmed Salem was working in the temporary clinic beside the mihrab. He spoke English well, and when I mentioned the funeral, Salem blinked and said that he had been too busy to pay attention. He had worked for two days with almost no sleep. He said that most of what he handed out consisted of Ventolin and Farcolin, for the tear gas, and he also distributed large amounts of polyvinyl alcohol eyedrops. The floor was littered with wrappers, vials, bottles, and other things; while we were talking, the pharmacist stepped on a syringe and sliced open his foot. He reached down and slowly applied a bandage, a remote expression on his face, as if he were scratching an itch. He was barefoot. Inside Omar Makram, many things were flexible, but one rule was never broken: nobody wore shoes inside the mosque.

On the sixth day of protests, the Nike sandals of a man named Salem Abd-Elsalem were stolen while he was praying in the mosque. "*Al-hamdulillah!*" he said warmly, when I met him at the back of the prayer room. "All praise be to God!" We chatted for a couple of minutes before he mentioned the theft. I couldn't imagine getting stranded barefoot on Tahrir, but Abd-Elsalem seemed perfectly good-humored. A volunteer caretaker at the mosque eventually found him a spare pair of slippers.

About a dozen young revolutionaries had offered to help out at the mosque during the protests. Most of them spoke no English, and after a week I hired a translator to accompany me on my trips to Tahrir. We often sat down with one of the volunteers, a skinny, sharp-eyed man named Waleed. He had come from the distant outskirts of Cairo, and like many of the activists he apparently brought nothing but the clothes on his back. Every day, he wore the same white sweater, and every day the sweater got a little dingier. At night he slept in the mosque. When the place was crowded, he rushed around the prayer room, distributing blankets, food, and other supplies that had been donated.

Such self-organization was a trademark of the revolution. Even during the first wave of protests, when Mubarak was forced out, there had never been any clear leaders of the movement. Most participants were young; in Egypt, more than half the population was twenty-five or younger. Activists often spoke proudly of the lack of leaders or parties, because in their opinion it reflected a more democratic generation. And the energy they invested in informal systems was part of this pride. At the clashes, teenagers with motorcycles evacuated people who had been injured or overcome by tear gas, and medical and pharmaceutical students staffed the field hospitals. There were even bands of young men with chisels and sledgehammers who broke up the sidewalks along Mohammed Mahmoud Street so people would have chunks of concrete to hurl at the police.

In addition to the other roles played by Omar Makram, the mosque had evolved into the main seat of justice on Tahrir. The relatively tolerant atmosphere that I had observed on my first visit seemed to be changing: now anybody who was caught committing a crime on the square was taken directly to the prayer room. If the violation was serious, the person's hands were bound, and he was locked in a side chamber. It was the volunteers' job to decide whether the accused would be released or delivered to a police station away from the square. I asked Waleed how he made this decision.

"It depends on how serious the crime is," he said.

Through my translator, I asked for specifics, but Waleed refused to clarify. Finally he stood up and retrieved two big plastic bags from behind a table where the volunteers sat. He dumped the contents onto the table—dozens of wallets, keys, and ID cards.

"This is the lost and found," Waleed said. "Many of these things have been confiscated from thieves. So you can see that this is a big problem, and we have to be harsh with the people we catch."

After a week of protests, some prominent sheikhs at Al-Azhar University, the most respected Islamic institution in Egypt, negotiated a temporary cease-fire at the Ministry of the Interior. During the truce, the army sent in soldiers to construct walls of concrete and barbed wire that blocked off the main approaches to the ministry. At this point, there was still no leadership among the activists that could issue a clear series of demands. The Muslim Brotherhood had refused to return to the square. Some younger Brothers had begged their superiors to participate, in part to institute some discipline that might reduce the violence. But the leaders held firm—they saw no benefit in getting involved with such a chaotic event. Early in the protests, the cabinet of Egypt's interim government had offered to resign en masse, which did nothing to diminish the anger.

But the walls worked. Before the barriers went up, the waves of protesters had been relentless: they rushed the ministry, retreated under pressure from the police, and then regrouped and charged again. But once the walls broke the rhythm of these attacks, it was as if a hypnotist had snapped his fingers. The young people lost focus; without a clear target, their energy spun off in different directions. There was a sudden surge in volunteer security guards, and checkpoints proliferated around Tahrir. Now, whenever my translator and I walked from the Qasr al-Nil Bridge, we were stopped seven or eight times by young people demanding to see our IDs.

The translator was called Mohamed, although he went by a nickname—Manu. Before the Arab Spring, Manu had been employed at a Cairo call center, using English to answer questions from mobile phone users in Dubai. Then he worked for a Dutch company that was building a new tourist resort along the Mediterranean. After the revolution began, the Dutch company abandoned its project, and the employees were laid off. Manu found whatever work he could around Tahrir, where there were always foreign journalists and photographers who needed translators. He seemed to take all of this in stride—in the span of a year, his work had gone from Dubai mobile phones to Dutch tourist resorts to helping foreigners make sense of Egyptian political events.

He was thirty years old, a handsome man with a shaved head and hooded eyes. One of my first impressions of Egyptians was that they had expressive faces, but I found Manu hard to read. He didn't smile too much, and initially he rarely spoke about his life. He was calm even when the volunteers at Tahrir checkpoints became aggressive. After these encounters, and before we entered the mosque, he often paused and smoked a Viceroy Blue. He did the same thing whenever we left the mosque. He always inhaled his cigarette deeply, as if he'd been holding his breath inside the prayer room. Once, I asked for his honest impression of the place.

"I don't like mosques," he said.

"So you're not religious?"

"No." He explained that as a boy he had often attended Friday prayers, but once he was older, he stopped going. Then, when he was a conscript in the Egyptian Army, he used to go to the mosque on the base, in order to take naps. "It was the only place where I was left alone," he said.

"You disliked the army?"

"Yes."

"But you disliked the mosque less than you disliked the army."

Now he smiled. "That's correct. At least you could sleep in the mosque."

I asked if he had worried that sleeping in the prayer room, in uniform, would be considered disrespectful. I had assumed that what I was witnessing in Omar Makram, where people sprawled across the floor at all hours, was an anomaly of the revolution.

"No," Manu said. "Go to any mosque on a hot day. You almost always see somebody sleeping. But this other stuff is not normal." He gestured broadly—the mosque, the square, the fighting, the checkpoints.

Manu had participated in some of the early Tahrir protests, and he had been thrilled by the fall of Mubarak. But he said that now the feeling was different. Many people at the mosque echoed his remarks. "In January, it was the upper and middle class," a Quranic teacher named Sheikh Samy told me. "They were asking for social justice and freedom. But now it's a revolution for the poor people. These are people who have nothing." The sheikh was originally from the Nile Delta, where he worked in a religious school. Since the November protests began, he had taken up residence in the mosque, and he often led the prayers. He said that many of the young people fighting on

Mohammed Mahmoud Street had muddled ideas, but they still deserved sympathy. "They don't come just to cause trouble," he said. "They have hard lives and a lot of anger."

In Egypt, all major mosques are directly administered by the government, which appoints imams and pays their salaries. At Omar Makram, the imam was Sheikh Mazhar Shahin, a telegenic man in his thirties who often preached a relatively liberal interpretation of Islam on talk shows and popular religious programs. He had become a celebrity during the early part of the revolution, when he supported the Tahrir movement. On the first day of the November protests, at Omar Makram, Sheikh Mazhar had delivered a fiery sermon. He told the crowd of activists, "We want a civic democratic state with an Islamic vision that allows people to practice their rights and democracy."

But since that sermon, I hadn't seen Sheikh Mazhar at the mosque. The law stated that a government-appointed imam was required to be at his mosque between the sunset and evening prayers, and Manu and I often visited at that time. "I wish he was here," Sheikh Samy said. "Somebody should be in charge." During this period, the imam continued to appear on television, where he made a public offer to mediate between the demonstrators and the police. But on the ground he was nowhere to be seen.

On the tenth day of protests, a man was brought into Omar Makram after getting caught with scissors in his possession. Scissors were considered contraband because thieves used them to slit open pockets. A small mob dragged the man through the prayer room and began beating him in the washroom that was used for ritual cleansing before prayers. Manu and I were sitting about fifteen feet away, talking with Waleed, and periodically we had to stop the conversation because of the man's screams. A couple of people knelt nearby, trying to pray. By now, Waleed's white sweater had turned completely gray. All the volunteers shared the same look: day by day, their clothes got dirtier, and their faces drew tighter.

I asked Waleed what they planned to do with the accused thief, and he said they would tie him up for a while. Like other places on the square, the mosque had received a sudden influx of self-appointed security guards. They kept themselves busy by asking questions of anybody who seemed suspicious, and they often beat people who had been detained, in hopes of extracting confessions. Some newcomers had equipped themselves with padded martial-arts sparring vests that were decorated with an image of the Rising Sun. When these warriors stalked around barefoot, it felt as if the mosque had turned into a Tae Kwon Do studio.

A couple of guards were starting to press Manu for more information about me. There were no longer any older people in the mosque; Sheikh Samy had returned to his home in the Delta after getting injured while trying to break up a fight. Thefts seemed to happen constantly, along with other crimes. One young man was caught impersonating a doctor in the mosque's medical clinic, and several volunteers reported that a large amount of donated medicine had been removed without permission, probably to be sold on the black market.

On the tenth day of the protests, after we had stepped outside the mosque, and Manu had inhaled his customary Viceroy Blue, he said that maybe it would be better if we stayed away for a while.

The parliamentary elections began the following morning. Across Egypt, the election was peaceful, and more than half of eligible voters participated. I spent the day visiting polling stations around Cairo, and at every site the lines were long but orderly, divided by gender. At one polling station in the suburb of Maadi, I counted more than twelve hundred women waiting patiently in line. It was the first truly free election in Egyptian history.

The Muslim Brotherhood won 47 percent of the seats nationwide. The Nour Party, which represented the Salafis, the most conservative Islamists, finished a surprising second. Together these two Islamist groups were set to dominate the new parliament, and no left-leaning party won as many as 10 percent of the seats.

The Brotherhood's leaders had apparently made a shrewd political decision. By avoiding the protests on Tahrir, they had been able to focus on the final stage of the campaign. When I interviewed leaders of the organization, they claimed that the authorities had deliberately antagonized the protesters, in hopes of causing a disruption to the transition to democracy. But there were a few prominent Brothers who disagreed. Mohamed Beltagy, who won a parliamentary seat in a poor district in eastern Cairo, said that he had made a personal visit to Tahrir. He told me that he had been dismayed by the violence.

"I agree with the other Brotherhood leaders that it was a fake situation," Beltagy said, when we met in his campaign office. "It was made up to distract people from the path of the election. And the Brotherhood thought that if this is a fake situation, then we should stay away. But I thought we should be there because there was a lot of bloodshed. With all these young people, somebody should have been there to guide them."

For a while, I struggled to reconcile the two things I had witnessed. On the square, inside the mosque, I had watched a small community develop and then collapse, a victim of poor leadership. But I also saw an orderly, peaceful, national vote—a democratic dream fulfilled. Sometimes I thought the mosque was too small to represent anything larger; at other moments, I sensed that the ritual of an election was shallow. But that was the nature of a city like Cairo: there were many parts, many realities. Even a commemorative date on a bridge—6th October, 15th May—might mean completely different things to different people.

That year, Manu and I often worked together on covering the political events, and sometimes we met socially. He liked going to informal hangouts, and on weekends he was often downtown, in small, furtive-looking bars that didn't have signs in front. Near my apartment building, there was a place that he called the Doormen's Bar. It was nothing but a gap between two buildings where a man in a traditional galabiya gown had arranged a few chairs and a refrigerator full of cheap Egyptian Stella-brand beer. Some local doormen drank there in secret, because the place couldn't be seen from the street.

One evening, Manu called and said he wanted to tell me something in person. He suggested meeting in another informal spot, on the quiet northeastern corner of Zamalek. There weren't any shops or restaurants on that part of the island, and groups of young people often gathered in parked cars, drinking beer and smoking hashish. Couples held hands while sitting on a fence that overlooked the Nile. Some nearby residents had tarred sections of the fence, in hopes of driving off the lovebirds, but for the most part the hangout was tolerated. It reminded me of growing up in the American Midwest, where small towns always had a cruising strip that allowed teenagers to escape their families.

Manu and I found an empty spot beside the fence, and we opened some beers that I had brought. Nearby, in the shadow of a tree, a couple stood close to each other, talking in low voices. The woman wore a *hijab* and her dress went to her ankles. Many of the women who came here with their boyfriends dressed conservatively. I sensed that they belonged to an in-between group: liberal enough to want to be alone with their boyfriends, but not so liberal that they did this in a restaurant or other public place. I never saw these women drinking alcohol.

Manu and I chatted for a while, and then he said that he had recently had trouble with the police. He believed that the problem had been resolved, but he wanted me to know that he might be targeted again. "I'm gay," he said. "I don't know if you guessed this."

I hadn't. He had never referred to a girlfriend, but young men in Cairo were often single. Nothing in his mannerisms had tipped me off, and now I realized that this was the reason I had found him hard to read: he had learned to be careful. I told him that I appreciated his honesty.

"Does it bother you?" he said.

I couldn't tell if he was referring to his homosexuality or to the possibility of problems with the authorities. Or perhaps these things were indistinguishable in Cairo.

"No," I said. "Of course it doesn't bother me."

He told me that his closest friends knew that he was gay, and I asked about his family. He clicked his tongue, an Egyptian *tsk tsk* that indicates a strong negative. "I can't tell them," he said.

He had grown up in Port Said, a city on the Suez Canal, and in the past he had told me how relieved he was to have escaped provincial life. I asked how openly gay he could be in the capital.

"Not fully open," he said. "But not closed. There are places I can go."

"Are there gay bars?"

"No," he said. "But there's a café where gay people go. And there are bars where young liberal people go, and maybe some of them are gay. And there are other places in the city."

"Is this one of them?" I motioned to the couples standing in the shadows.

He clicked his tongue again. "No," he said. "The gay place is the Qasr al-Nil Bridge. Or Ramses Square. Men go there late at night if they want to pick up somebody."

I asked if the bridge had become a gay spot because of the Tahrir movement.

"It was already like that before the revolution," he said. "I don't know how long gay people have been going there. Maybe for a long time."

We talked for a while, and then Manu got in a cab to meet some friends downtown. I walked back to the spiderweb building. I thought about all the times I had crossed that twice-named bridge, never suspecting its other identity. After Manu told me, there were evenings when I returned late from downtown, and on my way home I saw young men on the Qasr al-Nil Bridge. Some were single, and some were in pairs; they walked slowly above the nighttime river.

In December 2011, after the first round of the parliamentary elections had concluded, Manu and I made a final trip to the Omar Makram Mosque. The city had entered the pleasant Egyptian winter, and the sky was a perfect dome of blue. The northern breeze had washed away the dust and the smell of tear gas. Most protesters had left, and the violence on Mohammed Mahmoud Street was long finished. All told, an estimated forty-seven people had died. It was hard to say if anything significant had been accomplished by the movement, although SCAF had agreed to hold presidential elections before the end of June.

When Manu and I visited the mosque, the imam still hadn't returned. Some of the young volunteers remained, but I didn't see Waleed. I asked about him, and an activist named Mohammed Sultan gave a short, bitter laugh. "Waleed is gone," he said. And then he told the story: A couple of nights earlier, Waleed had collected more than ten cell phones and the equivalent of three hundred dollars from people who were sleeping in the mosque, explaining that he would keep these things safe for the evening. And that was the last time anybody saw the phones, the money, and the dirty sweater. One of the victims later told me that he had been forced to borrow money just to get home. Sultan said that I should write an article about the protests titled "Waleed the Fraud."

But Waleed's crime, and all the other problems on the square, still hadn't ruined Sultan's faith in the Arab Spring. He was glad that he had taken time off from his job as a driver in order to participate in the November protests. But he acknowledged that the movement had deteriorated. "At first, it was handled by real men," he said. "But now there are people who bring down the revolution."

Ahmed Salem, the young pharmacist who had sliced open his foot on a syringe in the early days of the protests, was also still in the mosque, and he agreed with his compatriot's assessment. In Salem's opinion, the young people on the square had been pawns in some larger game that he didn't understand.

"We're still in the same circle as we were in January," Salem said. "Maybe we don't know how to take the next step. We are just youth. The older generation is still directing us as if they were chess players." He smiled grimly. "We are the chess pieces right now."

CHAPTER 4

In *The Buried*, the majority of objects that were excavated from the looters' pits consisted of trash. Cigarette butts and cellophane packages were particularly common, because most thieves smoked while digging. They also discarded soda cans, food wrappers, and plastic water bottles. Sometimes they abandoned their tools after being scared off by the site guards, and now the objects were uncovered by the excavations. The archaeologists also occasionally found tiny beads made of faience, a pretty blue ceramic material that dates to pharaonic times. One looters' hole contained the torso of a mummy that had been ripped apart.

Each morning, the archaeologists started work at six o'clock, in order to avoid the heat. There's no shade in the necropolis, and clouds are rare; the average annual precipitation for this region is around one-tenth of an inch. When the ancients looked up at that vast blue sky, they saw water. They believed that the earth existed in a kind of bubble surrounded by a liquid universe. Every heavenly body—the sun, the stars, the planets—skimmed across the surface of the sky on boats. Somewhere in the distant south, there was a hole in the bubble, and water poured out into the desert. One hole, one river: the Nile. How else to explain a world with no rain but plenty of water?

In 1991, excavations turned up a fleet of a dozen ships that had been buried in the necropolis. These boats were located near the Shuna, the ancient mud-brick enclosure, and all of the crafts pointed toward the distant river. A boulder had been positioned on the stern of some boats, like an anchor that prevented them from drifting off into the sand. The ships averaged about sixty feet in length. Eventually, two more were discovered, and the fourteen vessels are believed to have been part of the burial offerings for a king of the

First Dynasty. The ceremonial crafts were fashioned more than five thousand years ago, from coniferous wood that had been imported from abroad, and they are among the world's earliest known built boats. It's possible that they never touched water.

Boats in the desert, boats in the sky: the Abydos landscape is full of miracles. One king of the First Dynasty was buried with seven pet lions; another was accompanied by a dog named "The Fast One." There's a royal tomb that contained enough offering jars for forty-five hundred liters of wine. Archaeologists have discovered bodies adorned with amulets of lapis lazuli, as blue as the watery sky, which prove that even in the days of the earliest pharaohs there were already trade routes that connected to Afghanistan. In 1899, when William Flinders Petrie opened the grave of a king named Semerkhet, the British archaeologist could still smell the ointment that had been poured into the tomb some fifty centuries ago.

Kings of the First Dynasty were also buried with individuals who seem to have been killed in order to serve the ruler in the afterlife. Some of the dead have court titles, and they obviously represent an elite class of society. They have good teeth and strong bones. They are adorned with ivory bracelets, lapis lazuli amulets, and other marks of finery. It's unclear how they died. "There's no evidence of physical trauma," Matthew Adams said one morning at the site. "No broken bones. The best we can surmise is that they were poisoned. A number of early states had this phase at critical moments. It happens in Mesopotamia; it happens in China. It's a way of defining the nature of royal power at a critical moment. I can't think of a stronger statement than the power of life and death over people."

Kingship was an Egyptian invention, along with the nation—the idea of people with a common identity sharing a political territory. In Mesopotamia, civilization developed around city-states whose temples and high priests held great authority. In Egypt, though, all power lay with the king. Violence was fundamental to his identity: the first known image of an Egyptian ruler, a man named Narmer, portrays him smiting his enemies. This exact motif—a king striding, his mace upraised, while his other hand grasps the hair of a captive—was repeated countless times for the next three thousand years. We know few details about Narmer, although the Greek historian Herodotus, who called the king Menes, left a brief, anticlimactic description: "He made a foreign expedition and won renown, but was carried off by a hippopotamus."

Post-hippo, the next king was Aha, who was accompanied in death by more than forty retainers. The number rose to six hundred for his successor, King Djer. This practice of ritual killing seems to have been adopted around the time that Egypt was unified under dynastic rule, and then, after an initial increase in sacrifices, the numbers became smaller. In less than two centuries the practice was abandoned entirely.

"It was somehow no longer necessary," Adams said. "There might have been a certain motivation not to dispatch your best and brightest every generation. It's not an effective way to run an administration. But it's what they were doing at this critical moment. It's as if they were working out what kingship is."

There's no evidence that victims resisted. Some were court retainers, but many of the dead were individuals under the age of twenty-five, and they seem to have been selected on the basis of youth and health. Adams speculates that these young people might have gone willingly to their deaths because they believed so strongly in the god-king. But it's impossible to know, and we lack even the language necessary to describe what happened. "I don't like to call this human sacrifice," Günter Dreyer, a German archaeologist who has excavated a number of First Dynasty tombs, told me. "A sacrifice is different. That's a deal—maybe it's with a god, and you give something in order to get something. But this is killing people to serve the king in the afterlife. It's equipment for the afterlife, but it's not sacrificial. There is no word for it, actually."

Early one morning, Matthew Adams gave me a tour around the Shuna. Nowadays, the enclosure's walls are the same sandy color as the Abydos cliffs, but in ancient times they were painted white. The facade had a series of sharply defined vertical buttresses that, beneath the cloudless sky, would have thrown dramatic shadows across the structure. A similar technique was used in some Mesopotamian buildings, and the Egyptians expanded this feature and made it central to their royal architecture. Other ancient cultures in sunny climates later built monuments with the same effect—for example, the prominent pillars of Greek temples. Some architectural details that we now consider modern, like the clean vertical lines of the Art Deco style, are descended directly from ideas that shaped the Shuna.

The kings of the First Dynasty, and the initial two rulers of the Second, built their tombs in another section of the Buried, about a mile away. They seem to have used structures like the Shuna for ritual offerings during the ruler's lifetime. Each king built an enclosure, and then, after his death, the building was ritually demolished.

"We think of Egyptian kings as building for all eternity," Adams said. He pointed out the areas where some of the other enclosures once stood—now there were no traces aboveground. "The idea of kings building temporary monuments seems strange. But they build these monuments, and they stay for ten or twenty years, until the rise of the next king. And then they are very carefully prepared. They sweep it clean, and they bring in sterile sand."

This powdery white sand was spread beneath the walls of the dead king's enclosure, like a kind of bed. Then the walls were toppled and interred. Subsidiary burials were located nearby: offering jars, animals, courtiers, young men and women. In the 1980s and 1990s, David O'Connor, an archaeologist at the University of Pennsylvania, directed a series of excavations that uncovered the remains of these buried buildings. Adams worked on many of these digs, and the Pennsylvania team also found the buried boats.

"There only would have been a single monument standing at any one time—the monument of the living king," Adams said. "It's not a monument to his memory. It's a monument in which his kingship is celebrated during his life."

We walked to the back of the Shuna, where birds fluttered around the high walls. In the great chain of construction that shaped this part of the necropolis, the Shuna represents the final link. It was built by Khasekhemwy, the powerful last king of the Second Dynasty. Before Khasekhemwy, royal enclosures were part of *neheh* time: they came in cycles, like the seasons and the Nile floods, and they weren't permanent. But Khasekhemwy seems to have been struck by the idea of building for *djet*. He made the walls of his monument much thicker than those of his predecessors, and after his death the building was left to stand.

This simple act triggered something powerful in the human imagination. Djoser, the son of Khasekhemwy, took another critical step, working in stone instead of mud brick. On the Saqqara Plateau, south of present-day Cairo, Djoser constructed a building of six terraced levels surrounded by an enormous stone version of the Shuna. This structure is now known as the Step Pyramid, and it's the world's oldest monumental building of stone. When Djoser's successors built their own memorials, they refined this shape to that of a true pyramid with smooth sides. All told, it took barely more than a hundred years for the Egyptians to proceed from the 40-foot-high enclosure of Khasekhemwy to the limestone-encased Great Pyramid of Giza, which stands 481 feet tall. More than forty-three centuries would pass before anybody on earth constructed something taller.

From the modern perspective, the magnificence of the Giza pyramids can be misleading. We tend to focus on the physical structures and objects of ancient Egypt, and we see the culture as an almost miraculous source of planning, construction, and craftsmanship. But the more interesting truth is that ancient Egyptians weren't intent on what we would consider progress. For most of their history, they made little effort to irrigate their land, relying on the Nile's natural flood cycles. They planted only a single grain crop per year. The population grew slowly; even in the late New Kingdom, nearly two millennia after the country had been unified, there were probably no more than four or five million people, compared with more than ninety million today. The first evidence of a simple irrigation tool doesn't appear on the historical record until seventeen dynasties have come and gone. The Egyptians constructed the Great Pyramid of Giza centuries before they used the wheel. They collected taxes, and they traded for goods all around the region, but they never invented money—the coins discovered in the Buried had been minted under Greek rule. In ancient times, the hieroglyphs contained an alphabet, but the Egyptians seem to have preferred not to use this simpler way of writing. For three thousand years, artists drew hieroglyphs in remarkably stable forms.

When ancient Egyptians produced things at industrial scale, like the baking of bread for city residents, their instinct was rarely to innovate. Rather than create larger ovens, or develop assembly-line methods, they simply built a lot of small ovens. "They expected logic to have only local application, to come in small packets," the Egyptologist Barry Kemp writes in *The City of Akhenaten and Nefertiti*. Efficiency wasn't valued; technology wasn't the goal. They certainly could handle numbers: the Great Pyramid contains some 2.3 million carved stone blocks, each of them weighing on average more than a ton, and the structure is oriented so precisely that it faces true north with a divergence of only one-twentieth of a degree. But the Egyptians of pharaonic times never practiced the subject of mathematics as we would understand it. There seems to have been no desire to develop abstract theories or standardized problem solving. Sums could be absurdly complicated. With the exception of $2/3$, ancient Egyptians wrote all fractions with a numerator of one. If they wanted to express $3/4$, they had to write $1/2 + 1/4$. The fraction $6/7$ was $1/2 + 1/4 + 1/28$. For $8/9$ they wrote $1/2 + 1/4 + 1/18 + 1/18 + 1/36$.

Why did they do this? Nobody knows; the ancient Egyptians weren't inclined to explain themselves for our benefit. Hany El-Hosseiny, a professor of mathematics at Cairo University who has examined the way the ancients performed calculations, told me that he was baffled by their approach. "They must have had abstract thinking, because they put problems that are similar in one group, and they solve them in the same manner," he said. "But they never state the method abstractly. They treat this problem, and then they treat that problem, and then they treat another problem. They never say there's a general principle."

The ancients didn't focus much on improving systems, and even the word may be inappropriate. "In recent years archaeologists have shown an interest in regarding aspects of ancient societies as 'systems,'" Kemp writes. "It is a valuable perspective, but it carries a semantic pitfall. We may identify systems in the workings of ancient societies, but they need not have been at all systematic, for the latter word implies a prominent degree of reason and order." This has been true for most of history, in most of the world, and often it's the way things still work today. As Kemp writes of the ancients, "They exemplify a general characteristic of cultures: that systems tend to be adequate for the demands placed upon them. People cope."

The true genius of the ancient Egyptians was directed elsewhere. It wasn't so much the structures they built, or the systems they designed, as the force of their imagination. They developed an expansive view of time, the universe, and political power. Inventing the abstract notion of the nation was probably more important than building the actual structures of that nation. Somehow, Egyptians created a powerful faith in themselves as a country and in their ruler as a god-king. They envisioned a fundamental tension between chaos and order, a dichotomy that must have been inspired by the divided landscape. River and desert, *neheh* and *djet,* life and death, male and female, Osiris and Isis, Horus and Seth—such pairings were fundamental to Egyptian thought. They were brilliant at creating traditions. Some of their concepts—the day of judgment, the holy image of a mother and child, the story of a god who dies and is resurrected—eventually became fundamental to Christianity. The annual mass pilgrimage to Abydos is often viewed as a precursor of the Muslim hajj.

The ancient Egyptians were also remarkably skilled at the use of political symbols. They are believed to have invented the crown and the scepter, and they understood the power of architecture. At the heart of their capital, they painted the king's residence white, the same color as the Shuna, and they referred to this royal residence as the "White Wall"—a distant ancestor of 1600 Pennsylvania Avenue.

Within the Shuna's walls, the sounds of nearby villages disappear, and all that's visible is the cloudless sky. Nobody knows the rituals that once happened here, but their power seems to have resonated for centuries. Ancient Egyptians dug graves all across the necropolis, but for more than seventeen hundred years they refused to touch the area inside and around the Shuna. And the early practice of ritual killing faded away around the same time that serious monument building began. Perhaps all that energy and faith needed an outlet: rather than putting hundreds of retainers to death, kings organized the construction of unbelievably large buildings. "What we see here in Abydos is the ancient Egyptian kings developing the vocabulary of royal power," Adams said, standing inside the Shuna. "They are developing the ideology of kingship, and we are observing this process on the ground."

Adams pointed out a spot where Petrie, the British archaeologist, lived in a small hut during some of the time when he excavated here, from 1900 to

1904. Petrie pioneered a more scientific approach to excavations, and he was meticulous, tireless, and tough-minded. Like Adams, he applied the techniques of archaeology to the tracks of looters and thieves, but his goal was punitive. His autobiography recounts an incident:

> *One stormy night a man carried off a statue of over a hundredweight from our courtyard. I tracked him and made drawings of his feet from various impressions, as the toes were peculiar. I got a local man to tell tales which led to identifying the thief. He was arrested; at the police court his feet exactly tallied to my outline.*

Petrie's frugality was famous. At the end of a season, he buried his leftover canned food, and then he excavated the tins when he returned for the next campaign. His method for assessing whether a can had gone bad involved striking it against a wall to see if it exploded. In recent years, Adams has found tins and other objects that Petrie left behind.

The possessions of earlier archaeologists often turn up in digs, and there's something touchingly humble about these modern artifacts. In one looter's pit, Adams's team discovered a laundry list of clothing items, written in an elegant hand, which was probably discarded by Arthur Mace, a British contemporary of Petrie's. Adams also found a container of hemorrhoid cream that was used by John Garstang in the early twentieth century. One Abydos dig turned up an old-fashioned house key that was lost more than a hundred years ago by Charles Currelly, a Canadian excavator.

In 2010, a team from the University of Pennsylvania was excavating some tombs from the Middle Kingdom when they stumbled upon the corpse of a modern teenage girl. The scene suggested that she had been murdered and then hastily interred at some point within the past half a century. The cause of death was strangulation—a cord was wrapped around the girl's neck. She appeared to have been about fifteen years old.

The archaeologists reported it to the local police, who expressed no interest: to them, the case was as cold as that of the six hundred retainers who accompanied King Djer into the afterlife. And so the Pennsylvania team reburied the girl in the same place where they had found her. She might have been the victim of a rape, or perhaps an honor killing, a practice that still occasionally occurs in the clannish villages of Upper Egypt. Ritual, sacrifice, the vocabulary of power—maybe we have words for what happened here, or maybe we don't.

Not far from the girl's grave, the Pennsylvania archaeologists found the remains of a lightning strike from a rare and recent storm. The bolt had hit an exposed piece of bedrock, which caused the electricity to flare out in all directions across the sand. The moment of the strike was perfectly preserved: everywhere the lightning ran, it fused the sand into delicate tubes of glass, creating a crystal web atop the desert. When the archaeologists tried to lift this artifact of the sky, it shattered into dust.

CHAPTER 5

IN LATE AFTERNOONS, SAYYID OFTEN STOPPED BY THE SPIDERWEB BUILDing for a break, because he knew that Leslie and I both worked at home. When I opened the door, he would greet me, and then he would call out to Leslie, "Two spoons, please!" This meant that he wanted a cup of tea with two spoonfuls of sugar. In Sayyid's world, this was the role of a wife: she provides male guests with tea and other refreshments.

After Leslie heard the command a few times—"Two spoons, please!"—she asked me to explain to Sayyid that in our household a woman was not expected to act as a waitress. But I worried that I couldn't yet communicate such a message with the proper nuance. So I delayed until my language skills improved, and in the meantime I made a point of fetching the tea myself. And sometimes Leslie sat with us in the front room of the apartment, where Sayyid sipped the drink and recovered from his labor.

During our early months in the neighborhood, he was the first person with whom we had long conversations in Egyptian Arabic. He was curious and patient, and his lack of education seemed to make him sympathetic to our struggles. Mostly, he was an attentive listener. I suppose that this was a natural response to illiteracy; he was accustomed to receiving much of his information aurally. If Leslie or I used a new term or grammatical structure, Sayyid invariably noticed, and he would encourage us by saying, "Bravo!" He even recycled the new words and phrases back into the conversation, the way a good teacher does.

We always had plenty to talk about, because he often arrived with things that he had excavated from the garbage. Once, he brought seven unopened bottles of wine: a Grande Marque Bordeaux, a Marqués de Cáceres, a Domaine de Moulines, a Château de Maligny Chablis, a Vin d'Alsace Muscat, a

Champagne Liébart-Régnier, and an Antonin Rodet Bourgogne Pinot Noir de Vieilles Vignes. I looked all of them up online, to check prices, and then Sayyid asked me to store them in the apartment until he could transport them home in the dark. He had discovered the bottles in the trash of an elderly Egyptian. Sayyid assumed that the man had given up drinking for reasons that were either religious or health related.

His finds sometimes included strange currencies, and at various points I looked up the values of Moroccan dirhams, Swedish kroner, Chinese yuan, Mexican pesos, Macanese patacas, and Canadian dollars. After Sayyid discovered a bill that said "10,000," he rushed to the spiderweb building in a state of high excitement, only to be deflated when I explained that there are thirty thousand Iranian rials to a dollar. Identification cards also frequently found their way into the trash. Sayyid brought me the current ID of a German diplomat, and I delivered it to the embassy, which was located a few blocks away. There were some Latvian diplomats in my neighborhood, and I became convinced that their embassy lacked any protocol for the destruction of official documents. Over time, Sayyid brought me an expired Latvian diplomatic passport, a Latvian school application, an ID for the adviser to the minister of defense and resource issues at the Latvian embassy, and another ID for the first secretary of the Permanent Delegation of Latvia to the NATO headquarters in Belgium.

There were a number of benefits to being friendly with the local garbageman, including the fact that at any moment I could embark on a new and fully licensed life in Riga. I also became an expert on cheap erectile dysfunction medications. Some of these drugs had wonderful names: Durjoy, which was manufactured in Bangladesh, and Virecta, which came from India. Chinese aphrodisiacs often included the character for "dragon," and they were spectacularly packaged in red and gold. But Sayyid was most watchful for anything blue. In another moment of excitement, he arrived with an untouched foil pack of Aerius desloratadine, whose pills were the color of Viagra. But I went online and learned that it was actually an anti-allergy medication—for Sayyid, a disappointment as crushing as that of the Iranian rials.

Sayyid taught me the Arabic word for sex—*gins*—as well as slang terms for various body parts. "*Andee zabala fil mokh,*" he often said. "I have garbage in the brain." He was only half-joking; his livelihood, after all, forced him to spend much of his time thinking about trash. In conversation this topic was often combined with women and money. After a while, I realized that all three things—women, money, and garbage—were interconnected in Sayyid's mind. They represented the trinity of his material world.

It was women and money that had led him to garbage in the first place. Sayyid's father had grown up in a village near Qena, a city in Upper Egypt, and like many southerners of his generation he migrated to Cairo. In the city outskirts, he worked as a watchman, and meanwhile he engaged in a series of rapid-fire marriages and divorces. For a Muslim man, divorce is legally easy, although in theory it costs money because of various fees that are supposed to be paid to an ex-wife, along with child support. None of this deterred Sayyid's father, who had nine wives, or ten if you count the Coptic woman he married briefly. When I met Sayyid's siblings and neighbors, they spoke of his father as a legendary figure. People said that he had Bedouin blood, which supposedly explained his restlessness and his sexual appetite. They always mentioned the numbers—the nine wives, or ten if you count the Copt. It was clear from the way they said this that nobody counted the Copt.

The number they didn't know for certain was how many children the man fathered. The total was somewhere around twenty, but most marriages were brief, and often there was little or no contact between half siblings. Virtually all of these kids grew up in poverty, and Sayyid's situation had been particularly dire, because his mother was the ninth and final wife (or the tenth, if you count the Copt). By that point, his father was well into middle age, and he died suddenly when Sayyid was six years old.

After the death, Sayyid had no choice but to work in order to help support his mother and two younger siblings. He never attended a day of school, and he gravitated to the garbage industry because it required neither education nor connections. His first childhood job involved sitting on the donkey cart of a *zabal,* or "garbageman," to make sure that nobody stole the trash while the man did his rounds. Over time, Sayyid worked his way into better jobs, until as a teenager he became the main assistant to a Coptic *zabal* named Salama.

Like Sayyid's father, Salama was a man whose life was shaped by an abundance of women. But Salama's abundance was of a different sort. He married only once, and his wife gave birth to eight daughters and no sons. This also conferred legendary status onto Salama, and people talked about how hard he worked to prepare his daughters' dowries. In an Egyptian marriage, a groom is expected to purchase an apartment and major appliances, while the bride acquires kitchenware, bedroom furnishings, clothing, and other household goods. For the family of the bride, these resources are essentially lost, because after marriage she becomes part of her husband's clan.

Salama's lack of sons also meant that there was no male heir to his garbage route. After Salama died, his family decided to subcontract the route to Sayyid, who had proven himself loyal through years of service. But there were strict conditions. In return for the privilege of collecting Zamalek garbage, Sayyid agreed to pick out all paper, plastic, glass, and other resalable commodities, and he delivered them to the husband of Salama's eldest daughter. Sayyid collected no fee for these materials. "I give it to him like a peeled banana," he once said.

With the examples of his father and Salama in mind, Sayyid's approach to marriage was strategic, assertive, and patient. He trusted nobody, not even family. For Upper Egyptians of his class, family elders typically arrange marriages between cousins. The risks of consanguinity are poorly understood, and the goal isn't to diversify the gene pool—it's to conserve resources. The choice is simple: you can watch your daughter's dowry vanish into a stranger's home, or you can effectively keep the goods by marrying her into your extended family. As a result, approximately 40 percent of Egyptians are married to a cousin.

Sayyid's mother came from a village near Beni Suef, another city in Upper Egypt, and when Sayyid was a teenager, the clan identified a younger cousin as his match. The girl grew up expecting to become Sayyid's bride, and he found her kind and attractive. But he developed his own ideas about cousin marriage. In Sayyid's analysis, it would be more difficult to control a cousin-wife, because she could complain to her father or another male elder, who would then put pressure on the husband. "I thought that if I married a stranger, then I'd be able to tell her what to do," he said.

Marrying outside the family, though, was more expensive. And that brought Sayyid back to the material trinity: in order to find a woman, he needed money; in order to make money, he needed more garbage. He picked up the rights to other buildings whenever he could, often paying for the privilege. He also practiced every form of thrift imaginable. He was one of the few Egyptian men I knew who didn't smoke, and he rode a bicycle between home and work, a sacrifice of dignity that is intolerable to most Cairenes. (Despite the city's flatness, it has very few cyclists.) Sayyid leveraged his finds for everything they were worth, cutting deals all over the neighborhood. If the trash contained bread or meat that was still good, he gave it to various doormen and laborers, who rewarded him with other favors. Sayyid also fished clean newspapers out of the garbage and delivered them to the local tea man in exchange for free drinks.

By the end of his twenties, Sayyid had saved enough to build a modest two-story building in Ard al-Liwa, a district on the Giza side of the river. After that, he started to look for a wife, in the most literal sense of the term. A glimpse, a glance—such things matter greatly in a society in which there is little casual contact between men and women. One morning, near the home of an older brother, Sayyid saw a young woman hanging laundry on a balcony clothesline. She was tall, fair, and strikingly pretty. Sayyid learned that she was a native of a village near Aswan, in Upper Egypt, and she had moved to Cairo to live with relatives. Her name was Wahiba.

She was much better educated than Sayyid. She had acquired the degree of *diplom,* a trade school that rural Egyptians often enter after middle school. Family marriage also hadn't worked out for Wahiba; she had been engaged to a cousin, but the agreement collapsed in some family dispute. When Sayyid approached Wahiba's male elders, they were impressed with his financial stability, and soon the wedding was held. He was thirty-one; she was barely eighteen. By the time I got to know Sayyid, they had been married for five years, and Wahiba was pregnant with their third child. Sayyid told me proudly that after marriage his wife had started wearing the *niqab,* the black full-face covering of conservative Muslims. The experience that first sparked Sayyid's desire—a glimpse of Wahiba's face—would not be repeated by other strange men.

For much of our first year in Cairo, Leslie and I attended a two-hour tutorial in Egyptian Arabic every weekday. My language skills improved steadily, and it wasn't long before I was capable of having that planned conversation with Sayyid about my wife's not serving as a waitress.

But by that point he had long since stopped asking Leslie for tea. He must have sensed our discomfort, and I noticed that he made other adjustments on his own. Cairo is notoriously difficult for foreign women, who have to deal with the sexual harassment that's common in public places. But the Egyptian male response to women also veers to the opposite extreme. If Leslie and I were together in the neighborhood, polite men usually addressed all conversation to me, carefully avoiding eye contact with my wife. This was intended as a form of respect, but it was part of the strangeness of being a woman in Cairo: sometimes she stood out, the object of leers and catcalls, while at other times she became invisible.

With Sayyid, though, the dynamic was different. He seemed to realize that I wasn't threatened by his speaking to Leslie, and the three of us could sit and chat without any of the imbalance that usually affected mixed-gender conversations. I knew that he didn't behave this way in his own community; he often spoke bluntly about the need to control and sequester his wife. But nevertheless there was an openness to his character, and he was capable of adapting to the expectations of people with different values.

This sensitivity, rather than the physical labor, was actually the most demanding part of Sayyid's job. There was no government oversight of his work, and no system or structure guaranteed him payment. Like many people in Cairo, he liked to chat about the ongoing revolution, but he never connected it to his own life. He had no real interest in national events; he was entirely focused on the neighborhood where he worked and on the things that he gathered. Sayyid picked up garbage, but he also picked up on the garbage—he had to be alert to clues that helped him understand the residents and persuade them to pay him. This was one reason why he wore filthy clothes: his appearance reminded people of the work that he did on their behalf. He took his midday breaks at the H Freedom kiosk in part because it was a prominent place that gave passersby the opportunity to see him, feel obligated, and pay their monthly fees.

If I was curious about anybody in the neighborhood, I always asked Sayyid. One evening, he stopped to chat with Leslie and me, and we mentioned a rich middle-aged woman who lived on the street. She was notoriously stingy, and she had never married, although she was well educated. I asked Sayyid why somebody with such advantages had become a spinster.

"There's a proverb," he said. "'If you befriend a monkey for his money, then tomorrow the money will be gone, but the monkey will still be a monkey.' That's what it was like with her. Nobody wanted to marry her."

I remarked that the woman was overweight, and I wondered if this had been another factor. But Sayyid shook his head. "She used to be pretty," he said. "I've seen pictures of her from fifteen or twenty years ago. She looked so different. Beautiful!"

"Where did you see the pictures?"

"In the garbage," he said. "She threw them away."

I asked why she had done that.

"Maybe she didn't want to remember those times," he said quietly. "Maybe the pictures made her sad."

On weekday mornings, Leslie and I took a cab west across the 6th October Bridge to a small language school called Kalimat. Before moving to Cairo, we had completed Middlebury College's intensive summer course in *fusha,* the classical Arabic that is used as a literary and formal language across the Arab world. But the Egyptian dialect is so different that even some of the basics—*How are you?*—are difficult to understand for somebody who has studied only *fusha*. And so in Cairo, I essentially started over, at the age of forty-one, with a beginner's course in Egyptian.

When you move to another country as an adult, the language flows around you like a river. A child can abandon himself to the current, but most older people, at least in the beginning, take more tentative steps. Maybe they get their feet wet; maybe they go waist-deep; maybe they occasionally have a few hours in which they're fully immersed. Along the way, they fish out the words and phrases that seem to matter most, and in Cairo I kept a notebook for vocabulary. Some lists came from drinking tea with Sayyid:

sex	جنس
difference	إختلاف
to hit	يضرب
regretful	ندمان

to burn	يحرق
to be burned	يتحرق
he burned the garbage	حرق الزبالة

Other lists came from work. In December 2011, after I had spent an afternoon at the Omar Makram Mosque, my notebook read:

imam	إمام
sheikh	شيخ
beard	دقن
carpet	سجادة
forbidden	حرام

Sometimes the words created a kind of narrative. As my Arabic improved, I occasionally went to Tahrir alone, as a way of practicing. In January 2012, after a group of activists became suspicious of me, the trajectory of their paranoia was laid out in my notebook:

agent	عميل
embassy	سفارة
spy	جاسوس
Israel	إسرائيل
Israelis	إسرائليين
Jew	يهودي

In February, I added "*tear gas*," "*slaughter*," and "*Can you speak more slowly?*" "*Conspiracy theory*" appeared on the same day as "*fried potatoes*." Sometimes I wondered about the strangeness of my Arabic and what it would have been like if I had arrived before the Arab Spring. But it would have been different at any time, in any place; you can never step into the same language twice. Many of my notebook words were relics of the revolution, and after the Muslim Brotherhood won control of the parliament, the list read:

people with the beards	أصحاب الدقون
Ministry of Media	وزارة الإعلام
authentic	أصلي
fake, false	مضروب
to stop (something)	يبطل
illusion, not real	وهم

One of my earliest lessons was that this particular instant, for all its intensity, would eventually pass. The notebook contained many words specific to the Arab Spring, but they were surrounded by terms and sayings that felt timeless. After I started to understand the political talk shows that cabbies played on their radios, I realized that callers and hosts exchanged polite Islamic greetings for much of a minute before they embarked on angry arguments about the revolution. My Egyptian textbook was titled *Dardasha*—"Chatting"—and the first chapter included a set dialogue that showed the proper way to greet a casual acquaintance. Soon I found myself repeating this conversation with neighbors, line for line, using phrases that would never be touched by Tahrir:

"Peace be upon you!"	السلام عليكو!
"May peace, mercy, and the blessings of God be upon you."	وعليكم السلام ورحمة الله وبركاته.
"How are you?"	إزيك؟
"May God grant you peace! Are you well?"	الله يسلمك! وإنتى بخير؟
"Praise be to God."	الحمد لله.
"Go with peace!"	مع السلامة!
"Go with peace!"	مع السلامة!

Arabic was the second language that I had studied as an adult. In high school and in college, I never traveled overseas, and then, as a twenty-seven-year-old, I signed up to teach in the Peace Corps. I was sent to China, where I lived in a small, remote city on the Yangtze River. After I finished my Peace Corps service, I stayed in China for another nine years, to work as a journalist. The language became part of my basic thought: certain words and concepts came to me in Chinese rather than in English.

Naturally, some of my perception of Arabic passed through a Chinese lens. I couldn't live beside the Nile without remembering what I had learned on the Yangtze, and one of the first qualities that impressed me was Egyptian politeness. In China, I had used a beginner's textbook titled *Speaking Chinese About China,* and the early lessons spent virtually no time on niceties. On the first page of the first dialogue, a student said to his teacher, "*Tell us about the Yellow River.*" No "*please,*" no "*thank you*"—the Chinese rarely used such terms, and they were known for directness.

In *Dardasha,* though, the first vocabulary list read:

Please, come in!	إتفضل!
sorry	معلهش
God willing! (hopefully!)	إن شاء الله!
Nice to meet you!	فرصة سعيدة جداً!
Thank you!	شكراً!

Many early lessons introduced phrases that varied depending on gender or class. The sociolinguistic rules were so complicated that even a thirty-second dialogue required a note of exegesis:

> *You might have noticed in the dialogue that when Hassan asked Ali about his wife, he did not use her name even though the dialogue sounds friendly and informal. In Egypt, you have to be a very close friend or a relative to use the names of others' spouses or female relatives in particular.*

Dardasha's approach was prescriptive: with every interaction, there were right and wrong responses. One chapter explained that when somebody visits an Egyptian home, the host will offer food and drink, but the guest should refuse repeatedly. The text instructed, "*After a few times of being offered and politely declining, the guest accepts the offer.*" Another chapter described the "evil eye," the belief that envy can cause misfortune. In *Dardasha,* icons of little bombs with burning fuses had been printed next to the kind of phrase that, even during a revolution, qualified as explosive: "*Your son is really smart, Madame Fathiya.*" Fortunately, this compliment-bomb was promptly defused by a corrected version: "*This is what God has willed, Madame Fathiya, your son is really smart.*"

I often heard that phrase—*masha'allah,* "this is what God has willed"—when I was out with my daughters. Occasionally, an elderly person smiled at the toddlers and said, "*Wehish, wehish!*"—"Beastly, beastly!" This confused me until somebody explained that a reverse compliment is another way of deflecting the evil eye. There were so many rules about social interactions that even *Dardasha*'s prescriptions weren't adequate. At the Kalimat school, one of our teachers, Rifaat Amin, prepared a five-page supplemental handout titled "Arabic Expressions of Social Etiquette." It listed the proper response whenever people blessed my daughters: *allah yakhallik,* "may God keep you."

Rifaat's handout included a salutation for somebody who has just returned from a trip, and another phrase for greeting a person who was recently sick. Anytime the name of a dead man came up, it was necessary to say *allah yerhamoh,* "may God rest his soul." Beggars could be rebuffed with a piece of deferred responsibility: *allah yasahellik,* "may God make things easier for you." One greeting—*shofeitum*—was used when somebody returned from the toilet. There was even a phrase for greeting a person who has recently received a haircut.

My Zamalek barber had been saying *na'iman* at the end of every trim, but I hadn't understood. After studying Rifaat's handout, I went to my next haircut and finally responded correctly, and the barber beamed. It was the kind of concept that hadn't existed in my mind until I had the word, and then suddenly the need was obvious. How had I lived on this earth for forty-two years without any dedicated post-haircut vocabulary? From that point on, the Zamalek barber and I always followed the script:

"*Na'iman.*" "With blessings."

"*Allah yin'am alik.*" "May God bless you."

Rifaat Amin's ancestral village was Abydos. His father was born there, the son of a farmer, and he became a contractor who specialized in water towers.

During the 1950s and 1960s, when Egypt's population grew rapidly, he built more than three hundred towers, all the way from Aswan to Alexandria. It seemed the perfect specialty for a son of Abydos—having grown up beneath that perfect dome of blue, in a place of buried boats and ancient imagination, he put the water back into the sky.

He became successful enough to construct a six-story building for his extended family in Cairo. Rifaat grew up in this complex, surrounded by aunts and uncles and cousins. He spent his childhood summers with his grandparents in Abydos, where he played among the ruins at the edge of the Buried. By the time he was in his fifties, when Leslie and I came to know him, his grandparents were long gone, and he rarely returned to the south. But he remained proud of his Abydos roots. He often said that he was descended from the Egyptians of pharaonic times, and he looked the part—his features could have been sketched from a carving on a temple wall. He was very thin, with an erect, stern carriage, and his thick white hair contrasted with his dark skin. He had high cheekbones and intense, deep-set eyes. He was fiercely patriotic. Like many Upper Egyptians whose families had risen in social class during the mid-century, he was a staunch adherent of Gamal Abdel Nasser, who had also come from the south. Rifaat had been only twelve years old when Nasser died of cancer, in 1970, but he remained nostalgic for the Egypt of that earlier era. At ten o'clock every evening, Rifaat watched the Rotana television channel's rebroadcast of a concert from the 1950s or 1960s by the great Egyptian singer Umm Kulthum. Once, Rifaat prepared a worksheet for our tutorial that included the sentence "*There is not a real Egyptian who does not love Umm Kulthum.*"

But Rifaat had other qualities that seemed out of place in today's Egypt. He was Muslim, but he drank alcohol, avoided mosques, and ate freely during Ramadan. He ignored the daily calls to prayer; for him, the only ritual that was followed religiously was the ten o'clock Rotana rebroadcast. He remarked that the hajj pilgrimage to Mecca was a waste of money that would be better spent on the poor. Since his teenage years, he had followed a mostly vegetarian diet, which is extremely rare among Egyptians. Rifaat's siblings told me that their father often shouted at him when he first refused beef and lamb, but the boy held firm. As an adult, one of the few meat dishes that he enjoyed was chicken prepared by his older sister, Wardiya, who removed the skin in a special way.

Wardiya sometimes delivered meals to Rifaat's apartment, because he was a man without a woman. He had left the family compound when he was young and single, citing a need for privacy, which is also unusual in Egypt. He lived alone in an apartment in Mohandiseen, a middle-class neighborhood on the Giza side. In his early thirties, he had been briefly engaged to a foreign woman, although now he didn't seem to take this episode very seriously. "I never got married, *al-hamdulillah*!" he often said to Leslie and me. "All praise be to God!"

A decade before he became our teacher, he had had lymphoma. While he was undergoing chemotherapy treatments, Wardiya delivered meals to him every week. These siblings were extremely close despite vastly different lifestyles and opinions. Wardiya was devout, and she disagreed with her brother about both God and gender relations. Rifaat believed that men and women should be equal, an idea that Wardiya refused to accept. But she admitted that she was influenced by her brother. He had pushed her to give the best possible education to her two daughters, and eventually she agreed. Rifaat's argument was to think of a woman's schooling as a weapon—it was a form of defense if her husband let her down.

Rifaat was natural in the presence of women, which was one reason Leslie and I had classes with him. For our tutorials, he liked to prepare lessons that reflected his social criticisms. Sometimes he wrote dialogues in which boorish men were denied names:

> ***Huda:*** *What are you tired about? You don't do a single thing at home.*
>
> ***Her husband:*** *What do you mean?*
>
> ***Huda:*** *I mean that you should help me a little with the housework.*
>
> ***Her husband:*** *Look, your work isn't necessary, and you spend half your salary on transportation and the other half on makeup.*

When we had a class on Umm Kulthum, who had married late in life and never had children, Rifaat mentioned that she was probably a lesbian. He admired such iconoclasts, and he valued personal freedom; he was an enthusiastic supporter of the Arab Spring. The lists of words from his tutorials often reflected a higher plane of discourse: "*confrontation,*" "*intellectual,*" "*de-*

veloping countries," "*social class.*" But he also had the traditional Egyptian love of a strong leader, and he proudly called himself a Nasserite. When Leslie and I pointed out that Nasser had thrown dissidents, intellectuals, and Islamists into prison, Rifaat claimed that the dictator's crackdown had been justified, because the country needed to be unified after the revolution of 1952.

He believed that today's Egypt urgently needed major social change, and he described family relations as stifling. But he also drilled us on the "Arabic Expressions of Social Etiquette." In terms of language, he had a traditional streak, and one of his handouts outlined the proper ways to address Egyptian women:

> Ya madam—*to married or engaged lady in Western clothes (look for ring)*
>
> Ya ʿanisa, ya madamwazel—*to unmarried, un-engaged young girl in Western clothes*
>
> Ya sitt—*to married woman in traditional dress*
>
> Ya sitt hanim *(very respectful)*—*to married women*

Sayyid and Rifaat were both second-generation Upper Egyptians who lived in Cairo, and they became the people with whom I most frequently spoke Arabic. Despite their differences in education and social class, they had one thing in common: a powerful sense of contradiction. Each man combined rigid tradition with ideas that could be surprisingly open-minded or nonconformist. Over time, I came to recognize this tendency for contradiction as part of the national character—it was just as Egyptian as those figures on the temple walls. The modern country had a dominant religion, a powerful nationalism, and patriarchal family structures that could be claustrophobic. But there was also a counterstrain of individualism, and many Egyptians were simply natural-born characters. Rifaat's quirks and inconsistencies seemed so innate that Wardiya and his other siblings had wisely chosen to accept them.

Rifaat liked to create his own materials for class, but in the beginning I insisted that we study *Dardasha*. My years in China had left me with a fascination for language textbooks, because they teach much more than just vocabulary and grammar. When I first studied *Speaking Chinese About China,* in the fall of 1996, the country's economic reforms were starting to accelerate, and the national priorities were reflected by the book's lessons. A sentence that appeared in lesson 3 ("*He works very hard at his job*") became more complex in lesson 4 ("*Everyone is working very hard; as a result, the output has been doubled*") and then reached new heights of sophistication in lesson 5 ("*We have realized that only by developing production can we raise the people's living standard*"). Along the way, it was never clear who the people were, or what they were producing, or why they were working so damned hard. They were led by shadowy political figures who were unnamed but every bit as diligent. (Lesson 3: "*Do the Chinese leaders themselves really participate in physical labor?*")

Fifteen years later, in another country in transition, *Dardasha* introduced me to a completely different world. The Egyptian text had no production quotas, no economic plans, and no infrastructure projects. The word "factory" didn't appear in the book. Nobody talked about doubling output or raising living standards, and characters in dialogues said things like "Ya hag, *I'm an engineer, and after five years of university I'm working as a waiter in a restaurant.*"

My Chinese text had been cagey toward its foreign readers—there wasn't a word of negative commentary about China or the Chinese people. But *Dardasha* was never shy about bad behavior. This was the flip side to the book's emphasis on politeness: it illustrated the many ways in which actual life failed to live up to beautiful phrases. *Dardasha* even included a dialogue of a bizarrely tenacious wrong-number conversation. Ever since Leslie and I had acquired Egyptian cell phones, we had been puzzled by all the calls we received from people asking for strangers, or demanding weird things, or saying nothing at all. *Dardasha*'s unit 8 prepared students for the experience:

Ali: *Hello!*

Khamis: *Hello! Is Mr. Gumaa there?*

Ali: *No, wrong number.*

Khamis: *Yes? How? I want Mr. Gumaa.*

Ali: Ya habibi, *there is nobody here called Mr. Gumaa.*

Khamis: *I'm Khamis. He knows me.*

Ali: *Again? Wrong number. Good-bye.*

Khamis: *Fine! But he knows who I am.*

Ali: *Good-bye.*

When we covered this lesson at Kalimat, Rifaat was away, and our teacher was a friendly man named Sami. To me, the dialogue seemed straightforward and fairly uninteresting. But Sami read it like a Hemingway story: the things that had been left out were the things that mattered.

"I think that Mr. Gumaa is actually there," Sami said seriously. He expounded on the various reasons why Ali might be lying on behalf of Mr. Gumaa. Perhaps Mr. Gumaa owed Khamis money, or maybe Khamis was trying to ask for a favor. Sami said this kind of behavior is common in Egypt.

"Sometimes we hide what people want," he said. "Sometimes we say he's not here, when in fact he's here."

I asked him where this deception comes from.

"From seven thousand years," Sami said. "Always a dictator. Always we are afraid. So we don't trust each other."

Now I reread the nine lines with new paranoia. Why did Ali call him *habibi*? Why did Khamis speak with such familiarity? "*He knows me.*" And what about that cryptic closing sentence? "*But he knows who I am.*" That was the day's lesson: in Egypt, nothing is too small for a conspiracy theory.

It took *Dardasha* a long time to get to numbers. The words for one through ten weren't introduced until the third chapter, and then the text waited another three chapters before continuing with the higher numerals. By the time a student learned to say "*eleven,*" he had already mastered such critical vocabulary as "*cute girl,*" "*engaged,*" "*marriage registrar,*" and "*Star of the East,*" which is the Egyptian nickname for Umm Kulthum. (The singer was covered in chapter 5.)

I had never been anywhere in the world where numbers seemed to inspire such discomfort. First of all, it was a shock to realize that the things that I considered Arabic numerals are in fact not standard in many Arab countries, including Egypt. The term is a misnomer; technically, they're the Hindu-Arabic numerals, because the system originated in India and then was introduced to Europe by the Arabs. Egyptians and many other Arabs use a different system, the Arabic-Indic numerals, which also came from India. As if these terms aren't confusing enough—Hindu-Arabic, Arabic-Indic—there's enough overlap between the shapes of the symbols to throw off any foreigner. I had to learn to read ٤ as 4, and ٥ as 5, and ٦ as 6. In an Arabic book, words are read from right to left, but numbers move in the opposite direction. If the flow of a text leads you to a figure, you spin around and go upstream. Egyptian license plates follow the same system:

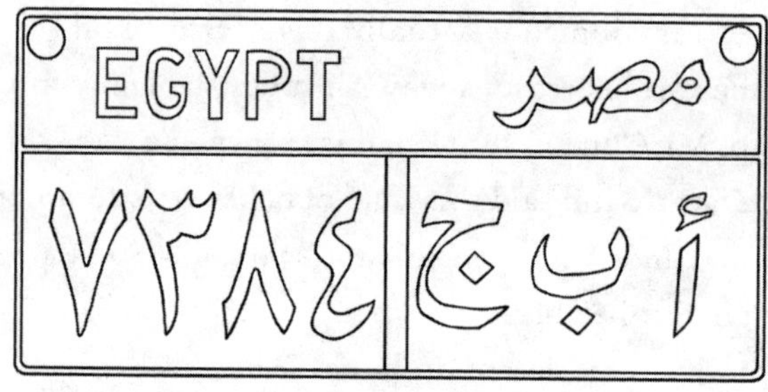

Every time I read a plate, I went cross-eyed: letters from the right, numbers from the left. Could this possibly affect comprehension? Egyptian schoolchildren learned to shift back and forth, juggling two directions of a text and two numbering systems. In public schools, all textbooks used the Arabic-Indic system, and math formulas were written from right to left. But if a student entered a math program in a public university, both the lettering and the direction changed. Formulas appeared in Latin and Greek letters, from left to right. During the student's third year, the curriculum shifted entirely to English, in part because there were no Arabic-language textbooks suitable for this level. Hany El-Hosseiny, a mathematics professor at Cairo University, told me that he noticed students struggling with each of these transitions. In his opinion, it hindered their progress, but he didn't see an easy solution. It was a remnant of nineteenth-century colonialism, when educators introduced technical subjects in English or French, and over time this became entrenched in the curricula.

Even on the street, Egyptians seemed uncomfortable with numbers. They hated to bargain, which surprised me, because I had arrived with preconceived notions about Middle Eastern bazaars. And after China, where bargaining is a national sport, I was trained in all the standard moves: the walk away, the "last price, my friend," the denigration of goods you hope to acquire, the misdirection of bargaining for A when in fact you intend to purchase B. But to do such things in Egypt was like tackling somebody in a game of touch football. During one early bargaining session with a Cairo shopkeeper, I was just getting warmed up when the man made an exasperated face, looked to the sky, and said, *"La ilaha ill'allah!"*

This phrase—*"there is no God but God"*—was also listed on Rifaat's handout. In class, he explained that an Egyptian sometimes repeats the Quranic verse if he's trying to control his temper. I had bargained somebody to the point of prayer! After that, I approached Egyptian transactions like a pregame practice—no pads, no contact. Everything had to be half-speed or slower, and it was wrong to ask many questions about money, which embarrassed Egyptians and made them fear the evil eye. They were easily overwhelmed by figures. At shops, Leslie and I learned to check the change, because merchants made so many mistakes. This wasn't necessarily a way of cheating the foreigners; if anything, the errors were more often in our favor. After eleven years in China, I couldn't recall a single instance in which a Chinese shopkeeper gave me too much change. But in Cairo this happened more times than I could count. It also wasn't unusual to hand an Egyptian clerk a hundred-pound note for a thirty-five-pound charge and see him reach for a calculator.

In some ways, it was a relief after China, where the obsession with money could be tedious. And the flip side to Egyptian math weakness seemed to be a strength with languages. In part this was another relic of colonialism, but I suspected it had more to do with the spontaneity and gregariousness of so many Egyptians. They were natural language learners; I often met people like Manu, who had acquired excellent English without any formal instruction. In my experience, this was rare in China, where people tended to have trouble with languages. They tried to learn them the way they learned math, through rote memorization and repetition.

When I mentioned these issues in class, Rifaat said that Egyptian math failures were both cultural and political. "There's no *nizam*," he said. This word appeared early in my language notebook, as one of the terms of the moment. On Tahrir, protesters used it in the sense of "regime." The most powerful slogan of the Arab Spring—"*the people want to bring down the* nizam"—was first chanted in Tunisia, and then it was picked up by Egyptians and others. But the word can also describe any kind of system, and Egyptians often used it when criticizing their society.

"There's no *nizam* in education," Rifaat continued. "Everything is chaotic and broken down—you see what the schools look like. The books are bad and teachers are poorly trained, so people don't learn to think logically. That's why they can't do math."

In Rifaat's opinion, the issue ran deeper than education or postcolonialism. He remarked that many Egyptians conducted their daily lives without any sense of system. He often harped on this point: people woke up late; they ate meals at odd hours; they socialized past midnight. An entire section of my notebook was dedicated to the vocabulary of lateness:

I'm going to be a little late

I came early

Can we push the appointment back a little?

What a terrible day!

Are you coming on time, or are you late?

I'm not coming on time

Can we delay the appointment?

Such phrases had never appeared in my lists in China, where people had strict ideas about when to sleep and when to wake, and nobody was late to appointments. After I started studying Egyptian, I became curious about these contrasts, and I reread *Speaking Chinese About China*. I was struck by how many Chinese lessons featured formal institutions and structures. In the early sections, the vocabulary included "*National People's Congress,*" "*socialism,*" "*United Nations,*" "*Women's Federation,*" "*vice-premier,*" and "*chairman of a committee.*"

In *Dardasha,* though, there was no sense of a larger *nizam*. The text referred to leaders like Mubarak, but not to institutions or structures, and government jobs were described in strictly negative terms. In dialogues, characters referred to *wasta,* a word that's difficult to define. The text translated it as "connection/favoritism":

> ***Father:*** *What about your friends from university—what do they do for work?*
>
> ***Mahmoud:*** *They all work at big companies.*
>
> ***Father:*** *And why don't you work there?*
>
> ***Mahmoud:*** *All of them had* wasta.

The Chinese have a similar concept: *guanxi,* or "connections." But *guanxi* can be developed, learned, and manipulated; it's a full-fledged social system. At times, it's terribly corrupt, but it's also flexible: anybody with skills and savvy can build *guanxi.* Egyptian *wasta,* on the other hand, impressed me as far more static. It seemed to reflect social class rather than a constructed and cultivated network, and it had a way of ending conversations—either a person had *wasta* or he didn't. Somebody like Sayyid, who worked hard and managed an impressive range of relationships, never described this as *wasta.* He could maintain his route and make small improvements in his life, but there wasn't a clear path to bigger success. The significant things that real *wasta* could provide—new jobs, true security, better schools for his children—were beyond the scope of Sayyid's network. He didn't see his garbage route as part of some larger system.

In *Dardasha*'s dialogues, even educated people expressed frustration that they had no options other than calling on *wasta* or leaving the country. Schooling seemed to have limited value, and nobody expressed faith in institutions of the state. Family mattered above everything. The text included side notes on structures of the clan:

> *As you might have noticed from the dialogue, the behavior of one member of a family tends to reflect on the entire family. . . . Within the ordinary Egyptian family, it is assumed that there is a hierarchy of knowledge in that the older members are believed to be wiser.*

The key words here were "assumed" and "believed." In *Dardasha,* elders could be generous and wise, but they could also be ridiculous and petty. A husband might behave worse than a child:

Ali: *What's for lunch today?*

Fatma: *Stuffed chicken, just the way you like it.*

Ali: *I don't want chicken. Every day, we have chicken.*

Fatma: *Fine, what do you want, Ali?*

Ali: *I don't know. But I don't want chicken.*

Fatma: *Tomorrow, God willing, I'll make whatever you like.*

The book also wasn't shy about the negative aspects of Cairo. It introduced the conditional tense with a series of open-ended sentences:

If only I knew who was calling the telephone every day . . .

If only I could see the child who rings the doorbell and runs . . .

If only I knew which of the neighbors listens to loud music all night long . . .

One exercise was called "You Are Irritable." The instructions read, "*Work in pairs and ask your partner the following questions to find out whether he/she has an irritable personality or not:*"

You have an appointment with a friend at five o'clock. At six o'clock your friend is still not there. Do you get angry and leave?

You are going to your friend's and you have an appointment, but he is not at home. Do you get angry and leave?

You are on the internet and each time the telephone rings and the same person calls with a wrong number. Do you get angry on the telephone?

When Rifaat taught this lesson, his answer to every question was: Yes. He was the most *'asabi* person I knew, although it's hard to translate a word that's so specific to the Egyptian experience. The English "irritable" lacks context;

it seems unfair to describe somebody as *'asabi* without also conveying everything in Egypt that might make a reasonable person *'asabi*. Perhaps it's best to say that this word describes the type of man who teaches Arabic by asking his students to translate the following: "*It seems no one in this country knows how to celebrate without a microphone and five loudspeakers.*"

Rifaat urged us to finish *Dardasha* as quickly as possible, because he loved creating his own dialogues in which Egyptians behaved badly, antagonized relatives, and turned minor issues into major problems. When Leslie and I first got to know him, we struggled to understand his patriotism, because he complained so vociferously about so many aspects of Egyptian society. But as time passed, we realized that there was the Egypt inside, and then there was the Egypt outside—these things weren't necessarily the same. The sense of being Egyptian ran so deep that it had little to do with the structures, or the lack of structures, of the actual country. This was one reason why the place felt so coherent, and held together so well, despite a remarkable lack of governance.

And it was another example of the national tendency toward contradiction. The people I met in Cairo tended to be deeply patriotic, but they also enjoyed criticizing themselves, their government, and their society, especially if this could be done with sarcasm or some other form of humor. Somehow, Egyptians could be at once proud and ashamed, optimistic and cynical, serious and joking. They loved their strongmen leaders even while complaining about what these figures had done to the nation. After one of our Arabic classes featured the glories of pharaonic history, a new phrase appeared in my notebook:

Egypt has been robbed for seven thousand years, but she is still rich.

CHAPTER 6

IN MARCH 2012, I CROSSED THE QASR AL-NIL BRIDGE, PASSED THROUGH TAHrir Square, and entered Egypt's parliament building, in order to meet with one of the legislative leaders of the Muslim Brotherhood. The new parliament had been in session for less than two months, and it was convening in the old parliament building, which before the revolution had been home to a series of assemblies that were closely associated with the term "rubber stamp." The building itself was quite impressive. The exterior was in the neoclassical style, with marble pillars and a domed roof that sat above a spacious meeting chamber. The parliamentarians took their breaks in an adjoining room that was called the Pharaonic Hall. Inside the Pharaonic Hall, pillars had been painted to resemble palm trees, in the manner of an ancient Egyptian temple. A bronze statue of Horus sat on a throne against one wall. Behind Horus's throne, there were several dirty rags, half a dozen cans of shoe polish, and four old pairs of shoes.

I was scheduled to meet a Muslim Brother parliamentarian named Sobhi Saleh, and he was running late. His assistant had called with one of those textbook phrases—"*Can we push the appointment back a little?*" I waited in the Pharaonic Hall, watching the dozen or so legislators who sat around the room, talking in low voices. An elderly man shined shoes, and waiters carried silver trays from which they served tea, sandwiches, and cigarettes.

Of everybody in the hall, the shoe-shine man seemed most at home. With each customer, he followed a ritual: he removed the man's shoes, replaced them with a temporary pair, and then vanished behind the statue of Horus. After a moment he reappeared with a rag or a can of polish. I watched him do this a few times, and then I became curious and walked over to look behind the statue. His stash of equipment was arranged neatly: the rags, the polish, the extra shoes.

I struck up a conversation, and the shoe-shine man told me that he was named Rifaat Mohammed Ahmed, and he had been shining shoes in the Pharaonic Hall since 1964. "I was here during Nasser, and I was here during Sadat," he said. He was about five feet tall and thin as a rail, with hands that had been stained the color of mahogany. His right eye was permanently closed. When he spoke, he leaned forward and tilted his head to the left, squinting through his good eye.

"There were only eighty-eight Muslim Brothers in that last parliament," Rifaat said. Like every assembly since Nasser, it had been dominated by the National Democratic Party, or NDP. The NDP had ruled what was effectively a one-party state, although the Brotherhood and some other groups had been allowed to take a limited number of seats in the assembly.

"Sometimes the NDP members wouldn't show up for a vote, so they wouldn't have enough for a majority," Rifaat continued. "One day, this happened, and Ahmed Ezz came running in here to tell the NDP members to get in the chamber and vote. And he shouted at me, 'You, Rifaat! If you keep delaying members with your shoe shines, I'll complain about you to the speaker of the parliament!'"

Ahmed Ezz had been a wealthy businessman and one of the most powerful figures in the NDP. That last parliament had been dissolved in February 2011, after Mubarak resigned, and now Ezz was serving a ten-year sentence for corruption in Cairo's notorious Tora Prison. Rifaat squinted and waved a polished finger, as if Ezz were still standing in front of him: "I said, 'I don't care. I'm not afraid of you.'"

The little man puffed out his chest. "I remember saying that this parliament will not continue," he went on. "I knew that something would happen. For ten years I had been saying that there would be a revolution."

While we were talking, Sobhi Saleh arrived, and all at once Rifaat abandoned the defiant pose. He dipped his head, smiled, and stepped back politely while Saleh took his seat. Saleh apologized for being late, explaining that he was the head of a committee charged with writing Egypt's new constitution. He said that recently he had been reviewing a study of 194 world constitutions, prepared by Princeton University, and he felt intense pressure from the public. "Their ambition has no ceiling," he said. "A revolution by definition is ambition."

Rifaat stood nearby, head bowed. Now Saleh gestured for him to take his shoes.

"This is the best man in the parliament," Rifaat said, kneeling beside Saleh. "He is honest and clear in his speeches. And he is a decent, good man."

Saleh waved off the praise, but he was smiling.

"He has no equal in the assembly," Rifaat continued. He took Saleh's shoes, and then he retreated to the statue of Horus.

Saleh was in his late fifties, with dark skin, thick gray hair, and heavy eyebrows. He smiled more easily than most Muslim Brothers I had met. They often had a stiff, formal air, and some Egyptians claimed that they could pick out a Brother by his proud posture. But in truth there was no clear sign of membership, which added to the organization's mystique.

As a newcomer to Egypt, I quickly learned to look for outward features that reflected a person's faith or class, because these signs were essentially part of the national language. An elite woman often left her head uncovered, whereas somebody from a conservative middle-class background was more likely to wrap her *hijab* tightly around her chin. In lower-class parts of the city, it was more common to see women in *niqabs*. For men, devout Muslims tended to cultivate prayer bruises on their foreheads, and Salafis wore bushy beards with the mustaches shaved. Virtually every Coptic Christian, both male and female, had a small cross tattooed on the underside of the right wrist. But there was no mark for a Muslim Brother. They tended to be solidly middle-class professionals, and some had beards while others were clean-shaven, like Saleh. His iPhone's home screen featured a picture of his own face, which lit up every time a call came in. He was smiling on the iPhone, too.

We talked for a while, and then Rifaat returned from Horus with the shined shoes. I asked Saleh about the presidential campaign, which was finally under way. The Brotherhood had promised not to field a candidate, because they wanted to reassure Egyptians that the Islamists intended to share control of the government. I asked if the Brothers might change their minds.

"Never," Saleh said. "Never. We will not nominate somebody." The iPhone lit up; Saleh looked at his smiling face and declined the call. He went on, "We want to send a message to every party to make them realize that Islamists are not seeking to dominate the power. As our historic slogan says, 'Participating, not dominating.'"

Muslim Brothers often told me that everything I needed to know about their politics could be found in the Quran. This was a common claim of Islamism as a whole: supposedly, the political movement reflected some essential and eternal quality of the faith. But this was as misleading as trying to understand the politics of American evangelicals by reading the New Testament. The book was one thing, and history was something else; any social movement was a product of its time and place.

The Society of the Muslim Brothers had been established in 1928, in the Suez Canal city of Ismailia, by Hassan al-Banna. Banna grew up in a village in the Delta, where his father was an imam who followed a conservative school of Sunni Islam. The boy—serious, devout, and obsessed with a strict interpretation of Islamic rules—became a teacher of Arabic. For his first job, the government assigned him to a primary school in Ismailia.

No other Egyptian city could have provided a more jarring environment for a young man like Banna. Ismailia was the headquarters of the British-run Suez Canal Company, and all the best villas were inhabited by European employees. Street signs were in English; outside town, an imposing British military base controlled the region. Like other Egyptian cities with foreign residents, Ismailia had a segregated legal system, with separate courts to handle any case involving a foreigner.

For an educated Egyptian, such humiliation was only the most recent chapter in a long decline. The last native to declare himself pharaoh had been defeated by the Greek Ptolemies, in 186 BC, and from that point until the middle of the twentieth century there wasn't a single Egyptian ruler. Egypt had invented the concept of the nation, and it defined many basic terms of kingship for Western civilization, but it lost the ability to govern itself. For more than two millennia, a series of foreign overlords took power along the Nile: Greeks, Romans, Byzantines, Persians, Arabs, Ottomans.

In the early nineteenth century, Muhammad Ali, an Albanian who ruled

Egypt on behalf of the Ottoman Empire, became determined to reform the country. He came to power immediately after Napoleon's invasion and brief occupation, which convinced Ali and others that the country needed to be modernized. Ali expanded the military, restructured the government bureaucracy, introduced elements of European law, and redirected agriculture toward cash crops like cotton. He was succeeded by his sons, grandsons, and other descendants, many of whom tried to continue the reforms.

To a large degree, these attempts at development were funded by another modern innovation: foreign loans. With overseas money, the various members of the Muhammad Ali dynasty built schools, palaces, and military barracks, and sections of downtown Cairo were redesigned along the Paris model. They excavated the Suez Canal, where brand-new cities sprang up in the desert. Port Said, on the northern end of the canal, was named in honor of one of Muhammad Ali's sons, and Ismailia took its name from a grandson, Ismail Pasha.

All of these projects, and the canal in particular, eventually bankrupted the nation. By the end of the nineteenth century, the Ottoman Empire was so weak that Egypt was ripe for another overlord. But this time the invasion was carried out by bankers rather than soldiers. The British simply purchased the country's debt. They took control of the Suez Canal Company and nearly all its profits, and over time they began to manage key government institutions, until, at the beginning of World War I, the British ruled Egypt directly.

On the banks of the foreign-run canal, Hassan al-Banna issued the founding statement of the Muslim Brotherhood: "We are weary of this life of humiliation and restriction." The movement is best understood as a reaction to colonialism, capitalism, and the way that traditional culture was breaking down in the late nineteenth and early twentieth centuries. In that sense, the Brotherhood was similar to Communism and fascism, which also gained strength around the same time in other parts of the world. But unlike the Communists, who attempted to create new and utopian structures for society, Banna turned to an existing faith.

He often used the word *nizam,* "system," to describe the ways in which Islam could be applied to solve all problems of contemporary society. This word never appears in the Quran, and scholars of comparative religion have described Banna's use of the concept as anachronistic. For him, Islam became a *nizam* not because this was the actual content of the Quran but because this was what he believed the modern world demanded. Brotherhood leaders weren't known as deep thinkers or theorists; Richard P. Mitchell, who wrote a seminal early history of the organization, remarked that "neither Banna nor the movement produced any work remotely identifiable as theology or philosophy." Instead, their main achievement was bureaucratic. Banna created a system of linked five-member groups, which resembled the cell structures of early Communist and fascist organizations. The Brotherhood's leadership was strongly hierarchical, and this sense of structure and discipline proved to be deeply appealing in a society searching for *nizam*. Within twenty years of the Brotherhood's founding, there were between 300,000 and 600,000 members, and they became active in mosques and charities.

But the Brotherhood's fundamental purpose was never as clearly defined as its structures. Banna spoke vaguely about inspiring the "Islamization" of Egypt, and he warned the Brothers that they were not a political party. Their activities, though, were often political, and they sponsored militias in Palestine during the early part of their history. Some members engaged in assassinations and other violent acts in Egypt. Brotherhood leaders eventually rejected such violence, but the Egyptian government responded to the group with repression. The secret police assassinated Banna on a Cairo street in 1949, and the Brotherhood was banned for most of its history in Egypt. All of these events increased the organization's tendency toward secrecy and paranoia.

Even after the fall of Mubarak, when the Brotherhood was participating in a newly opened political system, leaders refused to answer basic questions. The organization's finances were a mystery, as were total membership numbers. In the spring of 2012, I often asked leaders and spokespeople how many Brothers there were in Egypt, and I never heard the same thing twice. Their answers ranged from 400,000 to more than 2 million, and they invariably said that they didn't know the exact figure. This seemed unlikely for an organization that maintained an intricate cell structure and collected money from all members.

Rifaat, my Arabic teacher, loathed them. "*Kedebeen!*" he said, whenever the topic came up in Arabic class. "Liars!" This was a standard criticism, along with the idea that the Brothers had a hidden agenda. It was in part to allay such fears that the organization's leaders had declared that they wouldn't seek the presidency. "We sent this message to tell everybody that we do not want to be alone in power," Yasser Ali Elsaid, a Brotherhood spokesman, told me the same week that Sobhi Saleh said much the same thing in the parliament building. Less than two weeks later, the Brotherhood announced that it would field a candidate after all. In terms of reassuring critics, they accomplished exactly the opposite of what they had originally set out to do. But now they had a chance to control the presidency as well as the parliament.

That spring, as part of the new post-Tahrir openness, all legislative sessions were broadcast live on a show called *The Voice of Parliament*. For many Egyptians, this was the first glimpse of the fruits of the revolution, and the show seemed to play on every television in Cairo coffee shops and cafés. I usually watched it in Manu's apartment, taking notes while he translated. Sessions were shown without commentary, although legislators were interviewed during breaks:

> ***Q:*** *As we heard earlier, there are a lot of institutions and factions and people like Bernard Lewis around the world who have plans to divide Egypt into many small countries. As a Nubian, what do you think of that?*
>
> ***A:*** *Our culture is seven thousand years old.*

Before coming to Egypt, I had heard that conspiracy theories were prevalent among average people, but I didn't realize the ways in which they bubbled upward through society, like water from a spring. On *The Voice of Parliament*, political leaders didn't necessarily set the tone; instead, they often amplified the things that came up in talk shows and street discussions. One afternoon in February, a legislator stood up and said, "A lot of people are talking about the old regime manipulating and controlling everything from inside Tora Prison. How do we know whether this is true?"

This was a common pattern: a lawmaker would bring up some supposed threat, and others would chime in, and then, before anything was resolved, the topic was dropped. One day it was the Tora Prison; another day it was the low quality of government-subsidized bread. Who was responsible for the bad bread? Was there a conspiracy behind the incompetence? A member rose and delivered an impassioned speech about how he had offered some government bread to a hungry cat, but the animal refused, which apparently pointed to only one possible conclusion. ("There's a mafia involved in every facet of production, from supply to transport to the bakers.")

Certain themes repeated like clockwork. During virtually every session, some Salafi parliamentarian would stand up and announce that it was a crime that the holy city of Jerusalem remains in the hands of the Jews. The speaker of the assembly, a capable and long-suffering Muslim Brother named Dr. Saad el-Katatni, who looked as if he had acquired his prayer bruise from banging his head against a wall in frustration, would remind everybody to stay on topic. Members offered proposals; some were good and others were not so good. ("We have eighty-five million people in Egypt. If we got ten pounds from each of them, we would get a lot of money and we could solve all of the problems we are talking about.") The most outspoken legislators were Muslim Brothers, and Salafis were also vocal. The few liberals and secularists seemed subdued. During one two-day stretch, Manu and I watched for nine hours before a woman said a word. Only 2 percent of the legislators were female.

Nobody was under any illusion that this was good for Egypt. One day, a parliamentarian stood up and pleaded, "Let's stop this broadcast. When the people see what we are doing here, and all the fighting, they will lose trust in us." But it was too late; tens of millions of Egyptians had already tuned in. Anybody could recognize the revolution's lack of direction, along with the inefficiency of having a legislature without a new constitution or a new president. Parliamentarians were prominent but powerless; they had a platform but no preparation for what they were doing. They were essentially playacting an imported democratic ritual—a neoclassical dome propped awkwardly above a Pharaonic Hall. "Do you know what this government reminds me of?" one legislator said, during a session in late April. "Do you remember when we were kids playing hide-and-seek, and we were counting down from ten, nine, eight? Are there police yet? No. Is there bread yet? No. Are there schools yet? No. The thieves have fooled us."

Manu and I watched the show in the neighborhood of Dokki, on the Giza side of the river, where he shared a run-down apartment with a few young foreigners. He once remarked that his father used to spend hours watching the Mubarak-era parliament, a ritual that Manu never understood. In those days, the parliament was completely controlled by the NDP, and Manu's father would become incensed by the craven politicians and scream obscenities at the television. "Maybe that was the point," Manu said. "It made him angry."

Manu had grown up in Port Said, where the Suez Canal meets the Mediterranean. Like Ismailia, the city that inspired the founding of the Brotherhood, Port Said had initially been viewed with great promise. In the 1860s, Frédéric-Auguste Bartholdi, a French sculptor, proposed the construction of a monumental statue in Port Said that would rival the Great Sphinx. Bartholdi's working title was *Egypt Bringing Light to Asia,* and he designed the figure of a ninety-foot-tall Egyptian peasant woman, her arm upraised, with a torch in hand. But Egypt's financial collapse scuttled the project. Bartholdi eventually took his idea across the Atlantic to another promising port, where the Egyptian peasant woman was reimagined as the Statue of Liberty.

Over time, Port Said became a city of missed opportunities: neither as prosperous as it should have been, nor as open as one might have expected. In its early history, the place was cosmopolitan, but this was the shallow cosmopolitanism of a colonial outpost, and nearly all resident foreigners left after Nasser's revolution. Under Sadat and Mubarak, the port was granted some preferential trade and investment policies, but they were sapped by corruption and Egypt's general economic malaise. When Manu was a boy, Port Said felt isolated, a drab backdrop to the ships that passed through en route to more interesting parts of the world.

Manu's father ran a successful coffee shop, but the demands of the business seemed to weigh on him. He treated his staff harshly, and he screamed about Egyptian politics; in the evenings, he tried to relax by smoking hashish. He often beat his youngest son. Manu learned to avoid speaking with his father, because even a casual conversation could lead to violence. In school the boy was an indifferent student. He had a gift for languages, but he lacked an outlet; when he asked to be enrolled in a local English school, his father refused.

Manu began his first sexual relationship toward the end of middle school. Like all Egyptian public middle schools and high schools, classes were segregated by gender, and boys generally had little contact with girls. As the male classmates proceeded into their teenage years, their socializing and roughhousing often had a sexualized element. Sometimes a boy would act like a girl, in a half-joking way, and the others would touch and grab him. It wasn't unusual for boys to proceed from such roughhousing to more intimate activities, in private. Manu found himself obsessed with a good-looking classmate, and soon they were having sex. The relationship lasted for two years, on and off, and then Manu paired up with another male classmate.

He had no words for what he was doing. In Port Said, during the 1990s, there was no proper Arabic term for a gay person, other than *khawwal*. It was an old word: in the eighteenth and nineteenth centuries, a *khawwal* was a cross-dressing male dancer. These figures were common in Egypt, performing at weddings and festivals, and they were often seen as sexually available to other males. Now those dancers no longer existed, and the word had devolved into a slur: "faggot." *Shez ginseyan,* the more formal Arabic term that was often applied to homosexuality, literally meant "sexually abnormal." As far as Manu was concerned, "abnormal" hardly applied to an activity that, in his estimation, was enjoyed by more than half the boys in his high school class.

With Manu's second partner, the sex was intense but silent, and they never spoke about it directly. Their private code word was "football." "Let's play football," one would say, if he was in the mood. The other boy seemed tortured by his passions, and periodically he became upset and cut off the relationship. But invariably, over a period of four years, he always returned to the code: *let's play football.*

Years later, like most homosexuals in Cairo, Manu incorporated the English words "gay" and "straight" into his Arabic. But he disliked such labels. The terms imply fixed identities, whereas his early experience in Port Said had convinced him that sexuality is much more fluid. From what Manu observed, if men are surrounded by men, and if there's a tacit acceptance of contact between them, then these men are likely to have sex with each other. Later, if society demands some version of traditional marriage, then the vast majority of these same men will settle into heterosexual lives.

When Manu returned to Port Said as an adult, he occasionally ran into his old high school partners. Neither of them ever said a word about what they had shared, but their reactions were different. Manu found it easy to have a casual conversation with the first friend, who had apparently dismissed the relationship as a fling that happened long ago between two very young people. Now he was married to a local woman, and they had small children.

But the second friend never married, and he never had a girlfriend. To Manu's knowledge he no longer engaged in male sex. Eventually, he left to work in Saudi Arabia, which, even in a region known for sexual repression, stands out for rigid conservatism. A couple of times, Manu encountered this old partner on trips back to Port Said, and the interactions were brief and awkward. Afterward Manu felt depressed. He sensed that his friend's desires, which had once been silent but powerful, were now also numbed: no words, no feelings.

Of the young Egyptians I knew, Manu seemed to be the only one who lived fully for himself. He wasn't interested in acquiring a permanent home, and he felt little obligation to family. His older siblings tried to introduce him to potential brides, but he found it easy to make excuses about why the timing wasn't right. He rarely talked about the future. On weekends, he drank heavily, and he had an active sex life; sometimes he picked up men in bars or on the Qasr al-Nil Bridge. He had friends of all types. Many came from social groups that I would have expected: foreigners, liberals, activists, gay men. But he also associated with people whose identities were surprising. Sometimes I stopped by his apartment and found him hanging out with a group of young police academy students whom he had met in the neighborhood. They seemed like typical macho, conservative cops, but they enjoyed Manu's company. There was also a young member of the Muslim Brotherhood, a man I'll call Tariq, who came to parties held by Manu and his roommates. Everything that went on at these events—the drinking, the presence of homosexuals, the casual mixing of unmarried men and women—should have been anathema to an Islamist. But Tariq was always there, enjoying himself.

I sensed that Manu's separation from normal society was attractive to such young people. And perhaps he projected a self-knowledge that was unusual for somebody his age. For many Egyptians, the twenties and thirties seemed like difficult years; people felt pressured by their families and frustrated by the lack of professional opportunities. Sexual repression was a constant weight on their psyches. Young men in particular conveyed an unsettled, slightly volatile air, and it was no surprise that they had been the driving force behind the protests that overthrew Mubarak.

Sometimes they found an outlet in religious groups like the Brotherhood or the Salafis. Tariq, the Brother who attended Manu's parties, told me that he had become attracted to the Islamists in his early twenties. Faith wasn't the main reason; he described himself as only moderately religious. His uncle was a dedicated Brother, and the older man introduced him to the organization. "I was lost, and I wanted to find something," he said. "I wanted to find somebody like a godfather. I wanted someone to guide me."

During the spring of 2012, we met regularly. Tariq was the only Muslim Brother with whom I ever drank alcohol. He also smoked heavily, which was frowned upon within the organization—some strict interpretations of Islam are antitobacco. Tariq had been educated in English, and he had a good job with a tourist company; he was comfortable around foreigners. But as the spring progressed, and as the Brothers' political ambitions grew, he became more serious about quitting his vices. By early April, when I saw him at one of Manu's parties, he was no longer drinking.

Like many young Brothers, Tariq could be critical of the organization's leadership. He had been disappointed by their refusal to attend the November protests on Mohammed Mahmoud Street; in his opinion, the Brothers' discipline could have reduced the casualties. He was also wary of the heedless way in which the organization was entering politics. "It's like a hunger of having everything at once," he said. He was working on the campaign for Mohammed Morsi, the Brotherhood's candidate for president, but he wasn't personally impressed. He had recently met Morsi at a campaign event. "I realized that he is less than normal," Tariq said afterward. "He doesn't have the qualifications or the charisma."

Nevertheless, he predicted that Morsi would win. Tariq said that even if the candidate was weak, the Brotherhood's strategy was shrewd. For the election's first round, they were delivering a conservative message, in hopes of appealing to the Salafis, who had no candidate of their own. Later, if Morsi made the final round, the Brothers would present themselves as more moderate. Tariq acknowledged the cynicism of this strategy, but he believed that it would work in Egypt's unsophisticated political climate.

Tariq was much more forthcoming than other Brothers I met, but nevertheless he held things back. I couldn't figure out his status within the organization, or even if he had yet become a full member, a process that was famously demanding. He spoke enthusiastically about the Brotherhood's charitable activities, but when I asked to see projects, he always found excuses and broke appointments. I noticed a similar response with other Brothers. I suspected that this part of their reputation—that the organization provided significant social services—was exaggerated.

On the whole, the Brotherhood didn't feel like a true political group. Its orientation was too internal: members focused on the organization rather than on society at large. Undoubtedly, this quality had helped the Brothers survive decades of repression, but it also prevented them from reaching out. Young people who felt unfulfilled by Egyptian family life were often attracted to the Brotherhood, but it wasn't really an alternative; instead, it was just another version of the clan. Even the five-member cell that represented the basic building block of the organization was called an *'usra,* a "family." And Brotherhood structures replicated the flaws of traditional Egyptian patriarchy. The leadership was entirely male, and the most powerful figures were always older. Women couldn't become full members. Once, I attended a Morsi campaign rally in the canal city of Ismailia, and the event began with the celebration of three marriages that involved Brotherhood families. But the brides weren't even allowed onstage; they followed an unusually conservative version of the ceremony in which the father of the bride stands in as a proxy, exchanging vows with the groom. I found this spectacle oddly gripping: six male Muslim Brothers, arranged into pairs on a stage, vowing eternal love and companionship.

When Tariq complained about Morsi's candidacy, I asked him why he was working so hard to elect somebody whom he didn't respect. "It's something in my blood," he said. "It's a faith in the Muslim Brotherhood. It's like getting pissed off at your parents. You get angry and you want to go away, but you always come back."

At the end of April, with less than two months to go in the presidential campaign, a poll conducted by the government-run Al-Ahram Center for Political and Strategic Studies showed that only 3.6 percent of respondents supported Morsi. He was last among the six major candidates. The Egyptian press referred to him as "the spare," because he had been rolled out like an extra tire when the Brotherhood's original candidate, Khairat El-Shater, was disqualified on a technicality.

Morsi was overweight, bespectacled, and bearded, and relatively few Egyptians had heard of him before the election. He had grown up in a modest home in the Nile Delta, where the agricultural regions are generally more prosperous than those in the south. Morsi studied engineering at Cairo University, and he joined the Brotherhood near the end of his college years. But he reportedly became more conservative after moving to the United States, where he attended graduate school at the University of Southern California.

This pattern of coming into contact with the West, and then rejecting its values, was common in the Brotherhood. Sayyid Qutb, who was perhaps the most important thinker associated with the Islamist movement, had followed this path during the previous century, with tragic results. In 1906, Qutb was born into a prosperous family in Upper Egypt, and after completing his schooling, he went to Cairo to work for the government's educational bureau. But he never felt comfortable in the modernizing capital. In his words, he was an "exile" from the traditional south.

Like Hassan al-Banna, the Brotherhood's founder, Qutb envisioned Islam as a *nizam,* or "system," that represented an alternative to Western modernity. He was especially critical of the way that Egypt had haphazardly imported fragments of foreign ideas and institutions, ranging from the mixed educational curricula to the muddled legal apparatus. "A given society is a *nizam* that operates consistently as long as its parts fit," Qutb wrote. "When a component of this *nizam* is replaced with a part from a different model, it loses balance and even ceases to function, even if the part is more valuable than the original."

Qutb wrote beautifully in classical Arabic, and he had many penetrating insights about Egypt's struggle. But he also wore the blinders of a zealot, and at heart he was a frustrated, angry man. He never married and was probably a virgin for his entire life. In 1948, the Egyptian educational authorities sent Qutb on a yearlong study mission to America, which became a tour in reinforced prejudice. Nothing about the United States was too petty for Qutb to complain about: He hated the weather; he despised American barbers; he declared that suburban gardening was a symptom of abject materialism. American football and professional wrestling reflected a savage culture. Church socials mixed the sexes in immoral ways. In the short, bitter book that he published about his experience, he wrote, "I fear that when the wheel of life has turned and the file of history has closed, America will have contributed nothing to the world heritage of values."

Back in Egypt, Qutb became a member of the Brotherhood's highest council of leadership. In the early 1950s, Brothers joined with other Egyptians in fighting against the British troops stationed along the Suez Canal, and they contributed to Nasser's revolution. But shortly after Nasser came to power, he decided that he couldn't trust his Islamist allies, and he instituted a vicious crackdown. In 1954, Qutb was arrested, and he spent a decade in prison, where he was often tortured. Here he became truly radicalized: he came to believe that there were only two kinds of societies, the Islamic and the barbaric. He developed a theory of jihad, or "striving," that justified violence against political entities that didn't fit strict definitions of Islam.

In 1964, Qutb was released, but he immediately became involved in a plot to acquire weapons. He was arrested, tried, and executed by hanging. He became a martyr to the growing Islamist movement, and over time other radicals expanded on his foundation. Qutb never advocated for the killing of innocent civilians, but his bifurcated worldview prepared for such a step. Osama bin Laden, Ayman al-Zawahiri, and other key leaders of al-Qaeda were all inspired by Qutb's words. And while the Brotherhood officially rejected violence, there was a history of young members becoming radicalized and then leaving the organization for more extreme groups.

Mohammed Morsi admired Qutb's writing, and he shared some of his formative experiences. In the United States, Morsi acquired a Ph.D. in materials science, and for a while he taught at California State University, Northridge. But he was reportedly disgusted by many American values, ranging from the use of alcohol to the casual ways in which men and women interacted. After returning to teach in Egypt, he was imprisoned twice by the Mubarak regime. The second arrest happened at the start of the Arab Spring, and Morsi was being held in the Wadi al-Natroun Prison when it was overrun by civilians who freed all the inmates.

Many Brothers shared his basic profile: a man of science or medicine who had suffered political repression. During the first year of the Arab Spring, there were eighteen men in the Brotherhood's Guidance Bureau, the top tier of leadership, and fifteen were engineers, doctors, or scientists. Fourteen had served time in prison. Very few had backgrounds in humanities or politics. The desire for *nizam* ran deep in these technically minded men, but they could also ignore science and evidence when it suited them. Many Brothers did not believe in evolution, and they often denied that the 9/11 attacks had been carried out by Muslims. Morsi, whose academic specialty involved precision metal surfaces, claimed that planes alone could not have brought down the World Trade Center. "Something happened from the inside," he said. For Egyptians attuned to such coded comments, the culprit was clear: the Jews. Prior to running for president, Morsi had referred to Israel's citizens as "killers and vampires." He had also declared that neither a woman nor a Christian should be allowed to serve as president.

When I met with Manu's friend Tariq, he downplayed the violent ideas of Qutb and others. In Tariq's view, Brotherhood members would become more moderate as they moved into power. Despite his reservations about Morsi, he didn't want to be left behind during the Brotherhood's rise to power.

Many young Brothers had responded to the revolution like Tariq, by increasing their commitment to the organization. But some quit entirely. They often remarked that spending time with other activists on Tahrir had opened their eyes to new possibilities. Dr. Mohammad Affan, an insightful man in his thirties who had co-founded a new political group, the Egyptian Current Party, was one of the Brothers who had left. He told me that his joining and eventual departure were part of a long search that had started when he was a teenager. After flirting with Salafi ideas, he had shifted toward the Brotherhood, which seemed more directly engaged with political life. "They were heroes, because they stood up to the previous regime, and they went to jail,"

Affan said. Like all new members, he underwent months of training and testing, and he endured a fake police raid that his Brotherhood superior orchestrated as an elaborate test of loyalty. To a young man in his twenties, all of this made a profound impression.

But eventually Affan outgrew the Brotherhood. "They are not Machiavellian, which is what people seem to think," he said. "Actually, they are unsophisticated. They are not political at all. They are very clever in elections—they only know how to make people vote for them, full stop. All the other issues—how to choose candidates, how to choose a political platform, how to manage a political party—with all of those things they are unprofessional."

In the days of Mubarak, Affan had been active in the Brotherhood's political wing. He was a medical doctor, but he decided to go back to school to study political science. This decision mystified his superiors, who found him too theoretical. Affan believed that the group's preponderance of doctors, scientists, and engineers contributed to a lack of creativity and strategic thinking. They had developed an empty *nizam*—an elaborate structure that lacked real content or purpose. It was another example of a certain Egyptian genius: people could be brilliant at creating a sense of identity and purpose even while they neglected the on-the-ground details.

"In 2007, I asked the political leaders in the central committee about setting up a ministry for a shadow government," Affan said. "My leader said, 'It's not urgent.' I said, 'We are the main opposition movement here in Egypt, and we should prepare this government in case things change.' And now, four years later, the Muslim Brotherhood is asked to prepare a real government, not a shadow government. I hope they catch up."

Morsi's polling numbers had started to rise, and Affan was concerned that he would win and then botch the presidency. Affan viewed the Brothers as social and religious reformers who masqueraded as political reformers. "Political reformers think about how to build a system, how to manage a state, how to regulate political powers," Affan said. "These questions are very vague in the Brotherhood."

That central issue—how to construct a new *nizam*—was never articulated by either the Brotherhood or its candidate. In interviews Morsi could be incoherent. Like all leading Brothers, he knew the catchphrases of democracy and development, but it was unclear how much he truly understood. In 2012, during an interview with *Time* magazine, Morsi proclaimed Egypt's new democracy a success. "This stems from belief," he said, in English. "Islamic belief, freedom for everyone, freedom of belief, freedom of expressing their opinions, equality, stability, human rights. ERA. It's not only in America. Equal Rights Amendment. Everyone."

Even after the interview switched to Morsi's native Arabic, he spoke strings of words that connected to nothing. "Development with its comprehensive overall meaning," he said. "Human development. Industrial productive development. Scholarly research. Political development. International relations balanced with all different parties, East and West." After repeating dozens of such phrases, he explained that the modern world is complicated. He said, "It's a spaghetti-like structure."

One evening that year, Manu was returning home from a friend's house, and a young man on the street struck up a conversation. He said his name was Kareem and he was a conscript in the army. He offered Manu a Marlboro from a pack he had just opened.

The brand should have been a tip-off—no conscript was likely to smoke something so expensive. But it was late at night, and close to Manu's home; he wasn't particularly alert to the possibility of trouble. He accepted the cigarette, and Kareem kept talking.

Later, Manu had trouble describing the man's appearance. He was slightly shorter than average height, and slightly muscular. His skin was neither particularly dark nor particularly white. He wasn't good-looking. The main thing that stayed in Manu's mind was his story: Kareem had had a conflict with his commanding officer, who kicked him out of the barracks. He wouldn't be allowed to return until morning, and the night was cold; he wished there was a place where he could sit down for a while. Manu, who remembered well his own miserable military service, invited the young man back to his apartment for a cup of tea.

Once Kareem was inside, he started asking about Manu's possessions. How much did that computer cost? What about that mobile phone? Manu started to feel uncomfortable, and he made an excuse about being sleepy. Finally he asked Kareem to leave.

Now the man's demeanor changed completely. He told Manu that he knew he was a *khawwal*, a faggot, and he was going to expose him. Some of Manu's foreign roommates were home, and he asked one of them, a large Austrian, for help. By this point, Kareem was shouting that Manu had tried to assault him. The Austrian roommate finally picked up Kareem and forcibly removed him from the apartment.

A couple minutes later, Manu looked out the window to the street below. He felt a wave of panic when he saw Kareem talking on his cell phone.

It was three o'clock in the morning. Manu grabbed a coat and ran out of the apartment. A single car was moving slowly on the street, and Manu waved it over to ask for a ride, hoping to get out of Dokki. The driver took one look—a running man, looking scared—and accelerated. Manu heard shouting behind him; he ran as fast as he could. After a few strides he was tackled from behind.

The cops marched Manu back to his apartment. They passed a kiosk where he often bought things, and a group of neighbors were standing there; a couple of them hissed the word *khawwal*. Kareem accompanied the police to Manu's home. Now it was clear that the young man worked for the cops—the whole thing had been a setup.

The police seemed to know what they were looking for. They confiscated Manu's research notebooks, along with the business cards that he had picked up from interviews with foreign journalists. Then they transported Manu to the local police station and locked him in a holding cell.

On the other side of the bars, officers worked on the crime report. Every now and then, one of them looked at Manu and said, "*Hatroah fi dahya*. You're going to a disaster." They read sections of the report aloud—one part quoted Kareem's description of what he claimed had happened in Manu's apartment:

> *He brought me a cup of water, and then he took off his jacket and his pants. . . . He asked me to sleep with him. I told him no, I cannot do this. But he had two friends and they grabbed me.*

At first, the report described the foreign roommates as having participated in the alleged assault, but then an officer pointed out that this might cause their embassies to get involved, so the detail was changed. After the report was finished, one of the officers said, "Take him to the hospital to do an anal exam."

In 2010, in Alexandria, police brutally beat to death a twenty-eight-year-old named Khaled Saeed, who had been sitting in a cybercafé. Later, some officers claimed that Saeed had been in possession of hashish, while others mentioned a weapons charge, but nothing was ever proven. Saeed had no criminal history, and he had studied computer programming in the United States. He lived with his widowed mother. The authorities failed to carry out a proper autopsy on Saeed's body, but his family was able to get a photograph of his badly broken face in the morgue. Eventually, the photo was posted online, and Saeed's name became a rallying cry for activists. His brutal, pointless death was one reason why the first protests of the Egyptian Arab Spring took place on January 25—National Police Day.

After the fall of Mubarak, two officers were sentenced to short prison terms for their roles in Saeed's death, but the larger question of police reform remained unresolved. Part of the problem was that Egyptian authoritarianism wasn't really a *nizam*. It was more an atmosphere than a system: it enveloped the country like a low-hanging cloud, and repression had the unpredictable quality of a weather event. It could strike at any time, for no obvious reason. People in authority often behaved the way they did simply because they were in authority, and not because they had been issued clear commands or were following a real protocol. This made reform difficult—it wasn't enough to simply remove a leader or a group of leaders. The entire atmosphere needed to change.

In the Egyptian criminal code, there was no law against homosexuality. But gay men were often prosecuted under a charge of "debauchery," which could be applied to almost anything. Every now and then, the police carried out a bust on the Qasr al-Nil Bridge or some other gay hangout, and they routinely forced suspects to submit to anal examinations. After Manu was arrested, he started to think about suicide, because he knew he couldn't survive as a gay man in an Egyptian prison.

He was handcuffed to a sergeant. The cops marched him down the street to a public hospital, where the staff said they weren't equipped to handle an anal exam. They walked to another clinic. After they arrived, Manu was seated in the waiting area, and he was too far away to hear the conversation between the police and a doctor. But he could read the disgusted expression on the doctor's face. Manu guessed what he was probably saying: *I'm not going to touch that* khawwal.

They were about to go to a third hospital when the commanding officer decided that the exam had to be postponed. They had an appointment at the office of the prosecutor, who would formally declare charges. Back at the station, Manu was herded into a police van, along with a dozen or so other men who had been arrested. Manu was handcuffed to a filthy man who seemed incoherent.

Of all the people whom Manu encountered that evening, the prosecutor was the most hateful. "A normal man would approach girls on the street," he said. "Why would you approach guys? You fucking *khawwal.*" He told Manu that he stood accused of attempted rape. But he couldn't finish the proceedings until he received a statement from Kareem, and the young man was nowhere to be found.

By now, it was late morning. The cops handcuffed Manu once more to the filthy man, and the two of them sat outside the prosecutor's office. While they were waiting, a subofficer came back with Manu's cell phone. "Your father called," he said, and he laughed. "I told him that we found you with a man. Sleeping with a man!"

But then the subofficer handed him the phone. "Find someone to help you," he said. Manu called Tariq, his friend in the Brotherhood, and he called a foreign roommate who had contacts at Cairo human rights groups. Tariq telephoned a lawyer friend and drove into Dokki, where they started negotiating for Manu's bail. There was another appearance before the prosecutor, but Kareem was still absent. Finally, after nearly twenty-four hours in detention, the bail was accepted and the cops released Manu. They had never been able to organize the anal exam.

Outside the station, Tariq and a few friends were waiting. There was also an uncle who had been alerted by Manu's father. Now Manu knew that the subofficer had told the truth about outing him, and he realized that he could never show his face in Port Said again.

Over the next few weeks, the lawyer periodically asked Manu for money, in order to pay bribes. The fees totaled three thousand American dollars, and then the lawyer said that the police were no longer pursuing the case. But Manu knew the charges must still be on the books, somewhere, and he moved out of the Dokki apartment.

He was never certain what had initiated the bust. Perhaps his neighbors had alerted the authorities, or maybe the police had become aware of Manu's work with foreign journalists. Maybe the goal was to gain leverage and force Manu to inform on people he worked with. But if everything was part of some elaborate plan, then why didn't the cops follow up immediately and put pressure on Manu? And after Kareem went to all the trouble to entrap Manu, why didn't he show up at the prosecutor's office on time? Why was the police report so amateurish? Why did the subofficer out Manu to his father and then allow him to call for help? But such questions were unanswerable in a place where authority was environmental rather than systematic. There wasn't any point to the brutality—it served no larger purpose. And incompetence was another defining quality, which was one reason why police abuse under Mubarak had eventually served to undermine the state rather than sustain it.

Throughout this period, Tariq often checked in with Manu, and he monitored the lawyer's work. He never said a word about Manu's being gay. For a Muslim Brother, the issue should have been unequivocal: the organization's leaders had declared that homosexuality was not to be tolerated. During the spring of the presidential campaign, people wondered if a Morsi victory would lead to an immediate crackdown on the things that the Brothers considered immoral.

Not long after Manu's arrest, I met Tariq for coffee in Zamalek, and he spoke about his friend in protective terms. He believed that Manu had been targeted because of his work with journalists, and his friendliness made him an easy mark. "He's too trusting," Tariq said. "He should be more careful. But he's a good person."

I couldn't tell if Tariq pretended not to know about Manu's sexuality, or if he simply avoided mentioning it. Even a relatively short time in Egypt had taught me that people often had an impressive capacity for contradiction. Sometimes this felt like hypocrisy, but often it was simply a way to survive in a flawed world. And perhaps in certain cases it represented a form of human decency.

At the end of May, in the first round of the election, Morsi won nearly a quarter of the votes. In less than a month, he had risen from sixth place among the candidates to first. For the final round, he would face Ahmed Shafik, a former commander of the Egyptian Air Force who had been the last prime minister under Mubarak. For any Egyptian who had been inspired by the promise of Tahrir, these were the options: a seventy-year-old retired officer who had described Mubarak as "a role model," or an Islamist with a Ph.D. in materials science who denied that two Boeing 767s had brought down the World Trade Center.

Rifaat, my Arabic teacher, reluctantly planned to vote for Shafik. Despite his hatred for the former regime, he was too much of a Nasserite to support a Muslim Brother. Sayyid told me that he would vote for Morsi. "He has a beard, and he's religious," he said. He believed that a devout Muslim would be more honest in office.

Many young activists had decided that they would write in a candidate or spoil their ballots, but Manu believed that this was a demoralizing way to respond to the first free presidential election in Egyptian history. And he saw no point in looking backward to a figure from the old regime. For better or for worse, this was one miracle of the new democracy: a gay man who lived in fear of moralist authority felt compelled to cast his vote for the Muslim Brotherhood.

On June 24, in the early afternoon, Manu and I caught a cab in Zamalek and headed toward Nasr City, in eastern Cairo, where the final election results would be announced. The roads were packed, because so many people were trying to get out of the city center. At the Qasr al-Nil Bridge, traffic ground to a halt, and passengers jumped out of cabs and buses in order to continue on foot.

By this point, everybody knew who had won the election, but nobody knew who the winner would be. The vote had been held a week earlier, during a period of increasing chaos. On June 13, the provisional government declared that Cairo was under martial law, and the next day the Supreme Constitutional Court disbanded the parliament. The court had determined that one-third of the parliamentarians had been elected in violation of the rules. There was little doubt that the decision was politically motivated, and it sent a message to the Brothers: the *feloul,* or "remnants," of the old regime still had influence.

But even in this environment, the election had proceeded peacefully. Independent monitors were allowed at polling stations, and there weren't any reports of significant fraud. Ballots were counted in front of representatives of both candidates, and afterward the Muslim Brotherhood announced that Morsi had won, with over 51 percent of the vote. They released detailed counts from every district in the country.

And yet for a week the election commission delayed the official announcement. Shafik's campaign had also declared victory, although they gave no evidence for their claim. Supposedly, the election commission was investigating accusations of fraud, but most analysts believed that the military was preparing to steal the election for Shafik. In our cab, Manu and I passed Tahrir, where a crowd of Brotherhood members had camped out with flags and banners. They had sworn to occupy the square until the rightful victor was declared.

The announcement was going to be made at the State Information Service, and when we arrived all roads had been blockaded by soldiers and police. Manu and I got out of the cab and continued on foot. We passed through a complex of government offices and entertainment facilities, some of which had been built as boondoggles during the latter years of the Mubarak era. At the Ministry of Defense Morale Affairs Department International Bowling Center, a Sphinx-sized bowling pin stood at the entrance. On both sides of the massive striped pin, policemen in black uniforms had been lined up. Nearby, the doorway of the State Information Service had been decorated with the official logo of the presidential election commission. The logo featured an enormous white hand placing a presidential ballot atop the Great Pyramid of Giza.

They had restricted the announcement to registered journalists, so Manu waited outside, next to a few squads of young army conscripts with nervous faces. An elevator took me to the seventh floor. The elevator operator was a skinny old man who sat on a wooden stool, smiling happily, as if this were just another day spent pushing buttons. He told me that he had no doubt about the election. "Shafik is going to win, *insha'allah,*" he said. "Morsi could never be president of Egypt."

The chairman of the election commission began the event by intoning, "I meet you at the end of a critical phase of building the Egyptian democracy." He sat beneath another banner of the godlike hand stuffing a pyramid ballot box. About three hundred journalists, almost all of them Egyptian, had crowded into the auditorium. People looked tense, and there had been a couple of scuffles over seats before the event started.

Like many Egyptian officials, the chairman relished the spotlight, and he rambled on without mentioning who had won. He praised the election commission ("they fear no one but God"), and he read through an interminable list of districts in which totals had been adjusted after the discovery of mismarked ballots and other minor problems. One city had originally declared 42,508 votes for Shafik, but the final figure was 42,607; another town had Morsi at 683 when it should have been 685. The chairman droned on and on—50,428 instead of 50,228; 4,097 instead of 4,279—and in numerophobic Egypt it seemed a form of torture, to gather an auditorium full of nervous people and then shower them with statistics. It took most of an hour before the chairman finally announced the key figures: 25,577,511 legal votes, with 12,347,380 for Shafik. I was writing everything down, and doing the math in my head, and suddenly I realized it was over. I looked around me—no reaction; everybody had been numbed by the numbers. It wasn't until the chairman's next statement—"48.27 percent"—that the place erupted.

Manu and I caught a cab downtown. The streets were still mostly empty, apart from a few people who were driving with Egyptian flags hanging from their windows, honking in celebration. Manu told me that outside the State Information Service, the young conscripts had looked relieved at the announcement, which meant that they wouldn't be fighting the Islamists tonight. But at the head of every squad, an older officer wore a look of undisguised anger. They were imagining four years spent taking orders from a Muslim Brother.

Downtown, we entered the headquarters of the Freedom and Justice Party, the Brotherhood's political wing. Supporters were whooping and chanting Morsi's name. All sorts of people poured in off the street; at one point, Manu and I were seated next to a poorly dressed man who happened to be named Mohammed Morsi. He was showing his ID to anybody who would listen, explaining that he had the same name as the new president.

A couple of Japanese journalists were already waiting to interview a spokeswoman, and I got in line. After a few minutes, I was ushered into a room with Dr. Nussaiba Ashraf. She looked to be in her thirties, and she was dressed conservatively, with a long skirt and a beige *hijab* that wrapped tightly under her chin. The Brotherhood had a number of young spokeswomen, in part to convey the idea that they valued both genders.

Ashraf told me that until the last moment she had had no idea who would win the election. "We were worried," she said. "There were many indicators that there would be some manipulation."

She explained that Morsi had officially resigned from the Brotherhood, to demonstrate his independence. This would be a new era—a time of cooperation rather than conflict. "The president will establish a coalition government," Ashraf said. "The Freedom and Justice Party will not have a majority in the ministries. Other political parties and groups will be in charge of some ministries. It's not going to be a government controlled by the Freedom and Justice Party."

She continued, "It's not a victory for the party, and it's not a victory for Dr. Morsi. It's a victory for the revolution." She smiled and said, "The old regime will not be coming back."

Part Two

THE COUP

To whom shall I speak today?
Brothers are mean,
The friends of today do not love.

To whom shall I speak today?
Hearts are greedy,
Everyone robs his comrade's goods.

To whom shall I speak today?
Kindness has perished,
Insolence assaults everyone.

—"A Dialogue Between Self and Soul,"
Twelfth Dynasty, c. 1991–1778 BC

CHAPTER 7

IN ABYDOS, IT TOOK ALMOST A YEAR FOR THE RITUALS OF THE ARAB SPRING to make their way upstream. In December 2011, ten months after Mubarak's resignation, villagers finally held their first demonstration. About a thousand people gathered in front of the Temple of Seti I, which, along with the Shuna, is the most prominent local monument. The protesters' main complaint involved the erratic distribution of subsidized cooking gas. They demanded that the government solve the problem, and they called for the resignation of the village *rayis*. This word is an Egyptian colloquial version of "president," but it describes the leader of any group: "chief," "head." The Abydos *rayis* was Hussein Mohammed Abdel Rady, who had been appointed under the Mubarak regime. At the local demonstration, people chanted Tahrir slogans and held banners that read "The Youth of Abydos: We Want to Change the *Rayis* of the Village."

The demonstration lasted for a few days. Finally, some officials came from the district of Balyana, the next level of government. The Balyana officials met with some of the protesters, and they promised to improve the distribution of cooking gas. They also heard from villagers who complained that they should be allowed to enter the Temple of Seti I without paying the high prices that were charged to foreign tourists, and the officials agreed to figure out a new pricing arrangement. Finally, they announced that the *rayis* was being forced out. For protesters, the removal of the *rayis* followed the appropriate pattern of the Arab Spring, and they dispersed peacefully. After that, there weren't any more demonstrations in Abydos.

For my first few trips to the region, I flew from Cairo to Sohag, which was the capital of the governorate, the Egyptian equivalent of a state or province.

The airport in Sohag was brand new—it had opened during the last year that Mubarak was in power. In May 2010, the president had traveled there for the inauguration ceremony, and he had named the complex in honor of himself. The Mubarak International Airport was situated in the desert halfway between Sohag and Abydos, in part because officials hoped that foreign tourists would start visiting the ancient site in larger numbers. In front of the terminal, atop a sandy hill that faced the expanse of the Western Desert, ten-foot-tall white letters spelled out "MUBARAK AIRPORT." The letters were tethered to the earth with steel rods that were strong enough to withstand the Sahara winds.

After the first wave of the revolution, airport workers knocked over the "MUBARAK." It was replaced with another series of letters that read "SUHAG." The city's official English name is spelled with an O, not a U, but apparently the airport authorities decided to recycle whatever vowels they could. They left the consonants lying on the ground. The first time I approached from the air, I looked down and was able to make out an M, a B, and a K. Windblown sand had already started to cover the prone letters.

Upon arrival, I caught a cab to Abydos, and along the way we passed two road signs for the airport. On the first, the word "Mubarak" had been scratched out. But the name remained intact on the next sign, which could be reached only with a big ladder. By my fourth visit to the region they had finally gotten around to removing that higher "Mubarak." It usually took about forty-five minutes to drive from the airport to Abydos. The route passed King Djoser Road, which was named in honor of the ruler who had built the Step Pyramid, and then it connected to King Menes Road. Menes was the king who had first unified Upper and Lower Egypt, more than five thousand years ago, before he was carried off by a hippopotamus.

When I started traveling regularly to Abydos, it had been almost two years since the removal of Mubarak, and the story of his fall had become polished, like a coin that's passed through many hands. All over the country, people said the same things: in the beginning, Mubarak was a good leader, but then he lost his touch. Part of the problem was his wife. Suzanne Mubarak's advocacy for women's issues endeared her to Western officials, but these things hadn't appealed to most Egyptians. They blamed Suzanne for promoting the political career of Gamal Mubarak, the couple's second son. President Mubarak had never named his successor, and in the waning years of the regime he seemed to be grooming Gamal for the highest office. It would have been the first Egyptian family dynasty since King Farouk abdicated in 1952.

When citizens spoke of Mubarak's failure, they usually focused on his relationships rather than on the details of his regime. They rarely talked about systemic problems; instead, they complained about Suzanne and Gamal, and they said that corrupt officials and businessmen had taken advantage of the aging president. The terms were personal, but the blame was not; if anything, Mubarak had simply been too trusting. Perhaps this reflected some deep pattern of the human mind, because I remembered hearing similar things when I lived in authoritarian China. Old Deng Xiaoping couldn't have commanded soldiers to fire on student protesters in Tiananmen Square; his underlings must have made that decision. Mao Zedong was a good leader until his wife, Jiang Qing, gained too much influence. People said she must have been responsible for Mao's Cultural Revolution. That was another common tendency: somehow, even in these male-dominated dictatorships, people often found a way to blame a woman.

Under the Mubarak regime, the government had initiated the construction of a new visitors' center in Abydos. Along with the airport, it was part of the ambitious plan for increased tourism. But the industry had collapsed in the wake of the revolution, and by the time I started traveling to Abydos, there was no money to complete the project. The unfinished visitors' center was located on the same street as the Temple of Seti I, and it was possible to see the outlines of an exhibition hall and a cafeteria, although both these rooms lacked ceilings, floors, and windows. Piles of bricks and tiles lay in the sun. Everything was covered with a thin layer of windblown sand, which gave the visitors' center the same tan color as the temple and the Shuna. The center looked like another ancient ruin; from the outside, it was impossible to tell whether it was half-built or half-collapsed.

The Temple of Seti I was constructed during the thirteenth century BC, in the Nineteenth Dynasty, in the heart of the New Kingdom. All of these identifiers would have been meaningless to ancient Egyptians. Their vision of time—the cycles of *neheh,* the permanence of *djet*—is incompatible with the dynasties and kingdoms that are now used to describe their world.

During the third century BC, after the pharaonic age gave way to the Greek Ptolemies, a priest named Manetho created the first Western-style history of ancient Egypt. He organized the past kings into thirty dynasties, although some of his divisions now seem capricious. Khasekhemwy is the final king of the Second Dynasty, while his son, Djoser, is the founder of the Third. What's the difference? Father built the Shuna, and son built the Step Pyramid—the transition from mud to stone deserved a new dynasty, at least in the eyes of Manetho. He felt the same way about the construction of the first smooth-sided pyramid, and so King Sneferu is honored as the founder of the Fourth Dynasty. Some supposedly consecutive dynasties in Manetho's scheme are now known to have been concurrent, and at least one dynasty, the Seventh, never existed at all.

In the nineteenth century, Western historians further subdivided the dynasties. They created a series of "kingdoms"—Old, Middle, and New—that are separated by two "intermediate" periods of national disunity and chaos. For the modern sensibility, these classifications make it easier to keep track of the enormous spans of time that constitute ancient Egyptian history. But this system is also a reminder that Egyptians have rarely been in charge of their own past. It's not like China, where dynasties saw themselves as such and chose their own titles: the Tang, the Song, the Ming. Chinese history was first written by the Chinese, whereas Egyptology began as a colonial endeavor. To some degree this remains true today. Many of Egypt's most important sites are still excavated by foreigners, who make decisions about where to dig and when to publish. The Egyptian Ministry of Antiquities has to approve projects, and it issues the necessary permits, but the overall direction at many sites is established by outsiders. Sometimes they express discomfort with this colonial inheritance. "It's not our past," Matthew Adams once remarked. "It belongs to the people of Egypt. We're guests here."

Adams said he was embarrassed by his poor spoken Arabic. But it's rare for foreign archaeologists to speak the language well, and it isn't required in Egyptology programs, a reflection of the divide between the pharaonic past and the Arabic present. "Can you imagine somebody specializing in South American archaeology and not being able to speak Spanish?" Adams said. "It's impossible. Arabic should be required." He went on, "Egyptologists as a group have not been too interested in dealing with the Egypt of today. The Egypt of today is sometimes seen as an impediment to the Egypt of the past."

He believed that at some point there is bound to be a nativist movement that seeks to drive out the foreigners who dig in Egyptian soil. But Tahrir didn't provide the spark. Ironically, the revolution made the foreign archaeologists even more crucial, because the Ministry of Antiquities had no money to support its own digs. In the past, the ministry was funded entirely by proceeds from tourism, but now it needed injections of cash from the Finance Ministry in order to maintain basic operations. It also needed foreigners, and foreign institutions, to keep the excavations going. And foreigners contributed crucial funds for site guards and other protective measures.

Inevitably, the traditional dependence on outsiders has helped perpetuate a foreign perspective on the past. Any timeline or history of ancient Egypt reflects a Western sensibility: families rise and fall; numbered dynasties come and go; the kingdoms proceed in order from Old to Middle to New. But this straight line of history implies other values—progress, improvement, advancement—that probably mattered little to the ancients. And it obscures their true imaginative power, which was more likely to envision a state of *djet* permanence rather than some upward trajectory.

The Temple of Seti I reflects this vision. It was constructed early in the Nineteenth Dynasty, as the country was emerging from political chaos. During the previous dynasty, a king named Akhenaten attempted to radically change many basic traditions of Egyptian faith. His project ultimately failed, and his successors—Tutankhamun is the most famous—were all short-lived. The family's reign ended around 1306 BC, with what was possibly the first military coup in human history. Horemheb, the former chief commander of the army, ascended to the throne, and he named another military officer, Ramesses I, as his successor.

Seti I was the son of Ramesses I. The family had no royal blood and no legitimate claim to the throne. But they had military strength, and they understood the power of symbols. When Horemheb took power, he declared a *wehem mesut*, or "renaissance." Egyptian kings often used this phrase after a period of disunity. As part of the rebirth, Seti I chose to build a temple to Osiris in the time-honored landscape of Abydos.

The temple's design makes brilliant use of the desert environment. The entrance features a high-pillared front chamber that's full of light, but as the visitor proceeds into the complex, ceilings drop lower and rooms grow darker. The sounds of the outside world disappear. Deep within the temple, a wall carving portrays King Seti I's eldest son reading from a papyrus scroll. The scroll is inscribed with the names of sixty-seven kings who have ruled Egypt, arranged chronologically, beginning with King Menes and ending with Seti I. Such "king lists" have been found in a few places around Egypt, and they provided some of the data that allowed Manetho to create his chronology. But the Abydos wall isn't a history in the modern sense. The list excludes Akhenaten, Tutankhamun, and others from that royal line. All kings of the Second Intermediate Period are gone. Hatshepsut, a powerful pharaoh who happened to be female, is missing. For Seti I, the goal was to portray *djet* rather than the ebbs and flows of power.

Did it work? Seti I's son—the reader of the scroll on the wall—became Rammesses the Great. He probably completed construction of the Abydos temple, along with many other monumental structures. The family's dynasty, the Nineteenth, proved to be powerful. All told, the Egyptian pharaonic state lasted for three thousand years—the longest-lived political entity in human history. Such success can seem unsettling to moderns who believe in progress, technology, and system. The Egyptologist Barry Kemp writes,

> *But rational knowledge has proved to be far more fragile than knowledge about the deeper meaning of things that people feel is conveyed by religion. The latter kind has a staying-power and a vigour that suggest that it lies close to the heart of the human intellect. It is part of basic thought. Anyone who doubts this should ponder on one of the most significant developments in the contemporary world: the re-emergence of Islamic ideology as both a politically and an intellectually powerful force.*

Two months after the demonstrations at the Temple of Seti I, the village *rayis* quietly returned to his old office. Hussein Mohammed Abdel Rady told me that he had spent his exile working in Balyana. "It was for my own safety," he said. "And then I came back. People welcomed me. The people said it wasn't about me personally. It was just my position that they were attacking."

When I first met Rady, Morsi had already ascended to the presidency. Now that the Muslim Brothers were in power, they had declared that they would implement a development plan called *Al-Nahda:* "The Renaissance." It was essentially the same word as the *wehem mesut* declared by Horemheb and other pharaohs who came to power after a period of chaos. In Abydos, the *rayis* wouldn't speculate on what the renaissance might mean for the area, and he had no comment on Morsi. "I don't talk about politics," he said, as if he were involved in something different. Locals seemed to agree. They rarely connected their *rayis* with either Morsi or Mubarak, and they almost never said negative things about him. A number of people told me that the temple protests had taken place only because the village youths were briefly led astray by the example of Tahrir.

The *rayis* was a large man with a fleshy, pockmarked face, and he wore the style of well-trimmed mustache that is common for Egyptian police, soldiers, and government officials. During my trips to Abydos, I often stopped by the office, and the *rayis*'s eyes always looked exhausted. In addition to his government job, he ran a small farm not far from Abydos, on the eastern bank of the Nile. He grew bananas, wheat, and clover. Someday, he said, he would live full-time on the farm beside the river, which was exactly what Egyptian government officials did in retirement four thousand years ago.

On the *rayis*'s desk, a copy of the Quran sat next to a box of aspirin labeled, in English, "Provide Relief of Pain for Up to Three Days." Behind the desk there was an empty nail on the wall. When I met with officials in the region, I learned to look for that empty nail, which was where the state-produced portraits of Mubarak used to hang. If a room had big windows, the nail was surrounded by a small rectangular patch that was a shade darker than the rest of the wall. Thirty years in the sun is a long time. I was curious to see how many months it would take for Morsi portraits to appear. Even when I visited the new governor of Sohag, who had been appointed by Morsi himself, he had yet to hang up his patron's picture.

The governor was the only official I met in the region who had a computer on his desk. Even the Abydos administrator who handled the subsidized-bread registrations for sixty-eight thousand citizens lacked a computer. His room was drowning in paper; when I visited, an old woman appeared with three more forms to be stuffed into file cabinets and boxes. The administrator said that he wanted to computerize his system, but the government lacked funds, so he did the best he could with the paper files.

In the office of the Abydos *rayis,* there was one technologically advanced feature: a small electric button that had been installed near his right hand. Whenever the *rayis* pushed the button, a buzzer sounded, and an old man with a brown face and a white turban entered the room and asked the *rayis* how many cups he wanted. Heavily sugared tea is the lubricant to any interaction in Upper Egypt, and every government office employed some individual who brought in the cups.

Another standard feature was the line of citizens outside the office. I met with the *rayis* at all times of the day, in all seasons, and he was never alone. His responsibilities, like the expanse of blue sky above, had no limit. Without any real system of governance, there was no way for citizens to register complaints or make requests, other than showing up outside the *rayis*'s door. They asked about building permits, plumbing problems, and school issues. They wanted the *rayis* to resolve disputes between different clans. At one point, Abydos had been a small village, but over the last century the population had grown until multiple settlements sprawled across the valley floor. The *rayis* administered nine villages, with a total population of around seventy thousand.

Even acts of God fell under his jurisdiction. One morning, after a windstorm had toppled a tree on government land, I watched the *rayis* deal with the aftershocks. First, the electric company had to be alerted, because the tree had pulled down some power lines. Then a carpenter cut up the tree. After he was finished, he came to the *rayis*'s office in order to negotiate a price for the government-owned wood. The *rayis* wanted two hundred pounds, the equivalent of around twenty-five dollars; the carpenter offered one hundred and fifty. In the tradition of Egyptian non-bargaining, they went back and forth: Two hundred. One hundred and fifty. Two hundred. One hundred and fifty. At last the carpenter said, "One hundred and fifty. That's all I have." He held out the cash; the *rayis* recoiled. "There's a foreigner here. Don't make it look as if you're trying to bribe me!"

After that, the next issue was a butcher who had formerly worked in the shade of the toppled tree. Now the shade was gone. The sun was hot. Heat was bad for meat. Could the *rayis* do something? Finally, his exhausted eyes snapped wide in annoyance: "Tell him to make an umbrella!"

As a doctoral student, Matthew Adams excavated an ancient town site at the edge of the Buried. Such projects are rare, in part because ancient Egyptian settlements were usually located in the valley, where they were subject to *neheh* time. The Nile's annual floods, and the shifting path of the riverbed, destroyed most evidence of the places where people lived.

But Adams studied a slightly elevated settlement site that hadn't been destroyed. It dated to the First Intermediate Period, which spanned a century from around 2160 BC to 2055 BC. In traditional historiography, this period has always been associated with chaos. The great age of pyramid building was long gone, and dynasties became fragmented. One ancient source famously claims that seventy different kings ruled during a stretch of seventy days. "Behold, things have been done which have not happened for a long time past; the King has been deposed by the rabble" reads a text known as the Ipuwer Papyrus. "The land has been deprived of the kingship by a few lawless men."

More than a hundred miles south of Abydos, a provincial governor named Ankhtifi served during the First Intermediate Period. Archaeologists have excavated his tomb, whose inscriptions describe the routines of an official far from the capital:

> *I gave bread to the hungry and clothing to the naked; I anointed those who had no cosmetic oil; I gave sandals to the barefooted; I gave a wife to him who had no wife. . . . All of Upper Egypt was dying of hunger and people were eating their children, but I did not allow anybody to die of hunger in this [district].*

During Adams's excavation of the Abydos town site, he found no evidence of warfare, starvation, or political chaos. He uncovered private workshops that had clearly been busy manufacturing jewelry used for burial goods. The local economy appeared to be self-sufficient: households maintained their own granaries, and agriculture and trade seem to have been thriving. In recent years, other excavators have made similar discoveries elsewhere in Egypt, calling into question the authority of texts like the Ipuwer Papyrus.

One morning, Adams took me to see the settlement site. It was located near the Shuna, although any features of the ancient town had long since been covered by the sandy soil and the growing modern village. Adams noted that our imagination tends to accept the royal perspective, because kings and officials were skilled at portraying their power in symbolic ways: an inscription on a tomb, a king list on a temple wall. But those words and pictures don't necessarily correspond to the material we find beneath the earth.

"The evidence suggests that local society was locally oriented," Adams said. "In many respects the high-level political events did not affect their lives. It's very different from the model we get from the texts and the monuments. That model says that when the pyramids disappeared, then Egyptian society collapsed, and there was famine and chaos."

He noted that probably only 5 percent of ancient Egyptians were literate, and officials like Ankhtifi had an incentive to make the national situation look worse than it really was. "The evidence that we see from area to area is that people seem to be doing their own thing," Adams said of the First Intermediate Period. "And I wonder frankly if that's been true for much of Egyptian history, not just pharaonic times." He continued, "When they had the protests here in the village, their concerns were very local. They didn't have anything to do with Cairo."

The only demand of the Abydos protesters that was fully resolved was the issue of admission to the Temple of Seti I. Villagers were allowed to enter for a fraction of the tourist price; eventually, an Egyptian ticket cost ten pounds, versus one hundred for a foreigner. To Westerners inspired by democratic dreams of the Arab Spring, this may seem like a trivial outcome, but locals take the temple's power seriously. Whenever a wedding is celebrated, the bride and groom drive three times around the road in front of the temple, a ritual that is supposed to make pregnancy more likely. Other points of magic are situated within the temple itself. Foreign guidebooks direct tourists to the king list, the Second Hypostyle Hall, and other famous features, but villagers have their own unwritten itinerary. Certain stones and pillars have been worn smooth by repeated touching.

In 1910, Arthur Weigall described villagers carrying out similar rituals during his excavations in Abydos, Luxor, and other sites. More recently, when Matthew Adams was excavating in the Buried, locals requested permission to escort two newlywed women around the dig. Villagers who walk past the Shuna often stop, insert a pebble into a gap in the mud-brick structure, and then continue on their way. "They say it's magic," Adams said. Such folk beliefs are separate from Islam and long predate the religion. Adams continued, "There's a vague sense of lingering magic or power in ancient places."

After the demonstrations, the distribution of cooking gas remained erratic, but it didn't inspire another round of activism. Villagers kept going to the temple, and the *rayis* kept coming to work. The same office, the same tired eyes, the same endless line of supplicants. Different requests—this one from an old man trying to figure out the rules for utilities.

"About this law, article number 119, does it apply to houses on the canal?"

"No," said the *rayis*.

"I checked and it does."

"No, it doesn't." The *rayis* produced a tattered law book and recited the law. He explained, "However, houses in that area that have not been included in the past will never get the services."

The old man stood dumbfounded. "But—this law is horrible!"

"Yes, it is, and the guys who made it are now in prison," the *rayis* said. "Hopefully, they won't come out."

The old man couldn't help but laugh. The *rayis* suggested a different registration form that would allow them to skirt the bad law. He produced more papers, and the old man signed them and left, satisfied. Next request. Press the buzzer—more tea. Same desk, same copy of the Quran, same box of pills. "Provide Relief of Pain for Up to Three Days." Same empty nail on the wall.

CHAPTER 8

After Sayyid finished with the morning's garbage collection, he usually drank tea in the shade at the H Freedom kiosk. The kiosk had been built against the far side of my garden wall, next to the wrought-iron spiderwebs, and I could see it from the windows of my study. If Sayyid telephoned around midday and hung up before I could answer, I knew that I should look outside. Usually he was waving above the garden wall. This was his way of inviting me over without paying for a connected phone call.

When we sat at H Freedom, Sayyid would point out the neighbors who walked past. His descriptions tended to be brief, informative, and grounded in the material evidence of personal consumption. "She's a doctor," he said one day, after a middle-aged woman crossed the street. "She smokes Merit Blue, the ones that cost thirty pounds per pack. But she pays me only ten pounds every month." Another time, a foreigner shuffled past. "He lives in that building across the street," Sayyid said. "His wife is Egyptian. They have money. He drinks whiskey; I find the bottles in the trash."

Once, a young foreign artist from my building stopped to greet me, and Sayyid discreetly covered his teacup with his hand. "This used to be her cup," he explained, after she left. He pointed to a chip at the cup's base—the reason it had been discarded. After deciding that the cup was still serviceable, he had donated it to H Freedom. He portrayed the artist and her roommate with characteristically broad strokes: "They're nice. They pay me well. Their trash is full of cigarette ash. They don't seem to eat very much."

After I got to know Sayyid well, I occasionally tagged along for his morning rounds. In every building, he climbed to the top of the fire escape and then descended, filling a huge canvas sack while talking about the inhabitants. These were vertical narratives—each landing introduced a new character.

"Madame Heba," he said, at the top of a fire escape in a building a couple of doors down from mine. "She's a good person. Her husband is dead." He grabbed her plastic garbage bag, tossed it into his sack, and descended to another story: "This is Dr. Mohammed, an Egyptian. He's rich. He doesn't pay me enough. Only fifteen pounds." Next landing: "This one's a priest, Father Mikael. He's very cheap. He gives me only five pounds a month." Sayyid pointed at the Copt's garbage; he had twice as many bags as the others. "He says he doesn't have any money, but I see all the boxes and bags from the gifts that he gets. People give him things all the time because he's a priest."

We had started well before dawn, following a twisting, hidden route through the structures. Many of them, like the spiderweb building, had a fading glory, and Sayyid led me through marbled Art Deco lobbies where the stone had turned gray. We ascended back staircases with wrought-iron railings. Sometimes we climbed to an open rooftop, and the view of the city opened before us. As the dawn came and went, the color of the Nile changed: now gray, now orange, now a sun-dazzled blue. And every rooftop glimpse of the bright Egyptian morning was followed by another climb down a dark metal stairway. Many fire escapes were enclosed within narrow, chimneylike atriums, and the shadows lengthened as we descended, until at the bottom it felt like night.

We reached a gloomy landing full of rotting food and trash. "This one's a foreigner," Sayyid said. "I'm not supposed to touch her garbage. The landlord isn't happy with her; there's some kind of fight." Sayyid explained that in the same way that people paid him to take their garbage away, a landlord could also pay him to allow somebody's trash to accumulate. The filth was leverage: once the dispute was resolved, the landlord would give Sayyid some money to clean up the mess.

At the next landing, Sayyid dropped his voice: "She's Muslim, but she drinks too much. There are always bottles in her trash." He ripped open the woman's bag and showed me the empties: cheap Auld Stag whiskey and Egyptian-made Caspar wine.

Across the street from the drinker, Sayyid opened another bag. "This is Mr. Hassan," he said. "He's sick." He rooted inside and pulled out a pair of used syringes. "I think he has diabetes. Every day there are two syringes in the garbage. He takes one in the morning and one at night." Another time, we came to a landing, and Sayyid whispered that a resident was a sex-crazed Lebanese. Then he ripped open the trash and found an empty bottle labeled "Durex Play Feel Intimate Lube."

Sayyid could haul more than seventy pounds in his canvas sack. Within the atriums, he descended through scattered sounds of morning routines: running water, hissing stoves, crackled voices on the radio. Occasionally, an early riser heard Sayyid's footsteps and opened the kitchen door to greet him or offer tea. One morning when I was accompanying him, an elderly woman presented him with four hamburger patties in a plastic bag.

Many staircase stories described such acts of kindness. Sayyid introduced one landing as the home of a dentist who had recently arranged to have one of Sayyid's cavities filled, free of charge. Another fire-escape door led to the home of a petroleum engineer who once threw away his wallet by mistake. Sayyid found the wallet and returned it, and the engineer was overjoyed to recover his driver's license and other documents. The wallet contained only twenty-five pounds, the equivalent of less than three dollars, but the engineer rewarded Sayyid with a pair of hundred-pound bills.

This spirit of generosity, and the personal touch of *zabaleen* like Sayyid, were the main reasons that the Cairo garbage-collection system continued to function despite decades of government neglect. As usual, the word "system" was deceptive; garbage collection was better described as a series of layered relationships that had developed without any plan or oversight. In the early twentieth century, migrants arrived from Dakhla, a remote oasis in Egypt's Western Desert, where the water source had started to diminish. These environmental refugees became known as *wahiya*—"people of the oasis"—and they found a niche as trash collectors. They used flammable refuse for street carts that cooked *ful,* the inexpensive fried beans that are a staple in Egypt.

In those days, much of the trash was flammable, and the *wahiya*'s dual industries functioned in harmony. But inevitably the city's population grew at a rate that upset the delicate balance between trash and beans. During the 1930s and 1940s, another wave of migrants arrived from Asyut, a governorate in Upper Egypt. They were Copts who carved out a Christian-specific niche in the garbage world: they raised pigs that ate organic matter. Soon the original *wahiya* evolved into middlemen, managing access to buildings and collecting fees, and some of them entered the recycling business. Meanwhile, the Christians, who became known as *zabaleen,* did most of the hauling and sorting of trash, and they earned extra money by selling pork to tourist hotels.

These relationships worked well through an era of rapid growth. In 1950, the population of Greater Cairo was only 2.8 million, but it grew sixfold over the next six decades, to more than 17 million. The garbage network proved to be remarkably flexible, in part because there were always more Upper Egyptian migrants like Sayyid who were willing to work. In 2006, an article in the journal *Habitat International* declared, "Over the course of five decades the *Zabaleen* have created what is arguably one of the world's most efficient resource recovery systems." The *zabaleen* recycled roughly 80 percent of the waste they collected—more than twice the current rate in the United States.

But government officials tended to perceive *zabaleen* as symbols of backwardness rather than as community resources. In 2003, the government gave fifteen-year contracts to European waste-management companies, which would supposedly implement cutting-edge practices throughout the capital. Like so many attempts at modernization in Egypt, this reform introduced enough systematization to disrupt native traditions but not enough to result in true efficiency. The plan was underfunded, and the foreign companies had trouble negotiating the complex cultural landscape of the existing *wahiya* and *zabaleen*. Company trucks were too big to fit into many narrow streets. When the foreigners installed European-style dumpsters around the city, the *zabaleen* responded by immediately collecting these metal containers and selling them for scrap.

In 2009, during the worldwide epidemic of swine flu, the Ministry of Agriculture ordered the slaughter of all Egyptian pigs. There was no evidence that the animals were spreading the disease, which in fact had not affected a single Egyptian at the time of the decree. But the government went ahead and killed as many as 300,000 pigs. Some believed that the decision was driven by a desire to appease the Muslim Brotherhood and other Islamist opponents of the regime. But even if the Islamists had hated pigs more than they hated Mubarak, this hardly outweighed the costs of disrupting the city's sanitation system. Hundreds of angry *zabaleen* held demonstrations, and they started tossing organic waste into the streets, because now they couldn't feed it to the pigs. The declining hygiene of the capital, and the unrest of the *zabaleen,* contributed to the growing unhappiness that culminated in the revolution.

In Cairo, I met with Hassan Abu Ahmed, a spokesman for the Cairo Cleaning and Beautification Authority, a name that rang with the spirit of *insha'allah.* This government department ostensibly handled waste management, although in practice it had little control over huge swaths of the city. Ahmed acknowledged that the pig massacre had been a disaster. "The government has since said that the pigs had nothing to do with the swine flu," he said. "It was a mistake to slaughter all of them." But the government still hadn't allowed the *zabaleen* to resume raising animals, probably because now the Islamists were winning elections. Ahmed told me that the post-Tahrir economic collapse had resulted in the city's falling behind on tens of millions of dollars' worth of garbage bills. In response, the foreign companies had cut back on services, and the recycling rate was dropping. "The companies recycle 40 percent of the trash," Ahmed said. "They collect fifteen thousand tons every day, and three thousand tons are recycled."

I stopped writing in my notebook. "That's not 40 percent," I said. "Three thousand isn't 40 percent of fifteen thousand. Do you mean that they are recycling 40 percent or that they are recycling three thousand tons every day?"

"Yes," Ahmed said.

Fortunately, I always brought an interpreter when I interviewed officials. It took a while to establish that Ahmed had intended to say that six thousand tons were being recycled every day. But who knew for certain? Interviews often became entangled in Egyptian math, and while I always tried to clarify the figures, I wondered about accuracy. *Mafeesh nizam,* as my teacher Rifaat always said—there's no system.

Improved sanitation was supposed to be one of the five main pillars of the Muslim Brotherhood's Renaissance Project. But no detailed plans had been unveiled, and Morsi's public comments were low on practical application. ("Cleanliness comes from faith," he declared in a radio interview, when the topic of garbage collection came up.) I asked Sayyid if he was concerned about possible change, and he laughed. "*Kalem bas,*" he said. "It's just words."

In any case, his attention was devoted entirely to a single section of a single island in the Nile. He collected from twenty-seven buildings, which were subcontracted from seven individuals, of whom the most important was Aiman. Like many *zabaleen,* he went by a nickname: Aiman the Cat. Sayyid had also worked for Aiman the Cat's cousin, who was part of a three-generation line of *zabaleen* who went by the nicknames *Limoun, Zaitoun,* and *Filfil*—Lemon, Olives, and Pepper. Sayyid had no idea what had inspired these oddly culinary monikers, and he also couldn't explain the Beast and the Fox. The Fox subcontracted seven buildings to Sayyid; the Beast provided one more. Another *wahi* had been dead for a decade, but his son, a government clerk, retained garbage rights, so he collected a monthly fee from Sayyid. Sayyid also sent one hundred pounds every month to the widow of a *wahi* who had negotiated a deal before his death.

Sayyid kept track of all these relationships, and the tips of more than four hundred residents, by memory alone. There were no formal contracts for anything. Meanwhile, he also conducted his ongoing public relations campaign in the neighborhood. During Muslim holidays, he went to the mosque on Ahmed Heshmat Street and prayed ostentatiously so that other celebrants might be inspired to give him a bonus. He always wore his worst clothes and stood in prominent locations during the Eid al-Adha festival. One year at Eid, I was talking with Sayyid near the spiderweb building, and a retired diplomat walked by. The well-dressed man greeted Sayyid politely and handed over a twenty-pound bill. Then he looked at me.

"*Mish mehtegu,*" I said awkwardly, when the man reached into his pocket and pulled out another twenty. "I don't need it." He gave me an odd look and continued on his way.

"He thinks you're a *zabal*!" Sayyid said. It became a favorite story; he often repeated it to the men at H Freedom. He liked to relax at the kiosk, which was also a place to pick up information about the neighborhood. Occasionally his alertness backfired. Once, he was hauling trash at night when he saw the college-age daughter of a doorman kiss a boy. Sayyid immediately told the doorman—he said later that it was out of respect for the family's honor. But undoubtedly he was also motivated by the possible benefits of the doorman's gratitude. This turned out to be a miscalculation: the daughter denied everything, and the doorman was so embarrassed that he barred Sayyid from collecting the building's trash. Sayyid told me that he should have minded his own business.

Like so many aspects of Egyptian society, the garbage world involved endless complexities of social class, faith, and language. The first time Sayyid invited me to his neighborhood to watch a soccer game with his *zabaleen* colleagues, most of whom were Copts, he prepped me carefully. He warned me not to say *salaamu aleikum* to a Christian, and he reminded me to address any priest as *abuna,* "our father." At all costs I should avoid using Muslim interjections like *la ilaha ill'allah*—"there is no God but God." I enjoyed the strangeness of this exchange: the Muslim garbageman instructing the former Catholic altar boy on how to avoid offending Coptic Christian sensibilities.

Sayyid never acquired a proper nickname, although after the election the Copts in his neighborhood started calling him "Morsi." In the same spirit, Sayyid referred to me as Abu Ismail. Hazem Abu Ismail was a radical Salafi sheikh who used Twitter to incite his followers to behave like maniacs and attack various enemies in the media and government. Sayyid decided that this was the perfect name for an American, and soon a few of the local doormen started calling out to me, "Abu Ismail! Abu Ismail!" When I accompanied Sayyid on his morning rounds, he introduced me as his intern. "I'm going to America next week," he would say with mock seriousness. "Abu Ismail will be picking up the garbage."

Every day, Sayyid paid for a truck to haul the trash out to his neighborhood in Ard al-Liwa, where he did most of his sorting. From Zamalek, the journey wasn't far—a little more than two and a half miles—but Ard al-Liwa felt like a different city. Streets were unpaved, and most structures were newly built; there were still narrow swaths of farmland where people planted clover. There was no subway stop or public transport. Residents relied on private minibuses and *tuk-tuks,* the little motorcycle cabs that were banned in Zamalek and other parts of central Cairo. Even the money they used in Ard al-Liwa was different. In Zamalek, nobody gave change in anything smaller than a half-pound coin, the equivalent of about six cents, but Ard al-Liwa shops used all the tiny denominations of piastre. Every time I visited, I returned to

Zamalek with a pocketful of coins that were effectively worthless in the place where I lived.

Beginning in 1985, and continuing throughout the 1990s, the government constructed the Ring Road, an eight-lane highway that encircled the city. It cut through the heart of Ard al-Liwa, but the planners had so little interest in the people who lived there that they didn't build an entrance ramp. The trains that passed through the neighborhood also didn't stop. Near the tracks, at the entrance to Sayyid's neighborhood, a line of vendors sold relatively intact objects that had been harvested by *zabaleen:* worn clothes, old toys, mismatched bowls and plates. The first time I visited, Sayyid pulled me aside to issue a warning: "Don't buy anything here."

When he guided me through the neighborhood, I felt as if we were descending through the circles of some consumerist inferno. The vendors and their goods represented the first line of useful garbage—the easy pickings—and then we proceeded to objects that required recycling. Big warehouses melted glass; other shops reprocessed paper. Hydraulic presses hissed while crushing plastic water bottles into pallets. Toward the back of the neighborhood, where land was less valuable, goods became increasingly obscure. One man collected nothing but plastic yogurt containers. Another group of recyclers gathered pieces of discarded bread, dried them in the sun, and ground them into pellets for chicken feed. Rotting vegetables were pulled out of the trash and fed to goats. A couple of entrepreneurs focused strictly on denim. In a city of seventeen million, everything happened at scale: the denim men had a pile of old jeans, skirts, and jackets that rose more than ten feet tall.

Most of these things were industrial, machine-made products, but now in Ard al-Liwa they were deconstructed with a kind of premodern attention. When Sayyid sorted his garbage, he picked out all the pull tabs from soda cans, because even these tiny pieces of aluminum had value. Once, I saw him divide dozens of dirty plastic forks and spoons on the basis of opacity: the clearer the plastic, the higher the grade. For the same reason, he disassembled every syringe that was tossed by Mr. Hassan and all the other injection-drug users who lived on my street. Sayyid removed the metal needles, separated the plungers, and placed the clear casings in a pile dedicated to high-quality plastic.

He frequently cut himself. On a trip overseas, I bought Sayyid the kind of high-tech gloves that are used by sushi chefs and others who handle sharp blades. To me, the gloves were a perfect solution: classified at level-five cut resistance, fully compliant with the European Standard EN 388. But Sayyid labored on the other side of technology. He told me that if he wore gloves, he lost his touch. He insisted on working bare-handed, despite the risks. In his part of Ard al-Liwa, there was no hospital, no government office, and no police station. I never saw anybody in uniform near Sayyid's home. If a *zabal* was badly injured or became very ill, he lost his route. There was no health insurance or pension. It was rare for *zabaleen* to work much beyond the age of fifty, because they developed so many back and knee problems.

Many took drugs. The most common was tramadol, a prescription painkiller that functions like an opiate. Cheap versions were manufactured in China and India, and they became wildly popular in Cairo, where pills were sold on the street for about forty cents each. The year that Morsi was elected, the United Nations Office on Drugs and Crime estimated that there were five billion tramadol pills in Egypt—around sixty tablets for each man, woman, and child.

Almost every *zabal* I knew took the stuff. They said it helped with the pain, and they also used it as a sex drug, because it had the effect of delaying ejaculation. If I visited Sayyid and his friends on a Thursday, they often showed me the cheap versions of tramadol or Viagra that they planned to take that evening. In Egypt, Thursday night is the beginning of the weekend, and men sometimes call it "the Devil's birthday," because it's a traditional night for having sex.

A number of times, Sayyid stopped by my apartment with tramadol pills that he had found in the trash. People discarded these things if they were trying to quit, the same way they did with alcohol. Sayyid occasionally took the drug, but he didn't seem to have a problem. Other laborers, though, were clearly addicted. One evening when I was in the garden with my daughters, a young *zabal* who worked in a nearby part of Zamalek appeared on the other side of the spiderweb fence. He looked awful; he was sweating heavily and his eyes were darting here and there. He told me that he couldn't stop taking tramadol.

He asked for advice, and I suggested caffeine and aspirin; I couldn't think of anything else. Not long after that, he disappeared from the neighborhood, and Sayyid said that he had entered a treatment program. The government had recently reported that 60 percent of the people admitted to rehab clinics were tramadol addicts. The young man was fortunate: he came from a relatively prosperous *zabaleen* family that could afford treatment. After he returned, he looked much better, and he told me that he had learned to manage his joint soreness with Panadol Extra, an over-the-counter pain medication. It had taken seventeen days of isolation in the treatment facility to break his tramadol habit.

In Arabic class, Rifaat taught us the untranslatable word for neighborhoods like Ard al-Liwa: *ashwa'iyat*. The term is often defined as "slum," which isn't quite accurate. The literal meaning is "informal," but it's used as a noun, and only in the plural. *Ashwa'iyat* are never singular: to speak of one is to imply all the others. In 1960, such places didn't exist, but now they are home to two-thirds of the people in Greater Cairo.

None of this was the result of policy. For decades, planning bureaus had been most interested in constructing new cities in the desert, a dream that was especially dear to Mubarak. In 1996, he told the parliament that he wanted more than "a token exodus into the desert." The Ring Road was part of this vision; the highway was designed to serve new satellite cities. The first desert city was founded under Sadat, and the project expanded under Mubarak to include eight settlements. Some of these places became popular with the ultra-elite, who built villas with lawns and swimming pools. But the majority of citizens never made the move. By the end of Mubarak's reign, only 800,000 people had settled in Cairo's desert towns, compared with the 11 million who came to live in *ashwa'iyat*.

In most developing-world megacities, basic economic forces would push a person like Sayyid into bad housing in the distant outskirts. But the Cairo outcome was the opposite. In Egypt, where only 5 percent of the land is arable, strict laws prevent urban development from infringing onto farmland. Much of Ard al-Liwa and other *ashwa'iyat* were originally classified as agricultural, and no bank or investor would have taken the risk of funding a high-end development without legal status. But average citizens were willing to do this on a small scale because of the weakness of local authority. People paid off farmers, and they grabbed tiny plots of land, one after another. It was the opposite of city planning: when millions of individuals make the same decision, and replicate the same structures, the phenomenon has all the force of nature. The *ashwa'iyat* grew as if they were living things.

The government response was to follow rather than to lead. After individuals constructed an illegal building, they typically connected it—also illegally—to government utility lines. Then the government came in, installed meters, and charged for use. In the view of overwhelmed local officials, at least they had saved the cost of hooking up buildings. And in a strange way, the government's neglect made the city more livable for the poor, at least in terms of location. They occupied relatively central parts of the city, like Ard al-Liwa, and meanwhile the wealthiest residents had self-exiled to the hinterlands.

If people in the *ashwa'iyat* had feared government crackdowns, they would have constructed low-cost shantytowns, the way that illegal residents do in most parts of the developing world. But decades of dysfunctional government had conditioned Cairenes to behave as if nobody were in charge, and they built for permanence. Most *ashwa'iyat* structures were of good quality: between three and five stories tall, with foundations of reinforced concrete and walls of red brick. Virtually all of them had electricity and running water; nearly 90 percent were connected to the city's sewage system. When I met David Sims, an American urban planner who lived in Cairo, he was positive about what the average people had accomplished in the capital. "Cairo provides better cheap housing through the informal sector than any other megacity in the developing world," he said.

Sims's book *Understanding Cairo* argued that the government should have accepted the reality of the *ashwa'iyat* and even embraced some of their outcomes. They were fortunate that Mubarak's plan failed: if the desert cities had attracted large numbers of people, the capital would have become a sprawling mess. Instead, the density of the *ashwa'iyat* meant that more than three-quarters of the residents of Greater Cairo lived within ten miles of the city's center. It should have been easy to alleviate the capital's notorious traffic problems, but Mubarak's officials preferred to pretend that the informal areas didn't exist. They didn't build Ring Road entrance ramps in places like Ard al-Liwa, and they didn't connect them to the subway system.

The *ashwa'iyat* followed the same basic pattern as the *zabaleen* network of garbage collection. If the government had responded to these informal systems with vision and competence, it could have harnessed their energy. But the Mubarak regime was authoritarian without much authority. And there was always a fantasist element—it was similar to the ancient period that Matthew Adams had studied, when official texts portrayed a vision of governance that had nothing to do with the evidence on the ground. Sims wrote of the *ashwa'iyat,* "In a way it seems that government planners enjoy going through a rosy design exercise in which they can conveniently forget the reality that is present-day Cairo and over which the government has so little control."

For residents of the *ashwa'iyat,* the concept of home ownership required another kind of fantasy. They hired lawyers, wrote up contracts, and bought and sold property, and these transactions were generally recognized by local courts. But usually there was no real legal basis, and the entire system could be disrupted by a new authoritarian regime that behaved as if it actually had authority.

After Sayyid and Wahiba had had two children, she secretly had the contract for their house altered so that it included her name. The system's informality made this possible: Wahiba took the contract to a friendly lawyer, showed proof of her marriage, and explained that as the literate member in the family it made sense for her to be listed as a legal owner. When Sayyid found out, he was furious.

His lack of literacy was his great weakness. He had believed that a wife like Wahiba—poor, young, and unconnected to his family—would be more submissive. But he hadn't anticipated the impact of his wife's superior education. She wasn't afraid to assert herself, and she was better equipped to figure out things like property contracts. She was brilliant at text messaging. After she had the contract changed, there was a period when they argued intensely, and Sayyid sometimes arrived at my door to show me a text on his phone:

> It's not your house, you thief, and you came back to me like a dog, as I wanted you to, and I will send you away as I wish.

Whenever Sayyid received a message, he had to approach a literate person in the neighborhood. Wahiba's texts served two purposes: they conveyed messages, and they could also shame Sayyid in front of his friends. During arguments, Sayyid often withheld money, and sometimes he stayed in Zamalek for a couple of nights, sleeping on a cot in the garage of a building on my street where the doorman was friendly. In a typical Egyptian cousin-marriage, Wahiba would have approached her male elders for help, but as an outsider she had to find other tactics. Her texts often mentioned the lack of support so that the people who read them would tell Sayyid to straighten up and pay for his children's care.

Leslie and I tried to do the same. Sayyid often came to the apartment to vent, and we would listen and then suggest that he return home and deal with his wife directly. But like many Egyptians I knew, he had a tendency toward escapism. He often claimed that he planned to take a second wife. An Egyptian Muslim man can legally have as many as four wives at once, but in practice polygamy isn't common because of the expense and the complications. In Sayyid's case, his wife was pregnant with their third child; the last thing he needed was to bring another woman into the mix. But he seemed to like pretending, in the same way that he liked to hear the prices that discarded goods could fetch in the United States.

His ideas about sex were also escapist. They weren't fantasies in the sense of something private or prurient; it was more an imagining of an entirely alternative world. He often asked me about sexual practices in America and China, and he reported absurd stories that he heard from various doormen and *zabaleen*. Once, he told Leslie and me that in other parts of Cairo there were prostitutes who paid their clients.

"So how does this work?" I asked. "A man finds the prostitute and has sex, but then she pays him?"

"Yes," he said.

"Sayyid, *inta magnoon,*" Leslie said. "You're crazy. Show me one woman who wants to work as a prostitute so that she can pay men to have sex with her."

But he insisted that it was true. I supposed that this was one response to living in a city of seventeen million: you could always pretend that in some obscure and distant *ashwa'iyat* people were doing incredible things.

In Sayyid's own neighborhood, one long-standing civic fantasy was the idea that residents could connect to the Ring Road. After the revolution, this suddenly became a possibility, although not because of some new democratic process or improved access to officials. Actually, it was the opposite: residents realized that the government was in such disorder that officials might not notice the construction of two illegal access ramps.

This endeavor was organized by a local mosque called Al-Mesgid al-Hidaya, or the Mosque of the Gift. The mosque was privately funded, and it was one of the neighborhood's most important institutions. Its sprawling facilities included a medical clinic, a nursery school, a wedding hall, and classrooms for tutoring programs. But until the revolution, the mosque was never involved in traffic infrastructure.

The administrators timed their project carefully. Megdy Abdel Raziq, the chief executive officer of the mosque's charitable association, told me that they started working on the highway during the Mohammed Mahmoud protests, in November 2011. "At that time there wasn't any security in Cairo," he said. "All the police were busy around Tahrir." The mosque hired architects and engineers to design the highway ramps, and after every Friday sermon the imam requested donations from the congregation.

"After we started, some people came from the roads administration department," Abdel Raziq explained. "I said, 'This is our right, to enter and exit the highway.' They sympathized with us. They said, 'Go ahead and do it—I don't see anything happening here.'"

I was visiting Abdel Raziq in his office, along with a translator. It was late at night, but our conversation was repeatedly interrupted by participants in a program that helped poor families prepare for winter. For every visitor, Abdel Raziq produced a form and handed over a wool blanket and thirty pounds in cash. Most were women who wore the *niqab,* and often they signed the forms with thumbprints, because they were illiterate.

"It took us six months to build the ramps," Abdel Raziq continued. "We finished in May." He said that they had worked quickly because the project was illegal, and they had spent only one million pounds, the equivalent of 125,000 dollars. He noted proudly that a government-built ramp would have cost twice as much.

Earlier in the day, I had visited the exit. On the ramps, the angle of approach seemed sharper than normal, and the side barriers were nothing but chunks of concrete strewn beside the road. But traffic moved smoothly, and recently the government had even posted a metal sign with a name: the Matamden Exit. I asked Abdel Raziq if the ramps had been granted legal status.

"*Yanni,*" he said. In Egyptian Arabic, it could mean anything from "*yes*" to "*sort of*" to "*let's pretend.*"

"The department of roads administration is maintaining it," Abdel Raziq said. "We hope they'll give it complete legal status, but you know that the government isn't stable yet. *Al-hamdulillah,* all praise be to God, there haven't been any accidents there! If something had happened right after it was built, the authorities would have shut it down."

While we were talking, another woman in a *niqab* entered the office. She said that her husband had kicked her out of the apartment after a fight. She came from a different part of Cairo, and a bus had dropped her off at the new exit. She carried a sleeping infant in her arms. "I was sitting by the Ring Road, and somebody told me to come to the mosque," she said.

Abdel Raziq asked whether she intended to return to her husband.

"I don't know," she said. "Right now I need something to help me get through a night, maybe two nights."

It was impossible to see her expression behind the *niqab,* but she sounded upset. Abdel Raziq said there were women at the mosque who could help with the baby, or introduce a lawyer.

"I don't want that now," she said. "I just want something to eat and a place to stay for a night or two."

"Well, you can always come back here if you need help," Abdel Raziq said. Then he opened his desk drawer and took out 120 pounds. The woman blessed him, hoisted up her baby, and walked back into the night.

At the end of August, Wahiba gave birth to a daughter they named Lamis. On the seventh day after the baby was born, the family held a traditional celebration called a *sebou,* and Sayyid escorted Leslie and me to his neighborhood. We walked past the lines of garbage processing—the street vendors, the glass recyclers, the denim men. Rats rustled through big piles of organic matter. Sayyid explained that ever since the pig massacre the *zabaleen* had been unable to process all of this stuff. This was where our own discarded food ended up: if our household's leftovers weren't good enough for goats or ducks, they rotted in a pile down the street from Sayyid's family.

They lived on a narrow, unpaved alleyway. All the buildings here looked the same: two or three stories, with gray concrete foundations and redbrick walls. Steel rebar poked out from the roofs like wild strands of hair. Nothing in the *ashwa'iyat* was ever complete, because people added levels to their homes over time as they saved money and as their families expanded. Sayyid told me that someday he hoped to construct two more stories for his sons.

The moment we entered the building, we left the *ashwa'iyat* behind. Before visiting, I had had a vague notion that the home would be furnished largely with things that had been harvested from the Zamalek garbage, like Sayyid's clothes. But all of the appliances and furniture were brand new. The couches were still wrapped in factory plastic, and the family had two televisions. A computer was being installed for the older son, Zizou. In the abstract, I had always known that Sayyid did fine; he usually earned at least five hundred dollars a month, which was about twice the average household income in Cairo. But I had never fully grasped how profitable Zamalek trash could be until I visited his home. He told me that the building and its furnishings had cost him the equivalent of thirty thousand dollars.

Wahiba was another surprise. When Sayyid showed us the building's second floor, she was standing on the stairway. She was strikingly pretty, with fair skin and a heart-shaped face that was free from makeup except for heavy blue eye shadow and black eyeliner. She wore a long gown embroidered with beads. Her figure was so slender that I couldn't imagine she had given birth to her third child only a week earlier.

She greeted Leslie and me warmly, saying that her husband had told her all about us. The couple seemed comfortable; there wasn't any evidence of the tension over the apartment contract that Sayyid had complained about earlier in the year. Wahiba was holding Lamis, and she gently handed the newborn to Leslie and excused herself. A moment later she returned with her face covered by a *niqab*.

As the evening progressed, I realized that our arrival had caught Wahiba by surprise. We had been the first guests to arrive, and she hadn't finished getting dressed. She had made up her eyes carefully because that was the only part of her face that was intended to be seen.

Relatives and neighbors filled the apartment, and some people began to dance to music that played on a small stereo. The mood was festive; Ramadan had recently finished. The holy month had fallen during the summer, and Sayyid hadn't fasted—laborers received an exception because of the heat. So did pregnant women, but Wahiba had fasted anyway. In August, the temperature had been over one hundred degrees Fahrenheit almost every day, but Wahiba, eight months pregnant, had abstained from all food and water from dawn until sundown. The apartment had no air-conditioning.

"She's *gamda*," Sayyid said, when he mentioned the fasting. The word has a positive connotation: tough, determined. Behind the veil Wahiba's eyes flickered.

"It wasn't so difficult until the end," she said. "Anyway, it's over."

Lamis was the one I wondered about. At birth, the baby weighed barely six pounds, and every time I saw her wrinkled face, I thought: *Please give that baby something to drink*. When Leslie had been pregnant with our twins, she had been forced to spend two months on bed rest in a Colorado hospital. Her diet was advised by a nutritionist; nurses carried out daily ultrasound tests. No fewer than nine physicians and nurses were in the delivery room at the time of the births. And yet here was a woman who had spent her ninth month deliberately avoiding food and liquids every day from four o'clock in the morning until six thirty at night. But the baby seemed fine. What was the lesson? I had the same question whenever I watched Sayyid handling used syringes and broken glass with his bare hands. He never seemed to get sick or hurt; every morning, as sure as sunrise, he was lugging his canvas sack around the neighborhood.

At the end of the *sebou,* Leslie and I thanked the couple and praised the baby. To guard against the evil eye, we used the various phrases from class: "*This is what God has willed*"; "*all praise be to God*"; "*it will happen with the will of God.*" Wahiba thanked us, her eyes proud. She had fasted all the way through Ramadan; the birth hadn't taken place until the day after the final festival. Even this new house was registered in her name, and that was *gamda,* too. Nearly three years would pass before we saw her face again.

CHAPTER 9

THAT SAME RAMADAN, A GROUP OF ISLAMIST MILITANTS ATTACKED AN Egyptian Army base in the northeastern corner of the Sinai Peninsula. The incident occurred at sundown, after the soldiers had sat down to break the day's fast. For years, Sinai had been poorly governed, and the region had become home to various militant groups, including some that were affiliated with al-Qaeda. The Ramadan attack took the soldiers by surprise, and the militants killed sixteen men and stole two Egyptian APCs. They drove the vehicles east across the border, hoping to attack Israel, but the Israel Defense Forces promptly annihilated the militants.

President Morsi had been in office for barely a month. At a Cairo prayer service for the soldiers, a crowd of angry mourners chased away the Egyptian prime minister, who was representing Morsi's government. After that, Morsi decided not to attend the military funeral that was being held for the soldiers. An official at the American embassy who was in close contact with Brotherhood leaders told me that Morsi feared for his safety. According to the American official, Morsi believed that individuals in the army and the police were conspiring against him.

One week after the Sinai incident, Morsi made the first major move of his presidency. He issued a presidential decree that effectively purged the military's top leadership. The minister of defense was forced to step down, and more than two hundred high-ranking officers were retired. As the new minister, Morsi installed a colonel general who had previously been unknown to the vast majority of Egyptians. His name was Abdel Fattah el-Sisi.

In Arabic class, the topic of the army came up so often that one of our instructors, Sami, dedicated a lesson to the vocabulary of military rank. In my notebook, I lined some of them up:

Second Lieutenant	ملازم
First Lieutenant	ملازم أول
Lieutenant (Three Stars)	نقيب
Major	رائد
Lieutenant Colonel	مقدم
Colonel	عقيد
Brigadier General	عميد
Major General	لوا

These words cropped up everywhere, from Upper Egypt to Tahrir to the *ashwa'iyat*—the name "Ard al-Liwa" means "Land of the Major General." Even a place like Sayyid's neighborhood—unplanned, unregulated, unpoliced—was full of people who had once been uniformed. Egypt practices universal male conscription, with the length of service depending on educational level. A male college graduate spends one year in uniform, while two years are required of a high school grad. Sayyid, as a man without any schooling, served the maximum: three years.

From my perspective, the most striking thing about Sayyid's service was that after 1,095 days in the army he was no more literate than he had been on day one. But for most Egyptians the army was above reproach. Cabbies often told me that the high quality of Egyptian soldiers is mentioned in a hadith, which is evidence that the army is blessed by God, *al-hamdulillah*. The revolution did nothing to shake this faith. Most public anger was aimed at the police, while the army was viewed as a savior for having forced Mubarak's resignation. Sayyid tended to be cynical about the government, but he had no complaints about the three years he spent holding an automatic rifle at a sentry post in Port Said. He was never offered a single course in basic literacy.

Traditionally, women did not serve in the army, and neither did Muslim Brothers. During the years that the Brotherhood was illegal, even the children of members weren't allowed to serve. Now that the Brothers had come to power, they planned to change these rules, but for the time being they had few allies in uniform. Morsi's appointment of Sisi was widely viewed as the first step toward creating an officer corps that would be friendlier toward the Islamists.

Before the revolution, Sisi had served as the director of military intelligence, a position with a low public profile. But once he was promoted, information slowly trickled out about his background. It was telling that the first personal detail I heard was that Sisi's wife supposedly wore the *niqab*. Rifaat and other teachers at Kalimat mentioned this, because one common way to evaluate a man's social class and faith was to look at the women in his clan. When Khairat El-Shater was put forward as the Brotherhood's original candidate for president, there was a flurry of articles in the press about how, if he won, his wife would be the country's first First Lady to wear a *niqab*. Morsi's wife didn't cover her face, but she wore a *khimar*, a conservative veil that falls to the waist.

Sisi was married to his first cousin. His wife was a homemaker, and so was their adult daughter. In the Egyptian press, I couldn't find evidence of any woman in the extended Sisi clan having a career. Sisi rarely talked in public about his immediate family, with the exception of his mother, whom he often mentioned. Like the cousin-marriage, this marked him as a traditional Egyptian male—he told a reporter that his mother was "an authentically Egyptian woman, in all the meaning of authenticity." Sisi was known to be a devout Muslim, but his wife's *niqab* turned out to be a false rumor. In truth, she wore a *hijab*, like most married Egyptian Muslim women, but her garment had received special attention. Fathy El-Sisi, one of the minister's cousins, told the newspaper *Al-Watan* that Sisi had twice turned down a promotion to serve as a military representative in the United States, because the Egyptian authorities requested that his wife remove her *hijab* while in the West. This wasn't uncommon in the Egyptian Army, which tried to promote a more secular image to foreigners.

Sisi tended to speak softly. He was small, with dark, alert eyes, and he smiled easily. Most people who met him were impressed by his intelligence, and one American official told me that he reminded her of a certain Washington archetype. "You have the political people who always want to be the loudest voice in the room," she said. "And then there are people who are creatures of the system, who are just as capable but not necessarily the loudest." She went on, "I also think the quiet, reserved posture is a forcing function to make people lean in and really think about what he's saying. What signal is he trying to send? Is there a deeper meaning?"

Five years before the revolution, Sisi had completed a course at the U.S. Army War College, in Carlisle, Pennsylvania. Such exchanges are an important part of the U.S.-Egyptian military relationship, which has been close since the signing of the Camp David Accords in 1978. As part of the agreement, the United States provides Egypt with substantial support. In 2012, the year of Sisi's appointment as minister, the United States gave more than a billion dollars in military aid, which represented about a quarter of Egypt's total expenditure on defense.

At the War College, Sisi wrote a thesis titled "Democracy in the Middle East." He was skeptical about such prospects: "Democracy, as a secular entity, is unlikely to be favorably received by the vast majority of Middle Easterners, who are devout followers of the Islamic faith." He promoted Islamist views of governance: "Ideally, the legislative, executive, and judicial bodies should all take Islamic beliefs into consideration when carrying out their duties." He never mentioned gender inequality or other prominent social issues, and the word "women" did not appear in the text. But he emphasized that if conservative Islamist groups like Hamas win elections, they must be allowed to govern. He wrote, "The challenge that exists is whether the rest of the world will be able to accept a democracy in the Middle East founded on Islamic beliefs."

Such ideas made Sisi trustworthy in the eyes of the Brotherhood. A senior official in the U.S. State Department told me that Sisi had played a leading role in secret talks during the tense period when it was unclear who had won the presidential election. "Sisi was the one negotiating with the Brotherhood," the American official said.

When I met with Mohamed Kadry Said, a retired major general who worked at a government think tank called the Al-Ahram Center for Political and Strategic Studies, he said that initially he had been surprised by Sisi's promotion. Sisi was only fifty-seven years old, and he had previously been ranked lower than sixtieth in the military hierarchy. “It’s not normal for the minister of defense to come from military intelligence,” Said explained. But the more he thought about it, the more he understood the reasons for elevating a spymaster during a revolution. “It’s a time for information,” Said remarked. “Morsi needs to know the armed forces. Sisi is helpful because he knows every name.” He went on, “Sisi has all the keys to all the doors. And right now war is not tomorrow. What’s important is to know what’s happening inside Egypt.”

At the beginning of the Morsi presidency, it was possible to go almost anywhere in the country. The revolution had stabilized, at least for the time being, but the new regime had yet to work out its relationship with the security state. People told me it was a good time to travel and look into sensitive subjects. Leslie and I rented a car and took the toddlers to Siwa, an oasis near the Libyan border, and I made a couple of trips to northern Sinai.

One morning during this period, I went to have lunch with a man who had helped assassinate President Anwar Sadat. Manu found a young driver he knew from his neighborhood, and we headed north from Cairo and then took a side road to a small village in the desert. During the Mubarak years, this village had been home to a foreign-funded agricultural project, but it had mostly failed and now many buildings were empty. It felt like a place of exile—abandoned streets, scraggly bushes, stunted trees.

Salah Bayoumi met us on a battered motorcycle at the edge of the village. He was forty-nine years old, with dark hair, a mustache, and a prominent prayer bruise the color of coal. His heaviness had the look of something recently acquired, like an ill-fitting suit of clothes that had been borrowed from another person. His stomach bulged beneath a white galabiya, and his face was so full that it appeared almost swollen. After Manu and I arrived, Bayoumi seated us for a large lunch of roast chicken, beef, and potatoes. He ate quickly with both hands and he didn’t stop until nearly all the food was finished. He said that he had gained nearly fifty pounds since being released from prison.

Most of his life had been spent in jail. Despite his bulk, he had the eyes of a hungry man, furtive and fast moving. He established that he didn’t want to talk about certain things. "The incidents of 1981," he said. "The incident of Sadat." Every time we approached the topic, he used that word: "incident."

An Egyptian journalist friend had introduced me to Bayoumi, and he warned me that the man was paranoid. I started our conversation by asking about more distant personal history. Bayoumi said he had grown up in Shoubra, the same Cairo neighborhood where my teacher Rifaat was from, and in his early teens he had been welcomed by some Salafis in the neighborhood mosque. Soon he came to believe in their ideas.

"In the days of Sadat, the regime was fighting Islam," he said. "In order to resist, we studied sharia law and the idea of jihad." At the age of fifteen, he learned that the army was allowing teenagers to sign up early, fulfilling their mandatory service, so he volunteered. He saw no contradiction in being both a soldier and a Salafi. "I believed that the army was also a way of jihad," he said.

He wanted to fight Israelis, but the military assigned him to its music department instead. He was taught to play the bagpipes. He had no interest in this foreign instrument, or even in music; Salafis are typically wary of its distractions and temptations. But he had to do as he was ordered. His job was to march in military parades, like the one that was held on October 6, 1981, on the anniversary of Egypt's invasion of Sinai. That turned out to be the last parade for both Sadat and Bayoumi the bagpiper.

"Then I was arrested and tried without justice," Bayoumi said. "But this is what I don't want to talk about."

I asked if he could explain why it was unjust.

"When they arrested me, I didn't have any weapons or any incriminating papers."

"Did you have something to do with what had happened on that day?"

"All I knew was that something was going to happen at the parade," he said, and then he clammed up.

For Egyptians, the death of Sadat wasn't fixed in their minds the way that the Kennedy assassination was for Americans. This wasn't for lack of visual reminders. The reviewing stand where Sadat was shot still occupies a prominent place in the capital, along the main route from the Cairo Airport to downtown. Every time I passed, I remembered images from newspapers and magazines during October 1981, when I was twelve years old. One photograph was especially vivid: in black and white, a soldier turned terrorist fires into a rostrum of mostly empty chairs. The chairs are empty because the leaders of the country have either fallen or flung themselves onto the ground. In addition to Sadat, ten others were killed by terrorists on that day.

A Cairo cabbie occasionally muttered a prayer when he drove past the reviewing stand, but most people showed no sign of recognition. They tended to talk about Sadat less than they did about the other two powerful men who had ruled during the half a century before the revolution. Mubarak wasn't charismatic, but his long tenure, and the recent drama of Tahrir, made him prominent in people's minds. And many Egyptians, like my teacher Rifaat, still idolized Nasser. You could describe a socialist as a Nasserite, and the capitalists who benefited under Mubarak were known as *feloul,* or "remnants" of the regime. But there was no word for anybody connected to Sadat—no Sadatites, no *Anwari.*

His background was by far the most modest of the presidential trio. He was the grandson of an African slave; his mother's father had been forcibly brought to Egypt during the period before the British ended the practice. Sadat's father eventually married eight times, and he had thirteen children. Despite the family's poverty, Sadat imagined himself to be a visionary anticolonialist, although many of his early ideas were muddled. He admired both Gandhi and Hitler; once, he wrote a fond letter to the dead führer ("I admire you from the bottom of my heart"). Sadat loathed the British, but it was his father's connections with an Englishman that allowed the young man to enter Egypt's Royal Military Academy.

Sadat thrived in the army, and along with Nasser he became one of the "Free Officers," a group of military men who led the revolution of 1952. Sadat was known for his loyalty, and Nasser picked him as his successor. When Sadat ascended to the presidency after Nasser's death, in 1970, the American intelligence community knew little about him. Most people assumed that he wouldn't last long in office.

But Sadat proved to be a more complex figure than anybody had expected. He arrested many of Nasser's corrupt friends, and he turned against the Soviets, expelling fifteen thousand Russian troops and advisers in 1972. The following year, on October 6, he launched his surprise invasion of Sinai, initiating the conflict that Israelis called the Yom Kippur War. But, a few years later, Sadat made an equally surprising offer to visit Israel's parliament. He was the first post-revolution leader to emphasize his faith—he called himself "the believer President"—and he instituted a more tolerant policy toward Islamists, who had been brutally repressed by Nasser. But Sadat's personal version of the faith was moderate, and his wife, Jehan, was educated, uncovered, and committed to her public advocacy for women's causes. Most strikingly, Sadat was willing to infuriate the Islamists by agreeing to the Camp David Accords. After rejecting the Soviets, he turned to the Americans, and he instituted free-market reforms that became known as the *Infitah*.

In geopolitical terms, Sadat was shrewdly flexible, and he seemed to have an instinctive grasp of long-term strategy. He realized that Nasser's planned economics were doomed, that the Americans would be more useful than the Soviets, and that Egypt would be better off at peace with its Israeli neighbors. But these all represented difficult transitions in policy, and Sadat struggled to handle the domestic reaction. He was particularly clumsy with the Islamists. He veered between tolerance and repression, and he had initiated a harsh crackdown the month before the assassination, which was carried out by al-Gama'a al-Islamiyya, a radical group that included many former Muslim Brothers. At the time of Sadat's death, he was extremely unpopular, and people sometimes still expressed pleasure that the president had been shot. Once, when I visited a poor city in Upper Egypt called Mallawi, locals told me proudly that it was the birthplace of Sadat's principal assassin, Khalid Islambouli. Their hometown boy was the soldier-terrorist in the black-and-white photograph, firing into the empty chairs.

Islambouli was executed, along with four others. Another terrorist was killed by security forces on the day of the assassination. But the plot had required the involvement of many others, because no soldier in the parade was supposed to carry a working rifle with live ammunition. In the end, seventeen men, including Salah Bayoumi, were sentenced to prison terms for their roles in plotting the attack.

In Bayoumi's home, after we talked for a while, the conversation circled back to 1981. He seemed more relaxed, so I pressed him. "You said earlier that it was unjust that you were imprisoned for so long," I said. "But you also said that you knew something would happen."

"I had a huge role," he said. "But we cannot talk about the details."

I told him I had seen a report in *Al-Masry al-Youm,* a prominent private newspaper, that mentioned that Bayoumi had helped supply working weapons for the assassination.

He was quiet for a while, and then he answered: "You can say it's accurate and inaccurate." But he wouldn't elaborate on that cryptic remark.

In prison, he had been tortured, and repeated beatings left him deaf in one ear. At the end of 2006, after serving twenty-five years, he was released, but security forces continued to observe him closely. He found work as a laborer in a marble quarry in Sadat City, one of Mubarak's new desert communities. If Bayoumi recognized any irony in this life path, he kept it to himself. He still spoke angrily about the former president. "Everyone hated Sadat because after the war he sought help from the Jews," he said. "And he gave speeches that accused Islamists of being backward. He referred to women in *niqabs* as 'tents.'"

In 2011, when the Tahrir protests broke out, the police rounded up many Islamists, including Bayoumi. He was in jail at the time of Mubarak's fall. Since Morsi's election, the active monitoring of Bayoumi had apparently been abandoned. But he didn't trust this period of relative quiet. "I am personally convinced that the old regime is still here," he said. "The revolution still hasn't happened yet." He feared that the *feloul* would find a way to remove President Morsi.

I asked if the assassination of Sadat had accomplished anything positive.

"No," Bayoumi said flatly. "Mubarak just followed the same pattern. He did everything that Sadat did, but even worse."

One lesson that Mubarak took from the assassination was that the army couldn't be fully trusted. In response, he built up the Ministry of the Interior as a bulwark of personal support, and he indulged the police's worst abuses. It was part of the fragmentation of Egyptian institutions—rather than creating a coherent system, Mubarak encouraged scattered fiefdoms of authority.

Army officers often disliked the police, because they believed the cops' brutality and lack of discipline had sparked the revolution. One senior official at the U.S. State Department told me that during a private meeting he heard Sisi criticize the police in the bluntest of terms. "It's a million-man mafia," said the new minister of defense. The army and the police shared a hatred of Islamists, but they also had reasons to distrust each other.

Bayoumi said that he no longer belonged to political groups, but he still followed Salafi ideas. Of the seventeen people who had received long prison terms for Sadat's assassination, he was one of the least known. My Egyptian journalist friend told me that supposedly Bayoumi had supplied firing pins for the weapons that killed Sadat. Another Egyptian journalist had reported that Bayoumi told him about a final role that he was supposed to perform on the day of the assassination. The plotters believed that after they killed Sadat, other army officers would support them in seizing power. Bayoumi was instructed to ride a bicycle along the Corniche Road to the state television building, where he would deliver news of the coup.

For some reason, I found the image of the bicycle messenger particularly depressing. The plan seemed delusional in all its assumptions: that Sadat deserved to die for negotiating with Jews, that Islam would countenance such an act, that the killers would rise to rule the nation. But the participants had taken this crazed idea further than anybody could have imagined. It was the ultimate example of how small people, and small acts, can have great consequences—the teenage bagpiper with some firing pins who helped change history. But changing history isn't the same as escaping history. At eighteen, Bayoumi had envisioned himself on a bicycle beside the Nile, delivering the glorious news of an Islamist coup to a welcoming nation. Thirty years later, the army was still the most powerful institution in Egypt, and Bayoumi was an ex-con in the desert, riding an old motorcycle to a tough job in Sadat City.

The driver from Manu's neighborhood was twenty-two years old, and he shared our lunch in Bayoumi's home. During the interview he sat quietly nearby. After a while, when there was a break, he spoke up.

"What did you do about sex in prison?" he said.

"Nothing," Bayoumi said. "There are no women there. I thought that I would never get married, and I accepted it. But now it has happened, *al-hamdullilah.*"

After his release, Bayoumi had married a much younger woman, and now they had twin babies. This was one reason he lived in the desert village, where she had a family connection. Bayoumi asked the young driver if he was married.

"No," he said. "But I wish I was." Shyly, the young man asked Bayoumi for advice about how to control sexual desires.

"It's all mental," Bayoumi said. "It's not physical." He warmed to the subject; he talked about avoiding sexual thoughts and how hormones can be managed through prayer. He quoted from a hadith: "*Whoever among you can afford it, let him get married, for it is more effective in lowering the gaze and guarding chastity. And whoever cannot, then fasting will be a restraint for him.*"

"So I have to fast?" the driver said, a little sadly.

"Fasting kills lust," Bayoumi said sternly. "Fasting is better for everything."

The driver nodded. He seemed instinctively to look up to the older man, as if he had gained great wisdom from his prison experience. During another break in the interview, the driver asked Bayoumi how to manage fears about death. The answer was always the same—prayer—but these exchanges clearly impressed the driver.

The next time I saw Manu, he mentioned the driver's conversation. "That was so Egyptian!" Manu said, laughing. "You meet a guy who helped kill Sadat and your first question is about sex."

By now, Manu was employed on a regular basis at the *Guardian,* and we worked together only if he happened to be free. Most of our contact was social, and on weekends we sometimes met at the bars he liked to frequent downtown. There was no sign that the police near his new residence had been informed about the arrest.

Manu's father had started telephoning him the day after the incident, pleading for him to visit Port Said. Manu felt that this was impossible, because he knew that the police must have described his sexuality, and the false crime, in the crudest of terms. But on the telephone his father seemed gentle. "I haven't told anything to anybody," he said. "Be easy and come home."

When Manu was growing up, he had relied on his mother for support and protection from his father's abuse. But now she had been dead for years. All of his siblings led lives that were completely different from his own. One of his sisters married a husband so conservative that he insisted that she wear a *niqab*. Manu's brother had become a staunch Islamist, and his wife also covered herself with a *niqab*. Once, when Manu was visiting his brother's home, he accidentally walked into a room before his sister-in-law was able to veil herself. His first reaction was shock; he hadn't seen her face since they were married, more than a decade earlier, and he was struck by how much she had aged. She quickly covered herself again, and Manu felt instinctively as if he had done something wrong. Then he thought about the ridiculousness of the situation. If it seemed absurd that a woman would worry about her brother-in-law seeing her face, then it was even more absurd that a woman would worry about her gay brother-in-law seeing her face. Of course, these were ideas that Manu could never share with family. In that sense, the arrest felt like something fated—the inevitable final break.

But his father kept pleading with him to visit. Finally, Manu made the two-and-a-half-hour trip from Cairo, and his father greeted him warmly. He never mentioned the arrest directly, but he made it clear that he was concerned. After that visit, Manu began to make more frequent trips back to Port Said.

Manu's father was in his seventies, and his health was declining. He had lost his thriving coffee shop as a result of a lawsuit filed by the heirs of his former partner. The lawsuit had sat in the courts for twenty-five years before it suddenly succeeded, which made Manu's father suspect that a judge had been bribed. He could have become a bitter man, and he could have taken it out on Manu. But instead there was a new tenderness in the way he treated his son. He never spoke about Manu's getting married, the way other family members did.

The father lived for only a few months after the arrest. In his will, he left his Port Said apartment to Manu alone. It was the kind of gesture that a father would make to a youngest son who had yet to get engaged, but this clearly wasn't his motivation. And Manu found himself saddened in a way that he wouldn't have been a decade earlier. He felt grateful for the time after the arrest—the only period when they had had a good relationship. It seemed a miracle, this sudden kindness that came out of a father's realization that his son was gay.

Of all the people I knew, Manu had the most insightful view of Egyptian male sexuality. In many respects, he was an outsider, because he wasn't trying to get married, and he had no interest in chasing or harassing women. He saw clearly both the abuses and the absurdities—the sister-in-law who wouldn't show her face, the twenty-two-year-old who asked a convicted Islamist terrorist for sex advice. But Manu's outsider status was by no means complete: after all, he had sex with men all the time. Many of these men, like him, described themselves as gay, but others did not. "This is just something that my cousin and I used to do in the village," one partner told Manu, by way of explaining that he wasn't a *khawwal*. Sometimes partners talked to him about girls they liked. They often had idiosyncratic ideas about what constituted a *khawwal*. A man might be interested in male sex as long as he wasn't penetrated, or as long as he felt that he was dominant. For them, male sex wasn't the same as gay sex, an attitude that has a long tradition in Egypt, as it does in many places around the world.

Manu might stay with a partner for weeks, or months, or longer; even some of the straight men were looking for a relationship. But there was always a chance of volatility, because these private practices clashed so strongly with the public homophobia. Sometimes a partner lashed out at Manu, verbally or even physically. "They love me, they care about me, but they also have this thing inside that makes them hate me," he explained. He found that this could occur with gays as well as straights, which was one reason he distrusted such labels. It was impossible to tell how much any individual's behavior reflected true desire and how much had been shaped by religion, family pressures, or the strict segregation of the genders.

Manu couldn't untangle these forces, just as he couldn't predict the moments when an interaction led to danger. The choice was simple: he could live a safe life, and stay closeted and closed, or he could accept the uncertainty and the risks of male relationships in Cairo. Even after getting set up by Kareem, and detained by the police, Manu remained open to meeting strangers.

One of these strangers was Ahmed. He was young and good-looking, and he lived near Manu's new apartment. They talked a couple of times in the street, and then they started to meet for drinks in a Dokki club that had a cabaret show at night. Soon they were having sex. "He wasn't gay, at least not according to the measures in Egypt," Manu said. "He was totally interested in girls." The fact that Manu wasn't interested in women didn't seem to bother Ahmed. "I'm sure he knew that we were different," Manu said. "He had this somewhere in his mind, but it wasn't in a dangerous place."

One evening when they were together in Manu's apartment, there was a sudden pounding on the door. "Ahmed!" somebody shouted. "Manu! Ahmed! I know you're in there!" It was a friend of Ahmed's, another young man who lived in the neighborhood. He had a thuggish air, and Manu had seen him involved in various altercations. Every Cairo neighborhood had such characters—underemployed men in their twenties who hung out in the street, talking loudly, smoking hashish, harassing women, and getting into fights.

The thug asked to talk to Ahmed. For a few minutes, they spoke heatedly outside the apartment, and then Ahmed went away. The thug accused Manu of corrupting Ahmed. "If I ever see you again, you fucking *khawwal,* then I will cut your ass," he said.

That night, Manu left the apartment. In Cairo, it wasn't unusual for a gay person to get beaten or even killed, and Manu knew that he couldn't go to the local police. But he called one of the young police academy students that he sometimes saw socially. He asked him to accompany him for protection on one last trip to retrieve belongings from the apartment.

Before they went, Manu explained that he was gay, because he felt that his friend needed to know the full situation. In the end, nothing happened, and Manu moved to another apartment downtown. He never saw Ahmed again. None of the police academy students ever mentioned Manu's homosexuality, and they continued to socialize with him. In a way, it was encouraging—Egyptian men often turned out to be surprisingly tolerant, at least in private. But it was never something to be talked about, and the process of coming out invariably came from a position of vulnerability. In so many cases it was the threat of violence or police harassment that forced Manu to tell people who he really was.

During the first half year of Morsi's presidency, I asked Manu to introduce me to his police academy friends, because I was curious to hear their ideas about the new government. We met late one night downtown, in one of the anonymous bars that Manu liked. There were three officers in training, all in their early twenties. Their course was highly selective; after graduation, these men would be in charge of squads of police recruits. In Egypt, conscripts with the lowest education levels were assigned to the police. This was another reason why the police were notorious—their crowd control depended heavily on conscripts. One of the tragedies of the revolution was that these young men—poorly educated and poorly trained—were pitted against their activist peers in street battles.

For decades, Muslim Brothers had been banned from the police, and recently the rule had been changed. But none of the officers in training knew of any Brothers in their class, or even anybody who sympathized with the Islamists. "They act like they are good Muslims, but they are liars," one young man said.

His classmate spoke up: "I hate the Muslim Brothers because they cooperated with al-Gama'a al-Islamiyya and they killed Sadat."

In truth, the Brotherhood had had nothing to do with the assassination, but many ex-members had joined al-Gama'a al-Islamiyya in the 1970s and 1980s. I asked about the Brothers' current attitude toward the police.

"They're scared of us," the first young man said. "Because they know that when the time comes, I will have the power to put them back in the place where they deserve to be—in prison."

Like the others, he believed a conspiracy theory that Morsi's election had been rigged. None of these young men had been allowed to vote; ever since Egypt's constitution of 1923, people in uniform had been denied the franchise, supposedly as a way of establishing neutrality. Now this law seemed a strange holdover from the days of authoritarianism and sham elections, and it might have impacted the post-Tahrir democracy. If the estimated two million members of the army and the police had had the right to vote, and if they had opposed Morsi at a rate of 73 percent or higher, he would have lost. Instead, these soldiers and officers were now expected to protect the winner of an election that had excluded them.

I had heard that officer academies were revising their training materials to make them less anti-Islamist. But the young officer candidates weren't aware of any such shift. When I asked if they could think of anything else that was handled differently since the revolution, one man said, "We use real bullets more in training now."

The relatively quiet period of Morsi's early term ended on November 22, 2012, with the second major move of his presidency. On that day, Morsi issued a presidential decree that temporarily granted himself broad powers beyond the reach of any court or judge. He claimed that this was necessary to prevent the courts from dissolving an assembly that was writing Egypt's new constitution. The president never gave any evidence that the courts were about to do this, but earlier in the year they had canceled the parliament, a decision that seemed to have been politically motivated.

After Morsi's decree, the assembly rushed to finish the constitution. The group was dominated by Islamists, and nearly all opposition members resigned in protest. Morsi announced that in two weeks the nation would hold a referendum on the constitution. In response, demonstrators surrounded the Presidential Palace in Heliopolis, a district in eastern Cairo. They established a Tahrir-style sit-in, erecting tents outside the palace walls.

On the afternoon of December 5, Muslim Brotherhood supporters attacked the unarmed protesters. They quickly drove them off, and then they tore down the tents. News of the attack spread on social media, and soon more demonstrators arrived to retake the lost ground. For hours, the two sides fought with rocks and clubs, and then guns began to appear. Ten people died, and more than seven hundred were injured, with the majority of casualties sustained by Brotherhood supporters. The police finally gained control the next morning and erected barricades around the palace.

The following day, the Brotherhood issued a statement claiming that its supporters had responded to a breach of security. "An armed unit was arrested trying to take over the Presidential Palace," the statement read. "They are now being questioned by the prosecution service." Morsi echoed these charges of a conspiracy, referring to "a fifth column." But the Brotherhood never provided evidence of such an attack, and prosecutors made no charges. Videos showed clearly that Morsi supporters had set upon the peaceful sit-in. Soon, victims and witnesses appeared in the media, testifying that the Islamists had detained innocent bystanders, sometimes torturing them in hopes of finding a conspiracy.

Amr Darrag, a Brotherhood leader, told me that the attack had been justified by the incompetence of the security apparatus. "It's better that this took place rather than involving the police and the presidential guard in a massacre," he said. Walid el-Bedry, a spokesman for the Brotherhood's Freedom and Justice Party, admitted to me that nobody had actually broken into the palace. But he said the Brothers had heard it was about to happen. "So we went there, and we removed the tents," he said. "There was no violence while we removed the tents."

"Did the protesters agree that you could take them down?" I asked.

"Of course they didn't agree," he said.

None of the leaders whom I spoke with seemed to grasp the significance of what they had done. Untrained men had played the role of law enforcement, bringing back memories of the Islamist militias of old. For more than half a century, the Brotherhood had tried to purge itself of this early history, and the organization had successfully maintained a stance of nonviolence through nearly thirty years of Mubarak's repression. But it took only five months in power for the Brothers to break this principle.

During the night that Morsi supporters fought with demonstrators, another mob attacked the national Brotherhood headquarters in the Cairo suburb of Moqattam. Hundreds of people overran the building, smashing windows and breaking doors, and they dragged furniture and documents into the street and set them on fire.

The day after the violence ended, I took a cab to the headquarters, where piles of half-burned material still covered the street. A couple of Egyptian journalists were gathering documents from the piles. During the first wave of the revolution, when many Cairo police stations were looted, journalists had uncovered some damning materials about the activities of the Mubarak regime. Now they were looking for similar things outside the Brotherhood building, and I joined them in rooting through the papers—another archaeology of the revolution.

For some reason I found a lot of material in English about chicken feed. Documents referred to silage, dry forage, and succulent forage. Another paper in Arabic was titled "A Report of What Was Achieved in the Bureau of Northeast Cairo." The paper didn't note many achievements, and its conclusion was terse: "The most important obstacles facing the plan: weakness of employment." Another page featured instructions on how to use a compass, which had been photocopied from *The Bader Encyclopedia for the Scout Movement.* I found a report from the Brotherhood's Renaissance Project: "How to Remove Trash from the Airport."

> *There should be trash boxes. The boxes should be closed, and there shouldn't be smells coming from them. The flies should not be allowed to gather. . . . The contractor should commit to providing services of safety and professionalism, and he should wear clothes, gloves, shoes, a head covering, and it should be unicolored.*

A young guard stood at the gate, fiddling with a string of prayer beads, but he didn't try to stop us. One of the documents I found was stained with blood. I also turned up a photocopied expense form with receipts from a restaurant called Le Flandrin, at 80 Avenue Henri-Martin, in Paris. A man named Abdel Hamid had eaten there on the evening of December 20, 2010. He had ordered *soupe de poisson,* two *belles soles,* and half a bottle of white wine. This was my most damning discovery: a Muslim Brother had been reimbursed for Chardonnay.

After leaving the headquarters, I went to the Presidential Palace. It had been more than a day since the police had regained control of the area, blocking off streets with barricades of barbed wire. Armed officers stood at the barricades, where crowds of protesters were chanting, "The people want to topple the *nizam*!"

At exactly seven o'clock, the soldiers moved. They were Republican Guards, administered by the army and assigned to protect the president. They clearly responded to some command; they cut the barbed wire, opened the barricades, and jogged away. They lined up along the street, rifles at their sides, standing at attention.

For a moment, the crowd seemed confused. Then people surged into the street, running past the soldiers. One group of young men separated and began spray-painting anti-Brotherhood slogans onto the walls in front of the palace. Another group staked out space for a new sit-in camp. More young men stationed themselves in front of the palace gates, to serve as crowd control. They wanted to make sure that nobody tried to breach the compound.

By now, after almost two years of the Egyptian Arab Spring, the revolution was like a portable kit: all the key pieces could be packed up and reassembled anywhere in the city at a moment's notice. Around the palace, vendors quickly appeared, selling the staples of revolutionary activity: sweet potatoes, bread, sunflower seeds. Old women dragged butane burners down the street and hawked hot tea and Nescafé. Others sold gas masks, chemistry-lab goggles, and high-powered green lasers that were made in China. One of the most eerily beautiful sights I had witnessed during nighttime clashes on Tahrir was when the police launched a tear-gas canister and half a dozen lasers homed in on the object, tracing a bright arc in the sky so that the crowd could scatter before it landed.

Tonight, though, there wasn't any tear gas. It was the first protest I had attended where none of the anger was directed at the police. After the Republican Guards opened the barricades, some police officers started to appear in the crowd, mingling with protesters. Near one side of the palace, I saw a heavyset officer talking in animated tones with a group of people, and I joined them, with my translator. The officer's epaulets identified him as a lieutenant colonel in the police's Central Security Forces. A young woman asked him why there had been so many instances of police brutality during the revolution.

"There are good people in the police, and there are bad people," he said. "It's just like anything else."

She mentioned the previous year's battle on Mohammed Mahmoud Street.

"Let's not talk about that," the officer said. "It was partly our mistake, and it was partly your mistake."

"The Brotherhood is going to send more people to attack us," a young man said. "Please just go and stand at the entrance to the street with six police trucks. It would be enough to stop them."

"I can't hold a sign saying that I'm with you," the officer said.

The young woman asked the officer what he thought Morsi should do.

"He has to step away from the constitutional declaration," he said.

"They don't believe in Egypt," she said. "They aren't human!"

"What goes around comes around," the officer said. "If you do something bad, it will come back to you."

"But if they hold a referendum, you know that everybody is going to say yes!"

Her point was valid: most average Egyptians would be inclined to approve whatever was put on a ballot, because it would be described as a way to move the country forward. The officer seemed to agree. "These protests alone aren't going to do it," he said. "You have to have a general strike. If you have a strike, it has to be everybody, like they did in Poland."

I asked the officer why the barricades had been opened at seven o'clock and why the demonstrators had been allowed to surround the palace. "I can't tell you why," he said, smiling. "But you should be able to understand on your own."

A couple of days later, the protesters erected a Museum of the Revolution in front of the palace. This was another part of the Tahrir kit; there was a museum just like it on the square. The palace museum was housed in a tent, and the curators wired into a nearby streetlamp for electricity. "We have plumbers, we have electricians, we have everything," Mohamed Ezz, a college student who was helping to curate the museum, told me. A sign at the entrance read "Please, We Ask Visitors of the Museum Not to Touch."

The exhibits memorialized each significant clash of the past two years, arranged in chronological order. Over time, many clashes had acquired epic names: the Battle of the Camels, the Day of Rage, the Friday of Purging. The Battle of the Camels had taken place before the fall of Mubarak, when the regime hired thugs on camels to fight with revolutionaries. In the museum, these early images were most striking in the lack of preparedness among protesters: no helmets, no gas masks, no lasers. The equipment improved quickly after the fall of the regime. The later photographs showed motorcycle ambulances, and emergency field stations, and battle-hardened demonstrators in protective clothing. There were images of people with their eyes shot out and of dying men stretched out in pools of blood. Cars were transformed into fireballs; buildings were pockmarked with bullets. Beneath every image, a caption identified the date and the event: the Incident of Maspero, the Incident of the Cabinet, the Incident of Mohammed Mahmoud.

But the museum wasn't really about history. There was no narrative and no analysis; the exhibits consisted of nothing more than scattered incidents. Since the start of the Arab Spring, clashes had occurred one after another, and meanwhile the government had cycled through five prime ministers without any clear sense of direction. Many of the most important interactions must have been happening in secret, between the police, the army, and the Islamists. Until these relationships were resolved, the museum was effectively telling a story that had no ending.

Sisi's connection with the Brotherhood remained a mystery. During the fight over the constitution, Sisi offered to host a dialogue "for humanitarian communication" between President Morsi and the leaders of opposition groups. But the meeting never took place. Most reports indicated that Morsi refused to attend because Sisi had overstepped his authority. Gamal Heshmat, a leader of the Brotherhood's political party, told an Egyptian newspaper, "The defense minister should be asked for the reason behind postponement." But Sisi held his silence. He didn't say a word about the new constitution.

In December, the public ratified the document with a vote of more than 63 percent. It was an easy sell: citizens were told that the constitution reflected Islamic values and that it was essential for stability and economic recovery. Legal experts were mostly scathing in their assessment of the constitution. "It gives a broad space for tyranny," said Gaber Gad Nassar, a Cairo University professor who was one of Egypt's top scholars in constitutional law. Nassar had originally been part of the constitutional drafting assembly, but he resigned in protest, along with about a quarter of the members, including all the Christians. Some key articles were changed two days before the final vote, after the opposition had quit. Nassar showed me one article that originally protected against discrimination on the basis of "sex, or origin, or language, or religion, or belief, or opinion, or social status, or handicap." All of those words had been removed, which laid the foundation for an Islamist parliament to pass laws that could lead to unequal treatment of Christians or women. Nassar pointed out another article about freedom of the press that had been changed to specify that the media should "serve the community" and respect "private lives" and "national security."

"Since 1923, no constitution of Egypt has had something like that," he said. "They can use it to shut down newspapers."

Nassar's experience on the assembly had convinced him that the Brotherhood wanted to take over the country. But he also believed that the basic character of the organization would prevent it from succeeding. In his opinion, the Brothers were too secretive and too closed; they were incapable of recruiting outside allies and experts. "This is what is standing in the way of the Brotherhood and control of the country," he said. "They don't have enough talent."

CHAPTER 10

THE KALIMAT LANGUAGE SCHOOL HAD BEEN FOUNDED BY RIFAAT AND HIS younger brother, who was named Raafat. Their father, in addition to building water towers across Egypt, had been a soccer fan, and he named these sons after his favorite players. Rifaat and Raafat had starred for different teams, and perhaps the father hadn't anticipated the confusion that would result when the names joined the same family. "At least I wasn't named Mohammed," Rifaat said once. "Or Mahmoud. Or Ahmed." This was one quality that Egypt and China had in common: so many people, so few names. My address book was stuffed with Mohammeds and Mahmouds, Xiaomeis and Xiuyings. How many different Mohammed Mahmouds had handed me a cup of tea? Where were all the Wang Weis of yesteryear? Eight of the eighteen members of the Muslim Brotherhood's Guidance Bureau were named either Mohammed or Mahmoud. I randomly encountered three Mohammed Morsis during the month of the presidential election; two of them were driving cabs. Once, in Abydos, I interviewed somebody named Mohammedain. The name means "Two Mohammeds."

Fortunately, Rifaat and Raafat looked nothing alike. Rifaat was slight and dark; Raafat was big and fair-skinned. Rifaat lived alone, while Raafat was gregarious, with an English wife and children. But their political ideas were as similar as their names. Both were liberals who idolized Gamal Abdel Nasser, and they disliked Islamists in general and Muslim Brothers in particular. One Kalimat teacher told me that Raafat had personally telephoned every member of the staff before the presidential election, begging them to vote against Morsi.

The revolution had once seemed promising to anybody who taught Arabic. In 2011, during the first summer of the Arab Spring, Leslie and I had been part of the largest group of introductory students that Middlebury College's summer Arabic program had had in years. There was a similar energy when we arrived in Cairo, and mornings were busy at Kalimat. But as the street incidents grew louder, the school got quieter. When I asked Rifaat how things were going, he often winced and mentioned that another college exchange group had canceled a term in Egypt. My vocabulary lists tracked the deterioration:

Ministry of the Interior	وزارة الداخلية
vandalism	تخريب
democracy	ديموقراطية
democratic	ديموقراطي
division	إنقسام
there is a division in Egypt	في إنقسام في مصر

In January 2013, shortly after the Brotherhood had rammed its constitution through the referendum, I learned "*greedy*," "*power hungry*," "*confrontation*," and "*frustration*." That same month, Rifaat taught us *meskeen*, "pathetic," because that was how he described Morsi. The president seemed overmatched by the job; Rifaat said Morsi should have been repairing shoes or working in a coffee shop. In class, on the day that we talked about the *meskeen* president, our list ended on a new word that had started to crop up in conversations:

to feel sorry for	صعبان
I feel sorry for Morsi	مرسي صعبان عليا
shoe repairman	جزمجي
coffee-shop worker	قهوجي
postman	بوسطجي
to have no choice	مسيّر
to have a choice	مخيّر
coup	إنقلاب

One of Rifaat's great qualities was that he could convey the depth behind those Tahrir words. When I came to class with *debaba,* or "tank," Rifaat told us that the word derives from an Arabic root that means "to step heavily"—a perfect image for a military vehicle. The term for "infidel"—*kefir*—comes from a root that signifies "cover." "It's because the infidel is covering Allah," Rifaat explained. The word for "moody" is *bighazela,* "like a gazelle," and if you want to express the feeling of being in love, you say, "I have nails in my heart." "Gambling" and "moon" share a root. "The moon makes you crazy, and gambling is crazy," Rifaat said.

He loved the quirks of Egyptian Arabic. The language shares the national appetite for opposites: tradition and novelty, order and chaos. Scholars of *fusha,* the classical form of Arabic, have always taken pride in its purity, but Egyptian Arabic is a river muddied by many tributaries. Some words come from Coptic, which descended from pharaonic Egyptian, but there are many more imports from Greek, Persian, Turkish, French, and English. Rifaat enjoyed Arab Spring neologisms like *yashayer,* which took the "share" from Facebook and conjugated it as an Arabic verb. He often pointed out English terms that originally came from Arabic: "elastic," "magazine," "sugar," "kismet."

The language is wonderful for *Wanderwörter.* In class, Rifaat told us that Arabic imported the word "shah" from the Persians, and then the phrase *al-shah mat*—"the king died"—became "checkmate" in English. Sometimes a single word had traveled across thousands of years, passing through multiple languages along the way. One morning, Rifaat taught us the word for "mud brick." In ancient hieroglyphs, it was *djebet,* which became *tobe* in Coptic, and then the Arabs, adding a definite article, made it *al-tuba,* which was brought to Spain as *adobar,* and on to the American Southwest, where this heavy thing, having been lugged across four millennia and seven thousand miles, finally landed as "adobe."

Surprisingly few Coptic words survive in Egyptian. During ancient times, Egyptians were famous for their attachment to their culture and language, even after the empire had fallen to outsiders. "The Egyptians avoid following

Greek customs, and in general, they are unwilling to adopt customs of any people other than their own," Herodotus wrote in the fifth century BC. Over time, there were some prominent exceptions to this trend, most notably the conversion of many Egyptians to Christianity not long after the time of Christ. But most Egyptians never learned the languages of their foreign rulers: the Greeks, the Romans, the Byzantines.

The Arabs broke down this resistance in spectacular fashion. In AD 639, the first Arab army arrived in Egypt, which at that time was a province of the Byzantine Empire. The Arabs had only four thousand soldiers, but within two years they conquered the country. Their linguistic takeover was even more impressive. This had less to do with conversion to Islam than most people would expect. Unlike the Byzantines, who persecuted heretics, the Arabs accepted subjects of other faiths, as long as they paid their taxes. But the Arabs rarely learned other languages, which gave their subjects an incentive to acquire the tongue of their overlords. Kees Versteegh, author of *The Arabic Language,* notes that "language became a binding factor for the Islamic empire to a far greater degree than religion."

In effect, Egyptians converted to Arabic long before they converted to Islam. In AD 706, only six decades after the first Arabs arrived in Egypt, the language of administration switched to Arabic. After another 150 years, Coptic had essentially vanished as a daily language in Lower Egypt. By the tenth century, a bishop named Severus complained that even Egyptian Christians could communicate only in Arabic.

The language spread in similar ways across the rest of North Africa and in some parts of Europe. As the Arabs became a more powerful and more confident empire, they sought to benefit from the cultures of these new territories. During the early ninth century, the Mu'tazila school of Islamic theology promoted a rationalist exploration of faith and other subjects, and Arabs began to search out the works of the ancient Greeks. They were especially interested in philosophy, because Greek ideas were useful in religious debates, but they also wanted to access the scientific and medical knowledge of the classical world.

In the West, these sources had become hard to find. Relatively few had been translated into Latin, because the Romans had read Greek well. After the collapse of the Roman Empire, literacy in Greek disappeared rapidly, and soon the knowledge of many classics was lost. Even in Byzantium such works weren't highly valued. When the Arabs started searching for these texts, they reported finding them in forgotten archives, often in poor condition. The Muslims saw themselves as the protectors of the classical tradition, and they had these works translated into Arabic editions. The translators were often Syriac or Hebrew speakers who functioned as linguistic middlemen, filtering the original Greek through two or three different languages.

After Christians began to reconquer the Iberian Peninsula, in the late eleventh century, scholars translated the Arabic versions of Greek classics into Latin. In western Europe, Arabic became so critical to the rediscovery of classical knowledge that medical scholars at the University of Paris called themselves *arabizantes*. Even as late as 1530, the Dutch physician Laurentius Frisius emphasized the importance of Arabic in his field. A number of our modern medical terms still bear traces of Arabic: "retina" and "cornea," for example, come from Latin translations of *shabakiyya* and *qarniyya,* Arabic words that were themselves translated from Greek texts.

When complex ideas wander through so many languages, distortions are inevitable. Eventually, Western scholars rediscovered the original classics in Byzantium, learned Greek, and claimed that many Arabic-based translations were flawed. By then, the Muʿtazila school had been superseded by more dogmatic interpretations of Islam, and Renaissance scholars came to view the Arabs as the defilers of classical texts, not their preservers. The motivation for learning Arabic also changed. Now Westerners studied the language in order to argue with Muslims and try to convert them to Christianity. The first Western analysis of Arabic words and grammar was published in Spain in 1505, and it had nothing to do with classical ideas of philosophy, science, and medicine. The book was a tool that priests used with Muslims who had been converted during the Inquisition.

When Leslie and I chose to study Egyptian Arabic rather than *fusha,* or classical Arabic, the issue of religion never crossed our minds. The decision was pragmatic: we expected to be in Egypt for five or six years; we wanted to talk to average Egyptians; we didn't plan on working outside the country. It made no sense to study *fusha,* which is significantly harder and tends to be more useful for a person who is traveling around the region or engaging primarily with texts. But our choice also meant that the language we studied was much less religious. We learned the *fusha* phrases for polite interaction—*this is what God has willed; all praise be to God*—but we didn't delve into the Quran. We rarely read anything that could be considered formal history or literature. After we completed *Dardasha,* we were essentially on our own; there weren't high-level textbooks for Egyptian. The language has a weak literary tradition, and most of what we covered was essentially oral. Rifaat came to class with lists of phrases that could have been shouted across a Cairo street:

Stop bragging.

I'm not in the mood.

He put me in a bad mood.

Show me the new bag that you bought yesterday.

Are you really stupid or just acting stupid?

For Rifaat, creating class materials seemed cathartic. Kalimat was struggling, and the Muslim Brotherhood infuriated him, and all of this fed into the dialogues and stories that he wrote for class. He arrived every morning bursting with enthusiasm for some new lesson about poverty, or rape, or children who have been recruited into criminal gangs. He wrote devastating little character sketches that began with sentences like "*Fareed is a very lazy worker who does not keep his appointments; he is always late.*" In Rifaat's lessons, petty criminals spoke like philosopher-kings ("*I'm not the only fraud in the country; there are many other frauds*"), and family members displayed their love and loyalty in energetic ways ("*I'm going to break her head for the honor of the family*"). For this lifelong bachelor, Egyptian marriage was a relentlessly dire subject:

I've had enough of the whole disgusting business of marriage.

I became sickened by this life.

I was tossing and turning all night long.

Don't worry.

I got my fill of beating him.

Rifaat often used radio broadcasts and films from the 1950s and 1960s, because he wanted us firmly grounded in the era of Nasser. We listened to pan-Arab programs, and we watched old movies, with Rifaat waxing nostalgic about the more cosmopolitan Cairo of the past. He described the cultural geography of his childhood, when he and his brothers used to go to different cinemas for glimpses of different cultures: Russian films at the Odeon, French movies at the Radio, Hollywood at the Metro.

One week, we watched *Cairo Station,* a 1958 film by the great Egyptian director Youssef Chahine. Set in the capital's train station, the movie deals with labor unrest, poverty, the disabled, and violence against women. Our vocabulary list was heavy with sex:

something embarrassing	حاجة تكسف
psychological repression	كبت نفسي
sexual repression	كبت جنسي
he is repressed	عنده كبت

"People used to talk openly about these things," Rifaat said. He spat out the word *haraam*—"forbidden." "Now it's always *haraam, haraam, haraam*! You didn't hear that word so often in the old days."

Sometimes, when he embarked on one of his antireligious rants, I teased him by saying that he was a *kefir,* an "infidel." "I'm a good Muslim," he insisted. He declared that after death he would go to *gana,* "paradise," and he had an extremely specific idea of what this would entail. The jihadis might have dreamed of their seventy virgins in the garden, but Rifaat's *gana* was a very different place. "There will be a big balcony," he said. "I'm standing there with Nasser, and we're drinking cold beer. And we are looking down on Mubarak and Sadat burning in hell. Because they're the ones who created this mess with the Muslim Brotherhood."

Rifaat swore that he believed in the Quran. For him, the book's divinity was linguistic: the language was so beautiful that it must have come from God. He often remarked on the Prophet's illiteracy and how, at the time of the revelations, in the seventh century AD, Arabic had had a weak literary tradition. Given these conditions, *fusha*'s logical grammar was nothing short of miraculous. "Arabic is like a computer," Rifaat often said. "Everything has a *nizam,* a system. It's not like English, with all these irregular forms."

In truth, much of Arabic's *nizam* was formalized after the time of Muhammad. When Islam began to spread, the written form of Arabic was still in the developmental stages, and scholars went about establishing rules for orthography, grammar, and other aspects of a text. Such a project isn't uncommon for a new empire. In China, many key dynastic traditions were established by the Han, who began to rule in 206 BC, shortly after the country was first unified. As part of the Han's empire building, they codified and standardized the Confucian classics, a process that helped set the terms for the writing system. By taking these centuries-old texts as their model of proper Chinese writing, the Han prescribed an idealized language—classical Chinese—that was probably never spoken in day-to-day life.

Early scholars of Arabic had a similar instinct to draw on the past. They wanted to codify the language in ways that corresponded to the Quran, but they lacked the wealth of historical material that had been available to more literate cultures like the Chinese. So the Arabs went to the desert instead. They sought out Bedouins, who were believed to speak a purer form of Arabic than city people did. The elite sent their sons to live with nomads so that they would learn to talk correctly, and grammarians employed Bedouins as referees in language disputes. Some Bedouins even set up camps outside cities, to make themselves accessible to scholars—these nomads made a living from herding words.

During the tenth century, a lexicographer named al-Azhari was so blessed—*al-hamdulillah!*—that he was kidnapped by a Bedouin tribe. This experience allowed him to produce a dictionary called *The Reparation of Speech.* The book's introduction, in a kind of grammatical Stockholm syndrome, effusively praises the kidnappers: "They speak according to their desert nature and their ingrained instincts. In their speech you hardly ever hear a linguistic or a terrible mistake."

This standardization of written Arabic was in some respects opposed to the spread of the spoken language. In provincial places like Egypt, natives learned Arabic in informal ways, and they simplified the grammar. In response, scholars moved in the opposite direction, developing a beautifully logical but extremely difficult version of the language. This form of Arabic had great status, and it was seen as the language of the Quran, but it might have never been spoken in everyday life. Charles Ferguson, an influential linguist at Stanford University, argued that today's dialects of Arabic did not descend from the classical language. In Ferguson's description, the spoken and the written forms were used "side by side," even in the early years of the Islamic empire.

This dichotomy is still apparent in every Arabic-speaking country today, and so is the contrast in status. The traditional written form of Arabic is called *al-lugha al-'arabiyya al-fusha,* "the eloquent Arabic language," or, for short, *al-fusha:* "the eloquent." Egyptian Arabic, on the other hand, is known simply as *'ammiyya:* "common." Over the centuries, Egyptian changed along with its speakers, and it accepted loanwords from many languages and periods. But *fusha* remained remarkably stable. It was like the Nile that flows through Egypt—a river without tributaries. Nothing entered *fusha,* because it wasn't an everyday language; it was used for Friday sermons, academic lectures, formal speeches, and writing.

Every Egyptian I knew harbored an insecurity about the language, which surprised me, because they were such natural polyglots. In Cairo, I often worked with Hassan, a man in his early twenties who could perform simultaneous translation. He rendered Arabic into English even while the person was still talking, which essentially cut the time for an interview in half. In America, this skill is taught at elite schools like the Middlebury Institute of International Studies at Monterey, but Hassan, who had gone to terrible Cairo public schools and dropped out of college, had taught himself how to do such translation entirely on his own. And yet he struggled whenever I asked him to translate a sermon from *fusha.* He often said that he hated the language; he found it much easier to communicate in English.

In the past, there had been times when Egyptians questioned the tradition of using this difficult form for writing and education. During the nineteenth century, as the pressures of colonialism and modernization intensified, some intellectuals advocated for writing in the colloquial. They believed that such a change would improve literacy rates while making it easier to incorporate modern terms and ideas. But traditionalists feared further damage to a culture that had already suffered so much foreign incursion. "It will not be long before our ancestral language loses its form, God forbid," an editor at the newspaper *Al-Ahram* wrote in 1882. "How can we support a weak spoken language which will eliminate the sacred original language?"

Similar debates occurred in other parts of the world that also struggled with transitions to modernity. Both Turkey and Greece used antiquated literary languages that were eventually abandoned in favor of colloquial forms. In China, during the second and third decades of the twentieth century, the Baihua movement helped to end the practice of using classical Chinese, replacing it with the vernacular of northern China. But this change was politically and culturally easier for the Chinese than it would have been for the Egyptians. The Chinese language was effectively limited to one country, which hadn't been damaged by colonialism to the degree of the Middle East. Most important, classical Chinese wasn't tied to a dominant religion or a divine text.

In the Middle East, the anticolonialist movement transcended national boundaries, and activists saw *fusha* as a unifying force. One of these movements became known as the Nahda, or "Arabic Renaissance"—the same word that the Muslim Brotherhood later applied to their own vision of rebirth. During the end of the nineteenth century, leaders of the Arabic Renaissance decided to modernize *fusha* without radically changing its grammar or essential vocabulary. New terms were coined using traditional roots: "telegram," for example, comes from "lightning." ("Isn't that cute?" Rifaat said, when we studied the word in class.) *Qitar,* the word for "train," was originally used for "caravan." Other neologisms were more imaginative. "Lead camel" was an inspired choice for "locomotive," as was "sound of thunder" for "telephone"—the perfect image for those wrong-number conversations.

Over time, Arabs associated any encouragement of vernacular writing with colonialism, and allegiance to *fusha* became central to Pan-Arabism. But Nasser, the greatest pan-Arab of all, had a schizophrenic relationship with *fusha* and Egyptian. When the president delivered public speeches, he typically began in *fusha,* and then he would start to sprinkle in the occasional Egyptian phrase. By the speech's climax, the *fusha* had disappeared, and the president was declaiming entirely in the language of the people.

Leslie and I often argued with Rifaat about Nasser. Sometimes this was sparked by Rifaat's class materials, in which a sentence that modeled the conditional tense could be a vehicle for bald-faced historical propaganda. (*"If not for Gamal Abdel Nasser, more people would have remained uneducated."*) But there was also something magnetic about this figure and his inconsistencies. Nasser was an anticolonialist who imported Western ideas about socialism to disastrous effect, and he was a secularist who helped create the perfect environment for Islamism. These contradictions were part of what made him quintessentially Egyptian—the first native to rule the country with any authority since the days of the pharaohs.

Nasser was born in 1918, the year after the British issued the Balfour Declaration. The declaration supported the formation of a "national home" for Jewish people in Palestine, and afterward there were outbreaks of violence from both Arabs and Jews. Nasser's parents weren't well educated—his father was a postal worker—but like many Egyptians of their generation, they became staunch supporters of the Arab cause. The couple named one of Nasser's brothers "Glory of the Arabs."

As a boy, Nasser participated in anti-British protests, and he eventually joined the army. In 1947, the United Nations announced that Palestine would be divided into three states: one for the Arabs, another for the Jews, and a third that would be internationally administered. Civil war immediately broke out, and in the spring of 1948 the Israelis issued a declaration of independence. Egypt, Jordan, and Syria responded by invading, which was Nasser's first experience of warfare. He was wounded, and the Egyptian Army recognized him for bravery, but he saw the Arab-Israeli War as an unmitigated disaster. The new Jewish state expanded into territories that the United Nations had designated for Palestinians, and approximately 700,000 lost their homes. For Arabs, this event became known as *Al-Nakba*—"the Catastrophe."

Nasser was convinced that the Egyptian government must be overthrown. Along with other military figures, he met secretly with leaders of the Muslim Brotherhood, which shared the dream of revolution. The Brothers organized street protests that helped undermine the regime, and in 1952, Nasser, Sadat, and the Free Officers successfully seized power. For a while, Nasser continued to work with the Brothers, but he eventually turned on them. This would become a standard pattern in modern Egyptian politics: at various times, Egyptian leaders and military men formed alliances with the Muslim Brothers, and invariably these alliances collapsed.

For Nasser, the partnership ended in 1954, when he was the target of a failed assassination attempt. There's some evidence that the assassination might have been staged by Nasser and his allies, because they wanted an excuse to get rid of the Islamists. Nasser responded with a vicious crackdown, and for the rest of his presidency he never allowed the Islamists to reenter political life. It was under Nasser's reign that Sayyid Qutb was arrested, tortured, and eventually executed, becoming the most important martyr to the Islamist movement.

Nasser's rejection of Islamism was part of what appealed to Rifaat. He believed that the president understood the true brilliance of the Egyptians: their cosmopolitanism and their open-mindedness, and the way they combined these qualities with a powerful sense of history and identity. Umm Kulthum's most famous concerts were held during the Nasser years, and the government founded community theaters and art centers around the country. The education system was expanded on a massive scale, with millions of Egyptians attending college for free. Nasser did more to encourage the education and employment of women than any Egyptian leader before him. He seized the assets of the rich, in hopes of a more equitable redistribution, and he strengthened rent-control laws in Cairo.

But his vision of a middle-class Egypt turned out to be a mirage. Pan-Arabism was a reaction to colonialism, and like so many reactions, it replicated old flaws in a new form. Throughout the Middle East, Western powers had redrawn national borders while disregarding cultural, religious, and historical differences, and now Pan-Arabism did the same thing by promoting the idea that all Arabs were essentially the same. Egypt denied some of its unique identity, including its language, and its army became involved in wasteful regional conflicts like the North Yemen Civil War. Colonial-style patchwork countries came and went, like the brief period from 1958 to 1961 when Egypt and Syria were united under Nasser's government.

Nasser seized control of the Suez Canal, and he stood up to the British and the Americans, but he adopted some of the worst Soviet ideas. Entrepreneurship collapsed; state-owned enterprises became inefficient and unproductive. Nasser drove out most Egyptian Jews, Greeks, and other long-term citizens with foreign roots, destroying the economy and the cosmopolitan character of cities like Cairo and Alexandria. The expansion of education turned out to be another failure. Schools grew too rapidly without proper reforms or teacher training; now Egyptians could go to college, but they didn't learn much, and they couldn't find jobs. Many of these new campuses eventually turned out Islamists. In the 1970s and 1980s, Upper Egyptian universities became the most important breeding grounds for terrorist groups like al-Gama'a al-Islamiyya, because young people arrived on campus and were quickly disillusioned about their prospects. And the rise of Islamism quickly undermined Nasser's advances in women's education and employment.

Whenever I mentioned these things to Rifaat, he blamed everything on Sadat. "He's the one who brought back religion," Rifaat said. "He let the Brotherhood out of jail."

Older Egyptians tended to take sides between Nasser and Sadat. Intellectuals and cultural figures were more likely to idolize Nasser, whereas those engaged in business, the military, and the police felt more of an affinity with Sadat. In truth, there hadn't been any tension between these men, and even their contradictory approaches sometimes led to the same outcome. Under Nasser's crackdown, Muslim Brothers and other Islamists fled to Saudi Arabia; a generation later, when Sadat began to release Islamist prisoners, many also went straight to the Gulf. All of these expatriate Egyptians had a tendency to return home and spread the ideas of Wahhabism. The economic policies of Nasser and Sadat seemed to be diametrically opposed, but both failed to produce significant improvement. For all the charisma of these men, they seem to have lacked the power, the vision, or the time that was necessary to turn Egypt around.

Rifaat and Raafat's family still owned the building that their father had constructed during the Nasser years. It was centrally located in the district of Shoubra, and it consisted of twelve flats and some ground-floor storefronts.

The family rented out seven apartments, along with two shops. These nine units produced a total monthly revenue stream that was equivalent to twelve American dollars.

In the city proper, about 40 percent of occupied units were under strict rent-control laws that had hardly changed in half a century. If a tenant of a rent-controlled apartment died, descendants usually tried to maintain residence, which often resulted in a lawsuit. During the entire time that I lived in the spiderweb building, the beautiful four-bedroom apartment across the hall was unoccupied, because one of these cases was crawling its way through the courts. The landlady told me that she expected it would take at least another decade to resolve. A number of other apartments in the building were rented for only a few dollars a month. It was hardly surprising that the place was poorly maintained, with an open-cage elevator that lacked basic safety features.

Once, I asked Raafat if this legacy of Nasser's bothered him, given his family's building. "People blame Nasser because he did this, of course," he said. "But if you have a law and it no longer works after five years, then why don't you change it? It's not a Bible or a Quran." And to some degree he was right. Cairo rents had been frozen during World War II, and the policy continued throughout the chaotic years of the Arab-Israeli War and the rise of the Free Officers. Nasser strengthened this policy, but he hadn't started it, and it continued for decades after his death.

In the same way, Nasser's failed educational expansion had to be seen in the context of a much longer tradition of national failure. He mishandled the Islamists, but everybody else did, too. And who in the region had responded in a productive way to colonialism? So much of what Nasser had inherited had been passed on to Sadat, and then to Mubarak, and now to Morsi. As time passed, it became clear that Egypt's two modern revolutions—the Free Officers in 1952, and the Tahrir movement in 2011—had both been too limited in scope. These were narrowly political events in a country that needed deep social, cultural, and economic reform.

And there had always been a tendency to seek solutions in two sweeping and simplistic political ideologies. That was the thinking: maybe Egypt needed Pan-Arabism, or maybe it needed Islamism. But shifting back and forth between these flawed ideas seemed to have resulted in a particularly unfortunate combination.

The people don't want to change," Raafat said, when we talked about Nasser and his legacy. "They need to reform the system, but they don't really want to do it." Like many Egyptians, he had a fantasy of starting over, and he had bought a house in one of Mubarak's desert communities. "Maybe when people go to a new place, a place that's clean, then they realize that they shouldn't throw garbage everywhere," he said hopefully. "You have to change the education and the culture in Egypt. Otherwise you can build something good, but some Salafi or other *mutakhelif* will come and blow it up."

That was a street word: "idiot," "retarded person." During the spring of 2013, Rifaat taught us how to say "confrontation," "civil disobedience," and "gunfire." Another word of the season was *azma,* "crisis," which was applied to shortages. *Azma* of gasoline, *azma* of electricity. In Cairo, it became common for drivers to wait for an hour or more at a gas station, and the black market flourished. We often lost electricity in our neighborhood. Some said it was because of the incompetence of Morsi's government, while others believed that suppliers were deliberately creating these crises in order to undermine the Brotherhood. Either way, the outcome was the same: people increasingly blamed Morsi.

A few times at Kalimat, we had class during a blackout. Whenever the electricity failed, we added the topic to our discussion, applying the vocabulary of shortage. No matter what happened, we kept going to class, and Rifaat kept preparing his lessons.

One day in spring, he gave a class about suicide. He explained cheerfully that suicide had never been common in Egypt, but now, at least according to Rifaat, it was happening much more than it did in the days of Nasser. Rifaat claimed that it is physically impossible for a person to commit suicide after listening to the voice of Umm Kulthum. In any case, he would never do it. "You know why?" he said, smiling. "Because death is coming anyway. It's coming soon enough."

He disapproved of the cowardice of carbon monoxide. Pills and guns were also for the weak of heart. If Rifaat absolutely had to kill himself, he would do it like Cleopatra, with the bite of a *kubra.* This word, he noted with pleasure, sounds the same in Arabic and English, with a shared Latin root. He ended class by giving us a new set of character sketches to study. They were titled "Victims of the System":

> *When Ibrahim was a 16-year-old high school student doing well in school he enjoyed the full confidence of his family and the freedom to come and go as he pleased. His friendship with a teacher only increased his family's confidence in him. And Ibrahim was so proud of his friendship that when his teacher asked him to help to rob the flat of a girl who had refused to marry him, he did not hesitate. . . .*

CHAPTER 11

DOWN THE ROAD FROM ABYDOS, IN THE DISTRICT CENTER OF BALYANA, there was another *rayis.* His name was Shaban Qandil, and like the *rayis* in Abydos he was a large man who wore the style of well-trimmed mustache that is common for Egyptian police, soldiers, and government officials. His desk also had an electric button near his right hand. There was an empty nail on the wall. A long line of people waited in the hallway outside the office. It was the end of April 2013, almost ten months after the presidential election.

One of the people waiting was a man in his early twenties whose arms had been amputated just below the elbows. When he entered the office he did not use any of the polite introductions that are standard in Egypt.

"I want an apartment, because I want to find a wife and get married," he announced. "I was injured in a train accident."

He had the stern look and the full beard of a religious man. I was sitting in the office along with Hassan, and we had come to Balyana in order to watch the petitioners. Often a citizen registered our presence, but the armless man ignored us. He wore a blue galabiya, the wide sleeves hanging slack like broken wings. Since the revolution, there had been a series of train accidents across Egypt, because safety systems weren't being properly maintained. The young man explained that he had been injured at a road crossing that malfunctioned.

The *rayis* said that the government was subsidizing the construction of some local apartment buildings, which would be sold at a discount to needy people. "If you're lucky, I can put you at the top of the list," he said. "How much can you pay?"

"I can't pay anything," the young man said. "I can't work without arms. Give me a piece of land to cultivate."

"Forget about that," the *rayis* said. "You're not going to work a piece of land. We can give you a kiosk with all the goods. You can just stand there and sell things."

The young man didn't hesitate. "I want a kiosk at the entrance to the city."

The *rayis* looked up—he seemed impressed by this boldness. "We can't do that," he said. "We're already removing all the kiosks at the entrance to the city. But we can help you." He said they would find a kiosk in another part of town.

"I don't want to sell cigarettes," the young man said. "It's *haraam*."

"You don't have to sell cigarettes. You can sell anything else."

"I want prosthetic arms, too. I want the kiosk and prosthetic arms."

An assistant to the *rayis* made a noise of exasperation. "Just work first, my son, and you'll get the arms!"

The *rayis* silenced the assistant with a gesture. He said, "You can bring the medical records tomorrow, and we'll take care of it."

"I have the records here," the young man said. "You can take them now."

He said the records were in the front pocket of his galabiya. He waited there, staring straight ahead, his chin held high while his sleeves dangled at his sides. Finally the *rayis* stood up, walked around the desk, and reached into the young man's gown. Something about the intimacy of this act silenced the room—I could hear the papers rustling in the *rayis*'s hand. Then his voice boomed out again. "Put him at the top of the list!" he said to his assistant. "Give him a flat with three bedrooms, a living room, a bathroom! You'll get married and enjoy yourself there!" He turned to the young man and said, "Pray for me every day!"

The young man said nothing.

"You're getting help—be nice about it!" the assistant said.

But the young man maintained his dignified silence. He gave a quick nod of his head and left the room.

In the office of the *rayis,* Hassan and I were served two cups of tea each in an hour. The tea man was called by the electric button on the desk, which made the sound of a bird chirping. I asked the *rayis* if the national political problems were affecting him, and he made a dismissive gesture. "I'm an executive!" he said. "I'm removed from the politics." He smiled. "If a cloud forms in Cairo, it evaporates by the time it gets here."

In Abydos, it had become common to hear gunfire at night. Upper Egyptians had a long tradition of hoarding weapons, although in the past they tended to be discreet, and the police periodically confiscated firearms. But now there seemed to be no control. In my hotel room I was often awakened by the staccato of automatic rifles somewhere in the Buried. On a couple of occasions, a driver showed me the 9-millimeter Ekol Jackal Dual that he kept beneath his seat. Those pistols were Turkish, but most Kalashnikovs and other larger weapons had been smuggled in from Libya, where the security apparatus had disintegrated after the fall of Muammar al-Qaddafi.

Sometimes I thought about the Yeats line: "*Things fall apart; the centre cannot hold.*" Every night, the electricity was cut off in Abydos, and usually there was a line of more than one hundred vehicles at the gas station. Along the main road, children sold milk cartons full of black-market diesel fuel, like some twisted version of a lemonade stand. But there was still essentially no crime. At night, with no electric lights, no police presence, and guns everywhere, I could walk safely in the village. *Things hold together; the centre doesn't matter.* In a country where systems and laws had always been weak, there were other forces that kept the place from collapsing.

Even the nighttime gunfire had little to do with violence. People in Abydos taught me to recognize patterns: a short series of shots usually indicated that a potential buyer was testing a gun somewhere in the Buried. Longer bursts of automatic fire tended to come from weddings or other celebrations. Guns had always played a role in such events, but now they had become more prominent. In a way, it was reassuring: when people gained access to firearms, their first instinct was to show off rather than to fight.

One evening, Hassan and I had a meal with Ahmad and Medhat Diab, two brothers who came from a prosperous local family. The Diabs belonged to a tribe known as the Hawwara, which considered itself the elite in this part of Upper Egypt.

"During the days of Mubarak, if you were in a wedding, the best man was the one who gave the most tips," Ahmad said. "But now the best man is the one who shoots the most bullets."

He said that high demand had increased the price of a bullet to as much as three dollars. "If you have a wedding, everybody comes with a weapon," he said. "The singer sings for a while, and then he'll say, 'Medhat!' And he'll shoot three bullets. Then the singer will say, 'Ahmad!' And I'll shoot ten. Whoever gets his name called shows that he has bullets."

At the dig house, the archaeologists had mentioned a recent evening when there had been so much gunfire that it sounded like a war. I asked the Diab brothers if this had been a wedding.

"That was ours!" Ahmad said proudly. "We did it on purpose—to show everybody that this is us."

I asked who had gotten married.

"Actually, it wasn't a wedding," Ahmad said.

"It was a circumcision," Medhat said.

"We were just looking for an excuse," Ahmad said. "Some kid got circumcised, so we did it. We shot so many bullets—there must have been ten thousand."

Medhat smiled and said, "People called to compliment us afterward."

In the Buried, the archaeologists worked throughout this period. They had increased the number of guards who patrolled the site, and now more of them were armed. At night, the dig house relied on a generator for power, and Ahmed Ragab, the manager, spent much of his time searching for supplies on the black market. In the past, the authorities gave the archaeological crews permission to purchase large amounts of bread from government ovens, but now they couldn't fulfill such requests. Ahmed drove from restaurant to restaurant, buying whatever was available. He carried his government-licensed pistol for protection on his journeys through town.

More than two years had passed since Ahmed built his fake APC, but he still kept a video from those days on his phone. In the video, the APC looked remarkably realistic: a dark, boxy shape with police lights spinning on top, bouncing with purpose over the low hills of the Buried. One evening, after Ahmed showed me the video, he said that he didn't think Morsi was strong enough to be president. "Many people now say that they need somebody who is *shadeed*," he said. "I liked Mubarak. He was like our father, our *rayis*. Because I saw many things he did for us. He came and opened our airport."

Shadeed means "hard" or "tough," and people often used this word when talking about a president. For a Cairo liberal, the fear was that the Muslim Brotherhood would abuse its power, especially after Morsi rammed the new constitution through the assembly. But Abydos concerns were often the opposite. Villagers believed that Morsi wasn't capable of engaging in the kind of strong-armed authority that, in their eyes, was necessary for the *rayis* of an Egyptian state.

"We can't have an easy man rule us," said a teenager who worked on the excavation crew, when I was visiting the site one morning. "We want somebody tough, like Sadat."

Another young worker agreed. "We're pharaonic people, so we want one person in charge," he said. "Somebody who tells us that one plus one equals two. We want somebody *shadeed*."

"Like Nasser," a third worker said.

The excavation crews could be as large as 150 people. In the field, they were directed by Ibrahim Mohammed Ali, who came from the small city of Quft, about seventy miles upstream from Abydos. In the late nineteenth century, William Flinders Petrie, the pioneering British archaeologist, had excavated around Quft, where he described the natives as "the most troublesome people that I have ever worked with." But Petrie discovered that there was more to the Quftis than their flaws. "Among this rather untoward people we found however, as in every place, a small percentage of excellent men," he wrote. "They have formed the backbone of my upper Egyptian staff."

Over time, the hiring of Quftis became a tradition among Egyptologists. Many digs include a Qufti foreman, served by a hierarchy of Qufti lieutenants. They oversee excavations, operating as intermediaries between local laborers and foreign archaeologists. Few are formally educated, but they have a deep field knowledge of archaeology.

In the necropolis, everybody referred to Ibrahim Mohammed Ali as "*rayis*." And like every local *rayis* I met, he had a powerful physical presence. He was a tall, thin man with dark black skin and a standard police-issue mustache. In the field, he wore a white turban, a tan scarf, and a flowing galabiya. His clothes were always immaculate. He handled men, not sand: this was clear at a glance. He wore aviator sunglasses and carried a metal-tipped walking stick, with which he swiped at any boy worker who lagged. ("You water buffalo! May

God destroy your house!") He told me proudly that his father had once met Nasser when the president visited a dig. The father had been the previous *rayis* in the Buried, and the father's older cousin had been the *rayis* before that. The father of the father had worked for Petrie in the 1920s. This modern Abydos dynasty of Qufti foremen had lasted longer than the Free Officers, the NDP, and the Egyptian military dictatorship.

Once, I asked the *rayis* if any Quftis might have been involved in the post-Tahrir looting of the Buried. The *rayis* looked at me for a long moment. Then he said, very quietly, "No Qufti would ever do that."

We were sitting on the porch of the Quftis' residence in the Buried, and the *rayis* was smoking from a water pipe. When the topic shifted to politics, he told me that Mubarak had been brought down by the corruption of his underlings, and now the same thing was happening with the Muslim Brotherhood.

"Any ruler depends on the people around him," the *rayis* said. "It's like Morsi. He's good, but the consultants and advisers aren't good. My job depends on the people around me, too. If there's something wrong, they tell me."

He mentioned the mass graves that he had helped to excavate around the Shuna, where dozens of people had been killed to accompany kings into the afterlife. This evidence of ancient political violence made the *rayis* think about current events in Cairo. "When we find the buildings of these people, we feel that everything we're doing is just copied from them," he said. In his opinion, rulers have a natural tendency toward violence, and sometimes they are encouraged by followers with ulterior motives. "The pharaohs were corrupted by the people around them, and now we find that history is being repeated," he said.

In Balyana district, Morsi won more than 56 percent of the vote in the presidential election. Across the entire governorate of Sohag, he performed even better: 58 percent. Upper Egyptian support had been critical to the Brotherhood's victory, and Morsi appointed a professor of engineering named Yehia Abdel-Azim Mukhaimer as the new governor of Sohag.

Mukhaimer wasn't a Brotherhood member, but he was an Islamist. As governor, he oversaw 12 cities and more than 250 villages, with a total population of more than four million. But he told me that not a single official had been dismissed as a result of the revolution. It was as if Tahrir and the Morsi election had never happened: all the *feloul,* the "remnants" of the old regime, were still in office, the same way that the Abydos *rayis* hadn't been unseated by the local protests. "I can't afford to get rid of somebody just because of his political past," Mukhaimer said. He explained that there weren't enough capable people to staff the positions.

Brotherhood officials in Cairo often talked about their extensive grassroots network, and in Sohag I decided to investigate in a systematic fashion, from the top down. In Sohag, the Brotherhood's political party had recently opened a small headquarters, and the party's top official, Youssef el-Sharif, said they had a string of offices that connected to the villages. "We have a presence all the way down to the neighborhood level," he said, and he mentioned one of the places in Abydos. "There's a party office in el-Araba."

But when I proceeded to Balyana, the next level down, the Brothers there admitted this was the last stop in a three-link chain: national, governorate, district. There was nothing in el-Araba or any other villages near Abydos.

The Balyana office was tiny, and the top official, a physician named Ayman Abdel Hamid, told me there were only 150 Brothers in the district. The number seemed shockingly small for a place with a total population of around 600,000. I had always wondered about the Brothers' refusal to answer questions about national membership figures, and now I suspected the truth: the organization was much smaller and weaker than people realized.

Their social and charitable activities also seem to have been greatly exaggerated. In Cairo, when I talked to people in Sayyid's part of Ard al-Liwa, nobody reported being served by a Brotherhood program. The leaders of the local mosque who organized the highway ramp construction said that the Brothers did nothing of substance there. People in Abydos said the same thing. In larger cities in Upper Egypt, I occasionally encountered some modest after-school tutoring programs sponsored by the Brotherhood, and they had a tradition of selling groceries at a discount before elections. But there was rarely any extensive program or sign of institutionalized services. The idea of the organization was much stronger than anything it actually did.

Only one Brother lived near Abydos. He was a bright young pharmacist named Mohamed Wajih, and he came from a village about two miles from the Temple of Seti I. Wajih was the head of media relations in Balyana district, and he said that he had been prevented from campaigning during the last election, although not by the police or the *feloul*. "I was banned from leaving the house because my father didn't want me clashing with other people in our clan," Wajih explained.

In Balyana, the Brothers barely had enough members to staff an archaeological dig, much less a real campaign, and their district head of media relations had been prevented from canvassing by his own family. And yet somehow this organization had won nearly 60 percent of the vote in the governorate. From the outside, such numbers seemed to reflect strong support, but the true key to the Brotherhood's success was weak competition. In a country with no tradition of democracy, a little organization went a long way, and allegiances came easily. But they could vanish just as quickly. By the spring, almost everybody I met around Abydos expressed disappointment with the Brotherhood.

In Abydos, the word *nizam,* with its two most common meanings, was appropriate only in the negative. There was no regime, and there was no system. The old National Democratic Party was gone, and the Muslim Brotherhood didn't really exist here. The usual labels—Islamist, secularist, liberal, conservative, revolutionary, *feloul*—were meaningless. Without the distraction of modern parties and definitions, it was easier to recognize the elemental quality of local politics. Everything was face-to-face; everything was personal. Every district, every village, and every work crew had its *rayis*. In Abydos, *rayis* wasn't really a title—it was a type. It described the way a man carried himself, the way he spoke, the way he wore his mustache.

Ancient Egyptians had a flair for titles. The pharaoh was served by the Chief Mouth of the Country, a wonderful way to say "spokesman." There was a Royal Seal-Bearer, a Gentleman of the Bedchamber, a True Scribe of the King. During the Old Kingdom, a vizier named Khentika was Chief of Secrets of the Bathroom, Administrator of Every Kilt, and Overseer of the King's Breakfast. One New Kingdom official listed more than eighty titles on his tomb. He was Overseer of Overseers; Leader of Leaders; Greatest of the Great; Regent of the Whole Land; One Who, if He Gives Attention to Anything in the Evening, It Is Mastered Early in the Morning at Daybreak.

We have the titles, but what were the types? In Matthew Adams's opinion, words from ancient Egyptian sources are misleading, especially in terms of politics. "Egyptologists have not really appreciated how personal things were," he said. "A lot of Egyptologists have developed ideas about the structures of ancient Egypt, and their understanding of how it worked draws on their own cultural ideas." Adams believed that the modern, urban concept of governance is so deeply entrenched in our minds that we have trouble imagining the way that power worked long ago, or the way that it still functions in many smaller places. "If some individual would stand before the vizier or the mayor, then that person's situation might be addressed," Adams said of the ancient past. "But there was no codified set of laws or legal procedures to be followed. It was all based on the circumstances right then and there."

Everything was of the moment—the way a supplicant spoke, the way he presented an injury or a disability. One of the few glimpses we have of such interactions comes from a classic text called "The Tale of the Eloquent Peasant," which dates to the Middle Kingdom. In this account, a rich man robs a peasant, who goes to the chief steward in search of justice. The peasant makes his case so beautifully that the chief steward reports it to the king, who instructs his official on how to treat the peasant: "As you desire to see me healthy, cause him to remain here, without replying to anything which he says. And so that he may keep on speaking, remain silent."

And that's how the story proceeds: the state is silent; the peasant speaks. He often uses the metaphor of a boat upon the Nile, reminding the chief steward that "you are the rudder of the entire land." But the chief steward does nothing to help. At one point he even has the poor man whipped. "You are an empty vessel!" the peasant shouts. He keeps pleading: "The sounding-pole is in your hand like an unused pole."

All of this entertains the king. Finally, after the peasant's ninth visit, the king instructs the chief steward to make a fair judgment. The man who harmed the peasant is forced to pay restitution in the form of servants, donkeys, pigs, birds, and crops. The moral of the story is generally taken to be positive: justice prevails; the sense of order is restored; the king behaves as a king should. But this is true only if one reads to the end. In the middle of the story, there is nothing but official neglect, the patience of the weak, and a state that seems lost in the current:

The gaze of the steersman is directed forward,
But the ship drifts of its own will.
The king is in the palace,
And the tiller is in your hand.

On the final night of the 2013 spring archaeological season, a group of looters appeared in the Buried. An armed watchman confronted the thieves and called the police. Officers responded quickly, despite the general lack of police activity, and the looters fled. Matthew Adams was optimistic that the new monitoring system would be adequate to protect the site.

On Adams's way back to New York, he stopped in Cairo, and together we visited Michael Jones, an Egyptologist and administrator with the American Research Center in Egypt. This institution supports the study and conservation of Egyptian antiquities, with funding that comes in part from the U.S. State Department. In Jones's office, the windows were covered with boards. The building was only a block from Tahrir, and the anti-Morsi protests had reached a point where people seemed to attack indiscriminately. Demonstrators threw rocks at the police, but they also tossed them at random buildings.

In the office, Adams and Jones chatted about archaeology, and Jones mentioned the field's speculative nature. "The ancient Egyptians have been dead for thousands of years," he said. "Nobody alive knows what they were thinking. We create an image of them, and it's based on our own ideas. It's a bit like looking in a mirror." He continued: "Most of what we find is broken. These are things that were thrown away. We're dealing with a jigsaw puzzle where you only have two or three out of thousands of pieces."

"We can only ever access the past through our own frame of reference," Adams said. "We can only process it through our own cultural framework. To some extent our interpretations are modern."

He explained to me that this is "post-processual theory," the archaeological version of postmodernism. Some believe that nothing we observe about ancient societies is accurate, because invariably we apply our own experiences and viewpoints. Others counter that the essence of the human mind has changed very little in thousands of years, and basic desires and instincts remain the same, with certain societal patterns repeated endlessly. Adams tended to agree with this approach, although he recognized the value of post-processual ideas.

"We're just a component of a much longer trajectory than we realize," he said. "We think that this moment is special, that everything has led to this point. But our here and now is just a blip along the continuum."

Jones said that the research center was considering moving its offices away from Tahrir. "We had the windows broken out, and tear gas filled the building," he said. "The nature of the flare-ups has changed. There used to be a kind of festive atmosphere. Now it's much more aggressive." Behind the boarded windows, we discussed the same things that people talked about all over the city: the rise of the Brotherhood, the mystery of Sisi, the uncertainty of the future. All of us had heard so many rumors and conspiracy theories; the modern politics had become almost as enigmatic as any strand of Egyptology. It was hard to believe that two years out of five thousand could feel so long.

CHAPTER 12

T*AMARROD* APPEARED IN MY VOCABULARY LIST ON MAY 22, 2013. THAT morning, during a break in class at Kalimat, I noticed Raafat photocopying petitions. The word—"rebellion"—had been printed in big letters above a series of statements:

Because security has still not returned to the streets . . . we don't want you

Because the poor still have no place . . . we don't want you

Because we're still begging from abroad . . . we don't want you

Because the rights of the martyrs still haven't been achieved . . . we don't want you

Because there is no dignity for me or my country . . . we don't want you

Because the economy has collapsed and now depends on begging . . . we don't want you

Because you follow the Americans . . . we don't want you

At the bottom of each page was space for a signature:

And so I, the undersigned, announce, fully aware and as a member of the general assembly of the Egyptian people, the impeachment of President Dr. Mohammed Morsi.

There was no legal basis for the petition, which had been started the previous month by a few young Cairo activists. Nothing in the new constitution, or, for that matter, in any of the previous constitutions, specified that an

Egyptian president could be impeached via a popular petition movement. Raafat told me that he didn't have any faith in the Tamarrod campaign, but he figured that signing the paper was better than nothing. "What else can I do?" he said. He was distributing the photocopied petitions to other teachers at Kalimat. Supposedly, the Tamarrod campaign would culminate in a protest on June 30, which would be the first anniversary of Morsi's inauguration. In my notebook, I added the word to the day's list:

rebellion	تمرد
to rebel	يتمرد
signature	توقيع
to threaten	يهدد
threat	تهديد
tension	توتر
tense	متوتر

By that point, the heat of the early Egyptian summer had settled in, and the demand for air-conditioning meant that we usually had four or five blackouts in a day. The *azma* of fuel was so bad that Cairo drivers sometimes waited four hours at a gas station. The Egyptian economy—*because we're still begging from abroad*—had long depended on aid from the Gulf countries, the Americans, and other foreigners. But even with all that assistance, the country's foreign currency reserves were dangerously low.

Morsi had inherited most of these problems. Nasser's socialist policies had expanded the government bureaucracy, which became even more bloated under Mubarak, who saw the stability of civil servants as a way of heading off unrest. When Morsi took office, the Egyptian government employed about six million people, not including police and soldiers—more than twice as many as the number of civil servants in the United States, a country that is three and a half times more populous than Egypt. The salaries for these government employees represented one-quarter of Egypt's budget. Another quarter went to interest payments for loans. Another 30 percent was spent on subsidies, largely for electricity, gasoline, and cooking gas.

If this sounds like a shell game, that's because it was. Much of the Egyptian economy was structured on getting aid from abroad, subsidizing citizens just above the level of poverty, and doing nothing to move forward. The country essentially had no money for infrastructure or development projects. And while Morsi had inherited these problems, his lack of political skill made them worse. His government negotiated for a loan with the International Monetary Fund, which demanded that the Egyptians show a commitment to restructuring their economy. Morsi decided to take the first step in December, during the conflict over the constitution. Street violence had just killed ten people, and eight of Morsi's advisers and aides had resigned in protest. Nevertheless, the president went ahead with his new economic policy, announcing major tax increases for gasoline, electricity, cooking oil, cigarettes, and alcohol.

The news broke at night. As a journalist, when I heard about some major event or policy change, I sometimes telephoned officials for a comment. But this time I went straight to the liquor store on 26th July Street in Zamalek. At nearly ten o'clock the place was mobbed; most of the refrigerators were empty and customers were arguing over the last bottles of Auld Stag. I was lucky to get my hands on two cases of Heineken half-liter cans. The frazzled clerk at the counter, like everybody who worked at the liquor store, had a Coptic cross tattooed on his wrist. I asked him what he thought would happen next. He said, "Somebody is going to kill Morsi, *insha'allah*."

Later that evening, at 2:13 a.m., Morsi posted a statement on his Facebook page that canceled all the tax increases. It was widely believed that other Brotherhood leaders had persuaded him to change his mind, although nobody knew whose idea it was to engage in major tax policy on Facebook, after midnight. A few months later, around the time that the Tamarrod campaign got going, the IMF announced that loan negotiations were effectively dead. The Brotherhood lacked the political strength necessary to engage in serious economic restructuring; they couldn't raise taxes now. Still, I didn't regret my panic purchase. A person couldn't have too much Heineken in the early months of 2013.

There was no schedule for the blackouts, probably because officials feared that if people knew a cut was coming they would blast their air-conditioning in advance. But officials also feared the people's anger, so individual cuts rarely lasted more than an hour, at least in Zamalek. In Ard al-Liwa, Sayyid lost power for four or more hours at a stretch, and in Abydos the cuts were longer yet. There must have been some hidden calculus at the Ministry of Electricity that estimated the political importance of different neighborhoods and regions.

Leslie and I kept candles and flashlights around the apartment, and sometimes we finished the twins' meals and baths in the dark. Fortunately, the spiderweb building had been constructed long before air-conditioning. The rooms had twelve-foot-high ceilings, with exterior walls that were more than a foot thick, and the building was arranged around a central atrium that functioned like a chimney. On the ground floor, we could open the windows to the atrium and the hot air would rise out. Even during blackouts the place stayed cool.

In addition to electricity, we spent a lot of time thinking about water. There were days when it was cut off completely; sometimes, the landlady was able to warn us in advance, and we would fill the bathtub and haul out bucketfuls whenever we needed to wash dishes. For drinking water, we had big bottles delivered by Nestlé, but then, in February, the bottling facility caught on fire. How flammable can a water plant possibly be? I had never considered this question until our delivery service was cut off. Nestlé's Cairo office sent a nice note:

> *Dear Valued Customer,*
>
> *Over the last few weeks, you have had to put up with serious hardship due to the disruption in the availability of your favorite Nestlé Pure Life resulting from a very unfortunate fire that happened at our factory in Banha.*

After Nestlé's water went up in flames, we bought little bottles of other brands at H Freedom. There was no sense in dwelling on such problems; we tried to find solutions and move on. During our first year in Zamalek, we had a serious rodent infestation, and both Ariel and Natasha were bitten while they slept. The girls were too small to tell us what happened; from the size of the incisor marks on their skin I assumed that the animals must have been rats. For a while, I set glue traps around the twins' bedroom, but I caught so many mice that I finally gave up. Leslie searched online and found an American woman who was returning home and wanted to get rid of two cats. We chose the larger one, a male whose tiger stripes formed the shape of an M on his forehead, a mark of the breed that's known as the Egyptian Mau. He looked like the cats that were portrayed on the walls of ancient tombs, and even the name was old: in pharaonic times, *mau* meant "cat."

We named him Morsi. At the time, it seemed like a good idea—the election had just happened and people were still surprised at the fairness of Egypt's first democratic vote for highest office. Morsi proved to be a brilliant mouser, and we never again had any rodent problems in the apartment. But as the political situation deteriorated, the cat took his share of abuse. "I hate this name," the local veterinarian, a Copt, told Leslie when she first brought the cat in for a checkup. "Your Brotherhood cat is doing a terrible job as president," Sayyid often said. It became a joke around the neighborhood; people often told me to get my cat to straighten up.

In late afternoons, I often took Ariel and Natasha for long walks around Zamalek. They attended a nearby nursery school in the mornings, and a nanny named Atiyat cared for them during the early part of the afternoon. As the girls got bigger, they started throwing tantrums if their outfits didn't match. Leslie and I didn't want to dress them alike, but there were so many other things to deal with that we quickly caved. We bought everything in pairs, and when the twins sat side by side in their stroller, wearing identical clothes, it felt like a kind of show.

Everybody in the neighborhood knew them. On my stroller walks I chatted with the various local figures: the silver-haired man who sat at the government bread stand, the tea man with his tray of drinks. Across the street, a friendly shopkeeper enjoyed teaching the girls new words in Egyptian Arabic. On the fourth floor of the spiderweb building, an elderly woman liked to feed Morsi and the stray cats that hung around the area, and we often saw her arranging bowls of cat food. She always smiled at the girls in their twinned outfits and muttered the phrase *masha'allah,* "this is what God has willed," as protection against the evil eye.

If Sayyid was working in the street, he greeted the girls by their Arabic nicknames: Aro for Ariel, Nush-nush for Natasha. Egyptians have a fondness for such monikers; it's one way to deal with all the Mohammeds, Mahmouds, and Mohammed Mahmouds. Atiyat had nicknamed the twins, and she spoke to them mostly in Egyptian Arabic. They preferred the language for certain things—colors, animals, basic sustenance. *Aish* for bread, *maya* for water. If I twirled one of them around, she'd laugh and shriek, "*Tani!*": "Again!"

In the spring of 2013, they started differentiating between "the good Morsi" and "the bad Morsi." I knew they picked this up from Atiyat, who was also a Copt. And who was I to blame her for her politics? In the past, Morsi had declared that neither a woman nor a Christian should be allowed to lead Egypt, and Atiyat lived in the kind of *ashwa'iyat* that suffered four-hour blackouts. One day I received an email message from the girls' nursery school:

> Due to the heavy smell of tear gas in Zamalek at the moment, we think it is safer for the children not to come to school today. . . . We are terribly sorry for the very short notice, but it is strictly out of our hands.

During this time, I started stashing large amounts of cash around the apartment. If things became unsafe, I had plans for an emergency departure: what we would pack, who would drive us to the airport. But who knew if the roads would be clear, or if flights would function? *We are terribly sorry for the very short notice.* In April, the government announced a policy of dimming the lights at the Cairo Airport to save electricity. Whenever I returned from a trip to Abydos, I left the Sohag Airport, where the desert was covering the last traces of Mubarak's name, and then I touched down in the Morsi-era twilight zone: darkened hallways, frozen escalators. *It is strictly out of our hands.*

That spring, when I renewed our residence visas at the Mogamma, the big government complex on Tahrir, I chose a day without protests. But the area still reeked of tear gas; by now, it seemed as if the flagstones had become so soaked with the stuff that they sweated it out in the heat. Inside the building, I handed our applications to an official. He studied the documents.

"Where is your marriage license?" he said.

This was what mattered at such a time? Even more absurd was how pleased I felt: finally, here was something we had successfully planned for! I returned to Zamalek, retrieved the Ouray County license with its absurd ye-olde script ("*Holy Bonds of Matrimony*"), and triumphantly delivered the document. The official seemed just as happy as me; the visas were processed without a hitch.

By June, Tamarrod petitions were everywhere. Shops in my neighborhood kept stacks on their counters, and most people I knew said they had signed one. Sayyid had voted for Morsi, but now he had a literate friend fill out a Tamarrod form on his behalf, and Sayyid applied a thumbprint on the signature line. When I traveled to Abydos, the young officers at the police station told me they had signed petitions. Mohamed Wajih, the only Brother who lived near the village, said that even his family members were involved: his brother-in-law had become the local contact person for the Tamarrod campaign.

Six days before the anniversary of Morsi's inauguration, I stopped by the Tamarrod national headquarters, where the staff told me that they had collected fifteen million signatures. They worked out of an apartment on the sixth floor of a grungy old building about two blocks from Tahrir. Petitions were stacked everywhere, in old cardboard boxes and plastic shopping bags. While I was there, a blind man dropped off four hundred more. He told me that he had collected them from the office where he worked as a clerk.

The apartment had previously been rented by an organization called the National Association for Change, which in 2010 had mounted a petition campaign that attempted to pressure Mubarak for political reform. The organization was no longer active, and its lease was about to expire, so it had lent the use of the apartment to Tamarrod.

None of the Tamarrod leaders seemed to know what they were going to do with the petitions. A couple of organizers talked vaguely about having them certified by the Supreme Constitutional Court. Others mentioned the United Nations, although I doubted that the UN wanted to receive fifteen million petitions that lacked any legal standing. Even the organizers acknowledged that impeachment wasn't really their goal.

"At first, when I went out with these sheets, people said, 'This is children's play—it's not what's going to topple Morsi,'" a young volunteer named Amr al-Hawat said. "My response was that we were able to topple Mubarak, and Morsi's regime is weaker than Mubarak's was."

He believed that if enough people showed up to the protest, then some other force—maybe the military, maybe the judiciary—would be compelled to act. To that end, Hawat had distributed petitions for more than two months in the Delta governorate of Dakahlia, where he lived. Like most people I met who were collecting signatures, he had paid for the photocopies himself. He was nineteen years old, and he hoped to become a journalist. When I asked whom he had voted for a year earlier, he winced.

"Morsi," he said. "I feel like I made a mistake, so I need to do this now."

The petitions had always impressed me as amateurish. The print quality was invariably terrible, and most forms requested the petitioner's name and ID number, but they lacked a space for phone, email, or Facebook contact. I asked Hawat why they hadn't gathered this information in order to build a database for future organizing. He said, "You expect me to call fifteen million people?"

Sisi had been silent throughout the spring. Nine days before the anniversary, the minister of defense finally made a public statement. He warned about a "split in society," and he called for compromise. Two days later, he said that if necessary the army would "intervene to keep Egypt from sliding into a dark tunnel of conflict."

There was only one point of absolute clarity in the statement: that the military was prepared to act. But the nature of that action and which side the army would support were left open to interpretation. "Sisi is a character that we trust," one Brother told me, noting that Morsi had appointed the minister. But the opposition seemed just as confident. "We know our army," Dowa Khelifa, a young woman who had helped found Tamarrod, told me the day after Sisi's speech. "We know they will side with us."

In this way, a statement that seemed like a warning actually functioned as an accelerant. Everybody welcomed the involvement of the army, because everybody assumed that the army would be on his side. Morsi supporters began to gather around the Rabaa al-Adawiya Mosque, in eastern Cairo, where leaders wanted to demonstrate their numbers. In revolutionary Egypt, this had become a crude instrument of democracy: news channels trained live cameras on major protests so viewers could assess the size and enthusiasm of a crowd. On the day of an important event, a split screen might show as many as six sites at once. Sometimes there was no commentary: a viewer watched the crowds in silence, like a mall cop with his closed-circuit screens.

Four days before the anniversary, Morsi gave a televised speech. Like any unskilled politician, he was always at his worst when he went off script, and that night he talked for more than two and a half hours. He acknowledged that he had made mistakes, but as the speech wore on, it became clear that the worst mistake, at least in Morsi's opinion, had been a reluctance to attack enemies. The president named a judge whom he declared to be "illegitimate," and he proclaimed two owners of liberal-leaning television stations guilty of tax evasion. He said that thirty-two families controlled the entire Egyptian economy. He spoke the language of conspiracy: "Egypt's enemies" and "invisible fingers" were attempting to bring down the state. Even his reassurances weren't particularly reassuring. "I promised a policy of no prison time for journalists," he said, "only waived in cases of personal insult."

Morsi declared that he and the army were working "in complete harmony." The speech was delivered to an auditorium that included a number of officials and military personnel, and Sisi sat in the front row. He wore a desert-beige uniform and an olive-colored cap. His face was calm. It was impossible to read anything from his expression.

Shortly before the anniversary, the National Police Association held a meeting about the planned demonstrations, and a video was posted on the association's Facebook page. In the video, an officer said that if any policeman tried to defend a Brotherhood office—"I swear to God almighty"—the policeman would be shot.

General Salah Zeyada, a major general on the association's board, said,

"We all agree, brothers, that there will be no security provided for the headquarters of the Muslim Brotherhood."

On the afternoon of the anniversary, Leslie and I went to Tahrir, and at the head of the Qasr al-Nil Bridge we ran into Raafat, the brother of our teacher. He was there with a friend, marching toward the square. There were so many people on the bridge that it was hard to move, although the mood was peaceful, even celebratory. Many protesters were women. Periodically, an army helicopter flew overhead, and the crowd cheered. Uniformed policemen marched alongside the demonstrators.

"It's not enough," Raafat said. Even amid this happy crowd, he looked grim, because he believed a violent conflict would be necessary. *"Ayz dem,"* he said. "I want blood. I want the army to come."

That day, Tamarrod announced a final count for its petitions: 22,134,465. The military estimated that more than fourteen million people had participated in nationwide demonstrations—more people than had voted for Morsi the previous year. On YouTube, the army posted aerial footage of Tahrir. That had been the purpose of the helicopters: they were filming the masses. The video was mesmerizing; on every corner of the square, and every street and bridge, people stood shoulder to shoulder. In the June sunshine it was possible to see the shadow of the helicopter slipping across the crowd.

Later that evening, men armed with assault rifles and Molotov cocktails attacked the national headquarters of the Muslim Brotherhood. People from within the building returned fire, and eight died. The police didn't move in until after the Brothers had abandoned their building.

The following day, I went to the headquarters with Hassan. Inspectors from the prosecutor's office were photographing the bullet holes that had been left in the walls of houses across the street from the headquarters. They seemed to be documenting these marks because they represented evidence that the Brothers had fired.

Near the back gate, I watched an officer pick up a shell casing. "Machine gun," he said. "Foreign made."

I asked him why the police hadn't been there the previous evening.

"Because the Interior Ministry announced that we would not defend their headquarters," he said. While we were talking, a private security guard from a neighboring building wandered over and mentioned that he had donated two cans of gasoline to the arsonists. This information didn't seem to interest the inspecting officer.

Egyptian journalists were already busy with their excavations. A young newspaper reporter had scavenged some English-language documents from inside the headquarters, and he asked me to look at a letter. My heart sank when I read it.

"Who is it from?" the journalist asked.

I didn't want to tell him, but I couldn't lie. "It's from an American official," I said. "The special inspector general for Iraq reconstruction."

He asked me whom the letter was addressed to.

"Hillary Clinton."

Dear Madam Secretary:

I write to provide you notice of obstructions to the execution of my statutory duty to provide oversight reporting to you and the Congress on the use of taxpayer monies in Iraq. These obstructions arose during the conduct of two SIGIR audits, one concerning security contractors in Iraq and the other addressing the continued training of the Iraqi police.

Later I learned that the letters were openly available online; they came from an unclassified audit of Iraq's Police Development Program. I had no idea why the Muslim Brotherhood had been collecting U.S. government audits of Iraq while their own country was in the midst of an economic crisis. In any case, now the documents would undoubtedly serve as fodder for more conspiracy theories. *Hillary's emails!* The journalist thanked me and wandered off to continue his search.

I spent more than an hour studying the relics of the fight. At the back gate, tangled steel belts sat in pools of black melted rubber—all that was left from tires that had been filled with gasoline, set on fire, and rolled into the compound. Random papers were scattered everywhere. I found some high school examination results for a boy from Minya: yet another Mohammed Mahmoud, this one distinguished by a score of 407. There were some internal Brotherhood reports on the Egyptian Arab Spring. One began,

> *When we started the revolution, it was God who made the revolution. God is great; he made it law. Who would have thought that Morsi would come? And who would have thought he would have made so many great achievements in only twenty-eight days?*

In the shade of a high wall, a dozen police conscripts rested while their commanding officers met nearby. The wall was riddled with bullet holes. The last time I had seen police at the headquarters, it was during the winter fight over the constitution, and the officers had been dressed in black. Now they wore white for the summer. Egyptian cops change colors twice every year, from black to white in the spring, and white to black in the autumn—the seasonal foliage of the police state. In the shade of the wall, two very young-looking conscripts untied their heavy leather boots and switched pairs. One of them was talking about how much his feet hurt.

Civilians drove past the gate, honking their horns in the rhythmic fashion that Egyptians use when celebrating: *duun duun dun-dun-dun; duun duun dun-dun-dun. . . .* One woman who appeared to be in her sixties rolled down the window of her sedan. "Do you have any rooms to rent?" she called out.

The officers looked up and laughed.

"By the honor of our martyrs," she shouted, "we will bring them down!"

The officers cheered and the woman drove off. The two conscripts were still talking about their feet. "Listen, man, we're going to get new shoes," one of them said. "It will be better, *insha'allah*."

Not long after I returned home from the headquarters, an announcer on Egyptian state television read a communiqué that had just been issued by the military. The armed forces gave President Morsi forty-eight hours to respond to the protesters' demands. If the president failed to address the issue, the army declared that it would "announce a road map for the future."

I went outside and caught a cab. The driver circled the western side of the island, heading south toward Tahrir. It was a little after five o'clock, and the sky was unusually clear; the water of the river looked blue in the angled light. Across the river, crowds had already started to stream into Tahrir. Horns rang out: *duun duun dun-dun-dun; duun duun dun-dun-dun.* I got out of the cab and continued on foot toward the Tamarrod headquarters. A neat line of Apache helicopters cruised low overhead, trailing Egyptian flags.

The headquarters was empty except for three young activists. They were watching television news in a darkened conference room.

"It happened faster than our expectations," a twenty-three-year-old accountant named Mohamed Nada said. "We said that it was going to take more than a week, maybe ten days. Sisi surprised us."

Nada and the others were certain that in two days the military would remove the president. "Tamarrod is only sixty days old," Mohamed Belkeemi, another volunteer in his twenties, said. "The Muslim Brotherhood has been around for more than eighty years. And yet it was destroyed by this sixty-day-old organization."

Since the start of the Egyptian Arab Spring, there had always been at least one point of optimism: the way that so many Egyptians, and young Egyptians in particular, had become politically engaged. People often remarked how back in the days of Mubarak nobody cared much about politics. Now it was easy to find inspiring examples: the young activist gathering petitions, the *ashwa'iyat* resident marching in the name of social justice.

But as time passed, I became warier of this surge into political life. Nothing had prepared citizens for their participation, and they tended to be distrustful of traditional tools and methods. They scorned any kind of negotiation, and they loathed parties; in their view, everything should happen at the personal level. "There should be no parties," Karim el-Masry, a twenty-seven-year-old lawyer who was one of the founders of Tamarrod, explained to me on my first visit to the headquarters. "We're just Egyptians. We don't want to divide the country."

More than forty years earlier, Samuel P. Huntington, the influential political scientist, described something that he called a praetorian state: a nation in which "participation in politics has outrun the institutionalization of politics." Without established parties and other organizations that handle the give-and-take of governance, the result is a series of clumsy maneuvers by inexperienced players. In a praetorian state, there's no essential difference between activists gathering petitions, or protesters taking to the streets, or a court canceling a parliament, or a military staging a coup. Huntington wrote, "Each social force attempts to secure its objectives through the resources and tactics in which it is strongest."

Even those who seem powerful may in fact have limited options. As the Egyptian conflict deepened, it was clear that Sisi had two choices: he could do nothing, or he could do everything. He didn't belong to a party, and he had no formal structure for participating in politics. He had never even cast a vote in his life. He could issue warnings and entreaties, as he had done during the fight over the constitution, but nobody had listened back then. The communiqué was meaningless without action, and any action on the part of the military was likely to be blunt, because it essentially had only one tool.

The day before Sisi's ultimatum expired, I visited Mohamed Kadry Said, a retired major general whom I had met in the past. He said he was impressed by the energy of the Tamarrod activists. "And also there is some smell of connection between them and the military," he said.

Recently, a handful of activists had quit Tamarrod because they believed that military agents had infiltrated the organization. This later proved to be true, and it turned out that some of the funding for Tamarrod had come from Saudi Arabia and the United Arab Emirates, both of which feared the Brotherhood's rise. But I didn't believe that the foreigners and the army had founded Tamarrod or been involved in its earliest stages, because the generals lacked the political instincts necessary to start such a campaign. They didn't think in terms of grassroots organization, and it seemed that two separate dynamics had converged. In November, the Brotherhood's response to the constitutional crisis convinced the army and the police that they needed to be ready to act, and then the various crises of the spring turned the majority of the citizens against the Brothers. Once the public campaign gained momentum, the army and the Gulf states latched on.

I mentioned this observation to Major General Said, who agreed. In his view, the army didn't give rise to Tamarrod; instead, Tamarrod gave rise to the army as a political actor in this particular conflict. "The military is depending on them," he said. "After a certain time, the military found them, and saw that they were good, and gave them some support."

I asked him whether he thought Morsi would make concessions. He shook his head—the president and the Brotherhood leaders were too bullheaded.

"What will the military do with Morsi?" I asked.

"They will put him in some place," the major general said. "They will find a reason."

I asked if he thought there would be violence.

"Yeah," he said softly.

There were reports that Morsi planned to address the nation once again. But by ten o'clock on the evening before the ultimatum expired, nothing had happened. I called Gehad el-Haddad, a Brotherhood spokesman, and I asked if Morsi was negotiating with Sisi.

"There is no dialogue with Sisi," el-Haddad said. "He is an arm of the state. He follows the leadership of his president, Mohammed Morsi."

I asked if the military had decided how to proceed.

"I think they realize their mistake," he said. "The leadership of the military knows that there is a constitutional leadership here. It's different from Mubarak, who was elected through fraudulent means. President Morsi was elected fairly."

I asked what the Brothers would do if the military removed Morsi from office.

"We will stand between the tanks and the president."

"Where is the president now?"

There was a pause, and then el-Haddad said, "I have no idea."

At ten minutes before midnight, Morsi finally appeared on television. He wore a black suit and a black tie, and he seemed energized by the conflict. For the Brotherhood, this was a familiar position: so many times in the past they had been cornered by various elements of the state.

Earlier in the evening, I had met with a foreign diplomat who told me that some prominent figures in the Brotherhood had approached sympathetic

Egyptian academics for advice. The academics recommended that Morsi offer some concessions quickly and publicly, as a way of gaining the moral high ground. But their advice had reportedly been rejected. "It's denial," the diplomat told me. I had observed the same thing in my conversations with Brothers. For months, they had overestimated their public support, and even now they seemed unwilling to acknowledge that the crisis had become existential.

In Morsi's speech, the key word was *shar'aiya*—"legitimacy." "The people empowered me, the people chose me, through a free and fair election," he said. "Legitimacy is the only way to protect our country and prevent bloodshed." His voice rose to a shout; he gestured forcefully with his hands: "If the price of protecting legitimacy is my blood, I'm willing to pay it!"

Immediately after the speech, a gunfight broke out near Cairo University, and eighteen people were killed.

The following morning, on the day that everybody knew would end in a coup, Atiyat arrived for work with her fingernails painted in the colors of the Egyptian flag. She took out some red, black, and yellow crayons, and she instructed Ariel and Natasha in the production of little Egyptian flags. People had hung flags all over the city, and periodically I heard the horn from a passing car: *duun duun dun-dun-dun; duun duun dun-dun-dun*. Should my three-year-olds be celebrating a military coup that hadn't even happened yet? But I was too distracted to worry about it; soon I would have to leave to report on the day's events.

By now it was too late to get the girls out of the country, and in any case I thought it was safer for them to avoid the roads and the airport. Outside their bedroom, while they made flags with Atiyat, Leslie and I ran through scenarios. What if it's impossible to make it home tonight? What if the cellphone system goes down? What if things get violent? We decided that in the event of gunfire the safest place in the apartment was the interior hallway. That was the plan: shut the doors, stay close to the floor.

There was always a plan. Old plans had a way of becoming irrelevant, but new plans were easy to make. Over the coming years Leslie and I would have other versions of this conversation. Once, the nursery school canceled class because the police found a terrorist dummy bomb a block away. Another time, an ISIS-affiliated group kidnapped a foreigner on the outskirts of Cairo and beheaded him.

Before moving to Egypt, I had imagined that we would establish clear protocols: If *x* happens, then we will respond by doing *y*. This was how embassies operated, and during the summer of the coup the American embassy in Cairo evacuated all nonessential personnel. But we had no connection to any institution that set such rules, and as time passed, I realized that we were more likely to respond as Cairenes did, with flexibility and rationalization. People tended to talk about events calmly, and they maintained a sense of distance. They told jokes—*your Brotherhood cat is doing a terrible job.* They focused on little things that they could control. They normalized any situation, and even a foreigner could quickly adopt this tendency. Just because a coup is about to happen doesn't mean that there will be violence. It was a dummy bomb, not a real bomb. The kidnapped foreigner was an oil worker, not a journalist. It happened only once. If it happens again, then we'll worry.

And the difficulties of everyday life were more than enough to keep people occupied. Even in a place like Zamalek, things went wrong all the time, and it usually had nothing to do with politics. In our neighborhood, the silver-haired man at the government bread stand died suddenly, at the age of fifty, from a heart attack. The shopkeeper who liked to teach the girls words in Egyptian Arabic was shot and killed near his home, reportedly after trying to mediate in some dispute. From my perspective, these were shocking events, but locals seemed more likely to view them as inevitable and fated. Death was simply a fact; there was no point in obsessing over the circumstances. That was one reason why the rote phrases worked so well: *this is what God has willed; may God protect us; may God rest her soul.*

One day, the elderly woman in our building put out some cat food on the fourth floor. She called to a cat on the landing below, but the animal didn't come. So the woman poked her head through a gap in the wrought-iron spiderweb gate, in order to look down the elevator shaft. Above her, on one of the upper levels, the heavy wooden box of the elevator was motionless.

At that moment, on the ground floor, somebody pushed the call button.

Afterward, the police interrogated the doorman, and he either quit or was fired. He hadn't been anywhere near the accident, and there was no indication that he was at fault, but he made for an easy scapegoat. The landlady had wire screens installed behind the spiderweb gates. On the fourth floor, the family of the elderly woman played recorded Quranic chants for months, to put her soul at peace. *Allah yerhamha, allah yerhamha, allah yerhamha.* Leslie and I told Atiyat never to allow the twins to go on the landing unattended. During these years of revolutions, and coups, and violent headlines, one of the things that scared me most was the elevator outside my front door.

In the days before the ultimatum expired, Sisi made no public statements. He had been in regular contact with only one American official throughout the spring. As U.S. secretary of defense, Chuck Hagel was Sisi's counterpart, and the standard protocol meant that these officials could communicate directly. Hagel first met Sisi in March, during a visit to Cairo. "Our chemistry was very good," Hagel said, a couple of years later, when we met in Washington, D.C. He believed that his status as a Vietnam War veteran made Sisi comfortable. "I think he saw me as someone who understood the military, who understood threats and war," Hagel said.

Hagel had received little prior information about Sisi. "Our military people did not know him well," Hagel said. Leon Panetta, who had been secretary of defense during the first year of the Egyptian Arab Spring and who had previously directed the Central Intelligence Agency, told me the same thing. "I can't tell you that I recall any kind of special attention in the intelligence summaries with regard to Sisi," Panetta said.

Given all the U.S. aid to Egypt, and all the military exchanges, it seemed remarkable that the Americans knew so little about this man who had risen at such a crucial time. Their sense of the grass roots was even weaker. The day before Mubarak resigned, in 2011, James Clapper, the director of national intelligence, testified before a House committee. He said, "The term 'Muslim Brotherhood' is an umbrella term for a variety of movements. In the case of Egypt, a very heterogeneous group, largely secular." Even when the Brotherhood proved itself to be anything but heterogeneous, secular, and benign, American officials seemed reluctant to criticize. In December, after Morsi supporters incited the battles at the Presidential Palace, the Obama White House issued an anodyne statement: "The President emphasized that all political leaders in Egypt should make it clear to their supporters that violence is unacceptable."

During this period, I occasionally met with officials from the U.S. embassy in Cairo. One of them told me that because the Brotherhood had played a role in maintaining order during the initial phase of the Egyptian Arab Spring, the Brothers felt compelled to behave as vigilantes at the palace. "They are coming at this from a perspective that that role is positive and appreciated," he said. It seemed naive, and over the course of months other meetings left me with the sense that American diplomats were too trusting of the Brotherhood.

Egyptians invariably attributed sinister motives to the United States, which was why the Tamarrod petitions included that line about Morsi: "*Because you follow the Americans.*" There were endless conspiracy theories about the United States, but from my perspective their flaw had more to do with wishful thinking. The Americans longed for some kind of *nizam*—they wanted to interact with systems, regimes, and organizations. The Brotherhood's hierarchy and discipline made it appear like an effective group, and it employed a handful of well-educated spokespeople who were skilled at telling foreigners what they wanted to hear. The Brothers portrayed themselves as moderate, responsible Islamists, which appealed to Americans who wanted alternatives to radical groups. And the Brothers invariably exaggerated their strength, although anybody who spent time outside downtown Cairo could see the truth.

The Americans, though, had no interest in local dynamics. This was part of their faith in *nizam:* they believed in top-down structures. In any case, there were so many security restrictions on embassy staff that they couldn't travel freely to rural places, small cities, or *ashwa'iyat*. An American officer's tour in Cairo usually lasted only two or three years, and he or she typically lived in a gated compound. They studied mostly *fusha,* not Egyptian Arabic. Their Egypt was to a large degree theoretical, and they imagined systems and structures in the same way that an Egyptologist might lose himself in the words of an ancient text. "We can't get caught up in the day-to-day," one U.S. embassy official told me in December, during the fight over the constitution. "We need to keep our eye on the long ball." As a philosophy, this might have been admirable, but sometimes there wasn't any long ball. No system, no regime—no *nizam*. Day-to-day was all that most Egyptians had.

This American flaw seemed endemic throughout the Middle East. In 2016, President Obama told the *Atlantic* that the Americans hadn't been prepared for the challenges of regime change in Libya. "The degree of tribal division in Libya was greater than our analysts had expected," he said. "And our ability to have any kind of structure there that we could interact with and start training and start providing resources broke down very quickly." In the same way, U.S. officials didn't take Tamarrod seriously, because it didn't behave like a real organization. On June 18, 2013, Anne Patterson, the U.S. ambassador to Egypt, gave a speech in Cairo in which she dismissed the upcoming protests. "Some say that street action will produce better results than elections," she said. "To be honest, my government and I are deeply skeptical."

Throughout the spring, Chuck Hagel spoke with Sisi on the telephone roughly every week. Hagel told me that during the final days of June he warned Sisi that if the Egyptian military engaged in a coup, U.S. law required an automatic end to military aid. "I said something to the effect of 'You don't want to start down a road that you can't retreat from,'" Hagel said.

But it was never clear whether Sisi was actually looking down the road—long ball—or simply reacting to the mood of the minute. I asked Hagel about the last conversation they had before the ultimatum expired. "'What can I do?'" Hagel remembered Sisi saying. "'I mean, I can't walk away. I can't fail my country. I have to lead; I have support. I am the only person in Egypt today that can save this country.'"

In the manner of Egyptian time—*"can we push the appointment back a little?"*—the coup was five hours late. The military communiqué had set an afternoon deadline of four o'clock, which came and went. Tens of thousands had gathered outside the Presidential Palace, and I went there with Hassan. Nobody we talked to was surprised that they were still waiting long after dark.

Finally, at nine o'clock, Sisi appeared on television. The crowd around me silenced. Most people held phones or radios to their ears, although a few had set up televisions in the street. On the screen, Sisi stood behind a lectern, dressed in a khaki uniform and a black beret. He was flanked by representatives from the military, the police, the Coptic Christian Church, the Al-Azhar

Mosque, and a prominent Salafi group. One of the young Tamarrod founders was also in the room. Four Egyptian flags hung behind the general. When he began to speak, his voice was steady, and he looked directly at the camera.

For days, Morsi supporters had gathered outside the Rabaa al-Adawiya Mosque, in Nasr City, and shortly before the coup the Egyptian security forces erected barriers around the neighborhood. After Sisi's announcement, Hassan and I went to one of the checkpoints. The soldiers let us through, and we continued down a long street that led toward the mosque where the Islamists had gathered.

Nasr City—the name means "Victory"—had been founded in the 1960s, in the desert east of Cairo proper. Many residents were middle-class Egyptians who had made some money working in the Gulf during the economic opening under Sadat. The place had an ambitious, overbuilt feeling, with concrete apartment blocks clustered between areas dedicated to military installations. Even in times of peace, there were troops stationed everywhere in Nasr City. It would have been hard to pick a worse place for a standoff with the army.

The evening was warm and pleasant, but the street was empty. It was so quiet that I could hear our footsteps echoing off the buildings that we passed. On television, Sisi had announced that the constitution was suspended and that an interim president would come from the judiciary. He said that the military had been forced to take this step because of Morsi's refusal to negotiate. No statement was made as to Morsi's whereabouts.

Hassan and I came to a checkpoint that was manned by the Brotherhood. Men sprawled on the ground, wearing yellow construction helmets and holding simple weapons: clubs, nightsticks, nunchakus. They looked stunned; somebody examined our IDs silently. Down the street, we talked with a thirty-year-old civil engineer and Brotherhood member named Ahmed el-Hawat. He carried a long club, but he had a friendly, gentle manner. His helmet made him look like a building engineer on-site: glasses, button-front shirt, slightly overweight.

He told us that all of Egypt's Islamist television channels had been shut down at the moment of Sisi's statement. While we were talking, another supporter wandered over, weeping, and began to pound on a parked car. The main crowd of Islamists was at the mosque, less than a block away.

"We will see more blood in all the streets of Egypt," Hawat said. "If we are assaulted, we have a huge number of people, and we are armed. This is the simplest tool that I'm carrying, but there are other weapons."

I asked him what they were.

"There are machine guns, shotguns, 9-millimeter pistols," he said. "Every one of us is already a time bomb."

He told me that the American government was responsible for the coup. "They planned it well," he said. "They gave the army the green light."

He pointed out that the roof of the building across the street was full of army snipers. I hadn't been able to see them as we approached, but now their silhouettes were clear. The spindly shapes of their guns stood out against the night sky. "They showed up a couple of hours before the military issued its statement," Hawat said.

Suddenly an angry roar came from the crowd at the mosque, and somebody opened fire with an automatic weapon. Hassan and I turned and walked away. "Don't run," he said. "Don't run!" He was afraid that somebody would panic and shoot us. We walked fast, heads down. More gunfire: probably they were just shooting into the air, but I didn't look back. Nobody else was on the street. After a few minutes, there was another explosion, this time from up ahead—fireworks. People were celebrating at the Presidential Palace. It was only three miles from the mosque to the palace—that was all the distance that separated the winners and the losers.

At the army checkpoint, Hassan and I showed our journalist IDs, and they let us through without any problem. I caught a cab downtown. The streets were loud: *duun duun dun-dun-dun; duun duun dun-dun-dun*. When I got home, I thought about the men in Nasr City, surrounded by snipers, and I turned on the news. But the live feeds from Rabaa had been removed from the state-run stations. All the Islamist channels were blank.

That week in Cairo, it was hard to tell that anybody was upset about what had happened. Egyptian flags were everywhere, and the mood felt more relaxed than it had for months. There weren't any lines at gas stations, and the blackouts ended; such problems seemed to magically disappear. Anybody in uniform had a smile on his face.

The Morsi supporters remained in Nasr City. After a day, the military relaxed the checkpoints, and the rooftop snipers vanished, and it was clear that the authorities had decided to allow the protest to continue, at least for now. As time passed, the sit-in changed in subtle ways. Before Morsi's ouster, I had visited the place a number of times, and almost everybody I met was a Brotherhood member. The energy often flagged; organizers were constantly running through the crowd, telling protesters to start chanting so that it would look better on television. But now I encountered more people without a formal Brotherhood affiliation, and they seemed more energized. Many were particularly upset because their demonstration was no longer on TV.

On July 5, two days after the coup, protesters crowded in front of the headquarters of the Republican Guard, where they believed that Morsi was being held. Some soldiers panicked and fired on the crowd, killing four. An hour after that event, I spoke with a man named Mohamed Ibrahim Ahmed who said that he had been standing next to one of the protesters who died. Ahmed was a retired air force veteran from the Delta city of Mansoura. "I'm not a Muslim Brotherhood member," he said. "You can't join if you're in the military. But I voted for Morsi. It's my right to defend my vote." He told me that the military shouldn't interfere in politics, and he believed that the Americans were behind everything. In the span of two days, the prevailing conspiracy theories had completely flipped. Before the coup, activists believed that the Americans supported the Brotherhood; now people like Ahmed claimed that the United States had removed Morsi.

I mentioned the speech in which Ambassador Patterson had criticized Tamarrod. "Why would she have said that if she wanted a coup?" I asked.

"Would she say openly that she's the one who supported all those protests?" Ahmed said. "So of course she said the opposite."

The last time I saw anybody in the Tamarrod headquarters was July 8. That morning, another fight broke out in front of the Republican Guard headquarters, and fifty-one civilians were killed, along with one soldier and two police officers. Most likely, some soldier had panicked and opened fire, and others responded in turn. It was the worst single episode of violence in Cairo since Mubarak had been removed from office.

I stopped by the Tamarrod office in the evening, and a young activist named Ahmed Salama told me that the Brotherhood was responsible for the deaths. In Salama's opinion, Brotherhood leaders were encouraging supporters to remain at protest sites where they were likely to be massacred, in hopes of winning sympathy for the movement. The United States still hadn't made a decision on what it would do with regard to its Egypt policy, but nobody in the Obama administration had used the word "coup" to describe what had happened. Saudi Arabia and the United Arab Emirates had announced that they were providing Egypt with a total of eight billion dollars in aid.

Salama had been involved in the protests that overthrew Mubarak, and now he recalled those days. "We were like kids in democracy and revolution," he said. "We are becoming mature now."

He had no plans to continue with Tamarrod, which never again had a significant impact on Egyptian politics. "Tamarrod was an idea instead of a political organization," he said. In his description, it was almost a kind of performance art. "It's a quick idea that comes and you do something," he said. "It's a tool." He rolled a cigarette and lit it up, ignoring a sign on the wall that said "Smoking Outside the HQ Only." The place was a firetrap: stacks of petitions rose six feet high around us. Salama said that most petitions were hidden in four locations around the city, although he wouldn't tell me where. No journalist or independent group had ever verified their existence. For all we knew, the reported number of signed petitions—22,134,465—was a complete fantasy.

Later that month, I stopped by the building again. The doorman was sitting in front, and he said that Tamarrod had left after its lease expired. He was a dark-skinned Upper Egyptian who wore a gray galabiya. He said that Tamarrod's presence had annoyed the building's residents. "There were too many people coming in and out," he said. Upstairs, activists had scrawled political graffiti on hallways, which the doorman had had to repaint. He kept complaining about all the people who had tramped in and out of the building; he was glad that now it was over. He said the apartment was available for rent if I was interested.

CHAPTER 13

NOT LONG AFTER THE COUP, SAYYID FOUND THE MOST MONEY HE'D EVER seen on a Cairo street. It was six thirty on a weekend morning, and nobody else was out; the money was lying in the gutter, bound with a rubber band. The total was fifteen hundred pounds, or nearly two hundred dollars—much of Sayyid's typical earnings for a month.

He delivered the money to the doorman who worked in the nearest building. Locally, this was the protocol for any discovery of a significant amount of cash. It was understood that the doorman had a week to see if anybody reported the loss. If the money wasn't claimed, then it was supposed to be returned to Sayyid.

The first time Sayyid described this process, I couldn't imagine that any doorman would give the money back. But over the years, Sayyid often found cash, and almost always it was returned. Even the fifteen hundred reappeared after seven days, bound with the same rubber band. Sayyid gave one hundred pounds to his mother, and he gave another seven hundred to his sister, who had recently incurred a series of medical expenses. He didn't tell Wahiba about the money.

In the immediate wake of the coup, Sayyid noticed that people on his route tipped a little more generously than usual. Most Zamalek residents opposed the Brotherhood, and they were relieved by the change in government. But soon their largesse slipped back to a normal level. Adly Mansour, a prominent judge, had been named interim president, and Egypt was supposed to hold another election in the near future. As for whom Sayyid wanted to become the next president, he had no names in mind, only a type. "I want somebody *mish toyib*," he said. "Not nice. I don't care who it is, as long as he isn't nice. He needs to be *shadeed*." That was the word so many Egyptians attached to their ideal president—hard, strict. "He needs to punish people," Sayyid said. "Morsi was too soft."

Sayyid's sister Leila lived with her three children in an *ashwa'iyat* not far from Ard al-Liwa. They had recently moved into the apartment of her widowed mother because of domestic problems. The tiny two-room apartment wasn't really big enough for five people, but Leila had to figure out what to do about her husband.

The husband was possessed by an *'afrit,* according to Sayyid. People in the community often told stories about the spirits, which could appear in different forms. Sometimes they were visible; one of Sayyid's friends saw an *'afrit* hiding in an irrigation canal, as plain as day. Other spirits appeared because of some incident. Once, two young men in Sayyid's neighborhood got into an argument over a foul while playing soccer, and things escalated off the field, where one of the men stabbed the other in the chest with a knife. The victim bled to death while being driven to the hospital in a small truck. Afterward, the vehicle became possessed. The truck would start by itself, and the lights would turn on and off for no reason. The owner tried to sell the vehicle, but whenever a potential buyer came to the neighborhood, people couldn't help but tell the story about the soccer game, the foul, the fight, the death, and the demonized truck. Finally the owner went to another part of Cairo and found a buyer. Sayyid couldn't remember the price. But he was certain that the demented truck was a Suzuki.

With Leila's husband, the *'afrit* had no origin story. The husband worked as a painter on construction crews, and he had never been very diligent or successful. He had a weakness for hashish, tramadol painkillers, and other drugs; this, apparently, was one sign of his possession. He also had a tendency to talk to himself. Another symptom involved unpredictable outbursts of violence. He got into fights with neighbors, and the smallest thing at home could set him off.

Ramadan was always a volatile month. During the previous year's holiday, the man became sick, and his nine-year-old daughter, Rahma, suggested that he eat something. Her advice was reasonable—sheikhs and imams often said that anybody who fell sick should take a break from fasting. But apparently the *'afrit* took offense at the child's suggestion. The father flew into a rage, attacking his daughter, and Leila stepped between them. She received the brunt of her husband's blows, and her arm was broken. At the time she was several months pregnant.

For Leila, that was the last straw. Along with the children, she moved in with her mother. Whenever she went outside, her arm in a cast, she sensed that some people took pleasure in her misfortune. And eventually she came to believe that her sister-in-law Wahiba was one of these people.

They had never had good relations. Sayyid's female relatives seemed hard on his wife, probably because she had been chosen over the cousin whom the elders had favored. Her beauty might have been another factor. After Sayyid and Wahiba were married, Leila encouraged the younger woman to start wearing the *niqab,* because she believed that her pretty face attracted too much attention.

Wahiba agreed to cover herself, and she never did anything remotely inappropriate, but Leila and other relatives remained judgmental. And after Leila suffered the injury, she was convinced that Wahiba had engaged in some form of the evil eye. Periodically, the women encountered each other, usually at their children's school, and there might be a wayward glance or comment. Sometimes a remark was made to somebody else, who then passed it on to a third party, and then to a fourth, and so on, until the barb reached its target. Sayyid often showed me texts from his wife:

> Yesterday you didn't fight for me. I'll do it myself and you will regret what I'll do.

Wahiba clearly felt frustrated by Sayyid's reluctance to support her. Meanwhile, Leila had plenty of reasons to be unhappy about her own situation. With both sides demanding sympathy, Sayyid's response was often to disengage. If the women were feuding, he spent a night in Zamalek, sleeping in the garage on my street. As the conflict grew, the texts incorporated random neighborhood figures:

> The prostitute whose reputation is on every man's tongue and who sleeps with the Christian Sammy is talking down to her betters.

Sayyid tried to explain the background of such messages, but I could never follow the thread. Each new participant dragged in baggage that had nothing to do with the original conflict, and there were various complications that had to do with people being Christian, or Muslim, or Upper Egyptian, or something else. Finally, it culminated one day outside the school. Wahiba was accompanied by some of her male relatives, and they encountered Leila and some members of her family. An argument turned into a brief scuffle, and somebody hit Leila in the eye with a stick. After everything that had already happened to this woman—the possessed husband, the pregnancy, the broken arm—her eye was damaged badly enough that it required surgery.

The first time I visited Leila, her arm and eye had both healed, and her new daughter was several months old. The fight with the husband was distant enough that the family spoke about it casually, like an old story that everybody already knew. Rahma, the oldest daughter, brought it up almost immediately after I arrived. "He tried to hit me, but my mother came to protect me, and he hit her instead," she said. The girl had striking features: dark eyebrows, tawny skin, and big eyes that lit up when she talked. Like all children, she loved telling a dramatic story that placed herself at the center of the action.

Sayyid and I had gone there for a lunch that was prepared by his mother and Leila. They must have worked on it for hours: roast chicken, *molokhiya* soup, fried potatoes, and rice wrapped in vine leaves. Sayyid and I sat on the floor of the main room, and the women served us first before sitting down. Like most Muslim women in the neighborhood, Leila wore the *niqab,* and with every bite she had to pull the cloth away from her mouth. The siblings teased each other throughout the meal.

"Do you want another wife?" Sayyid asked me. "She's available!"

His sister laughed behind her veil, and I said something about Americans being limited to one wife.

In truth, Leila was still married. Under Mubarak, women had finally won the right to initiate divorce; this, along with other women's rights, had been a prominent cause of Suzanne Mubarak's. But the law was still heavily weighted against women, who lost any alimony and other financial rights if they were the ones to file for divorce. And there remained a powerful stigma in conservative communities. So Leila had retained a lawyer, but instead of filing for divorce, he had been trying to force the husband to support his children. The man hadn't paid anything for months.

Sayyid did what he could to help his sister, and she worked in a small textile factory. Like her brother, she had never attended school, but she had become literate. She had accomplished this in part by listening to radio shows in which a holy man read from the Quran while she followed the text at home. She had also enrolled in literacy classes in the *ashwa'iyat* that had been offered by an American Christian NGO.

"They had a different class for men," Sayyid said. "They used to talk to us about how masturbation is bad." He said he had never gotten far with his studies.

Of all Sayyid's siblings and half siblings, Leila was the one with whom he was closest. Once, she talked to me about how difficult life had been when they were children. Their father died when Leila was less than a year old, and there was another brother between her and Sayyid. Their mother had been forced to find odd jobs on small farms in the area, and Sayyid often cared for his younger siblings, in addition to working for various *zabaleen*. "He was like the moon!" Leila said, using a common phrase that expresses beauty or decency. "Sayyid was only eight or nine, but he would feed us and get us things to drink. After he was about twelve, he told our mother, 'Now you don't work. You've done enough. It's my turn to support the family.'"

Whenever I visited Leila, I avoided mentioning Wahiba's name. At the time of our lunch, the women had reached a temporary détente, and Leila made only one offhand remark about her sister-in-law. The television played at high volume throughout the meal, and it was tuned to a drama that featured an exorcism. Such scenes seemed to appear with some regularity on Egyptian television; I had seen them during other meals with Sayyid. Today's possessed person was a woman in a nightgown who had been tied down in bed. One man tried to physically restrain the woman while a bearded sheikh read from the Quran. Every time the sheikh read a holy verse, the woman screamed and foamed at the mouth.

The family had seated me at the place of honor, facing the television, and for ten minutes I ate chicken and rice while trying not to watch the woman in the nightgown get exorcised. The sheikh seemed to be making very slow progress. Finally I asked Leila's son if he could change the channel, and he grabbed the remote and found a Bollywood movie. Nobody else seemed to care either way; they enjoyed the dancing Indians just as much as they had enjoyed the exorcism.

In Arabic class, I mentioned Sayyid's conversations about *'afrit* and *djinn,* another common word for spirits. There was a popular television talk show called *Cairo and the People,* and Rifaat taped an episode about possessions. The guests included a psychologist, a woman who claimed to be inhabited by multiple spirits, and a sheikh from Al-Azhar Mosque, the most respected Muslim institution in Egypt.

The sheikh explained that the Quran testifies to the existence of *djinn,* but the holy book describes them as invisible. The possessed woman disagreed; she said that she knew her own spirits so well that she could identify one that was Muslim and another that was Christian. The Christian *djinn,* she said, was better behaved than the Muslim *djinn.*

For Egyptians, it wasn't uncommon for spirits to cross religious lines. Once, a Muslim friend of Sayyid's became possessed by a Christian *djinn;* he was certain of the spirit's faith because he discerned a cross around its neck. It took them a while to find somebody who was willing to perform an exorcism, because there was some debate over jurisdiction. One Coptic priest said that he couldn't pray over a Muslim, while a Muslim imam explained that he had no power over a Christian spirit. Finally, Sayyid tracked down another priest who agreed to try an exorcism, and soon the possessed man reported that he felt better.

On the talk show, the psychologist spoke after the other guests were finished. "Why is it that *djinn* are here and not in other countries?" he asked. "This is because people won't accept that there's a possibility of a psychiatric illness. So they believe in *djinn.* It's a temporary comfort." His words occupied the heart of our vocabulary list for that day's class:

illusion	وهم
hallucination	هلوسة

justification	مبرر
we're the ones who are crazy	إحنا اللي بنخرف
exorcism	زار
exorcist (female)	كودية

I never met Sayyid's brother-in-law, and from descriptions I couldn't tell whether the man was psychologically troubled, or addicted to drugs, or simply inclined to violence. Regardless, all of these possible explanations, as well as most solutions, were effectively cut off by talk of *'afrit*. When a problem came from the world of the spirits, nobody was accountable, and nobody could do anything other than arrange for an exorcism.

Even everyday conflicts seemed to have limited options for resolution. After the fight between Wahiba and Leila became more serious, a neighbor in Ard al-Liwa organized an *'adit al-sulh,* or "reconciliation session." This practice is particularly common in Upper Egypt, and Sayyid seemed encouraged when I saw him the morning after the session. He told me that members of both families had attended, and they spent hours trying to work through the problem. One issue that came up was Sayyid's tendency to withhold financial support from his wife during conflicts. A neighbor offered Sayyid a piece of advice. "If your wife asks for a penny," he said, "give her two."

"Why should I give her two pennies?" Sayyid asked.

"Because the man with three pennies is standing outside your house."

Sayyid had to admit that this was wise. I asked him what Wahiba and Leila had said at the *'adit al-sulh,* but the question surprised him. "They weren't there," he said.

"Why not?" I asked. "Didn't they want to solve the problem?"

"Women aren't allowed at an *'adit al-sulh,*" Sayyid said. "It's for men only."

"But in this case the women are the ones who have the conflict."

"Yes," Sayyid said. "That's what we were trying to solve." He explained that if the women had participated, they would only have caused further problems. "They can't be controlled," he said. "They have long tongues, and they insult people."

During the *'adit al-sulh,* each woman had remained in her own home, surrounded by female friends and relatives. "They were encouraging them to keep fighting," Sayyid said. In his opinion, this was the problem: if the women would just back off, the men could solve the issue. I wasn't surprised when Sayyid soon appeared with more text messages—"*It's not your house, you thief. . . .*" From what I could tell, nobody ever focused on the most obvious root of the conflict: one man's violence against his pregnant wife, and the lack of support for this traumatized and burdened woman. But all of that had happened because of an *'afrit,* so it was essentially out of everybody's hands.

In Sayyid's community, men and women had little contact, at least in public, and their inequality meant that problem-solving tactics diverged widely. It reminded me of Huntington's description of the praetorian state: "Each social force attempts to secure its objectives through the resources and tactics in which it is strongest." For men, power often came from money or violence, while women turned to words: gossip, insults, text messages. An educated woman could also use the law or the government bureaucracy as a means of defense. After a while, Sayyid began withholding money from Wahiba once again, despite his neighbor's penny-wise advice. Wahiba responded by hiring a lawyer who filed three court cases, including one of nonsupport.

These actions forced Sayyid into a world that was especially hostile to an illiterate person. One morning, I accompanied him to the Real Estate Tax Authority, where he needed to file paperwork in order to fight his wife's claim on the apartment. The tax authority was situated on the Giza side of the river, in an old building whose hallways and waiting rooms were packed with people. Most of them looked poor, and they clutched official forms while waiting to be called by clerks.

Sayyid started on the second floor. He passed some forms through a barred window, where a clerk in a dirty blue shirt sat at a desk. The clerk glanced at the papers and said, "I want to drink tea."

Sayyid pulled out a twenty-pound note and passed it over. The clerk pocketed the money, marked the form, and instructed Sayyid to go to another office on the third floor. The third-floor clerk had gelled hair and sleepy eyes. He said, "Come back on Thursday."

"Is it possible to do it faster?" Sayyid asked.

"I have an itch," the sleepy-eyed man said, and Sayyid handed him a ten.

At every window, the clerk had his own euphemism for a bribe. The next one simply said, "I need something to speed it up." Five more pounds. Another window, another ten. After Sayyid had paid half a dozen clerks and collected all the necessary forms, he brought them outside the building, where a literate friend was waiting. The friend filled in the blanks, and Sayyid affixed his thumbprint on the signature lines. Then he went back inside the building to deal with more clerks.

In the past, when I saw statistics about government employment, I wondered what six million civil servants could possibly do all day long. But now I realized that legitimate tasks weren't necessary to create a bustling office. At some level, the place was productive: money constantly changed hands, and somebody like Sayyid moved briskly from window to window. Even the people who were too poor to pay bribes were useful. They became a kind of prop—the way they crowded the hallways, staring hopelessly at the floor, persuaded more prosperous visitors to be free with their money. And so Sayyid tossed off bill after bill, surrounded by crowds of people who could afford to spend nothing but time.

In the garage on our street, Sayyid slept on a cot. He had some bedding, a few sets of clothes, and an electrical outlet where he charged his phone. Sometimes he took a shower in my apartment, where he had a knack of stopping by around dinnertime. He shared enough family meals that my daughters knew him as *Amu Sayyid*—Uncle Sayyid.

For a period of months he didn't see his children. Wahiba made it clear that if Sayyid refused to provide support, then he couldn't visit his kids. Leslie and I often told him that he needed to meet his wife alone, without the distraction of relatives and neighbors. From our perspective, no single part of the conflict appeared insurmountable; it was more a matter of small slights and misunderstandings that had escalated. But it seemed impossible for them to isolate the fundamental problem.

On one of the national holidays, Sayyid invited me to accompany him to his mother's ancestral village near Beni Suef. We caught a microbus in Cairo and headed south, following the new road that ran on the desert highlands west of the river. After half an hour the driver pulled over at a gas station. He filled the tank with a lit cigarette in his mouth while the engine was idling.

We passed the Meidum Pyramid, less than two hours from Cairo, and then we descended into the river valley. The village was called Wasta, the word that means "connections" in Arabic. After we arrived, Sayyid's uncle escorted us into his home, where we were served tea. As guests of honor, we were seated in the *dawar,* the sitting room that occupies a prominent place in any Upper Egyptian home.

The uncle's home was prosperous because his adult sons had done well as migrant laborers in Libya. Over the past decade, it had become common for Upper Egyptian men to go there, usually to work construction jobs. But the fall of Qaddafi and the subsequent violence had caused most Egyptians to return home. One of Sayyid's cousins was now back in Wasta, trying to decide where to go next, and he drank tea with us in the *dawar.* Sayyid asked if anything had changed in Wasta after the coup.

"The police confiscated our gun," the nephew said. He explained that it was a Kalashnikov. "We shot it from an apartment, and that's why it was taken away. Somebody reported it."

"Where is it now?" Sayyid asked.

"It's here. We got it back. But we can't shoot it anymore. They're stricter now."

In the *dawar,* a text message popped up on Sayyid's phone, as if to remind him that even in Wasta he couldn't escape his problems:

> You're going to divorce me with your legs crossed over your head.

For the trip, Sayyid had dressed well, in a pair of jeans and a button-front shirt that had been discarded by a foreigner who lived on his route. I was accustomed to seeing Sayyid adopt a deferential posture toward Zamalek residents, where the doormen and other neighborhood figures sometimes teased him good-naturedly. But here in Wasta he carried himself like an elder. He sat in the *dawar* with a comfortable, casual pose, slumped against the cushions. When a younger nephew brought tea, Sayyid accepted it with a curt nod. He had brought a big-city gift for his uncle: a foil pack of five Indian-made tramadol tablets.

In the village, people often mentioned Sayyid's father. He hadn't come from this place, but his marriage to a local woman had clearly left a deep impression.

"He used to laugh a lot," one old farmer told Sayyid, when we went for a walk through the fields. "And he was married so many times! He even married a Christian woman. They had Atala."

"Atala was my brother?" Sayyid said.

"Yes, Atala was your brother," the old man said.

Sayyid shook his head thoughtfully while we walked away. "I didn't know Atala was my brother," he said. "He died a few years ago. He was as black as this jacket." One of Sayyid's older brothers had told me that even now, in middle age, he was occasionally surprised to meet some half sibling for the first time.

The village looked relatively prosperous, with new barns, chicken coops, and houses that had been built with remittance money from Libya. People said there had been a surge in illegal construction on agricultural land during Morsi's year in power. Sayyid told me that he had some business to handle on behalf of his recently divorced brother, and at the end of our visit we met another family elder in the uncle's *dawar*. A younger man served tea, and Sayyid brought up the subject of marriage.

"My brother is carrying a stick over his shoulder," he said.

"Get him a donkey from here," the elder said. He was in his late fifties, and his head was wrapped in a field-worker's turban.

"My brother has an apartment, a car, three daughters, and a son."

"I can help him find a wife," the elder said. "How old is he?"

Sayyid telephoned his brother in Cairo and put him on speakerphone. "How old are you?"

"Forty-seven."

"Are you *shadeed*?"

"I'm *shadeed*!"

"How many horsepower do you have?"

His brother laughed. "Sixty-four!"

Sayyid hung up and asked the elder what he thought.

"There are a couple of possibilities," the man said. "There's one who's dark-skinned, and there's another who's thirty-five years old."

"You'll be the middleman?"

"Sure, for two thousand."

"Two thousand?" Sayyid said, laughing. "Screw the bread and salt!" The phrase meant "*screw family!*"

The men shook hands, and Sayyid said he'd try to make a return visit with his brother. We caught a microbus back to Cairo after sunset. In the darkness, the driver entered the highway going the wrong direction, and another bus came upon us suddenly. Its headlights filled the windshield; our driver swerved at the last instant. Passengers lurched out of their seats, and afterward they called out the standard phrases: *al-hamdulillah,* "all praise be to God"; *rabina yustor,* "may God protect us." At a gas station, the driver filled the tank with the engine idling, just like the other microbus. Shortly after this trip, I decided that if I was going to continue to visit Upper Egypt, I wanted to be the one behind the wheel, and I acquired an Egyptian driver's license. *Rabina yustor.*

In Cairo, during late afternoon, I often took Ariel and Natasha into our garden. We had a swing set and a few other toys, and the girls would run around the narrow space that was enclosed by the spiderweb gates and the high brick wall. On the other side ran the bustling streets of Ahmed Heshmat and Ismail Mohammed. The place felt like an oasis: a tiny lot on a tiny island, surrounded by one of the most densely populated cities on earth.

One afternoon, Sayyid came by, and we chatted while the girls played. He asked me casually if I planned to have them circumcised.

I looked at Ariel and Natasha digging in the dirt near the spiderweb gate—they were all of three years old.

"No," I said. "People don't do that in America. It's against the law. People think it's terrible. It's bad for the girls."

"It's against the law here, but people still do it," he said.

The practice had been banned under Mubarak, in 2008, but it was still common. In 2015, a survey sponsored by the Ministry of Health and Population determined that 90 percent of Egyptian women between the ages of fifteen and forty-nine had undergone the surgery, which involves the partial or total removal of external genitalia. Opponents of the practice refer to it as female genital mutilation, and Egyptians typically have it performed when a child is between the ages of nine and twelve. The procedure is intensely painful, and sometimes girls are maimed or even die as a result of complications.

Long-term effects can include cysts, urination problems, and increased risk of complications with childbirth. There are no positive outcomes to the procedure, which seems to have appealed to male-dominated communities because it makes intercourse less pleasurable for women.

I asked Sayyid if he planned to have the surgery performed on his daughter.

"Yes," he said.

I told him bluntly that he shouldn't do it.

"We have to do it," he said. "Otherwise women are crazy for *dakar*." The word means "male." He continued, "They'll be running around outside the house, chasing men."

The subject came up again during a subsequent trip with Sayyid to his mother's ancestral village. We were sitting in the *dawar* with two of his cousins, one of whom had recently married. Somebody mentioned female circumcision, and I asked if the law deterred villagers.

"The law doesn't matter," the cousin said. He explained that now the surgery couldn't be performed in a hospital. "But there's a doctor who still does it," he said. "He just comes to your home instead."

I asked why people felt the procedure was necessary.

"Al maya sokhna," he said. "The water is hot." In his explanation, there was so much heat in Nile water that women developed powerful sexual urges, and the surgery was necessary to control them.

This social issue infuriated Rifaat. When we covered it in class, he worked himself into a frenzy, complaining about the stupidity of traditional-minded Egyptians. In his opinion, the mutilation of girls was wrapped up in superstition, sexism, religion, poverty, and the country's troubled transition to modernity. The day's vocab list tracked these factors:

female circumcision	ختان
pure	طاهر
to circumcise; to sterilize	يطَهّر
male circumcision	طهور

economic recession	كساد إقتصادي
psychologist	دكتور نفساني
the modern life	الحياة العصرية

Originally, mutilation had been an African tribal custom, and it became entrenched in many places, including along the Nile. During the modern era, Egyptian Islamists promoted the practice as an article of faith, probably because it was another way to manage women. But there was no basis for it in the Quran. Few Muslims in other parts of the world engage in the surgery, which is opposed by conservatives in Saudi Arabia and other Gulf states. In any case, the Egyptian practice is hardly limited to Muslims; Coptic Christians also mutilate their daughters in high numbers, especially in the south.

Government campaigns against the surgery have had significant success among educated residents in Cairo. But in the *ashwa'iyat,* people tend to have ideas and opinions that remain close to those in their ancestral villages. This is in part a function of geography. Egypt's layout along a single river valley allows for easy transport, and more than two-thirds of the population lives within a three-hour drive of Cairo. A person like Sayyid easily maintained links to the village—at any moment, he was never more than two hours removed from his family's rural past. Cairenes sometimes joked that the massive migration of Upper Egyptians and other rural people to the capital had turned the city into a giant village.

I often thought about how different the dynamic was in China. During the years I lived there, more than 150 million Chinese had left their homes in the countryside, which represented the largest rural-to-urban migration in the history of the world. Migrants flooded cities, but they didn't transform these places into villages, the way it happened in Egypt. The Chinese outcome was the opposite: the cities transformed the migrants into urban people. Again, some of this could be explained by simple geography. China is roughly as large as the United States, and its earliest development focused on coastal cities in the east and south. For most migrants, it was a long journey, and usually they made only one annual return visit to their hometowns. Few Chinese could follow Sayyid's pattern of making regular day trips back to see relatives.

And Chinese migrants tended to be institutionalized. They worked in factories; they slept in dormitories; they entered jobs with clear tasks and set hierarchies. Conditions could be brutal and abusive, but the industrial environment also taught people about system and process. Village time was gone: workers learned to live by the clock. Night schools and trade classes sprang up in factory towns, because education helped workers rise into management. Women participated in this process as well as men—in fact, female migrants generally outnumbered males, because they were preferred by most factories. Over time, their ideas and opinions tended to come from co-workers, dorm mates, and the media, rather than from village elders. Religion played basically no role in this process. But literacy did: virtually all Chinese migrants were already literate when they left home, which allowed them to process new ideas quickly.

All of this also required a strong economic and educational foundation. For more than three decades of the Chinese boom, when migration was under way, manufacturing averaged more than 30 percent of GDP. In Egypt—a young, populous country, with cheap labor, an easy geography for infrastructure, and great access to shipping lanes—manufacturing is only 16 percent of a weak GDP. The Egyptian government never effectively followed the strategy of China and other Asian countries, which invested heavily in public education while granting preferential policies to key cities that were well situated to attract foreign investment. In Egypt, they attempted to establish special manufacturing zones in canal cities like Port Said, but inevitably such projects were sapped by corruption and lack of government direction.

As a result, the Egyptian industrial sector remains largely based on energy extraction and production, which employs relatively few people. Foreign aid makes up the shortfall. The handouts come easily, but they don't create institutional change. Even in Cairo, between 25 and 40 percent of all workers are mainly employed in the informal sector. The rate is particularly high for uneducated Upper Egyptians: the *zabaleen,* the doormen, the deliverers, the construction-crew workers. They work informal jobs, and they live in the informal environment of the *ashwa'iyat.* And all economic movement is dominated by males: men leave the village for work, whereas women leave for marriage. The act of migration—a revolutionary social force in China and other parts of the world—actually reinforces traditional gender disparities in Egypt.

Sayyid's mother had an identical-twin sister who still lived in Wasta. Every time Sayyid took me to the village, we stopped in his aunt's home, and afterward he always remarked how much older she looked than his mother. On the farm, his aunt's face had been darkened by the Upper Egyptian sun.

As a foreigner, though, I was much more impressed by everything these women still had in common. After childhood, they had moved into different worlds: one twin migrated to the capital with a worker husband, while the other twin stayed behind and married a farmer. But their economic and social outcomes were basically indistinguishable. Neither sister developed a career, and neither worked in the formal economy. Virtually all their money came from males. They couldn't read; they couldn't drive; they rarely left home. They were equally religious. Both covered their heads with the same conservative style of *hijab,* and both wore long, heavy gowns, even in hot weather. They cooked the same foods, and at mealtimes the women always served the men, who always ate first. Forty years ago, Sayyid's mother had moved to the largest city in North Africa, and she had witnessed the capital's unprecedented growth. But even a megacity of seventeen million couldn't overwhelm the influence of this tiny place they called Connections.

CHAPTER 14

IN AUGUST 2013, I TRAVELED FROM FRANKFURT TO CAIRO ON AN EGYPTAIR flight so empty that the attendants wouldn't let anybody sit in the back of the plane. Passengers were distributed across the middle and the front, to maintain balance, and at most there was one person in a row. There weren't any couples or children. The only other time I had seen an international flight like this was when I flew into Tokyo shortly after the Fukushima reactor melted down, in 2011. On that flight, passengers had behaved the same way they did on the EgyptAir plane. There was no conversation, and nobody ate or drank very much. Most people lay across the empty seats and went to sleep. When I looked down the aisle, feet poked out the ends of the rows, as if everybody on this flight had collapsed.

The EgyptAir plane touched down after curfew. Anybody who showed up this late had to arrange a ride in advance, and Hassan was waiting for me in his car. As journalists, we had a vehicle permit that allowed us to drive in the evening.

The first checkpoint was right outside the airport. Police officers inspected the vehicle permit and our IDs, and they asked Hassan to open the trunk. After they waved us on, we drove for less than half a mile before we were stopped by the next group of police. The third checkpoint was even closer. Virtually no other cars were on the roads, and the police were visibly nervous. Most of them kept their weapons in their hands.

A few days earlier, on August 14, security forces had cleared the two main pro-Morsi protests in Cairo. Ever since the coup in July, there had been rumors that the police would act, and when they finally did, the violence was brutal. Human Rights Watch later estimated that it was likely that more than a thousand people died, the vast majority of them unarmed. The last time such a thing had happened in a major world capital was in 1989, around Tiananmen Square. After the Egyptian massacre, the government declared martial law, and a curfew was instituted in Cairo. Across the country, more than fifty officers and conscripts had died, many of them in guerrilla-style attacks of retaliation.

When the crackdown began, we were on vacation in the United States. Leslie and I decided that she would stay with the girls, and I would return to report on the events in Cairo. After Hassan picked me up at the airport, we tried to follow the usual route to Zamalek, but the main road was blocked. Nobody at the checkpoints seemed to know which streets were open. The curfew had been instituted suddenly, and many barriers were manned by conscripts who were so frightened and so poorly trained that they had no idea of anything beyond their immediate station. Each checkpoint was an island; the men behaved as if they had no communication with the outside world. They would inspect our documents and the trunk, and then they sent us off to drift until we reached the next island of uniforms and guns. The previous evening, at a checkpoint in the Delta, a group of police panicked and opened fire on a car that contained two Egyptian reporters. One journalist died—the fifth to be killed that week.

After crawling through eastern Cairo for most of an hour, in the stifling August heat, Hassan and I made two mistakes. The first mistake was rolling up the windows and turning on the air conditioner. The second mistake was switching on the radio. The radio wasn't very loud, but with the windows up it prevented us from hearing a policeman yelling on the street. There weren't any lights at his blockade. By the time we saw him, he had raised his Kalashnikov into the firing position.

Hassan slammed on the brakes. Now at a distance of thirty feet we finally heard the man. "This is your last warning!" he shouted.

We raised our hands. Hassan was yelling—"we've stopped, we're journalists!"—but the policeman seemed frozen. Everybody held still for a long five seconds. Then, very slowly, the policeman approached the car. He still had the rifle trained on us. He looked inside, and then he motioned for Hassan to roll down the window. Permit, IDs, trunk. All three pairs of hands were shaking when the documents were passed around. The policeman looked as if he were no older than nineteen.

The clearing of the sit-ins had apparently been scheduled in coordination with Ramadan. It happened a week after the holiday ended, and whatever planning had gone into the operation didn't seem aimed at minimizing casualties. The police never issued a clear public warning or deadline, and once the crackdown began, they failed to establish safe exits for protesters who wanted to leave peacefully. Their firepower was overwhelming—they behaved as if the people at the sit-ins had been heavily armed.

One of the Brotherhood's tactical errors had been to allow some weapons at the protests. It seemed that there had never been many guns, but they were certainly present; I had witnessed a supporter firing an automatic rifle on the evening of the coup, and other journalists also saw guns. Before I left for my summer trip, I had often visited the Rabaa sit-in, where patrols of Muslim Brothers regularly marched in formation, wearing helmets and carrying clubs. These patrols had no real security value, but they created a disturbing optic. For many citizens, such shows of force, along with the presence of weapons, justified the government's brutality.

Some believed that provocation had always been the goal. Before the crackdown, Ahmed Ragab, a young reporter for *Al-Masry al-Youm,* a private newspaper, had helped document abuses by the Brotherhood at the Rabaa sit-in. It was similar to what happened at many other Egyptian protests: over time, the Morsi supporters started to engage in mob justice. A number of random civilians were detained and tortured on vague accusations of being "agents." Ragab believed that Brotherhood leaders had tolerated such actions, as well as the accumulation of weapons, because they knew that such factors could provoke an outsized government response. "My personal conviction is that the Muslim Brotherhood leadership knew this was going to happen," Ragab told me. "They were hoping for a massacre. They hoped for it as much as the police hoped for it." It reminded me of Raafat's comment at the June 30 protest: *Ayz dem.* "I want blood." In the crude tactics of Egyptian politics, casualties were valuable, because they could inspire more support.

On both sides, the leadership was essentially passive-aggressive. Nobody truly led: instead, they gave their followers enough leeway to indulge in their worst instincts and behavior. And it was always easy to hide behind the incompetence of splintered institutions. During the weeks before the massacre, Chuck Hagel, the U.S. secretary of defense, had been in frequent phone contact with Sisi. Hagel later said that he had warned Sisi to control the situation. But Sisi always emphasized his lack of power.

"He would say, 'I've got problems because it's the police doing this, not the military,'" Hagel told me. "I said, 'You've got to find a way to handle this.' And that's when he would say, 'I don't control the police.'"

After the massacre, Hagel and Sisi spoke once more. "He said that he was sorry, so sorry," Hagel remembered. "He said he wished it hadn't come to this."

I asked what else Sisi had mentioned.

"He talked about his family, and he talked about his wife," Hagel said. It seemed remarkable that after initiating such a massacre, the general spoke fondly of family. Hagel continued, "He said his wife was very upset, and his family, to see all of this bloodshed. He didn't say they blamed him for it, but they were really touched by it. He said they were praying for everybody."

In the evenings, I went for walks around Zamalek. The apartment felt empty without Leslie and the girls, and during this period Morsi the cat left offerings beside the chair where I worked—a mouse, a spider. After dark, when I felt restless, I would walk to the northern tip of the island, where it splits the river like the prow of a boat. I returned on the western bank of Zamalek, looking at the lights of Giza across the water. Usually, Cairo feels alive at night, but now there was nobody out except the occasional patrolling officer. It was more common to hear the overhead whir of an Apache helicopter than the sound of a car.

During the day, city routines proceeded as they always had, but the facade of normalcy was brittle. Twice, I saw women in *niqabs* engage in fistfights, something that I had never witnessed before the massacre and something that I would never see again. One afternoon, I watched a furious cabbie chase his Salafi fare into the entrance of a charitable foundation that was attached to the Aziz Bellah Mosque, in eastern Cairo. The cabbie's mouth was bleeding; he ran after the bearded man and screamed, "Fuck your mother's religion!"

The mosque was known for conservatism, and it was located near Rabaa, where the worst massacre had occurred. Many Salafi members of the congregation had participated in the sit-in, and dozens of injured protesters had been brought to the small hospital that was attached to the mosque. One afternoon, Hassan and I stopped by to meet with the mosque's executive manager, a sixty-year-old named Ahmed Mohammed.

Mohammed was a retired major general in the police. It was common for people with security backgrounds to take administrative jobs at big private mosques, but Mohammed said he worked here because of his faith. When I entered his office, he was studying a transcript of a recent Friday sermon by a famous imam.

Mohammed said that he had opposed the removal of Morsi, but he also disapproved of the current anti-Sisi protests that were being held in some parts of Cairo. "Proper Islam is to not disobey the ruler, even if he's so bad and black that his head is like a raisin," he said. "It was wrong to oust Mubarak; it was wrong to oust Morsi; and now it would be wrong to oust Sisi." He spoke of Sisi as if he were leading the country, although technically he was still only the minister of defense.

Morsi's fate remained unclear. Thus far, the authorities had said only that the former president was being held at an undisclosed location. Mohammed had voted for Morsi, and the massacres sickened him. "They could have dispersed it over five or six days without killing so many," he said. But he also sympathized with the officers who had been commanded to gun down their fellow citizens. He said that when he was in the police, during the days of Mubarak, his greatest fear had been that he would be ordered to participate in a mass killing. Every day of his service, he had prayed that he would be spared from such a duty. "God answered my prayers," he said. "He kept me away from them. I had good intentions." He paused. "But there is some stuff that I hope God forgives us for. We were oppressed. We were forced to do it. And I made up for that many other times when I said no."

I asked what it was that still required forgiveness, and he fell silent. Then he looked up. "This had to do with the fixing of elections," he said.

"What did you do?"

He smiled a little sadly and said, "No comment."

None of the top Brotherhood leaders had been killed at Rabaa, but afterward the authorities quickly made arrests. When I telephoned prominent Brothers whom I had met in the past, I always got the same phone-company recording: *This number is not a working number. Please check the number you are calling. This is a recorded message.* Many of the lower-level Brothers whom I knew quietly slipped out of the country, if they had the means to do so. Mohamed Wajih, the Brother who lived near Abydos, fled to Kuwait, and Manu's friend Tariq ended up in Qatar.

After the massacre, there was a brief time during which people seemed unusually forthright and reflective, like the executive manager at the Aziz Bellah Mosque. But this period passed quickly, and then conspiracy theories became even more rampant than in the past. People exaggerated the number of weapons that had been found at Rabaa, and there was a common false story about the police discovering the corpses of innocent people at the site of the Brothers' sit-in. The state-run *Al-Ahram* newspaper ran a front-page story alleging that the United States had conspired with the Brothers in order to divide Egypt.

There had been scattered violence in other parts of Egypt, with some of the worst incidents happening in Minya, a governorate about two hundred miles north of Abydos. By many measures, it was the poorest part of the country, and mobs of Morsi supporters had responded angrily to the news of the Cairo massacres. They burned more than a dozen Coptic churches, and they overran and looted various government buildings and police stations.

In the spring, I went to Minya to try to meet with the governor. His name was Salah Zeyada, the former major general in the police who had gained a measure of fame in the waning days of the Morsi regime by declaring publicly that the police would not defend any Brotherhood headquarters. For this, apparently, he was awarded the governorship of Minya after the coup.

Zeyada's office was in a beautiful old British-built complex that faced the Nile. Hassan and I approached him the same way we did any *rayis:* rather than trying to make an appointment, we simply joined the line of random people outside his door. Soldiers with Kalashnikovs had been posted throughout the hallways of the capitol, because guerrilla-style attacks still happened periodically. After a while, an assistant escorted Hassan and me into the governor's office.

Zeyada greeted me warmly. He was a trim, handsome, gray-haired man, and he wore a yellow V-neck sweater and a standard police-issue mustache. He called briskly to his tea man, and after my drink arrived, the governor offered me a Marlboro. He lit one up himself. The office was decorated with two busts of Nefertiti, one of which was a copy of the famous painted sculpture that had been excavated from the southern part of Minya governorate. I didn't see a nail on the wall.

I asked who was responsible for the recent violence in Minya, especially the burning of Coptic churches.

"It was Obama," the governor said. "And all of the American politicians who have divided all of the world. They are the only people who supported the Muslim Brotherhood because they knew that the Muslim Brotherhood would destroy all of Egypt." He continued, "Ask Obama's spokesman about everything he said from June 30 to today. Ask him why they endorse the Muslim Brotherhood."

I said that Obama had never endorsed the Brotherhood.

"Then why did he cut the aid to Egypt?" the governor said.

The Obama administration had done nothing until the massacre, after which it suspended military aid to Egypt. But this turned out to be a temporary measure, and in any case the aid for 2013 was the usual amount—around 1.5 billion dollars. The Obama administration used semantics to dodge the American anti-coup legislation: they simply refused to apply the word "coup" to what had happened in Egypt. I mentioned this to the governor.

"I don't know exactly," he said, making a dismissive gesture. "I don't receive the aid myself." He told me that protests still happened periodically in the governorate because Qatar and the United States paid people to cause trouble. After a while his cell phone rang. He smiled at me and put the call on speaker.

"Governor of Minya?" a man's voice said. "Look, *Basha,* I work in the quarries. Are temporary workers being promoted to full-time now?"

The governor said that he had heard that some quarry workers were receiving full-time jobs. He asked for the man's name.

"Mahmoud Abdel Dayum."

"By this year, you'll be promoted, just ask God for it, and pray," the governor said. "Are you a Muslim or a Christian?"

"Muslim."

"Of course!" the governor said. "Would a Mahmoud be a Christian?"

Everybody in the room laughed.

"God bless you, Mahmoud!" the governor said. "If you ever need anything, come to me."

He hung up and turned to me. "You see how the governor talks to his people?"

His assistant spoke up: "Mr. Governor's number is with everybody."

We resumed the interview, and now the governor switched to English. He spoke the language well. He lit another Marlboro and mentioned that he had spent time in the States. "I went to New York and Chicago and Washington," he said. "Your American CIA, they know me very well."

I asked him why.

"Because I have traveled there, and I took courses."

"Where did you take courses?"

"The FBI," he said. "I was in the Marriott, in Washington, D.C. I was there for three weeks."

So this former officer and current conspiracy theorist had been another beneficiary of the U.S.-Egypt exchanges. I asked him if his country was now headed in the right direction.

"If the United States leaves us alone, we will go in the right direction," he said.

While we were talking, three more people called, and each time he put them on speakerphone. One caller wanted the address of a government building in south Cairo. Another caller wanted to talk about repaying a personal debt. "I know you're a thief, and you could steal a couple thousand more pounds while you're at it," the governor joked into the phone. "Come to the Friday prayers with me!"

He hung up and told me that all across the governorate they planned to build sixteen brand-new cities in the desert. Such fantasies had been reported in the press since the coup, as evidence that the Egyptian economy was on the verge of miracles. I asked the governor about the desert cities, but he abruptly changed the topic.

"Have you heard the joke?" he said. "About the ones who ruled Egypt?"

I said no, I hadn't heard the joke about the ones who ruled Egypt.

"They asked somebody to name the people who had ruled Egypt, and he said, 'Gamal Abdel Nasser, Anwar Sadat, Hosni Mubarak, and then . . .'" The governor paused for effect, taking a long draw on his Marlboro. "'And then, after Mubarak—a comedy break!'"

Leslie and the twins didn't fly back to Cairo until martial law was lifted. We had the usual discussions, and the usual rationalizations: once the checkpoints were gone, and the police seemed less likely to panic, then the children could come back.

After everybody returned, Leslie and I purchased a Honda sedan. There was something reassuring about the normalcy of this family routine: we took a cab to a big new Honda dealership in eastern Cairo, where we were greeted by a salesman in a dark suit with a firm handshake. His name was Mohammed Mahmoud. I added his contact information next to all the other Mohammed Mahmouds in my address list. During the test-drive, I rolled off the lot and cruised for a couple of miles on the Ring Road. When I came back, Mohammed Mahmoud was waiting in front of the dealership with a tight smile. He said their strict policy was that vehicles never left the lot before a purchase. He had been trying to yell at me to stop when I pulled away.

Leslie and I scheduled a meeting with an agent at the insurance company Allianz, but at the last minute he called to cancel, because he had just totaled his vehicle. Another agent stepped in. While handling our application, she mentioned that she herself no longer qualified for auto insurance from Allianz, because she had had multiple accidents every year for three consecutive years. She handed us a glossy brochure that read "Our own data shows that six out of every ten cars purchased in Egypt will either be crashed, damaged, or stolen."

I paid for the insurance. By now I was so nervous about the hour-long drive home that I asked Hassan to meet us in his car, and he guided me through rush-hour traffic, like a tugboat. I parked the Honda in a corner of our garden, behind one of the big spiderweb gates.

At this point, my Arabic was adequate for basic interviews, and I started traveling alone to Upper Egypt. On one of my first journeys, I stopped in the small city of Mallawi, which was located at a bend in the river in Minya governorate. Mallawi was a poor, remote place, but it had an unusually good museum, because it was situated across the river from the archaeological site of Amarna. In the fourteenth century BC, this place briefly served as the capital of Egypt under the pharaoh Akhenaten and his wife, Nefertiti.

During the period after the Rabaa massacre, when there was violence in many parts of Minya governorate, a mob overran and looted the Mallawi Museum. Everything portable had been stolen—the worst case of artifact looting since the revolution had begun.

I parked across the street from the museum, behind another vehicle. After I got out of my car, I realized that the other vehicle was a BMW sedan that had been set on fire. The windows were broken and the tires had been removed. This seemed like a bad sign, but I didn't see anywhere else to park.

Mallawi had a history of jihadi violence in the 1980s and 1990s: it was the hometown of the main assassin of President Sadat. But during the early phase of the Egyptian Arab Spring, Mallawi hadn't been a dangerous place, and the recent outbreak was something of a mystery. Near the museum, a pro-Morsi mob had burned down a Coptic church, and they set fire to a government building. A total of eight people were killed. On the day that I arrived, workers were repairing the government complex, but the ruined museum was still untouched. The front gate was broken and the door hung open.

Inside, the museum director, Ahmed Abdel Sabbour, sat at a desk with a smashed glass top that had been pieced together and covered with adhesive tape. He offered to give me a tour of the museum. By now, after all my visits to looted cemeteries, burned-out Brotherhood offices, and bullet-pocked scenes of massacres, this had become a subspecialty: the archaeology of political violence.

"This was where we had a statue of one of Akhenaten's daughters," the director said, when we entered the main exhibition hall. He pointed to the floor, where a rectangle was a slightly different color than the rest of the cement, like a Mubarak portrait palimpsest around an empty nail. Elsewhere on the floor, a pattern of scratches converged from all directions at the main entrance—ghost tracings of heavy objects that had been dragged out. "There was a sarcophagus there," the director said, pointing. Upstairs, some old-fashioned wooden display cases had been shattered into splinters, which still lay on the ground. "Ptolemaic coins were in that case," he said.

The museum originally had 1,089 artifacts, of which 1,043 had been stolen. The 46 objects that remained had been too heavy to be removed, although now they had been taken to a locked storage facility. In photographs of the emergency evacuation, the ancient coffins had been stacked like cordwood on the backs of trucks—probably they had sustained some damage during transport. The director escorted me into the museum bathroom in order to show how the metal doors had been ripped off toilet stalls. Even these modern artifacts had value, because looters could sell them for scrap.

The director had a notebook with a list of the missing pieces, and anything that had been recovered was marked in green. There were more green lines in the notebook than I would have expected. Later that year, in May 2014, I made a return trip, and the director reported that they had recovered 813 of the 1,043 lost artifacts.

He explained that a number of stolen pieces had been used as bargaining chips. Many people had been arrested after the violence, and sometimes a clan would negotiate for somebody's freedom by returning an artifact. This part of the process was slow, although the director was hopeful that they would eventually get almost everything back. Among the artifacts they had recovered thus far, about four dozen had been broken. The government planned to restore these objects and rebuild the museum.

On the day of the attack, the director had been taken to the hospital after getting struck on the head by a projectile. "It was either a rock or a bottle, I don't know," he said. He considered himself lucky; the museum's ticket seller was shot and killed. The ticket seller was in his mid-thirties, with two small children, and he had worked at the museum for fifteen years. Afterward, out of respect for the dead man, and in hopes of supporting his family, the government offered the ticket-selling job to his widow. But she requested and received a job in a different government bureau instead. There was too much history here; the widow couldn't bear to work in the same museum where her husband had been killed.

After meeting the director, I went back across the street to the burned-out BMW. It was parked in front of a *m'arad,* a kind of tented market that's common in Egypt. While I was studying the car, half a dozen clothes dealers and security guards came out of the *m'arad.* One of them explained that the BMW belonged to the son of the market's owner, and it had been set afire by Molotov cocktails. Most protesters had been peaceful, he said, but there were a small number of troublemakers. I asked who these people had been.

"They came from other villages."

"Which villages?"

"Nobody knows. Places far from here. They weren't from Mallawi."

"Why did they attack here?"

"Because they were paid to do it."

Others chimed in: the Qataris and the Americans were responsible, because they paid poor Egyptians to protest and riot.

In other parts of Upper Egypt, when I visited sites of violence, I often heard similar explanations. The narrative was like another artifact left behind in the wreckage: *Outsiders did this. Foreign agents paid them to do it. It wasn't locals; it couldn't be locals; why would locals do such a thing?*

The crowd around me swelled to more than twenty people. A police station was located a block away, and I wondered if somebody would report that a strange foreigner was in town, asking about the recent attacks. But the men were talkative and friendly, like most Egyptians, and they shot out questions: Do you own that car? How long did it take to drive here? Are you Muslim or Christian? At one point, a man in the back of the group said, "There's a Chinese man in the *m'arad*!"

He didn't know that I had any past connection to China. He simply thought that because I was a foreigner, and because we were talking about foreign agents, naturally I would be interested in the Chinese man in the *m'arad.* I asked what the Chinese was doing in Mallawi.

"He works here!"

"Can you take me to him?"

A dozen men led me inside the *m'arad.* Most of the stalls were stocked with cheap clothes, and everything was shaded by a heavy cloth roof propped on metal poles. This kind of tented shelter was adequate in a place where it never rained. At the end of a mazelike corridor, the men stepped aside.

They had stopped at a clothing stall whose brightly colored goods were displayed atop a table and on a big metal rack. There were silky nightgowns, and lace panties, and red brassieres; along the rack somebody had stretched out leopard-print thongs and hot-pink G-strings. Surrounded by all this finery, and sitting alone in the stall, was a very small Chinese man.

"*Ni hao,*" I said. "*Ni shi shenme difang laide?*"

His name was Ye Da, and he had come from Qingtian. The small city is located in southeastern China's Zhejiang province, not far from the city of Wenzhou, and I had been there many times when I lived in the country. Qingtian residents were famous for going overseas, especially to Europe, where they opened restaurants, shops, hairdressing salons, small factories—anything entrepreneurial.

Ye Da ran the stall with his wife, who was currently taking a break in their rented apartment. He said that he had relatives in other parts of Egypt, including a cousin in Minya, the next city upstream. I asked what the cousin was doing in Minya.

"He's selling the same stuff," Ye Da said. "Women's underwear."

"How did he get started?"

"There was somebody else from Qingtian selling it in Cairo."

He said that there was a chain of Chinese lingerie dealers in the upstream cities: Asyut, Sohag, Nagaa Hammadi, Aswan. I asked if I might be able to track down these other dealers, and he shrugged. "Go see my cousin," he said. "When you get to Minya, just tell a taxi driver to take you to the *ma la*."

The word was his approximation of *m'arad*. He spoke little Arabic, and he had moved to Mallawi shortly after the attacks. He had heard that some people died, but otherwise he knew little about the violence that happened across the street from his stall.

We talked for most of an hour, and I promised to come back. The Egyptians from the *m'arad* gathered around as I entered my car. They were pleased that

I had met Mr. Ye, and they gave me directions for crossing the river. The next time I visited Mallawi, I stayed longer, and the third time I spent the night.

Given the recent violence, and all the rumors about foreign agents, it seemed reasonable to assume that people in Mallawi would be suspicious. It also seemed reasonable to become suspicious of an American who showed up alone in a brand-new car, asked questions in Arabic about Islamist mobs, and then, after meeting a merchant from Qingtian, began speaking Chinese. But there was no indication that anybody reacted in this manner. The people in Mallawi always greeted me warmly, and the police never bothered to talk to me.

Egyptian conspiracy theories seemed to function best if enemies remained at a distance. It was similar to the *djinn* and the *'afrit:* the conspiracy theories were expressions of helplessness, and they also allowed for denial of responsibility. *It wasn't locals; it couldn't be locals; why would locals do such a thing?* Even the foreigner was transformed once he appeared in a familiar setting. Egyptians are naturally open and friendly, and people in Mallawi probably sensed that it would be unpleasant if they applied the conspiracy theory to the real-life individual who stood in front of them, speaking their language. *He wasn't an agent; he couldn't be an agent; why would an agent do such a thing?* On every visit, I parked behind the burned-out BMW, and the men happily escorted me back to Mr. Ye and his wife. Nobody was the least bit wary of the Chinese. If anything, the people at the *m'arad* seemed protective of this strange little couple who had appeared at their bend in the river.

The last thing that any driver sees when departing Mallawi is the dead. After my initial meeting with Ye Da, I took the bridge to the eastern bank of the Nile, where an elevated highway crossed a series of fields. I passed a small road, heading south, that led to the archaeological site of Amarna. To the north, a large modern cemetery had been built against the dry slope of the Nile gorge. Hundreds of domed roofs rose above small grave buildings. In the low afternoon light the domes were beautiful—a silent city of rounded shadows.

I followed the highway through a canyon, climbing steeply, and then the landscape opened onto the expanse of the North African plateau. After a dozen empty miles I reached a tollbooth. The police waved me on to the Cairo-Asyut Desert Highway.

I drove north. The desert here was absolute—too dry for even thorns and scrub grass. The road had three lanes in each direction, but there was so little traffic that nobody had bothered to erect billboards. A gas station materialized every hundred miles or so; shops and restaurants were even rarer. At various spots in the wasteland, the government had erected a series of metal propaganda signs that stood at intervals beside the road. The Arabic messages flashed by at seventy-five miles per hour:

EGYPT THE PATRIOTIC
EGYPT THE HISTORICAL
EGYPT THE FUTURE
EGYPT ALWAYS

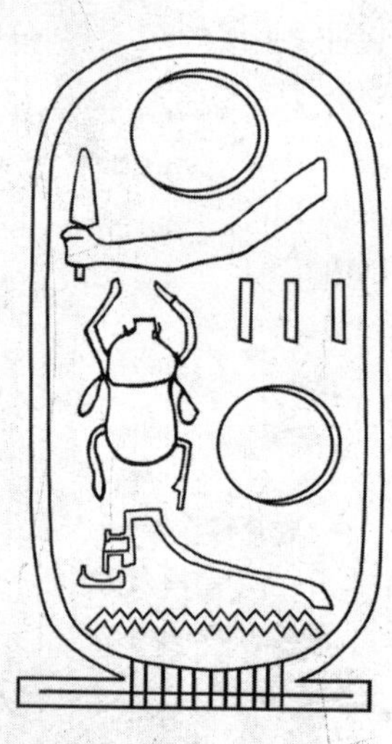

Part Three

THE PRESIDENT

The words that men say are one thing;
what the god does is another.

—The scribe Amenemope,
c. 1300–1075 BC

CHAPTER 15

THE HARDEST PART OF ANY JOURNEY TO UPPER EGYPT WAS GETTING OUT of Cairo. From Zamalek, I would drive to the bottom of the island, cross the Qasr al-Nil Bridge, and head south along the Nile. I passed Tahrir, and I passed Garden City, the old district of the British colonialists, and then I passed Fustat, where, more than a thousand years ago, Arab invaders founded the capital that eventually grew to become Cairo. The distance was only three and a half miles; on a bad day it took an hour.

Whenever the traffic bogged down, I read the cars around me. Egyptians liked to post statements in white decal letters on their rear windows, and usually they were the standards: *masha'allah,* "this is what God has willed"; *la ilaha ill'allah,* "there is no God but God." But sometimes a message had been designed for those godless moments when nothing moved. *Mafeesh Faida.* "There's No Use." *Ana T'aben.* "I'm Tired." The most memorable were often in English: "Real Women Hunt." "Love Story Jesus." "If Your Life Is a Minute, Live It as a Man." A Kia Cerato: "Try but Don't Cry." A Jumbo-brand bus: "That's What Friendship Leads to, a Court Case." A Nissan Sunny: "Police Is My Job, Crime Is My Game."

In the southern part of the city, I passed the high walls of the Tora Prison, home to Islamists, dissidents, and ex-parliamentarians, and from there it wasn't far to the Cairo-Asyut Desert Highway. At the tollbooth, I paid the equivalent of two dollars, the best money ever spent in Egypt. To the east rose low flat mountains of brown and red, their slopes barren. The highway skirted the lower flanks, and soon the hazy green of the river valley disappeared in the west. While driving, I studied Arabic by listening to recordings of Rifaat reading our vocabulary lists. His high-pitched voice, clear and adamant, reminded me of everything I'd left behind:

Please don't bother	بلاش تتعب نفسك
Don't ask me again	ماتسألنيش تاني
I don't need your services	مش محتاج خدماتك

High on the desert plateau, the road surface was excellent, and there were hardly any other cars. It never rained; the light couldn't have been better. Thanks to government subsidies, gasoline was cheaper than bottled water. On some sections of road I drove for fifty miles without seeing any vegetation.

Turnoffs were rare as trees. Some exits led to provincial capitals like Minya or Sohag, where I met with government officials, while other side roads took me to archaeological sites. A number of turnoffs deposited me in places where Chinese lingerie dealers had set up shop. The stories behind each exit might be different, but the geography was always the same. After a westward turn, a connecting road descended for ten or so miles, and then the green of the valley materialized like a mirage in the windshield. The exits were ports; the highway was the river. For the modern traveler, this was the country's new axis.

to flee	يهرب من
escaping	هروب
crisis	أزمة
feeling of loneliness	الإحساس بالوحدة

At seventy-five miles per hour, with vocabulary on the speakers and air-conditioning in the car, it was hard to imagine the desert journeys of old. In 1868, an Englishman named Edward Henry Palmer wrote in his diary, "Monday—Walked six hours; saw two beetles and a crow." Annie Quibell, 1925: "It is not the heat, not the glare, nor the sand storms, nor even the solitude, that become oppressive after a time; it is the utter deadness and the howling of the wind." For past travelers, the landscape was brutal, but they often found that desert solitude clarified the mind. "There is something grand and sublime in the silence and loneliness of these burning plains," Robert Curzon wrote, in 1833. A century later, Robin Fedden compared the view to "the cleanliness of a country under snow." He wrote, "You have the impression of looking upon places so stark and fresh that they can never have been seen before. By seeing them you create them; they owe their existence to you." Arthur Weigall, who excavated at Abydos and other sites in the early twentieth century, wrote, "The desert is the breathing-space of the world, and therefore one truly breathes and lives."

Such reactions were by no means limited to foreigners. In the late third century, after Christianity had swept across Egypt, there were two famous instances in which a wealthy young Egyptian left his comfortable Nile valley home for a life of prayer, reflection, and loneliness in the desert. According to tradition, Paul became the first Christian hermit, and Anthony the first monk. In this narrow river valley, neither man had to travel far to reach a site of desolation. And their relative accessibility allowed for occasional visitors, who informed the rest of Christendom about these holy men. The Egyptian desert—that breathing space of the world—inspired the Christian tradition of monasticism.

Around the year 1346 BC, in Upper Egypt, the pharaoh Akhenaten founded a new capital on a previously uninhabited shelf of desert above the river's eastern bank. Major cities had always been situated in the river valley, and even when kings built mortuary temples and monuments, they favored desert sites that were already sanctified by graves of the ancients. But the young king wanted a landscape uncontaminated by history or ritual. On the site, he erected a stele: "Behold, it is a pharaoh (life! prosperity! health!) who found it, when it did not belong to any god, nor to a goddess, when it did not belong to any male ruler, nor any female ruler, when it did not belong to any people to do their business with it."

By that time, the Egyptian faith had changed remarkably little for nearly a millennium, despite the lack of a central religious text—no Quran, no Bible, no Tanakh. "It says much about the unchanging rhythm of life in the Nile Valley," writes the Egyptologist Toby Wilkinson, "dictated by the annual regime of the river itself, that the resulting belief system remained so stable for so long." In a landscape of such simplicity and continuity, core beliefs didn't have to be written down. The Nile was the book.

But Akhenaten wanted a home in the desert, and he wanted a key text.

His long poem, now known as the Hymn to the Aten, celebrated the form of the god Re called the Aten, the disk of the sun. In all respects these words were revolutionary. They were written in a more colloquial form of the language than traditional Egyptian texts, and they celebrated the natural world:

The entire land performs its work;
all the flocks are content with their fodder,
trees and plants grow,
birds fly up to their nests.

The Hymn to the Aten has some parallels in imagery and concept to Psalm 104, and a number of scholars have theorized that the Israelite psalmists might have been influenced by Akhenaten's poem. Most strikingly, the hymn emphasized the Aten alone. For the first time in recorded history, an individual took a step toward monotheism:

Sole god, without another beside you;
you create the earth as you wish.

The king called his new home Akhetaten—"the Horizon of the Aten"—and within a few years it became home to an estimated thirty thousand people. Roads, palaces, temples, and government buildings were constructed at an astonishing pace. The scale was massive; one place of worship, the Great Aten Temple, was half a mile long. So many workshops produced crafts for the royal family that it resembled a factory town. "It is an overwhelming site to deal with," wrote William Flinders Petrie, who in the 1890s excavated at the place that archaeologists came to call Amarna. "Imagine setting about exploring the ruins of Brighton, for that is about the size of the town."

Akhenaten's great hymn, and the other texts he wrote to describe the site's boundaries, failed to mention one key detail: there was no potable water. Crops couldn't grow here. Traditional supply chains had never served this place. As the Egyptologist Barry Kemp writes, "The danger of being an absolute ruler is that no one dares tell you that what you have just decreed is not a good idea."

During one of my drives to Amarna, I pulled over at the site of the Great Aten Temple just after Barry Kemp had found a piece of a broken statue of Akhenaten. Kemp's crew was excavating the temple's front section, where he had spotted the fragment poking up through the sandy soil. The piece of statuary was a little less than a foot in length, but when he handed it to me, it felt heavier than I expected—granite. It featured the king's lower legs, and around the knee the figure had been struck with enough force to cause a sheer break. "This is not accidentally damaged," Kemp said.

Kemp was in his mid-seventies, and he had worked at Amarna since 1977. From the beginning, he had been drawn to the idea of a city in the desert. There's a long history of fascination with the figure of Akhenaten, and Egyptologists have traditionally focused on royals and other elites. But at the time of Kemp's student years at the University of Liverpool, the field of archaeology was changing, with a new emphasis on studying the tracings of everyday life. Amarna was the perfect site for such an endeavor. The city was occupied for twelve years at the most, and then, not long after the death of Akhenaten around 1336 BC, it was abandoned completely. Nobody came after the king for the same reason that nobody had preceded him: no water.

When Kemp started excavating at the site, he was a professor at Cambridge University. Like most archaeologists, he spent vacations and sabbaticals on digs. Eventually, he retired from academia in order to work more often in the field, where he was funded by private donors who contributed to the Amarna Project, which Kemp had established. Over the course of decades, he meticulously excavated sections of the city, hoping that small relics of everyday life would answer larger questions. How had the capital been laid out? How was it planned? What did the streets, homes, and public buildings say about ancient Egypt?

Kemp was tall and soft-spoken, with long gray hair that fell across his neck. He wore a full white beard that helped protect against the Amarna sun. He lived for much of the winter and spring in the no-frills dig house that was located on the southern edge of the site. He had spent more than three times as many years digging through the city as Akhenaten had spent building it.

Even after all that time, Kemp was surprised by some discovery almost every season. He had recently determined that the Great Aten Temple was completely demolished and rebuilt around the twelfth year of Akhenaten's reign. This was what had happened to the statue of the king with the broken legs—workmen must have smashed the figure and used the pieces as hardcore, or filler, in the new structure's foundation. Akhenaten frequently changed his mind about how he wanted to be portrayed, and apparently he had decided that this piece of statuary, like the entire temple, no longer matched his vision.

"This is beautifully finished," Kemp said, tracing the lines of the smashed statue. "It's an odd thing for them to have done, from our perspective. The statue is no longer needed, so they reduce it to hardcore." He turned the piece of stone over in his hands. "We have no commentary on what's going on."

Ancient Egyptians rarely explained themselves. They never identified why they built in the shape of the pyramid or what those monuments symbolized. We don't know how they moved two-ton blocks of stone to a height of more than four hundred feet. We can trace the architectural progression from the Shuna to the Step Pyramid to the Great Pyramid, but there's no contemporary source that describes this process. Even basic social traditions remain a mystery. Illustrations on tomb walls provide rich details about funerary practices, but we lack an equivalent source for weddings. In three thousand years of Egyptian history, there's no direct evidence that any marriage ceremony ever took place.

In ancient Greece and Rome, people left many contemporary commentaries about political and social events. "There's none of that in ancient Egypt," Kemp said. "You have to infer a great deal. And you infer with parallels in mind that you've picked up from more recent periods. It becomes difficult to tell how much support somebody like Akhenaten had. Was he totally unpopular? Or was he popular and the military removed all traces of that support?"

Without many sources, one inevitably excavates the imagination. In 1905, the Egyptologist James Henry Breasted described Akhenaten as "the first *individual* in human history," because the king stands out so brilliantly against the patterned past. Over the course of the twentieth century, the ancient king was portrayed variously as a proto-Christian, a peace-loving environmentalist, an out-and-proud homosexual, and a totalitarian dictator. His image was embraced with equal enthusiasm by both the Nazis and the Afrocentric movement. The Nazis connected the Aten to the Aryan tradition of sun worship, and they even convinced themselves that Akhenaten was partly of Aryan descent. In turn, black thinkers celebrated the king as "Blackhenaten," a symbol of African power and genius. Thomas Mann, Naguib Mahfouz, Frida Kahlo, and Philip Glass all incorporated Akhenaten into their creative work. Sigmund Freud was so excited by Amarna digs during the 1930s that he wrote, "If I were a millionaire, I would finance the continuation of these excavations." He once fainted during a heated argument with Carl Jung about whether Akhenaten had suffered from excessive love of his mother. (Freud's diagnosis: Akhenaten was oedipal, almost a thousand years before Oedipus.)

Dominic Montserrat, an Egyptologist whose Akhenaten book is subtitled *History, Fantasy, and Ancient Egypt,* noted that the king has become "a sign rather than a person." But there's enough evidence for a more grounded view of this figure. He was part of the Eighteenth Dynasty, which rose to power in conflict with the Hyksos, a group from the eastern Mediterranean that gained control of the Delta during the time now known as the Second Intermediate Period. In order to drive out the Hyksos and reconsolidate the empire, the forefathers of the Eighteenth Dynasty had to adopt key innovations from their enemy, including the horse-drawn chariot and the composite bow.

This struggle also motivated the Egyptians to professionalize their military. The Eighteenth Dynasty, which began in the mid-sixteenth century BC, became the first to maintain a standing army, and their empire grew until it extended all the way from current-day Sudan to Syria. Even as the empire expanded, the kings tightened their definition of family. They refused to allow their daughters to marry outside the clan, as a way of consolidating wealth and power. Kings often wedded their daughters, and brothers married sisters. Occasionally a royal branch ran straight for generations without a fork. Amenhotep I, the second ruler of the dynasty, married his sister, and between them they had two parents, two grandparents, and two great-grandparents: three successive generations of brother-sister marriages. Unsurprisingly, and probably for the greater good of Egypt, Amenhotep I and his sister-queen died without issue.

Despite such genetic pitfalls, the dynasty was brilliant at politics, and it produced many ambitious figures. One such striver was Thutmose IV, Akhenaten's grandfather. Thutmose IV wasn't in line for the throne, which he might have seized by having his brother killed. As with many key moments in Egyptian history, we lack outside commentary—all we have is Thutmose's own story about his rise. He claimed that while hunting on the Giza Plateau, he decided to nap in the shadow of the mostly buried Great Sphinx, which at that time was already more than a thousand years old. While the prince slept, the god Horemakhet visited him in a dream, declaring, "I shall give to you the kingship." The god instructed the prince to clear away the sand from the body of the statue. After this was done, and after the prince became king, he had the dream-story inscribed onto a stele and placed between the Sphinx's paws.

This shrewd political strategy—using the ancient past to justify acts of change, disruption, or even radicalism—was also applied by the king's descendants. His son Amenhotep III ruled during a period of unprecedented prosperity, and he built more monuments than any previous pharaoh. He sent officials to study Old Kingdom tombs and temples on the Giza Plateau, in order to incorporate ancient forms and traditions into new buildings and ceremonies. The Aten was one of these throwbacks; the sun disk had been more prominent centuries earlier. Amenhotep III began the process of elevating the god, and under his direction the style of court art began to change in ways that we would describe as more naturalistic.

Under Akhenaten, these changes became a full-blown movement—a revolution from the top. Other gods were first neglected, then attacked. After a few years at Amarna, Akhenaten sent teams of workers around the country, gouging out the image and the name of the god Amun in temples. Amun had been the state god of Thebes, in present-day Luxor, and Akhenaten's decision to move his capital might have been a way to break the power of the established priesthood.

The king constantly tinkered with the way he appeared in statues and portraits. His features were often strangely exaggerated: massive jaw, drooping lips, and elongated, otherworldly eyes. He was portrayed with his wife, Nefertiti, in unusually intimate and natural poses; one scene even features the king and queen about to get into bed together. In portraits they often kiss and caress their six daughters. Nefertiti was named co-regent, and she appeared in scenes that had previously been restricted to male kings: inspecting prisoners, smiting bound captives. The final lines of the Hymn to the Aten are devoted to her:

The Foremost wife of the King, whom he loves,
the Mistress of the Two Lands,
Nefer-nefru-Aten Nefertiti,
living and young, forever and ever.

Under Akhenaten and Nefertiti, the Egyptian faith was radically stripped down: fewer gods, fewer rituals. In the tombs that court officials commissioned for themselves on the cliff walls behind the city, there were no more references to Osiris, and no more depictions of the traditional afterworld. Akhenaten had temples constructed without roofs, to make sun worship more direct. Rituals must have been brutally hot. The king of Assyria wrote Akhenaten an angry letter: "Why should my messengers be made to stay constantly out in the sun and die in the sun?"

But for Akhenaten, the move to the desert was a return to a purer past. "He tried to be as ancient as possible," Christian Bayer, a German scholar, told me. "Of course he also wanted to do something totally new. He made a revolution out of something ancient."

By fashioning this revolution from the ancient, Akhenaten also intimated the future. He reminds us that the fundamentalist is never near the fundamentals—he's always at a distance, gazing back at the unattainable. Barry Kemp writes, "Akhenaten appears to represent an early example of a widespread trend in the history of piety, towards greater austerity in conceptions of the divine." It's similar to the modern Islamists, whose revolutions in Iran, Afghanistan, and Egypt always envisioned a return to some distant, purer past.

In building his new city, and in creating his new rituals, Akhenaten pioneered political techniques that are still effective today. Some slogans of modern political revolutionaries—"Make America Great Again"—echo the way that Akhenaten and other pharaohs manipulated nostalgia in order to justify change. Amarna tombs show the king reviewing military parades that foreshadow the October 6 rituals of Sadat and others. In these scenes, Akhenaten's bodyguards are prominent, their pose eternal: hunched over, eyes alert, weapons at the ready. Another innovation was the palace-balcony scene, in which the ruler looks down on admiring subjects, like Hitler above the Heldenplatz. In Akhenaten's new city, court officials erected garden shrines with pictures of the royal couple, the same way that Mubarak's portrait would someday hang on the walls of bureaucrats' offices. Kemp writes, "Akhenaten's kingship provides an unintended caricature of all modern leaders who indulge in the trappings of charismatic display."

We have no idea what average Egyptians thought while all of this was going on. Akhenaten died suddenly, in the seventeenth year of his reign. The city was still being constructed; the king's tomb was unfinished. The heirloom that he chose to be buried with was a thousand-year-old stone bowl inscribed with the name of the pharaoh who had built the Great Sphinx.

Akhenaten's revolution collapsed almost immediately. Two years after his death, the throne was occupied by his only son, Tutankhamun, who was no more than ten years old. Tutankhamun's mother was not Nefertiti, and clearly he was less committed to the new religious ideas. He issued a decree criticizing conditions under his father: "The land was in distress; the gods had abandoned this land." Soon, the Egyptians vacated their city in the desert.

Less than a decade into Tutankhamun's reign, he also died unexpectedly. He had been married to his half sister, and their only two children were both stillborn—finally, inbreeding put an end to the family's reign. After another king ruled for a brief period, Horemheb, the head of the army, named himself pharaoh—possibly the first military coup in history.

Horemheb declared a *wehem mesut,* but this renaissance was one of forgetting, not of remembrance. The king began to dismantle Amarna's royal buildings and temples, and his successors accelerated the destruction. They sent workmen to Amarna to destroy every statue of Akhenaten and Nefertiti that they could find. The king's coffin was smashed; royal names were obliterated from inscriptions. The rulers of the dynasty that succeeded Horemheb, the Nineteenth, referred to Akhenaten only obliquely, with phrases such as "the criminal" and "the rebel." They omitted the pharaoh and his successors from the famous king list in the Temple of Seti I at Abydos. This campaign of *damnatio memoriae* was so successful that Akhenaten disappeared from history for thirty-one centuries.

But by the time his name was rediscovered by foreign archaeologists, in the mid-nineteenth century, the world had caught up with the ideas of the rebel king. During an age of revolutionary movements, everybody wanted to claim Akhenaten. In particular, he appealed to groups that felt marginalized, and they applied the king's own strategy of seizing the past. If somebody wanted more acceptance for environmentalism, or gay rights, or Nazism, or racial equality, or some other issue, he could turn to the image of the iconoclast king as proof that such ideas were rooted in antiquity. Often the evidence was flimsy; largely on the basis of a few images that seemed to show Akhenaten holding hands with a male successor, many scholars speculated that he was gay or bisexual. (Nowadays, most Egyptologists believe that the other figure was in fact Nefertiti under another name.)

Part of the king's appeal was his survival: even the targeted campaigns of his successors weren't enough to destroy his memory. In some cases, acts of destruction actually turned out to be a form of preservation. Ramesses the Great dismantled more Amarna temples and palaces than anybody else, and he used the stone blocks that are now known as *talatat* for his own temples. Many Amarna *talatat* were beautifully inscribed, and Ramesses had them placed deep in the foundations of his structures as a way of burying the heretic king's work. But over the course of millennia, the temples of Ramesses the Great were themselves slowly dismantled, until only the foundations were left.

"It's a cycle of recycling," Raymond Johnson, an Egyptologist who directed the University of Chicago's research center in Luxor, told me. "The ultimate irony is that what Ramesses thought he was hiding away is now exposed. How could you hide it better than putting it in the foundation of a temple? But we know more about Akhenaten's temples than we do about Ramesses's. We inherit a puzzle, because we don't have any monuments of Akhenaten that are still standing. What we have are the pieces."

These pieces were scattered up and down the Nile, where the *talatat* were used in various construction projects. Then the modern age of archaeology and collecting sparked another round of diffusion. *Talatat* that had originally been adjacent in a temple wall might now be located in different collections on opposite sides of the world. After institutions digitized their holdings, Johnson spent hours online searching for matches. Once, when I visited him in his Luxor office, he had recently identified two blocks in museum collections in Copenhagen and New York City.

"They're four thousand miles apart, but I realized that they join," Johnson said. When the pieces were digitally placed next to each other, they revealed a surprising scene: Akhenaten was performing a ritual not with Nefertiti but with Kiya, another wife who might have been the mother of Tutankhamun.

Johnson had been trained as an artist, and he felt a deep connection with the Amarna style. He believed that Akhenaten must have been "wildly creative," despite his despotic tendencies. This is another reason that the period has always drawn attention: many artifacts, like the famous limestone bust of Nefertiti, are stunningly beautiful. Naturalistic scenes portray the changing emotions and appearances of the royal family; even Nefertiti—the name means "the Beautiful One Has Arrived"—is shown with wrinkles as she ages. In Johnson's analysis, this "sometimes painful truthfulness" was a way of transcending *djet* and *neheh* time. "This preoccupation with the present rather than the eternal is one of the hallmarks of Amarna art," he writes. "It is almost as if the two dimensions of Egyptian time—the eternity of the gods and the endlessly repeating present of nature and humanity—had converged."

While Akhenaten's faith was quickly rejected after his death, the art seems to have been irrepressible. The Amarna style influenced subsequent periods, including the court art of Ramesses the Great. And I noticed that scholars who focused on artistic representation, like Raymond Johnson, tended to have a softer view of Akhenaten than Barry Kemp, who dealt with the material traces of the city.

Marsha Hill, a curator at the Metropolitan Museum of Art, sometimes pieced together fragments of statues that had been destroyed during the anti-Akhenaten campaigns. She told me that handling the pieces made her feel positive about Akhenaten. "Everybody likes revolutionaries at some level," she said. "Someone who has a real good, strong idea that makes it seem like things are going to get better. I don't see him as destructive. Of course, it didn't work out. It usually doesn't. Steam builds up under the ground until it explodes, and then you have to put it all together again."

Early one morning at Amarna, Barry Kemp guided me to the spot where the famous bust of Nefertiti was discovered, in 1912, by a German archaeologist named Ludwig Borchardt. We started at the modern road that cuts across the site, and then we walked east. The ground was covered with pieces of pottery, most of them the pale, pretty color known as Amarna blue. Low brick walls appeared in rectangular arrangements, and it was easy to trace the shapes of former homes.

"The floor often isn't there," Kemp said, pointing to the ruins of a house. "It was a common practice to bury things under the floor, and the floors had been dug up all over the city." He believed that this had been the last act of many Amarna residents—all over town, they dug up their floors before abandoning the city.

We came to another rectangular wall. "This is a major house," Kemp said. "We don't know the name of the owner. It's one that the Germans excavated before the First World War. There's the house. It sat within a big enclosed wall."

We stepped over the remains of the wall—a low line in the windblown sand. Kemp continued to another cluster of ruins. "That's a mud-brick pylon. This nearer half is a garden with a little temple, or a shrine. It's a cult to the royal family, a sign of loyalty. And between the pylons and the temple there is a rectangular pit. It's a sunken garden that would have had water in it." At Amarna, people dug wells, but Kemp believed that the groundwater would have been saline, the way it is today—good only for plants and perhaps for washing. Drinking water would have been hauled in from the river, which was more than half a mile from where we walked. Other parts of the city were even farther from the Nile.

Nowadays, diesel-powered pumps and electric irrigation systems allow farmers to grow crops on the desert shelf, and people live all along the edges of Amarna. During the Egyptian Arab Spring, Amarna hadn't experienced intense looting, but farmers were making significant incursions onto the site. Kemp pointed out one illegal settlement where a shrewd farmer built a tiny mosque, knowing that the authorities would be reluctant to tear down a religious building. Mohammed Khallaf, the director of the office of antiquities in Minya governorate, told me that villagers around Amarna were legally limited to about three hundred acres of cultivated crops, but they had doubled that area through recent land grabs. He was powerless to do anything because the revolution had put so many other pressures on the police.

Villagers referred to the archaeological dig with the same term that people used in Abydos: *al-Madfuna,* the Buried. The sites are nearly two hundred miles apart, but in imaginative terms they make a natural pair. Amarna is on the eastern side of the river, while Abydos is on the west. Each has the feel of a natural theater, with cliffs rising behind a stagelike site. Every morning, the sun rises from behind the dry Amarna mountains, and every afternoon it sets beyond the barren cliff walls of Abydos. One site is a necropolis and the other is a city. Together they intimate other pairings: death and life, eternity and moment, monument and gesture. Abydos is forever—even now, more than five thousand years after the first king was interred, locals still bury their dead there. But the city of Amarna lived for only a fleeting instant. Norman de Garis Davies, a British archaeologist who worked here around the turn of the last century, described Amarna as "a chance bivouac in the march of history."

Kemp stopped in the sand. "This is where the head of Nefertiti was found," he said. Brick walls still rose waist high, and it was easy to see the layout of this complex, which is believed to have been the home studio of the sculptor who fashioned the bust. "This is the original entrance," Kemp said. "You'll find very shallow steps there. You turn in to a vestibule and there's a reception room."

He led me through the complex, pointing out details. And now the magnificent bust of Nefertiti vanished from my mind, replaced by more mundane artifacts: a doorway, a table, even a toilet. For the first time, I imagined real people living here, day after day, more than thirty-three centuries ago. "That's a piece of furniture," Kemp said, pointing. "It's a stone table. Those were stairs leading up to the upper story. This was the bathroom. Borchardt found an almost perfectly preserved bathroom here. It was a sandstone tray, with a little drain hole. When I came here it was already broken up. He left it here and villagers broke it up. In 1977, that had already happened. And the adjacent toilet had been destroyed before Borchardt's time."

The city of Amarna had one main avenue running parallel to the Nile. This Royal Road connected the various palaces and temples, and it was used by Akhenaten and Nefertiti during daily chariot processions. But other than that single road, the city's street layout follows no logic. There aren't any grids or quadrants, and districts weren't identified for specific industries.

"Amarna seems like the antithesis of city planning," Kemp writes, "a notable avoidance of what, to us, looks like a perfect opportunity to engineer a complete society." He describes it as an "urban village," and his excavations have shown that neighborhoods developed organically, with smaller houses often clustered around the residence and workshop of some key official or artisan. He writes, "This kind of plan—the fuzzy grid—tends to appear in the modern world, in informal settlements that develop in places where government control is weak."

One year, a professor in modern urban planning named Bill Erickson joined Kemp's archaeological team. At the University of Westminster in London, Erickson studies informal development around the world, and he noticed that Amarna followed the same patterns as modern slums or *ashwa'iyat*. "What you see in the modern slum is that they are not chaotic," he told me. "They are not stupid people. They're making rational decisions, but they're making them at the smallest scale. They have very immediate needs. They're not worried about whether you can run the sewer, or whether you can run a bus down the street, or whether you can get a police car in there. These are very localized decisions. They're thinking, 'I need to be next to my cousin or my aunt.'"

He believed that the mind-set was essentially the same at Amarna. There was the city of royal roads and palaces, and the city of average residents, and there was very little contact between them. "I don't think the city was designed to make people feel like citizens," Erickson said. "You are building this massive road where you can drive down in your chariot. It's exactly what Hitler tried to do in Berlin."

During one of our walks across the site, Kemp mentioned that the ancient Greeks built settlements differently. "The Greeks were very keen on geometric city plans and public buildings," he said. "The heart of the Greek city was the agora, the place where politics was discussed and trade was done. When you look at Amarna, it's hard to identify anything similar. There's no built marketplace. And there's the perfect opportunity to have one, in the central city, between the Great Aten Temple and the Small Aten Temple. It creates a natural frame for it. But it's not used as a political center, or as a place for any civic building. It's not a meeting point."

I asked what larger message was conveyed by the layout of Greek cities.

"Being a citizen was important," he said. "Engaging in city life was important."

"Why do you think it was so different in Egypt?"

He said that Egypt wasn't unusual: informal city planning was the trend across the ancient world, and it remains dominant in many places today. "You're faced with the question, why was Greek culture so different?" Kemp said. "It's different in ways that we are the heirs to. Where did it come from? They came to develop political philosophy. They thought about what the ideal society should be like. They wrote about it in an abstract way. They were able to detach themselves from how life was lived and imagine other possibilities. It's not something that the Egyptians and other ancient peoples developed. You can't find Egyptian sources that are the equivalent of Herodotus and Thucydides. With Thucydides, you can read it now and almost shiver at the coldness of the analysis. He's writing about what motivates men to go to war, and he's writing for the benefit of posterity. He realized the importance of the Peloponnesian War—he realized that men would always go to war. It's an incredible vision, even though he fought within this world. It's a different plane of thinking."

The painted bust of Nefertiti was removed from Egypt under an old system in which, at the end of each excavation season, foreign-funded archaeologists divided their finds with the Egyptian government. In 1924, the bust was displayed to the public for the first time, in Berlin's Neues Museum. It was an immediate sensation. And the feeling of Egyptian regret spread as quickly as the artifact's fame. Government officials requested the return of Nefertiti, as they have done periodically for nearly a century. Nowadays, any artifact excavated in Egypt remains in the country.

The Neues Museum also displayed a limestone bust of Akhenaten that had been discovered in the same sculptor's studio at Amarna. The Akhenaten bust had been shattered during the ancient campaign against the king's memory, but the Germans were able to piece it together, although most of the face remains permanently disfigured. Nobody knows why the Nefertiti bust survived in such pristine condition.

Legally speaking, the Egyptians have no case for demanding the artifact's return. The agreement was made according to national laws of the time, and all paperwork was handled properly. But the moral issue is murkier. The Egyptian government official who agreed to Nefertiti's removal was a Frenchman—in those days, much of the country's real authority lay with foreigners. It's understandable that many Egyptians see the queen's bust as a symbol of all the heritage and culture that were lost under colonialism.

In 1939, after World War II began, most artifacts in the Neues Museum were evacuated. First they went to bank safes, then to bunkers. As the war intensified, artifacts were moved farther from the Nazi capital. The busts of Akhenaten and Nefertiti were separated: the king traveled to eastern Germany, while the queen descended deep into a salt mine in the west. The Neues Museum was damaged repeatedly by Allied bombing raids. In 1943, frescoes along its central stairway were burned; in 1945, an entire wing of the museum was destroyed. Artifacts that had been too large to move were packed in sandbags, which in some cases proved to be inadequate. One beautifully inscribed Amarna stone doorway was never found—it must have been obliterated. In German, there's a word for such a thing: *Kriegsverlust*—"war loss."

After the war, the Egyptian royal couple was separated by the Iron Curtain. Nefertiti remained in West Germany, while Akhenaten was in Soviet hands. During the late 1950s, the piece was returned to East Germany, but the Neues Museum remained a bombed-out ruin for more than four decades. The building was finally repaired after the reunification of Germany, and the restoration deliberately left signs of damage throughout the complex.

Limestone columns at the entrance are charred and pockmarked with bullet holes. Inside the exhibition halls, many frescoes are broken, stained, or completely ruined by fire.

"The building itself is an archaeological object," Dr. Friederike Seyfried, the director of the museum, said as she gave me a tour. On the second floor, we stopped at the bust of Akhenaten. Seyfried explained that the object had been damaged in stages. It originally contained some metal ornaments, which she believed had been pried off whenever the sculptor's studio was abandoned. Later, during the ancient campaign of *damnatio memoriae,* workmen or soldiers returned to the sculptor's studio and deliberately smashed the king's bust. More than three thousand years after that, when the object was transported around wartime Germany, the lips and mouth fell off and disappeared—another small *Kriegsverlust.* Now the bust has replacement lips, and it sits inside a small cupola whose lower frescoes are also ruined.

"The damage of the building is telling a very similar story to the damage that occurred to some of the objects," Seyfried said. "We can't hide it. It's part of our history. People get a very good idea here that history is continuing and that it changes objects. They realize that damage can occur all over the world at any time." She went on, "This hall was ruined, and there were ruined buildings all over Berlin. And you know what happens after a war—looting was going on. It's the same as what would have happened at Amarna after the city was abandoned. History repeats."

The painted bust of Nefertiti sits in a large cupola with a skylight high in the ceiling. The queen is solitary; no other artifact shares this space. Above one entrance to the cupola is a faded inscription:

PROMETHEUS CREATED ART FOR THE MORTALS

The floor here was once a mosaic of yellow, red, and white, although most original pieces are gone. On all sides the walls are stained. The colors are rich and mysterious: a soft red, a deep, uneven green. Around the ceiling and the walls, at carefully calibrated angles, twenty-two high-tech spotlights point at the queen. Beautiful nose, perfect lips. The chin is delicate. Tiny wrinkles have been carved near the eyes. The long, graceful neck is marked by subtle lines of ligaments, their shadows cast softly under the lights.

Photographs are forbidden inside the cupola. For visitors, regardless of whether they are German or foreign, male or female, young or old, their behavior is so similar that it resembles a ritual. Invariably people fall silent at first sight of the artifact. Some approach the glass pillar that surrounds the bust, but most maintain a respectful distance of seven or eight feet. They stand perfectly still, facing the queen. Her expression conveys the hint of a smile, but almost everybody who meets her gaze is serious. They do not talk and they do not move. When a dozen stand together they could be a congregation at worship.

CHAPTER 16

DURING THE PERIOD IMMEDIATELY AFTER THE COUP, SISI SAID NOTHING about seeking the presidency. Most people I knew in Cairo believed he wouldn't run. Sisi was too smart, they said; he would have more power, and less accountability, if he stayed behind the scenes.

The general's first remarks about the presidency were issued unintentionally. In December 2013, almost half a year after the coup, somebody posted an audio recording that featured Sisi speaking with an Egyptian journalist named Yasser Rizk. Rizk specialized in military topics, and he was trusted by the regime. During their conversation the topic of dreams came up.

"I'm one of the people who have a long history of visions," Sisi said. "I have seen a lot of things that then happened."

Rizk asked for an example.

"This will not be repeated," Sisi said.

"It's not going to be mentioned in the interview," Rizk said. "I will use it when God wills it."

And then Sisi told a story. Many years ago, he dreamed that he was holding a sword inscribed with the Quranic phrase "There is no God but God." In another dream, he wore an Omega watch with a green star. The watch and the star, and the sword and the words, must have had symbolic significance, but Sisi didn't elaborate. He continued, "In the third dream, I was told, 'We will give you what we gave no one before.'"

Sisi repeated the phrase: *We will give you what we gave no one before.* "And then in another dream I was sitting with Sadat, talking with him," he said. "He told me, 'I knew that I was going to become the president of the republic.' And I said, 'I know that I'm going to become the president of the republic.'"

The recording had apparently been leaked without Rizk's knowledge. It was one of a series of audios and videos that featured Sisi and other military figures discussing key issues. The recordings became known as Sisileaks, and while Sisi's prime minister, Ibrahim Mahlab, denied the tapes' credibility, most analysts believed them to be authentic. Nobody knew how they had been made.

Many of the leaks were first revealed by an Islamist television channel in Turkey, and they were clearly intended to undermine Sisi. But the conversation about visions had the opposite effect. Now people spoke more openly about the general's becoming president, and they didn't seem bothered by his mystical streak. After all, it wasn't the first time in Egyptian history that a leader with questionable legitimacy had been endorsed by a dream.

Exactly four months and a day after Morsi vanished from public view, he was scheduled to reappear at the Cairo Police Academy, in a lecture hall that had been converted into a courtroom. I made sure to get there early. Any journalist or lawyer who hoped to observe the trial of the former president had to carry a stamped statement of approval from the Cairo Court of Appeals, and then he or she had to pass through four armed checkpoints and three metal detectors. Nobody was allowed to carry a camera, a voice recorder, or a cell phone. Journalists could not be accompanied by translators. Each attendee also had to hike for more than half a mile up a steep hill to the police academy, where roads had been closed to traffic. I started the walk behind a group of lawyers. They were heavyset men in black robes, and they trudged slowly with their heads down, like a line of crows too fat to fly.

The last robed lawyer was very overweight and breathing hard. I introduced myself, and he said his name was Said Hamid, and he was on Morsi's defense team. Morsi had been charged with a number of crimes, including murder, and today's case involved the fights that had occurred around the Presidential Palace, in December 2012. Hamid said the charges were trumped up. I asked if he had met with his client.

"No," he said. "We haven't been able to consult with him."

"Have you seen him at all?"

"The last time I saw him was on television," he said. "Before the coup." He made a point of using that word—*inqalab*—which had become taboo in most circles.

The Cairo Police Academy was located in the far eastern suburbs, near the top of a long incline that rose from the Nile valley into the desert. Beyond these neighborhoods, there was nothing but sand and rubble for seventy-five miles until the Suez Canal. Any political trial ran the risk of a terrorist attack, and the police academy had been chosen for its remoteness.

Beginning in the summer of 2011, Mubarak had been tried for crimes that ranged from corruption to inciting violence, and a police academy lecture hall had been converted to serve as a courtroom for his trial. Mubarak was sentenced to life in prison, but his lawyers appealed, and the case was ongoing. There were signs that eventually the authorities would release him, and it was rare to hear much public anger directed toward Mubarak anymore. But for now he remained in custody, and the two former presidents would be tried, at alternating times, in the same building on the edge of the desert.

Hamid stopped to rest. We were passing the police academy's high concrete wall, which was topped with metal spikes and razor wire. I asked if he was a member of the Brotherhood.

"Not at all," he said. "Actually, I'm a Nasserite."

I expressed surprise, and he smiled. "People don't always understand what that means," he said. "People now say that Sisi is like Gamal Abdel Nasser. That's a lie; Sisi is nothing like Nasser. Look at everything Nasser did: he built the Aswan Dam, he took control of the Suez Canal, he built factories. What has Sisi done? The only thing he's done is kill Egyptians."

I asked Hamid if he was religious.

"Not very," he said. "Some days I pray, and some days I don't." He said that he supported Morsi out of principle, because the president had been removed by illegal means.

At the entrance, lawyers and journalists had separate checkpoints, so Hamid and I shook hands and parted. I waited in line near a high brick wall covered with spray-painted slogans. The words had a timeless quality, like so much Cairo political graffiti; after all the cycles of revolution, no opinion seemed either totally current or totally obsolete. When had these slogans been painted? Maybe last year, maybe this morning, maybe a year from now:

MUBARAK WILL RETURN
MUBARAK IS INNOCENT
I LOVE YOU, MUBARAK!

The trial was scheduled for nine o'clock, but Morsi appeared an hour and a half late. *Can we push the appointment back a little?* Reportedly, the delay involved clothing—out of pride, the former president refused the traditional white clothes of an Egyptian prisoner. At last the court officials allowed him to wear a black suit without a tie.

The moment he appeared, the room erupted. A group of Morsi's lawyers stood up and shouted a soccer-style chant that had been common during the days of his campaign: "*Morsi-i-i-i-i-i-i! Morsi, Morsi! Morsi-i-i-i-i-i-i! Morsi, Morsi!*" Egyptian journalists also leaped to their feet, drowning out the lawyers with their own chant: "*E'adem, e'adem!* Death penalty, death penalty!"

I was sitting near the front of the room, and with everybody jumping around me, I stood on the seat of my chair in order to see the former president. Morsi was still bearded, and he didn't appear to have lost any weight. He held his head high, the way he had during his final televised appearance last July. After the noise died down, he shouted, "I am the president of the republic! I am the president of the republic! This is a military coup!" There was another outburst, and finally security men demanded that everybody in the room sit down.

The lecture hall appeared to have been converted with minimal effort. It was a long, spacious room with a wooden floor that descended steeply to a low platform. The place felt like a turned-around theater—here, the audience was elevated. All of us sat on rough chairs with attached writing surfaces, like students in a decrepit college. We looked down on the judge and the other court officials, who were seated at a long desk. Behind them a wood-paneled wall rose more than twenty feet high. This space was blank: no sign, no inscription, no national seal. There wasn't an Egyptian flag in the room. The only words consisted of a small engraving on the judge's desk: "Justice Is the Foundation of Governing."

It seemed remarkable that this building, which was hosting the most important Egyptian trials since the cases of Sadat's assassins, included no symbols of the state. But perhaps such abstractions were unnecessary when the functional tools of authority were so obvious. On the left side of the chamber, a pair of heavy black metal cages had been installed to hold defendants. One cage contained Morsi; the other was occupied by some Brotherhood leaders who were also being tried today. Dozens of security officers stood throughout the courtroom. At the back, young police conscripts rested their heads on the desks and went to sleep. They seemed capable of dozing through any amount of noise.

For more than half an hour, the chanting and shouting continued. There were few foreign journalists; a number of organizations had been denied accreditations. Family members of the accused had also been prevented from attending. Among the Egyptian journalists who had come, there was little pretense of neutrality; most of them stood and shouted, "Death penalty!"

The judge, a middle-aged man named Ahmed Sabry Youssef, repeatedly called for order. He didn't have a gavel; he banged on the desk with the flat of his hand, like a substitute teacher on a bad day. At last he declared a recess, and Morsi and the others were escorted out of the cages and into a side room. In the audience, a fight broke out between a female journalist and a man from Morsi's legal team. The woman was young and she wore a brightly colored *hijab;* she took off her shoe and brandished it at the lawyer, which was an insult in Egypt. The lawyer grabbed his own shoe and did the same thing. The two of them faced off, shoes in their hands, and other people joined the fray, shoving and slapping at each other. Finally police charged in and broke it up.

During the recess, two Egyptian journalists next to me talked about the last time they'd seen a former president in a cage.

"I was here when Mubarak appeared in court," one of the journalists said. "He didn't behave like this."

"Mubarak was polite," his colleague said.

"There wasn't all of this shouting, not from the president," the journalist said, disapprovingly. He wrote for *Al-Watan* and *Al-Masry al-Youm,* two private papers. I asked if he believed that Sisi would run for president. "I hope he runs," he said. "We need Sisi at this time."

Behind me, a young Chinese journalist sat rubbing his leg. Somebody had slammed him into a bench during one of the scuffles. He worked for China Radio International, a state service. We talked in Chinese, and he said he couldn't believe the scene. "This is totally chaotic," he said. "How can you tell who's who? In China, they'd have a sign for the prosecutor, for the defendant, for the lawyers." There had been no effort to separate the various groups, which was one reason why they kept fighting.

A little past noon, the proceedings finally resumed, but it wasn't long before Morsi interrupted. "I want a microphone!" he shouted. "I want a microphone so that I can say something to you! This is not a court, with all due respect to the members, this is not a court that can try the president of the republic! To try a president, this is a military coup! I am a representative of the state!" The chamber erupted once more; the judge slapped his hand uselessly on the desk. The Chinese journalist leaned over and said, "In China, something like this would never be public. It would be a secret trial."

The next day, I contacted Said Hamid, the lawyer on Morsi's team, and he said that the authorities had told them that from now on they would be able to meet with their client. Morsi was being held at the Borg al-Arab Prison, near Alexandria. It was the first time since the coup that the former president's whereabouts were made public.

Hamid said that during one of the breaks in the chaotic day at court the lawyers had finally been allowed to talk with their client. I asked how Morsi seemed, and Hamid said sheepishly that he had missed the brief meeting. After all these months, and after all the security hassles, the authorities had finally granted the meeting at the precise moment that Hamid was not in the chamber. He had just stepped outside to get a sandwich.

In January 2014, less than a week before Egypt was scheduled to hold a referendum for a new constitution, Sisi gave the first clear signal that he might run for president. "If I run, then it must be at the request of the people and with a mandate from my army," he said. He asked citizens to turn out and vote in favor of the constitution. "Don't embarrass me in front of the world," he said.

Since the coup, the new constitution had been prepared rapidly by a team of law professors and others. The preamble began with a simple sentence—"Egypt is the gift of the Nile for Egyptians and the gift of Egyptians to humanity"—and then, in translation, it flowed for another thirteen hundred words. Religious and historical figures were mentioned in the following order: Allah, Moses, the Virgin Mary, Jesus, the Prophet Muhammad, Muhammad Ali Pasha, Refaa the Azharian, Ahmed Orabi, Mostafa Kamel, Mohammad Farid, Saad Zaghloul, Mostafa al-Nahhas, Talaat Harb, Gamal Abdel Nasser, and Anwar Sadat. The Eloquent Peasant made an appearance. The Nile inundated three of the first six sentences. This wasn't just a preamble to the constitution; it was a preamble to civilization itself:

> *In the outset of history, the dawn of human consciousness arose and shone forth in the hearts of our great ancestors, whose goodwill banded together to found the first central State that regulated and organized the life of Egyptians on the banks of the Nile.*

The Morsi-era constitution had already been declared void, but in fact there were many similarities between the two documents. Under Morsi, the preamble also referred to "the timeless Nile," and it ran on for almost nine hundred words. It referred indirectly to Akhenaten, noting that the constitution was the product of the same civilization "that opened the way to monotheism and the knowledge of the Creator." Such statements now had the ring of hubris—so much history in a document that died in six months. The world's oldest functioning democratic constitution, that of the United States, has a fifty-two-word preamble that doesn't include a single mention of the past.

But Egyptian constitutions had a way of coming and going. Over the past century, there had been nine or ten of them, depending on how one counted. Since the start of the revolution, the country had held three constitutional referendums. With every document, the preamble got longer, and references to the past became more prominent. The newest one was explicit about the utility of history:

> *We believe that we are capable of using the past as an inspiration, stirring up the present, and making our way to the future.*

One historical reference, though, had been carefully excised. Unlike Morsi's constitution, the new version never mentioned the words "Tahrir Square." Now the political movement was described as "the January 25–June 30 Revolution," which connected the first protests of the Arab Spring with the protests against Morsi's regime.

In terms of the actual articles, there seemed to be some improvements in the postcoup constitution, including stronger references to women's rights. But the document still protected the military from civilian oversight, and it allowed for plenty of ways for the government to crack down on dissent. One sentence from Morsi's preamble was now conspicuously absent:

> *Our Armed Forces form a patriotic, professional and neutral national institution that does not interfere in political affairs.*

I never met anybody who voted against the constitution. Sayyid voted yes, as did Rifaat; both of them told me that it was necessary for the country to move forward. Manu, like others I knew who disapproved of the new regime, simply didn't go to the polls. Nationwide, more than 98 percent of the voters who did show up endorsed the new constitution. There was no sign of fraud, which had been true of every Egyptian election and referendum since the dawn of the Arab Spring.

By now, the repetition of these democratic rituals only made them more meaningless. Of the eight candidates who had been most prominent at the start of the first free presidential election, in the spring of 2012, three were now in prison, one was in exile, and another was dead. More than seven hundred people had been voted into parliament, and every one of them had been unseated. The only fairly elected president in history now made his public appearances inside a cage. Since the revolution started three years earlier,

Egypt had held seven national votes, all of them free from violence and fraud, but the country still did not have a single official at any level who had been democratically elected.

These days, Manu sometimes talked about going overseas. Such conversations were becoming more common among young people who had the means to travel. Elite Egyptian families often had a tradition of studying abroad, and dual passports weren't unusual among this class. As the revolution deteriorated, and as the economy grew worse, some of these people were leaving the country.

It wasn't so simple for Manu. He didn't come from a wealthy family, and he had been educated at a mediocre public university. He held a passport, but he hadn't been abroad other than a short vacation in childhood, and European countries tended to deny visas to applicants who seemed likely to overstay or become refugees. In any case, Manu wasn't certain that he could make it out of the Cairo Airport. Before his father died, the old man once mentioned the issue of the trumped-up police charge. He said there was no way of finding out in advance whether the charge was still on the books. "You'll know when you get to the airport," he said.

And so Manu made no plans. He still worked with the *Guardian,* and he still lived downtown. His gay life continued to be about as open as it could be in Cairo, although friends often warned him to be more careful, especially now that the political climate was changing. In downtown bars, Manu sometimes talked with older gay Cairenes who had survived for decades without significant problems from police, neighbors, or gay bashers. But these men tended to be extremely discreet; they never hung out in pickup spots like the Qasr al-Nil Bridge or Ramses Square, and they weren't involved in political activities or journalism. And even among the discreet there were still stories of men who had been disgraced or gone to prison.

Periodically, the police organized a sweep of the gay hangouts. One evening, Manu was chatting up another young man in Ramses Square when the cops came through. They grabbed Manu and his companion, but Manu played it perfectly. He showed his government-issued journalist pass, and he shouted at the police that he was working; he claimed to be interviewing the young man. He figured that outrage was the most effective response, and he knew that the officers might be intimidated by documentation from the Ministry of Media. So he brandished the pass, and he acted as if he were angry; but the more he acted, the more the anger felt real. What right did the police have to arrest him for talking to another man? After a brief exchange, the cops let him go. He insisted loudly that they release the other man, too—it was bold, but it worked.

The problems, though, were by no means limited to cops. Some of Manu's worst experiences came from people he brought home. During the time I knew him in Cairo, he was robbed of three computers and three cell phones, and another computer and cell phone that belonged to a roommate—all in his apartment. Occasionally, the culprit was somebody he slept with; he'd wake up and find himself alone, with his belongings gone. Other thieves had stayed with him as guests. Once, he met a young man who had just suffered a long detention after a crackdown on gay pickup spots. Manu let the young man take a shower in his apartment, and rest for a while; he gave him clothes to replace the filthy things he had been wearing. Later the young man grabbed a computer and a cell phone from the apartment and disappeared. Needless to say, Manu's response to such thefts was never to go to the authorities.

He said it was impossible to predict how any individual might behave, because gay life so often involved layers of deception and denial. "The guy you hook up with could be a police, or a thief, or somebody who beats you up," he said. "These are all options." He suspected that the worst problems came from straight men who frequented cruising spots, but even gays could be overwhelmed by self-loathing. "When they become thieves, or they hate you after sex, it has to do with guilt," he said. "They think I'm a *shoshar,* a cockroach. I'm very weak and they can do what they want. And I'm disgusting. I have to be punished."

I often worried about Manu—I had a feeling that someday I'd get a phone call from one of his friends, telling me bad news. Occasionally, I was tempted to give him advice: don't pick up straight men. But I realized the absurdity, because in a country where nobody could be openly gay, nobody could really be straight either. And Manu had already decided who he was; he had no illusions about the risks. It would have been just as useful to advise him: don't be young and gay in Egypt.

By the third anniversary of the Tahrir protests, on January 25, 2014, it had become rare for demonstrators to meet in public. After the coup, the interim government passed a law that required activists to register three days in advance of any protest, and everybody knew that the regime would reject such applications. Nevertheless, demonstrators declared that they would commemorate the anniversary with an unregistered meeting in front of the Mostafa Mahmoud Mosque, in Mohandiseen, just across the river from Zamalek.

I went to the demonstration alone. At one o'clock, a few hundred people gathered on a small grassy square in front of the mosque. During the early years of the revolution, marches had often started here and continued to Tahrir, but today the army had stationed more than a dozen armored personnel carriers at nearby intersections. Armed officers sat atop the APC turrets, and police stood in lines on the street.

There were two groups of protesters. A pro-Morsi faction shouted, "Down with military rule!" and "The people want to overthrow the regime!" Fifty yards away, members of liberal activist groups called April 6 and the Revolutionary Socialists began to chant against both the military and the Brotherhood. Others stood silent on the periphery, and I struck up a conversation with two of these men. They were in their twenties, and they lived nearby; they said that they didn't support either the Brotherhood or the activist groups, but they also disliked the idea of military rule. While we were talking, we were suddenly interrupted by gunfire.

Later, the state media reported that some Brotherhood supporters had antagonized the soldiers, and one newspaper claimed that a protester fired the first shot. But I saw no weapons in the crowd, which had been there for only ten minutes. There wasn't any warning by the security forces. The gunfire came in a cascade; they fired bird shot, and there was the heavy percussion of tear-gas canisters being launched. People began screaming, and the men I was talking to shouted, "Run!"

The security forces seemed to be firing above our heads. I ran with most of the crowd, heading south away from the square, and all at once I felt a piercing pain in my right foot and I stumbled to the ground. I didn't know what had happened; in the chaos of the crowd, I must have stepped awkwardly onto a curb or something. I got up and kept going, and I slowed to a walk once I thought I was out of range. But then I heard bird shot ripping through the leaves of a tree overhead, so I started running again.

I turned down the first side street. A protester was staggering alone, bleeding from the head, where he had been hit with bird shot. I asked if he was okay, and he waved me on: "Keep going!" This area was residential, and some locals stood at the entrance to their building, watching. I asked a man if I could sit inside.

"Get out of here!" he said. "Why do you Brotherhood people come here and cause trouble?"

I told him that I was a foreign journalist and my foot was injured, but the man pushed me hard. "Get out!"

The others looked embarrassed—Egyptians usually didn't respond this way to a stranger who was hurt. But nobody said anything as I limped away. Now I was certain that the foot was broken; the adrenaline was wearing off and every step was excruciating. Down the block, two other residents watched from behind a garden wall, and I told them what had happened. They opened a gate and let me inside.

The garden belonged to a banker, and his neighbor was a retired military engineer. The banker brought me a chair and a glass of water, and the three of us sat in the garden and waited. Sirens echoed all around; the police were patrolling side streets and arresting fleeing protesters. Both men spoke good English, and the engineer had spent some time in Fort Worth, Texas. The banker said that he had been scheduled for heart surgery today. "But the surgeon thought there would be trouble with the protests, and people would get hurt and have to go to the hospital," he said. "So they're going to do my operation next week."

Periodically, our conversation was interrupted by a volley of gunfire. It felt bizarre to sit with these educated professionals in the garden, sipping water, while beyond the wall officers chased protesters. Most people in this neighborhood were middle and upper-middle class; the district name, Mohandiseen, means "Engineers." But violence in nice neighborhoods was a general feature of the revolution. Over the years, the sites of most clashes were home to relatively prosperous people: the downtown neighborhoods near Tahrir, the suburbs around the Presidential Palace, the Nasr City community that included Rabaa.

Demonstrations rarely took place in the *ashwa'iyat*. Without parks, monuments, or other public spaces, political organizers couldn't find meeting points, even though *ashwa'iyat* residents had plenty of reasons to complain about the government. In the early phase of the revolution it had been common for the poor and the working class to travel to better neighborhoods in order to participate in marches and meetings. But as time passed, they stayed home. Geography was one reason why the revolution tilted toward the elite—most events happened in places where it was difficult to engage the poor.

Bill Erickson's assessment of ancient Amarna could also be applied to Cairo: the city wasn't laid out in a way that made people feel like citizens. For most residents of the modern capital, the environment was unplanned, and there were no anchors for the routines of civic life. Even in nicer districts like Mohandiseen, marches and demonstrations were often held around mosques. It seemed strange for a secular group like April 6 to schedule a protest in front of the Mostafa Mahmoud Mosque, but this was the area's most recognizable institution. The same dynamic had been common during both the early phase of the revolution and the Mubarak era. Without civic rituals, and without civic spaces, people were left with whatever the mosques provided: Friday sermons and prayer halls that were usually restricted to men. To at least some degree, the Islamization of Cairo politics had been encouraged by poor city planning.

It took an hour for the security forces to finish clearing the Mohandiseen streets, and the banker and the military engineer sat with me the whole time. Neither man supported Sisi; even the military engineer didn't believe the army should be involved in running the country. "They aren't supposed to attack Egyptian protesters," he said. "This is wrong. It's like Nasser."

He was a Sadat man—he told me that he admired the former president's efforts to build peace in the region.

I described what had happened at the protest, where the authorities hadn't issued a command to clear the area, or even fired a warning shot. The men asked if this kind of thing happened in China, and I found it hard to answer. I described the 1989 massacre around Tiananmen Square, when the Chinese authorities killed hundreds of unarmed protesters. Afterward, the government instituted a brutal crackdown, but it also trained police in the use of nonviolent methods to dispel demonstrations. For almost three decades, China had remained a strict one-party state, but there had never been another public massacre.

It seemed like a terrible thing to give them credit for. I felt like the Chinese radio reporter at the Morsi trial, who had remarked that in China a political case would be controlled and kept secret, as if this reflected a kind of decency. But even without moral decency, there was some value in coherence and predictability. In China, there was an actual system of governance, as well as a system of repression; it was venal, but at least people generally knew where lines were drawn. This was one grim lesson I had learned in Egypt: unstructured authoritarianism is even worse than structured authoritarianism.

And there was something particularly damaging about the rituals of public violence that had become so routine. It wore citizens down: after three years, they were desensitized to the terrible things that happened in even the nicest parts of their capital. On that anniversary, more than sixty people died, almost all of them shot by the authorities, but the news didn't linger. Few Egyptians seemed concerned that after three years of revolution the authorities still lacked a basic protocol for dealing with unrest.

When I returned home from Mohandiseen, I went to a doctor for X-rays—two broken bones. Later I called one of the men with whom I had been talking when the gunfire started. He said they had run in the opposite direction, but the outcome was the same; his friend fell and broke his foot. In Arabic class, Rifaat taught me how to say "crutches," which I added to my notebook, along with other anniversary words:

to threaten	يهدد
death	وفاة
suffering	معاناة
pain	ألم

I attended Morsi's second court appearance on crutches. It took a long time to get up the hill, but once I was inside the courtroom, the security people found me a good seat directly beside one of the cages. After the disaster of the first court date, the authorities had added a layer of soundproof glass to the enclosures.

Along with Morsi, twenty-one other men, most of them Brotherhood leaders, were scheduled to be tried today. This case was separate from the previous one. Now Morsi and the men were being charged with organizing the breakout of the Wadi al-Natroun Prison, which occurred during the early days of the revolution, in 2011.

The other men entered first, chanting slogans, but all we could hear was a muffled roar. After the men realized that the cage had been soundproofed, they began to make gestures. They sat with their backs to the judge, who was named Shaaban al-Shamy, and they held up a four-fingered salute that had come to represent Rabaa. A few Egyptian journalists responded by holding up two fingers in a victory symbol. Directly in front of me, a reporter with a shaved head stood up with his pinkie and forefinger upraised, like a metalhead at a concert. He held this satanic symbol next to the cage until a plainclothes officer came over and told him to stop.

"These are terrorists!" the reporter said. "I'm not afraid of terrorists!"

Mohamed Beltagy, one of the accused, began gesturing to me through the bars. During the early phase of the revolution, I had seen him at a number of events, and at the end of 2011 I interviewed him in his office. Back then, Beltagy was campaigning successfully for a seat in parliament, and I had asked if he believed the authorities would allow the Brotherhood to win a majority. "Any attempt to turn the parliament into a facade—it's unacceptable," he said confidently. "They can't go into conflict with the people. When there's pressure, they will respect it."

Now Beltagy caught my eye from inside the cage, and he smiled and made a series of exaggerated gestures. He drew a hand across his mouth—*silenced.* Then he patted his back and turned away from the judge—*boycott.* Clenched fist, crossed arms—*military.* Thumbs down, hands atop the shoulders—*oppression.* In an awful way, there was something clownish about the figure:

dressed in baggy prison whites, locked in a soundproof cage, smiling and miming as if he were playing some twisted game of charades.

Critics of the Brotherhood often accused leaders of protecting themselves while encouraging followers to take risks, but Beltagy had lost as much as anybody. His seventeen-year-old daughter, Asmaa, had been killed at Rabaa. Like many tragic public events of the revolution, this act was captured on video and posted to YouTube. In the video, a young woman stands at the edge of a crowd, listening to a sheikh preach a sermon. The scene is calm: nobody running, no sound of shooting. And then the girl drops as suddenly as if she's lost control of her legs. She was shot in the chest, apparently by a rooftop sniper. There was speculation that Asmaa had been targeted because of who her father was.

Asmaa died on an operating table at a Rabaa field clinic, and there was a YouTube video of that, too. Even at the end, the young woman is modestly covered in a red-patterned *hijab*. Her face is pale. She murmurs, "*Ya Allah!*" in a faint voice. "Oh God!" Her eyes are calm. By the time her father entered the courtroom cage, that clip had been viewed more than half a million times. Nobody had been charged with the crime.

Beltagy jotted something onto a piece of paper and held it against the glass. Another security officer quickly stepped over to block my view. The Egyptian reporter with the shaved head took out his own piece of paper and wrote two big capital letters: *C C*—shorthand for "Sisi." The reporter held the paper above his head, grinning, like a kid taunting a monkey in a zoo.

Morsi appeared a little before eleven o'clock. This time he had been forced to wear white, and he was escorted into the smaller cage. Until now, the judge hadn't switched on the cage's microphone. It was controlled by a button that had been installed onto his wooden desk. This arrangement looked exactly like the buttons that Upper Egyptian officials used to call for tea.

Now the judge pushed it. For the first time, we heard the voices of the accused:

Down, down with military rule!

Down, down—

The judge hit the button again, and the room went quiet. For the rest of the session, that was the pattern: the judge turned on the microphone, the men chanted, and almost immediately they were cut off.

Peering into the cage, I saw many people whom I had interviewed during the first year and a half of the revolution. There was Hazem Farouk Mansour; in 2011, when he was running for parliament, he assured me that the Brotherhood would win people's trust. "We have been underground for eighty years," he said. "When I speak to you now and I am under the light, then you can know me well." In the cage he sat next to Sobhi Saleh. I had met Saleh while he was having his shoes shined, in the parliamentary building, where he had promised that the Brotherhood wouldn't seek the presidency.

Many of the caged men had aged dramatically. I had trouble recognizing Rashad El-Bayoumi, a top leader who had talked with me in their national headquarters, and the same was true for Safwat Hegazy. At the time of Hegazy's arrest, his beard had been dyed black; today it was as white as his prison garb. I used to see Hegazy during the Morsi election campaign, when he served as a kind of Salafi hype man at rallies. By that point, the Brotherhood was no longer making any pretense of sharing power. At a rally in Ismailia, in May 2012, I had listened to Hegazy rail against minority rights. "Yes, we do want everything!" he shouted. "We want the parliament! We want the president! We want the cabinet and the ministries!" His voice rose to a scream: "The majority should have power! The minority opinions are not allowed to argue!" Now in the cage he slumped over in silence. Even if he had anything to say, nobody could hear him. His face looked old and tired.

The case itself was absurd. The trial began with a court official reading a twenty-three-minute statement claiming that eight hundred members of Hamas and Hezbollah had entered Egypt illegally and then helped coordinate the attack on the prison. More than seventy Palestinians were also being tried, in absentia, and all of them had been charged with "carrying out a plot to bring down the Egyptian state and its institutions." For good measure they were also accused of stealing chickens from the prison storehouse. One of the accused Palestinians, Hassan Salama, had spent every day of the last twenty years in Israeli prisons. Another Palestinian, Shady El-Sanea, had been dead when he allegedly helped organize the Egyptian prison break.

But the absurdity was part of the point of the case. It undermined the narrative of Tahrir as a homegrown movement, linking the Brotherhood to shadowy foreign agents, and it transformed a real historical incident into fantasy. Near the end of the session, Beltagy began pounding on the cage, and the judge pressed the button.

"So if there were eight hundred Hamas and Hezbollah members who crossed the border and came from Sinai to Cairo, and caused all of this to happen," Beltagy said, "then was it a revolution, or was it a military occupation?"

The prosecution's lawyer said calmly, "By responding to the allegations, Beltagy is acknowledging the case." The judge hit the button—silence—and a number of journalists applauded. But now Beltagy was enraged. He climbed the metal bars of the cage, trying to get closer to the microphone that was set into the glass ceiling. The cage rattled; Beltagy was screaming. Finally the judge pressed the button.

Beltagy bellowed, "From January 25 to January 30, was that a revolution or a military occupation?"

"I don't talk about politics," the judge said.

"This isn't politics!"

They went back and forth a few times until the judge hit the button. He gestured like a man brushing away a fly, and the audience laughed.

After the judge called for a recess, I hopped over on my crutches to study the cage. A man in a blue worker's uniform was doing the same thing. He was short and bald, and his company name was stitched onto an oval patch on his breast. "You can see how they installed this, between the wires," he told me, touching the glass. "And up there they joined it."

I asked if he was there to fix some part of the cage.

"Of course not," he said. "I'm the air conditioner repairman."

"What's wrong with the air conditioner?"

"Oh, there's no problem!" he said, looking surprised. "It's not even on."

This made sense—it was the last week in January. So why was he here? The court had banned cameras, voice recorders, and cell phones; the relatives of the accused weren't allowed to attend; few members of the foreign press had come. And yet the midwinter air conditioner repairman was mingling with Egyptian journalists and Islamist lawyers. I figured I might as well get his opinion.

"What do you think about this cage?" I asked.

"I don't think it's right," he said. "They should be allowed to speak, right?"

When the trial resumed, he took a seat directly in front of me. For the next two hours he listened intently. I never figured out why he had come, but I liked having the air conditioner repairman there in the courtroom. It was good to see somebody paying close attention.

In March 2014, Sisi finally made his announcement. It was never described as an act of ambition, or as the result of personal reflection or careful consultation. From the way Sisi spoke, he had no choice; the decision was as passive as a dream that comes in the night. He said, "I cannot turn my back when the majority wants me to run for president."

CHAPTER 17

WHEN THE GOVERNMENT NEEDED TO CONTACT SAYYID, IT SENT A LETter to the H Freedom kiosk. This seemed miraculous—the printed address consisted of nothing but his name, the name of the kiosk, and the names of the two streets that intersected there. But in this village of seventeen million, that was enough: four names, no numbers. The proprietor at the kiosk read the letter to Sayyid:

Ministry of Justice
Agouza Bureau
Regarding: Settling Family Disputes

Greetings:

Kindly appear next Tuesday at 10:00 a.m. in the Agouza Bureau for Settling Family Disputes. . . .

Sayyid knew exactly what it meant. "*W'allahy,* by God, she did it," he said. "She's filed for divorce. She knows that the kiosk is where to find me."

He had slept in the garage throughout much of the winter. As the months passed, he looked worse, and he ate most of his meals on the street. When he stopped by the spiderweb building, Leslie and I gave him leftovers, and we listened to him complain. Sayyid hadn't seen his kids for months, but he swore that his wife had filed the cases as a negotiation tactic. The best response, in his opinion, was stubbornness. He refused to pay anything to support his children until his wife dropped all disputes.

But now court appearances were being scheduled. The night before the first one, Sayyid went to see his lawyer, and I accompanied him.

The lawyer also represented Sayyid's sister in her battles with her estranged and *'afrit*-possessed husband. The lawyer's office was located in one of the dirtiest sections of Ard al-Liwa; we picked our way through piles of rotting food. Sayyid explained that the neighborhood had been like this ever since the great swine massacre of 2009. "*Zabaleen* come here to throw the garbage that they used to feed to pigs," he said.

On the ground floor of a decrepit building, there was a sign on a door: "Cassation Court Lawyer." Inside, the place was clean, and hardbound legal books lined a shelf. A set of scales was displayed prominently on a desk in the center of the room. Throughout the office, small religious signs had been arranged: "*Pray on Behalf of the Prophet.*" "*There Is No God but God.*" We sat on purple plastic lawn chairs that faced the lawyer's desk.

He opened a drawer and took out a set of court documents. One of them had a photograph of Wahiba stapled to it.

"Is this your wife, or is it an *'afrita*?" the lawyer asked. "Do you know what she's planning for tomorrow? She's requested a legal divorce."

The lawyer was a short, neckless man, and he leaned forward as he talked, shoulders level with his ears, as if prepared to ram his head into whatever stood in his way. "You have to tell me, do you want to leave the door open, or do you want to shut it?" he said brusquely. "You've been married for ten years, so you have to pay two years of support. If you leave it like this, it's going to cost you twenty-four thousand. I need to know—do you want me to leave the door open for negotiation?"

"No," Sayyid said.

"So we shut the door."

"Well," Sayyid said hesitantly, "maybe I'll negotiate." He looked tense; all the way to the office he had been working his jaw, as if chewing something that couldn't be swallowed. He had bags under his eyes and he was still wearing his dirty work clothes.

"If there's a one percent chance that she might change, then I prefer not to divorce," the lawyer said. "I hate divorce! I'm asking you, can she be treated and improved?"

Sayyid explained the various sources of tension: the way his wife had registered the house under her name, and the fight with his sister. He talked about the insulting text messages, and he pulled one up on his phone. The lawyer's eyes widened.

"She's calling you a dog!" he said, and now the talk of negotiation—the open door, the 1 percent chance—disappeared. "If she were my wife, I swear to God I would have shot her. Boom, I swear!" He shook his head. "She knows you can't stand in front of the judge. Her lawyer knows you can't attend because you're busy. And they think you'll get a bad lawyer for fifty pounds, not a good counselor like me. That's what they're counting on. You know, Joseph went to prison for seven years in Egypt."

Sayyid seemed confused by this Quranic non sequitur, but the lawyer kept talking fast. "What I care about, and what the law cares about, is paperwork," he said, brandishing a document. "The law has no heart. It has a brain, and the brain is papers. And this paper says that she can't live with you, she can't stand you."

Sayyid said, "Until now, I still don't want to humiliate her."

"Sayyid, this is love!" The lawyer told him sternly that he was being softhearted, and he held up another paper. "Look at this!"

"I can't read," Sayyid said.

"She insults you with nasty words! She writes these things—look at it!"

"I can't read," Sayyid said.

The lawyer took no notice; he waved the paper as if Sayyid had understood. "She insults you! She's filed three cases. Each one is a speed bump. Her goal is to make it so that either you don't go, or if you go, you can't work." Sayyid looked overwhelmed, but then the lawyer seemed to sense his panic. For ten minutes, he calmly asked questions, checking details on various forms. Periodically he flourished a document, and Sayyid said the same thing: *I can't read. I can't read.* The lawyer asked who had arranged the marriage in the first place.

"She was living near my brother," Sayyid said. "I saw her and I liked her."

"Does she pray?" the lawyer asked.

"She used to. She wears the *niqab*."

"She wears the *niqab*?"

"Yes."

"*Rabina yustor!* God protect us! Forget about looks—beards, *niqabs*. It's all in the heart. That's all that matters."

After a while, Sayyid mentioned that his wife had recently taken a job at a weaving factory, in order to support the children. The lawyer's eyes lit up.

"What's the factory address?" he said. "Tell me and I can have her arrested!" Triumphantly, he waved one of the papers that had been filed by Wahiba's lawyer. "It says here that she's not working. You see, the law is beautiful!"

"She was always asking me to work," Sayyid said. "I told her that when I die, she can work."

"So she was asking you to work?"

"Yes, but what am I, a child?" Sayyid said. "I can work. My wife doesn't need to work."

"You won't believe the cases I see," the lawyer said. He described another client whose mother had been flirting with her own son-in-law. "They get these ideas from watching television," he said. "Your wife, she's from Upper Egypt, and she's used to being behind a cow." He continued, "She came to Cairo, she got a television, she saw dancing—she wants all of this."

"I have two televisions," Sayyid said proudly.

"It's our duty to teach her," the lawyer said. "When we have a cow that's aggressive, what do we do? We put a ring through her nose. The problem with you is that you're kind. You're sweet."

He noted that Wahiba had hired a female lawyer, which, in his opinion, was an underhanded strategy. He expected the judge to be a graduate of the esteemed Al-Azhar University, and he said that any Azhar man was so decent and so pious that he was bound to be unnerved by the presence of a woman. "When this female lawyer talks to the Azhar judge, he'll stare at the ground," the lawyer said. "He'll be shy; he won't know what to do."

But knowledge of Wahiba's job was their ace in the hole. Legally speaking, an Egyptian woman is free to work, but in the Islamic tradition she must ask her husband's permission. This is often codified in marriage contracts, as it was in the agreement that bound Sayyid and Wahiba. "We'll go to the manager of the factory and say, 'You fire her, or you give us the proof of her working here,'" the lawyer said with a smile. "He has to do this. Otherwise we can shut down the factory." He continued, "In Islamic sharia, the woman is like an egg. Let's say you have ten eggs. Where would you put them? Would you just leave them lying around? No, you'd put them in the proper place: in the refrigerator. Women belong at home. They can go out of the house with their husband's permission, but that's it. Protecting the woman is what you do. She can eat, she can have fun—she's a princess in her own house! It's not abuse; it's not beating. It's not like a dog you keep at home, tied to the wall. She can enjoy herself."

Now the lawyer was in a philosophical mood, and he leaned back in his chair. In his opinion, marital tensions often resulted from women taking jobs. "The Egyptian woman who works usually compares her husband to a colleague," he explained. "The colleague will be really nice; he treats her well. And then she goes home after work and her husband says, 'Go make my tea, bitch.' This causes problems."

That was the issue—not the husband who calls his wife a bitch, but the polite work colleague who raises the bar. Sayyid listened intently; he seemed to calm down. He mentioned his sister's legal situation, and he said that there was a carpenter in the neighborhood who sometimes harassed her and behaved erratically.

"Does he take tramadol?" the lawyer asked.

"Yes," Sayyid said. "He's always lost in his head. He knocks on my sister's door at four o'clock in the morning and he says a lot of bad things."

"Bring me his name and address, and I'll deal with it," the lawyer said. He offered to threaten the carpenter with a lawsuit. He warned Sayyid not to tell anybody about the strategy of putting pressure on Wahiba's workplace. "Keep the secret between your teeth," he said. "That's why God made your mouth like this!" He continued, "You have to be smart. If you're among the wolves, then you have to become a fox."

"Now I'm a wolf," Sayyid said.

"You're a lion!" the lawyer said.

Whenever Sayyid met with the lawyer, he mentioned other cases that involved family or friends. Sayyid's sister had multiple cases pending, and a couple of his brothers were also dealing with the courts. Other *zabaleen* that

I knew mentioned legal complaints that they had filed or were trying to fend off. All of them worked in the informal economy, and they lived in the *ashwa'iyat,* where they had virtually no contact with government institutions. But they seemed remarkably litigious.

Most of this legal action, though, seemed to be directed at conflicts between family or neighbors; it rarely involved deeper questions of social and economic rights. Sayyid was perfectly comfortable working a job without any contracts, and he never complained about making payments to the people who supposedly owned the garbage rights on his route. For Sayyid, such unwritten traditions were easy to accept—he would never have imagined bringing a lawyer into his professional life. But when it came to a fight with his wife, or a problem with a neighbor who harassed his sister, legal representation seemed perfectly acceptable.

A significant amount of government activity must have been generated by such conflicts. A couple of days after the visit to the lawyer, a police officer came to Zamalek to interview Sayyid about his income, because Wahiba had filed requests for financial support. Various courts and legal departments sent a steady stream of documents to the H Freedom kiosk, and Sayyid made regular trips across the river to government bureaus. Whenever I accompanied him to government family law offices, the majority of visitors were men who were trying to sort out cases that had been filed against them. It seemed that women were more likely to initiate such actions, probably because they were mistreated and they lacked other forms of power.

Once the men were in the offices, they mostly dealt with female clerks. In Egypt, only about a quarter of women work, but government jobs are among the few positions that conservative families consider acceptable for wives and daughters. These jobs are perceived to be low stress, and they don't create the type of contact with strange men that might be seen as inappropriate. Of course, government jobs also have poor prospects. Within the bloated civil service, salaries are low, and there's little opportunity for a worker to show her skills or creativity.

I never saw these women bureaucrats demanding bribes the way the men did, but they seemed to make Sayyid nervous. One morning, I accompanied him to the Family Court in Imbaba, a district just across the Nile from Zamalek. Sayyid hadn't changed out of his filthy work clothes, which he described as a legal strategy. "The lawyer told me that the decision is fifteen percent better if you wear old clothes," he said.

We waited in line behind a man who obviously hadn't received the same advice. He wore a suit, and he spoke like an educated person. The clerks in this room were all women, and one of them asked the man in the suit about his lawyer.

"He's not here," he said.

"Why not?"

"It's just a small case."

"What's the small case?" the woman asked.

"It's just child support."

"Just child support?" She arched her eyebrows. "If child support is a small case, then what is a big case?"

"Well, divorce," the man said.

Sayyid whispered to me that all of this was on account of laws that had been changed under the Mubarak regime. He spoke angrily, as if this had been one of the injustices that had sparked the revolution. "Suzanne Mubarak invented divorce for women," he hissed. "The fact that they can file for divorce, the alimony—all of that happened because of her."

Sayyid's turn came, and the clerk, a woman in her forties, greeted him sternly. She flipped through some forms. "What's this about a kiosk on Ahmed Heshmat Street?" she said. "This is listed as your address. What's the street number? Do you work there?"

"I work in the street," Sayyid said. "I collect garbage from Ahmed Heshmat Street. But that kiosk is where I receive mail."

"What's the street address?"

"There isn't any address."

"Stop playing around!"

"I'm not," he pleaded. "There's no address."

It took a while to convince the clerk that the kiosk was the best way to contact him. She asked a series of questions, as part of his testimony, and finally she came to the issue of whether he agreed to the divorce.

"I don't want to divorce," Sayyid said. His lawyer had instructed him carefully on this point. As long as Sayyid didn't demand the divorce or agree to it, he wouldn't be financially obligated to Wahiba, who would also have to return a significant fee that he had contributed at the beginning of their life together. For an Egyptian woman, this was one reason why dissolving a marriage was so difficult.

While the clerk was recording Sayyid's legally savvy response, he couldn't resist another comment.

"But she's a tyrant," he said. "She ruined my sister's eye."

"Well, if she's that bad, why don't you divorce her?" the clerk said sharply.

Sayyid was taken aback, but then he recovered. "All I can do is say, 'Allah sufficeth me, most excellent he in whom we trust,'" he said, repeating a well-known verse from the Quran. "You can see my work clothes here. I work in trash. I clean the streets. But I thank God for everything; at least my income is *halal*."

"It's nothing to be ashamed of," the clerk said. She seemed softened by the verse and by the reference to his lowly job. "It's not *haraam* to do such work," she said gently.

While they were talking, Wahiba arrived. Both husband and wife had been scheduled to deal with the family law office at the same time, and now the clerk asked Sayyid to step aside while she questioned Wahiba.

Sayyid watched from across the room. Wahiba's face was covered by the *niqab*, and she was accompanied by all three of their children, along with her lawyer, a young, bright-looking woman. It was the first time Sayyid had seen the kids in months. The boys, Zizou and Yusuf, were both younger than seven, and they clung to their mother, looking frightened. They kept glancing across the room at their father. Sayyid's mouth was tense—once again, he was chewing the unswallowable.

After a while, Wahiba stepped aside, and the clerk called Sayyid over.

"Your wife wants to divorce you," the clerk said. "Are you sure that you don't want this divorce?"

"Yes," Sayyid said in a thick voice.

"If she initiates it, then she's going to win the case," the clerk said. "It's her right."

Sayyid said he understood. The clerk stamped a form and gave a date for the next court appearance. We took a ferry across the Nile back to Zamalek. It was a hazy morning, and the water was gray as slate. Sayyid looked stunned. "My heart was aching," he said. "I couldn't even say hello to the kids." We walked in silence back to the neighborhood. He went straight to the garage to try to sleep; he told me he couldn't bear to pick up trash after seeing the children that way.

When Sayyid stopped by at night, he often asked for advice, which was always difficult in Egypt. Even with Manu, who was easy to communicate with, I didn't know what to say, because there weren't any clear solutions to his problems. With Sayyid it was different: there were many obvious changes in behavior that were likely to improve his domestic situation. But his world was so traditional, and he was surrounded by so much casual misogyny, that any suggestions from Leslie and me were generally ignored.

And now that the conflict had entered the courts, I couldn't assess the real goals of the people involved. Egyptians often used the law in indirect ways, in part because the system was so incoherent. The influence of traditional Islamic sharia remained strong, especially with regard to family law, while codified laws in other areas were based on European models. Various rights, such as women's right to divorce, had been introduced relatively recently, and often they were legally enshrined but socially condemned. Other laws or customs still functioned in direct contradiction to these reforms, like the traditional requirement that a husband had to agree to his wife's taking a job.

Within this muddled system, people searched out inconsistencies that could be exploited. The law wasn't really a foundation; other traditions of family and faith ran much deeper. The legal apparatus often functioned more as a kind of parallel structure, and individuals used it as a way of bolstering other strategies. Christine Hegel-Cantarella, an anthropologist at Western Connecticut State University, spent time researching court cases in Port Said, where she tracked a number of unorthodox applications of the law. In poorer communities, when a young woman got engaged, her family sometimes demanded that the fiancé sign a commercial document. Such documents weren't supposed to be part of an engagement, but it was a way of strengthening the woman's position, because any broken promise would become a matter of criminal law rather than family law. Hegel-Cantarella also observed a number of instances in which a broken engagement was immediately followed by a formal charge of rape. Afterward, the accused rapist agreed to marry his victim, who then dropped the charges. It seemed that the women used the rape allegation not as a way of protecting themselves against sexual violence but as a tool of negotiation.

One of the many problems with these strategies was that they invariably pointed toward the same goal: marriage. The stigma of divorce was so powerful, and it was so unusual for women to support themselves financially, that even laws designed to free them from bad marriages were often most handy in terms of maintaining such unions. Women used the law to fight but not to escape.

Sayyid had always calculated that Wahiba wasn't really committed to a permanent separation. In any case, the system was stacked against her. By taking a job without Sayyid's consent, she had left him with a legal opening, and she couldn't afford to raise three children on her own. After months of court visits, and right before the separation would have been final, she dropped all of the cases against her husband.

For a while, Sayyid seemed chastened. I suspected that many Egyptian men would have felt emboldened and vindictive, but this wasn't his personality. I could tell that he truly cared about his wife and children, despite the way he sometimes treated them. After the cases were dropped, he returned home, and Wahiba stopped working the job at the textile factory. She had always complained that he spent too much time in Zamalek, and now he seemed to make an effort to change. I no longer saw him in the neighborhood at night. During weekends, he sometimes brought Zizou, his oldest son, to Zamalek, and the boy helped with the garbage collection. This was another concession to Wahiba, who had told Sayyid that he needed to spend more time with his children.

Eventually, though, Sayyid reverted to old patterns. If the couple had a fight, he slept in the garage; if the fight became serious, he withheld money. At one point, Wahiba came alone to Zamalek, complaining about Sayyid's lack of support to some of the respected neighborhood figures. A number of them, including the proprietor of H Freedom, spoke sharply to Sayyid, telling him to accept his responsibilities. But it seemed too easy for Sayyid to take the most obvious lesson from the previous court battles: he had the upper hand.

During one of these spells of conflict, I drove him to Upper Egypt, to make another visit to his mother's village of Wasta. While we were there, we went for a walk around the fields, and we passed the childhood home of the cousin who years earlier had been expected to become Sayyid's bride. The woman happened to be outside, but Sayyid didn't formally greet her. They acknowledged each other from a distance with the briefest of waves.

"I can't talk to her," Sayyid said, once we were out of earshot. "It's not appropriate." While walking, he told her story: The cousin had married a man who turned out to be physically abusive. After years of tolerating his behavior, she finally divorced him. Now she lived in her parents' home, with her young children.

"She'll stay there," Sayyid said. "She won't marry again." Under Egyptian law, a woman who remarries also loses the legal right to custody of her children. They are supposed to go to her mother or to her sisters, but if no female in her immediate family can take the kids, then the father can sue for custody. This law is in place because it's considered inappropriate for children to live in a home with a strange man, even if that man is now their stepfather. On the other hand, it's no problem for children to be with a stepmother. This is simply another way in which the law favors men.

Not long after our visit to Wasta, the cousin was killed in an auto accident. The news left Sayyid shaken, and he often talked about it, but he didn't make the two-hour trip back for the funeral. He told me it wouldn't have been right because of their history as a potential match. It was hard to imagine a much sadder life: a short, brutal marriage; a sequestered divorce; a sudden and violent death. And even after death there were still traditions that limited who could pay his respects to this poor woman's memory.

CHAPTER 18

AFTER MY FIRST TRIP TO MALLAWI, WHEN I MET YE DA, I STARTED searching for other Chinese merchants in Upper Egypt. Ye Da mentioned a cousin in Minya, so the next time I was in the city I stopped in a *m'arad* market downtown. The entrance featured a Quranic verse that warned against jealousy. Inside, at the back of the market, there was a shop called the Chinese Lingerie Corner. It was run by the cousin, Ye Haijun, and his wife. They told me there was a second Chinese-owned shop in a different part of the city, so I visited that one, too.

By now, I was growing more comfortable with Egyptian roads, and I often drove the Honda alone to southern archaeological projects. I would visit a site, and then, before returning to Cairo, I would spend a day or two looking for Chinese migrants. They were never hard to find. In the sprawling city of Asyut, which was home to approximately 400,000 people, I arrived in the outskirts, parked, and hailed the first cab I saw. I asked the driver one question: "Do you know if there are any Chinese people in town?"

He didn't hesitate. He waved me into his car, and we drove along Asyut's Corniche Road, past the central government building that faced the Nile. The river here was calm and wide; across the water, the steep, bare hills of the desert plateau were the color of sand. The driver followed a series of alleyways through the heart of the city, and then he stopped at a shop whose sign said *Linjer Seenee:* "Chinese Lingerie." Two other shops, China Star and Noma China, were less than a block away.

These three shops, like the two in Minya, and the single store in Mallawi, were run by natives of Zhejiang province. All of them sold the same products, many of which were inexpensive, garishly colored, and profoundly impractical. There were buttless body stockings, and nightgowns that covered only one breast, and G-strings accessorized with feathers. Transparent tops were decorated with plastic gold coins that dangled from chains. Brand names were often in English, and some of the popular ones included Laugh Girl, Shady Tex Lingerie, Hot Love Italy Design, and Sexy Fashion Reticulation Alluring.

It was rare for foreigners to live in these cities. Occasionally, traveling groups of Syrian traders passed through, and a handful of Westerners resided at the dig sites during the archaeological season, but otherwise it was only the Chinese. In Beni Suef, near Sayyid's ancestral village of Wasta, I found two Zhejiang underwear dealers who had somehow embedded with a group of Syrians who ran a *m'arad* called the Syrian Fair. In the city of Sohag, thirty miles north of Abydos, two more Chinese couples were selling thongs and nightgowns. They said they had come to this remote place because there were already too many Chinese doing the same thing in the north.

All told, along a three-hundred-mile stretch of the Nile in Upper Egypt, I found twenty-six Chinese lingerie dealers: four in Sohag, twelve in Asyut, two in Mallawi, six in Minya, and two in Beni Suef. Three more had just left the remote city of Nagaa Hammadi, where the local emporium was still named in their honor: *al-M'arad al-Sini*, "the Chinese Market." It was like mapping the territory of large predator cats: in the Nile valley, clusters of Chinese lingerie dealers tended to appear at intervals of thirty to fifty miles, and the size of each cluster varied according to the local population. Cairo was large enough to support dozens. In the capital, I met Dong Weiping, who told me that he had more than forty relatives in Egypt, mostly in Cairo and Alexandria, where they sold Dong's products. He had a small factory in eastern Cairo that manufactured lingerie under the brand name Hangzhou. Dong said that he had chosen the name, and the logo of a pagoda, because Egyptians associated Chinese lingerie with good quality.

In Cairo, the director of the China-Egypt Trade Association, Chen Jiannan, was also a former lingerie dealer. These associations exist in virtually every African capital, and they help Chinese businesspeople deal with local authorities. Chen was originally from Zhejiang, but he had lived in Cairo for fifteen years and he spoke Egyptian Arabic well. He enjoyed using the language cynically, in the spirit of a Cairene.

"*Inta Muslim?*" he asked, when I arrived in his office. "Are you Muslim?"

"*La'a,*" I said. "No."

"*Al-hamdulillah!*" he said. "All praise be to God!" Then he reached into his desk and pulled out two half-liter cans of Sakara beer. He pushed one in front of me, opened the other for himself, and handed over a business card. It listed twelve different titles; in addition to Chen's work with the China-Egypt Trade Association, he was heading something called the Egypt-China Peaceful Reunification with Taiwan Association. He had one factory that manufactured shoes and another that made PVC window frames; he also assembled solar panels. All of this Egyptian commercial activity had started with lingerie. When I asked him how he had figured out that this particular product would sell, he didn't say anything about market research or strategy.

"Somebody who does business just sees things differently," he said with a shrug. "It's like a hunter. A hunter goes out into the wild and he'll spot a rabbit, or a deer, or some other animal. He knows what he's looking for. It's the same for a businessman. He sees whatever is in demand."

The Chinese lingerie dealers of Upper Egypt followed their own sense of time. Unlike most Chinese, they slept late; they opened their shops in the afternoon and closed well after midnight. Most of their business took place at night, and summer was a better season than winter. Ramadan was especially good, and so was Eid al-Adha. They ignored the Spring Festival—the Chinese holiday meant nothing along the Nile. There were other days that inspired customers to shop: New Year's Day, the Prophet's birthday, Mother's Day.

But nothing compared with Valentine's Day. I liked going to the shops on busy evenings so I could watch the Chinese and Egyptians interact, and one year I drove to Asyut in order to spend Valentine's Day at the store called China Star. Just before the call for sunset prayer, a sheikh swept into the shop. He was tall and fat, with strong, dark features, and his galabiya was the color of turquoise. He wore a pair of heavy silk scarves, and his head was wrapped in a white turban. Two large women in *niqabs* followed him.

Periodically, one of the women would hold up an article of clothing, and the sheikh would register his opinion with a wave of his hand. They found two items that he approved of: matching sets of thongs and skimpy, transparent nightgowns, one in red and the other in blue. While they were shopping,

I chatted with the sheikh, who told me that he worked for the Ministry of Religious Endowments, where his job was to monitor mosques. He was friendly and talkative, but he said nothing about the women, which was typical in the south—Upper Egyptian men rarely mentioned the women in their family to strangers. With the sheikh and the women, I couldn't tell what their relationship was, which was one problem with the *niqab.* The garment made it impossible to guess a woman's age or expression, and invariably it left much to the imagination. Were these women the sheikh's wives? Was one to be dressed in red, and the other in blue, for Valentine's Day?

The sheikh began to bargain with Chen Yaying, the Chinese woman who ran the shop along with her husband. They went by the names Kiki and John, because they were easier for Egyptians to pronounce. Kiki was twenty-four years old, but she could have passed for a bookish schoolgirl. She wore rectangular glasses and a loose ponytail, and she was so small that she barely reached the sheikh's bright blue chest.

"This is Chinese!" she said in heavily accented Arabic, holding up one of the thong-and-nightgown sets. "Good quality!" The total price was 200 pounds, but she reduced it to 160, a little more than twenty dollars. The sheikh offered 150 and refused to budge. For a while, they engaged in Egyptian non-bargaining: One hundred and sixty. One hundred and fifty. One hundred and sixty. They were still separated by ten pounds when the call to prayer sounded.

The chanting was loud—the Ibn al-Khattab Mosque was directly next to the shop. "I have to go," the sheikh said, handing Kiki his money. "I'm a sheikh! I have to pray."

But the Chinese woman blocked his way. She slapped him lightly on the arm with the cash. "Ten more!" she said sternly.

The sheikh's eyes widened in mock surprise. A local woman would never initiate contact with a strange man in this manner, but Kiki's status as a Chinese made the slap a comic gesture. The sheikh responded in turn: with a flourish, he faced the direction of Mecca, closed his eyes, and held out his hands in the posture of prayer. Standing in the middle of the lingerie shop, he began to recite,

> *Subhan'allah wal'hamdulillah. . . .*

"Fine, fine!" Kiki said. The sheikh grinned as he left, the women trailing behind. Later, Kiki told me that she was quite certain that one of the women was the sheikh's mother and the other was his wife. From my perspective, this changed the narrative significantly, but it didn't make it any less interesting. Kiki, though, had nothing more to say about it. As far as she was concerned, the story ended the moment the sale was made.

The Chinese dealers rarely speculated about their Egyptian customers. In addition to lingerie, they sold light, nightgown-like dresses, which southern women wore when they were at home. The region is brutally hot—summertime temperatures often reach 110 degrees—but standards of morality require women to wear heavy, layered dresses in public. They buy the lighter clothes to change into once they are away from the eyes of strange men. This was one reason why the Chinese business was so profitable: Egyptian women essentially need two wardrobes, one for home and another for public use.

But the majority of the Chinese sales came from lingerie. Kiki said that some local women visited the shop several times a month, and she knew of individuals who had acquired more than a hundred sets of the nightgowns and panties. China Star, like all the Chinese shops, frequently changed its stock. When I pressed the Chinese to analyze the demand, they often said that it was because Egyptian men like sex, and they mentioned the restrictions on public attire. "If you never have a chance to look nice, it's hard on you, psychologically," Chen Huantai, another dealer in Asyut, said. "And they have to wear so many clothes when they're outside, so they have these other things to look prettier at home." There might have been some truth to this theory: the conservatism of exterior garments made Egyptian women more attentive to what they wore underneath.

But the subject didn't interest the Chinese. Most of them had little formal education, and they didn't perceive themselves as being involved in a cultural exchange. On issues of religion they were truly agnostic: they seemed to have no preconceptions or received ideas. "The ones with the crosses—are they Muslim?" Ye Haijun asked me once. He had been living for four years in Minya, a town with sectarian strife so serious that several Coptic churches had been set afire after the Rabaa massacre. During another conversation, I realized that he was under the impression that women who wore *hijabs* were adherents of a different faith from those who wore the *niqab*. It was logical: he noticed contrasts in dress and behavior, so he assumed that they believed in different things. A monolithic label like "Islam" meant nothing to him.

Initially, I wondered how the Chinese dealers survived with so little knowledge and curiosity about their cultural environment. Even their discovery of this odd product line had been accidental. In Asyut, the small Chinese community was pioneered by Kiki's father, Lin Xianfei. In the 1970s and 1980s, Lin grew up on a half-acre farm in Zhejiang, where poverty forced him to drop out of school after the fifth grade. He migrated to Beijing, where he found modest success trading clothes to buyers who came from other countries in the region. But after the Asian financial crisis struck, in 1997, most of Lin's clients stopped coming to China.

He heard that some people from near his hometown had gone to Egypt and succeeded as merchants. He studied a map and decided that he would settle in Asyut, because it was one of the most populous cities in the south. He couldn't find an affordable Arabic class in Beijing, so he signed up for English lessons instead.

"I knew I'd be the only Chinese person there," Lin said, when I asked him why he had chosen Asyut. "If I stayed in Cairo, there would have been more Chinese, so I would have had to deal with more competition."

In Asyut, he set up a stall in a *m'arad*. Initially, he sold three Chinese products: neckties, pearls, and underwear. These products had been chosen not because they were known to have any special appeal to Upper Egyptians but rather because of their size. "They were easy to pack in a suitcase," Lin explained.

He quickly realized that few Asyut natives were interested in pearls, and nobody wears a necktie with a galabiya. But women's underwear sold briskly. Lin traveled repeatedly to China, packing lingerie in his luggage, and then he started sending containers full of underwear across the Indian Ocean. His wife, Chen Caimei, came over, and eventually they moved out of the *m'arad* and rented a proper storefront.

Lin took no special pride in what he had accomplished. He used the word *suzhi,* which literally means "quality" but has connotations of class. "If my *suzhi* were higher, then I could have stayed in China," he said. "Only somebody with low quality comes to a place like this." Such remarks were typical of the lingerie dealers, who, like many Zhejiang entrepreneurs, were masters of the lateral product transition. Prior to selling lingerie in Upper Egypt, one man had sold winter coats in Siberia, another had dealt construction materials in Azerbaijan, and a third had harvested crabs in the East China Sea. In every case, they had left for the same reason: too many Chinese showed up. "I knew if I came to a bad place like this, then there wouldn't be any other Chinese people," a dealer in Sohag said. But even in Sohag, two more Zhejiang merchants quickly materialized to compete with him.

I never met a Chinese in Upper Egypt who had studied Arabic formally. In fact, none of them even owned a Chinese-Arabic dictionary, phrase book, or textbook. They acquired the language entirely by ear, and the results were idiosyncratic—I came to think of it as the lingerie dialect. In the lingerie dialect, even men spoke in the feminine voice. Mandarin and other Chinese languages are not inflected for gender, and traders had trouble grasping the way that Arabic distinguishes between the masculine and the feminine. The vast majority of their customers were women, so the Chinese naturally picked up their speech patterns.

In the lingerie dialect, one important phrase was *fee wessa'a*—"there is a bigger size." Chinese dealers used this phrase a lot. Egyptians tend to be big, especially in the south, and often they have a natural charisma. Like many people in the Mediterranean region, they gesture constantly. In conversation, an Egyptian will mimic a movement for prayer, or rub his fingers to indicate money, or tap his head and roll his eyes to express craziness. My favorite Egyptian gesture is when a man brings his fingers together and slowly pulls his hand down, as if tugging a helium balloon toward earth. It means "calm down."

The Chinese have no equivalent. They rarely speak with their hands and bodies, and they shy away from physical contact. The typical Egyptian greeting between male friends—a kiss on the cheek and a big swinging hand slap that makes the palms pop—would virtually constitute assault in China. Whenever I sat in China Star, observing the Egyptians and Chinese interact, I couldn't imagine two more different cultures.

But somehow these contrasts were perfect for the exchange of lingerie. The Chinese lack of physical presence made it easier for them to stay out of the way while Egyptian women looked at intimate garments. There was something disarming about the Chinese men speaking in the feminine voice, and they didn't have to feign a lack of prurient interest. They knew little about Egyptian culture and traditions, and they cared even less, which seemed to put customers at ease. In this remote region, a lack of cultural awareness actually functioned as an effective business strategy.

The Chinese shops usually employed young local women as assistants. In the conservative south, it was especially rare for women to work, and most of the assistants had been forced to find jobs because of desperate family circumstances. In Minya, at the Chinese Lingerie Corner, a woman named Rasha Abdel Rahman had started working almost a decade earlier, after her mother died and her father was crippled in an auto accident. Rasha had four sisters, and thus far she had earned enough money to pay the dowries for three of their marriages. At the age of twenty-seven, she remained single. I suspected that being employed in the lingerie shop probably damaged her marriage prospects, but she was sacrificing herself for the sake of her sisters.

Rasha had been employed by two different Chinese shops, and she said that after this experience she would never work for an Egyptian. She described the Chinese as direct and honest, and she appreciated their distance from local gossip networks. "They keep their secrets," she said.

In her community, many lingerie stores were also run by Egyptians, but Rasha said that local men could never sell the product as effectively as the Chinese did. "I can't describe how they do it," she said of the Chinese. "But they can look at the item and give it to the woman, and that's it. An Egyptian man would look at the item, and then look at the woman, and then he might make a joke or laugh about it." She talked about her previous Chinese boss. "He didn't have anything in mind while he was selling," she said. "When you buy something, you feel the thoughts of the person selling it. And with the Chinese, their brains don't go thinking about women's bodies."

The most important word in the lingerie dialect was *arusa,* or "bride." The Chinese pronounced it *alusa,* and they used it constantly; in Cairo neighborhoods, there were Chinese who went door-to-door with sacks of dresses and underwear, calling out, "*Alusa! Alusa!*" In Chinese shops, the owners used it as a standard form of address for any female customer.

On Valentine's Day, not long after the turquoise sheikh left, a genuine *arusa* walked into China Star. She was nineteen years old, and the wedding was scheduled for later in the year. The *arusa* was accompanied by her fiancé, her mother, and her sixteen-year-old brother. Kiki began picking items off the racks.

"*Alusa,* do you want this?" she said, producing a box labeled "Net Ladystocking Spring Butterfly." First the *arusa* studied the Ladystocking, which was then passed to the fiancé, then to the mother, and finally to the younger brother. The box featured two photographs, front and rear, of a Slavic-looking model who stood behind a bookshelf of leather-bound volumes while wearing high heels, a neck-to-ankle lace bodysuit, a G-string, and a vacant expression. The teenage brother studied the box for a long time. It went into a pile for approved items.

In an Egyptian marriage, where the goods to be contributed by each side are codified in a contract, clothing and lingerie are part of the *arusa*'s responsibility. This was one reason why the market was so significant; Dong Weiping, the manufacturer I met in Cairo, told me that he imported ten shipping containers of women's underwear every year from China, in addition to the items that he made in his factory. At China Star, the *arusa* and her family spent more than an hour picking out twenty-five nightgown-and-panty sets, ten additional pairs of underwear, ten brassieres, and one Ladystocking. The mother paid the equivalent of 360 dollars, a large amount of money in Asyut, which was among the poorest governorates in Egypt. The mother said they planned to visit two or three more clothing shops before the wedding.

They were appreciative shoppers. At one point, they broke into spontaneous applause when Kiki displayed a nightgown. "What do you think?" she said, holding up a transparent top with a pink G-string.

"*W'allahy, laziz!*" the fiancé said. "By God, it's beautiful!" He was a lawyer in Asyut, and the *arusa* studied law at the university. She was well spoken and modestly dressed, with a heavy green coat covering her clothes. She wrapped her *hijab* tightly under the chin in a conservative style.

They impressed me as a traditional upper-middle-class family, and nothing seemed awkward about this shopping expedition. If anything, the mood was innocent and joyous, and the *arusa* didn't appear the least bit embarrassed. I was certain that even the most self-confident American woman would be mortified by the idea of shopping for lingerie with her fiancé, her mother, and her teenage brother, not to mention doing this in the presence of two Chinese shop owners, their assistant, and a foreign journalist. But I had witnessed similar scenes at other shops in Upper Egypt, where an *arusa* was always accompanied by friends or family members, and the ritual seemed largely disconnected from sex in their minds.

And there was something about the status of an *arusa* that demanded an audience. Chinese dealers sometimes told me that Egyptian women bought these things because they did belly dances for their husbands at night, a theory that I suspected had more to do with movie images than it did with actual behavior. But it might have been true in a more figurative sense. Whenever I saw an *arusa* shopping for lingerie with friends or family, I sensed that the woman was on display and preparing for a future role. At China Star, I asked the mother if her daughter would work as a lawyer after the wedding.

"Of course not!" she said. "She'll stay at home." She spoke proudly, the same way that Sayyid and other men did when they said that their wives didn't work. In Egyptian Arabic, another meaning of *arusa* is doll—children use this word for the toys that they dress and undress.

When Lin Xianfei and Chen Caimei were building their China Star business, they noticed a lot of garbage lying around Asyut. They were not the first people to make this observation. But they were the first to respond by importing a polyethylene-terephthalate bottle-flake washing production line, which was manufactured in Jiangsu province and allowed an entrepreneur to grind up plastic bottles, wash and dry the regrind at high temperatures, and sell it as recycled material.

In Lin's description, plastic was simply another lateral product transition. "I saw that it was just lying around, so I decided I could recycle it," he said. He returned to southern Zhejiang province, where he visited some established recycling plants and studied the machinery. In order to set up the equipment, he paid for a Chinese mechanic to come to Asyut for a few weeks. But Lin's goal was to handle most maintenance himself. Just like in his Arabic, he had never received any formal training in engineering or manufacturing.

One day not long after the factory was established, there was a problem with one of the industrial grinders, so Lin turned it off. He put his hand inside the machine. While he was feeling around the blades, a worker turned the machine back on.

For twenty days Lin lay in a hospital bed at Asyut University. His right arm was broken in five places, and huge swaths of skin had been ripped off. He also suffered bad cuts along his shoulder, neck, and face, because the blades had pulled him into the machine. At the hospital, Egyptian doctors took skin from his left thigh and grafted it onto his right arm. The surgery took eight hours. After Lin was stable enough to travel, he flew to southern Zhejiang, where he recuperated for a couple of months. Then he returned to Asyut and went back to work on the machinery.

Lin and Chen's plant became the first plastic-bottle recycling facility in all of Upper Egypt. Lin handled the machinery, and Chen took care of many of the financial aspects of the business. Soon, people were carting in bottles from places as far away as Aswan, and the plant had more work than it could handle. It was located in a small industrial zone in the desert west of Asyut city. The first time I visited, so many bottles were waiting to be recycled that they formed a pile more than a story tall.

The plant washed and ground up four tons of plastic every day. It employed thirty people, and Lin sold the processed material to other Chinese in Cairo, who used it to manufacture thread. This thread was then sold to entrepreneurs in the Egyptian garment industry, including Dong Weiping, the lingerie manufacturer. When a bottle was tossed beside the road in Asyut, it was possible that the plastic would pass through three stages of Chinese processing and manufacturing before returning to town in the form of lingerie, also to be sold by the Chinese.

Lin's arm was covered with rubbery skin and he had a bad scar across his face. The arm lacked full mobility, but Lin was able to work without too much problem. He shrugged when I asked about the quality of the care he had received at the local hospital. "It cost only ten thousand pounds," he said. The price seemed good to him—fifteen hundred dollars. As far as he was concerned, he had only himself to blame for the accident. "I'm stupid," he said. "I don't have enough education to do this work."

At the factory, Lin and Chen netted between 50,000 and 200,000 dollars a year. This success inspired an Asyut businessman to poach some of the Chinese couple's workers, and he opened the second plastic recycling facility in Upper Egypt. But there was more than enough plastic in the south for both businesses to thrive.

Lin and Chen lived in an apartment above the factory floor, amid the roar of machinery. Like the home of every Chinese entrepreneur whom I visited in Upper Egypt, their apartment was furnished with plastic lawn chairs. The only decoration on the wall was a clock. They had an old Panasonic TV, and their Egyptian satellite dish picked up China Central Television, which they watched constantly when they were at home. They bought pork from the local Copts. The Chinese could live without many things—neighbors, friends, furniture—but pork was virtually a necessity.

Lin was in his early fifties, although he looked a decade older. He often complained about stomach pain; like any Chinese entrepreneur of his generation, he had shared a lot of heavy drinking and eating with associates. He rarely said much. Once, when he was driving me through Asyut in his beat-up Nissan, I asked casually what he considered the biggest problem in Egypt. The forcefulness of his response surprised me.

"Inequality between men and women," he said immediately. "Here the women just stay home and sleep. If they want to develop, the first thing they need to do is solve this problem. That's what China did after the revolution." He often made this point, emphasizing that Chinese women had also been sequestered not long ago. At the turn of the last century, it was still common for a wealthy Chinese man to have multiple wives and concubines, and women rarely worked. The Chinese practiced their own fetishistic equivalent of female genital mutilation, breaking the bones of girls' feet and keeping them painfully bound throughout adulthood. Such practices were opposed by various political drives in the early twentieth century, including the May

Fourth Movement, and then the Communist revolution ended them for good. As far as Lin was concerned, Egypt was still waiting for a real revolution. "It's a waste of talent here," he said. "Look at my family—you see how my wife works. We couldn't have the factory without her. And my daughter runs the shop. If they were Egyptian, they wouldn't be doing that."

In Upper Egypt, almost all Chinese lingerie shops were run by married couples. This arrangement functioned well: the husband dealt with Egyptian male landlords and suppliers, while the wife had more intimate contact with female customers. A couple of times at China Star, I saw an Egyptian woman turn her back to John and me, and then she lifted her *niqab* so Kiki could catch a glimpse of her face. It was a way of establishing a more personal connection that wouldn't have been possible with a male shopkeeper.

When I first lived in China, in the mid-1990s, I was a single man in my twenties, teaching at a small college. The little restaurants and shops around campus were all managed by couples. I often saw a husband and a wife working together in a rice field; on local microbuses, a man drove while his wife collected fares. The society still had serious problems with sexism, and the top government leadership and the executives of virtually all large corporations were males. But in daily life, there was often a sense of shared purpose between men and women. In my first book, I described sitting on the banks of a river at dusk, watching two people on a sampan:

> *They were husband and wife, like so many of the pairs that worked the small fishing boats. The woman stood sculling in the stern with the long oar while her husband worked the nets at the prow. They did not speak to each other. I wondered what that would be like, to be married to somebody and spend all day working together on a boat that was fifteen feet long. The couple on the sampan seemed to be handling it all right.*

A decade and a half later, that description made me laugh. In Cairo, Leslie and I had set up offices in adjacent rooms in our apartment, where both of us worked on books about Egypt. The distance between our desks was roughly the length of a sampan. We alternated research trips; if she needed to go to Alexandria or Minya, I stayed in Zamalek with the twins. Because of Egypt's stark gender division, our material naturally separated as well: Leslie spent most of her time with women, while the majority of my research involved men.

Outside the spiderweb building, none of the nearby restaurants and shops were managed by couples. In rural Egypt, farmwork was segregated, and usually it was male only. Among the Coptic *zabaleen,* the women sorted the trash that their husbands gathered. Sayyid and the other Muslim *zabaleen* didn't allow their wives to do this work, and even the Copts maintained a strict gender division in terms of labor. A Christian wife was allowed to sort the trash, because that could be done at home, but she would never work in public with her husband, driving a truck or hauling garbage from buildings.

It wasn't until I started visiting the Chinese shopkeepers in Upper Egypt that I realized how much I had missed seeing men and women together. It was relaxing to spend time with the Chinese—I could sit and talk with Kiki without worrying about her husband's reaction or whether my male presence might damage her reputation. Those bizarre little shops, with their erotic products and their off-kilter mix of languages, came to feel more like oases of normalcy. Even the Egyptian assistants seemed to sense this. All the women who worked in the shops were unmarried, and invariably they were fascinated by the relationships of their foreign bosses. "They're equal," Rasha, the assistant at the Chinese Lingerie Corner, said about the couple whom she worked for. "And they discuss things. They have arguments, but they talk about it. Egyptians just try to dominate."

In general, the people in the communities seemed to like the Chinese merchants, and they respected their toughness. During one of my visits to the Asyut recycling plant, Chen Caimei was running the place by herself, because Lin Xianfei had gone to China to see a specialist about his stomach problems. Chen was handling purchases of material to be recycled, and two young men from a nearby village arrived at the factory gate in a truck. The bed of the vehicle was full of bottles in burlap sacks.

One of the men was named Omar, and he said that in the past he hadn't had regular work. After the Chinese opened the plant, he started scavenging for plastic, and eventually he partnered with the truck owner. Now they subcontracted to village children who picked up plastic around town. Omar usually earned the equivalent of around thirteen dollars a day, which was double the local wage for a laborer.

While we were talking, Chen burst out of the factory gate. She wore a flowered apron that said, in English, "My Playmate," and her face was a picture of perfect rage.

"Why are you bringing water?" she screamed. She hurled a couple of one-liter bottles at Omar and his companion, who scurried behind the truck. "You're bad!" she shouted in broken Arabic. "Ali Baba, you Ali Baba! I'm angry, angry, angry!"

Chen had discovered the bottles of water in a sack of empties: the recyclers were trying to tip the scales. She kept screaming, "Ali Baba, Ali Baba"; in Egypt, the Chinese often used this *Arabian Nights* reference to call somebody a thief. Omar stayed out of range until Chen stalked back inside the gate.

"By God, I hope a car hits her!" Omar said. "She threw bricks at us once."

A factory foreman named Mohammed Abdul Rahim said something to the effect that Omar deserved to be pelted with whatever he hid in his sacks.

"I'm not the one doing this!" Omar said. "The little kids do it—the kids who collect the bottles."

"He knows what he's doing," Mohammed said to me. He explained that invariably some foreign object was hidden in the sacks, and Chen always discovered it. "It's her right to treat you like that," he said to Omar. "People here would eat her alive if she didn't do this."

Soon Chen reappeared and engaged in another round of Ali Baba abuse. After ranting for a while, she finally sat down and negotiated heatedly with the bottle collectors for a price per kilo. The total for the truckload came to a little more than a hundred dollars. When Omar's partner insisted on receiving the last pound, the equivalent of about twelve cents, Chen slammed the coin on the table like a rejected mah-jongg tile. The young Egyptian made a show of inspecting the bills until he found a fifty that he claimed was too tattered to accept.

"*Filoos muslim!*" Chen shouted. "Muslim money!" But she replaced the bill. The moment the bottle collectors were gone, her anger evaporated, and she talked to me calmly. Like the Egyptian's inspection of his money, Chen's rage had all been a performance.

She wore her hair pulled back in a bun, and she had the broad, weathered face of a Chinese farmer, as well as the reflexive modesty. Once, when I remarked that Chen had been brave to move to Asyut, she brushed aside the compliment. She said that she hadn't had any choice in the matter, because she was uneducated. She was of the generation that had grown up before the economic boom improved education. "I can't read," Chen said. "I didn't go to school at all, not for one day."

Her husband often made similar remarks, referring to the couple's low *suzhi*. But every time I visited, I thought: Here in Egypt, home to more than ninety million people, where Western development workers and billions of dollars of aid have poured in for decades, the first plastic recycling center in the south is a thriving business that employs thirty people, reimburses others for reducing landfill waste, and earns a significant profit. So why was it established by two lingerie-fueled Chinese migrants, one of them illiterate and the other with a fifth-grade education?

CHAPTER 19

WHEN THE POLICE FINALLY GRABBED SAYYID, THEY USED GARBAGE AS bait. The doorman in my building helped set the trap. He saw Sayyid working down the street, and he told him that our building had some trash that needed to be gathered immediately. The moment Sayyid walked through the spiderweb gate, two cops surprised him with a court document.

I was out on an errand, and by the time I returned, the story was everywhere. "Did you hear about Sayyid?" the proprietor of H Freedom asked me. He held out his arms, crossed at the wrists, fists closed. The doorman made the same gesture: handcuffs.

In the end, it had nothing to do with divorce, or child support, or house ownership. Wahiba had found a much more obscure and brilliant way to manipulate the law. Like Sayyid, I had assumed that she had given up, but now she outflanked him with the final move.

I rang Sayyid's number. I got the same automated message that I heard whenever I tried to contact Brotherhood leaders who had vanished into the justice system. "*This number is not a working number. . . .*" I called Sayyid's sister Leila.

"*Sigen,*" she said. "Jail. Sayyid's in jail."

After the police arrested and handcuffed Sayyid, they transported him to the station in Qasr al-Nil, across the river. The cuffs were removed, and Sayyid's phone was confiscated. The officers let him keep his money. They said he was going to need it.

He was placed in a room that served as a holding station, and it was packed with forty detainees. Several had been arrested for selling hashish or tramadol. Other men had been caught with guns. There was one purse snatcher and a couple of drivers who had committed traffic violations. A group of bearded men had been arrested at a small protest in support of Morsi.

When Sayyid entered the room, a very large man told him that it cost twenty pounds to sit on the concrete floor. The very large man had prominent scars on his face and arms. Sayyid paid the twenty pounds. He sat down. One of the bearded Brothers asked him why he had been arrested.

"Exchange of furniture," Sayyid said.

Wahiba's lawyer had come up with the idea. Egyptian marriage contracts are meticulous in recording the various objects contributed by each spouse, which was why any *arusa* in Upper Egypt was so intent on acquiring and documenting the appliances, clothing, lingerie, and other items that she brought to the union. The contract protected assets in the event of a divorce, but it also guarded against rash actions during a fight or separation. Any attempt by one party to remove the goods was against the law.

The lawyer calculated that charging Sayyid with such a violation might be the quickest and most effective way to pressure him. So she filed papers claiming that Sayyid had removed a television, washing machine, stove, and bedroom furniture, all of which were listed under the charge of "exchange of furniture." Of course, none of these things had actually been removed, and in any case Sayyid would have had nowhere to put them, given that he was sleeping on a cot in a garage in Zamalek. But all that mattered was that the charge put into motion the Egyptian law, with all its flaws and corruptions. After the charge was filed, a report went to Sayyid's lawyer, who failed to notify his client. Nobody from the police bothered to check to see if any furniture had actually been removed. Meanwhile, Wahiba's lawyer had a *wasta* connection at the Zamalek police station, so she was able to persuade them to detain Sayyid.

Once Sayyid was in custody, officers immediately started shaking him down for cash. They charged him to use his cell phone to call his sister, and then, after she arrived, they charged her for delivering home-cooked food to Sayyid. The officers began to negotiate a price for his release, but they drew out the process, knowing that a little time in custody would make Sayyid more willing to spend for his freedom. His sister asked me not to go to the station, because the presence of a foreigner would only jack up the price. She seemed calm; like many families in the *ashwa'iyat,* they had had experience with cops and jails. One of Sayyid's half brothers had recently spent more than a year in prison on a charge of selling hashish.

After one night at Qasr al-Nil, Sayyid was handcuffed to another prisoner and transferred to a station in Abdin. Then the usual lack of system led to an argument, because the officers couldn't decide on which side of the river to put Sayyid. They discussed it for a while and then cuffed him and sent him across to Giza. With every transfer, there were new demands for money, and Sayyid was placed with a new group of detainees. They always asked the same question, and he always gave the same response: "exchange of furniture."

Finally, he was deposited in Kirdasah, an *ashwa'iyat* on the Giza side with a bad reputation. There had been some recent high-profile traffic accidents involving drivers who were high on tramadol and other drugs, and the police were cracking down with random drug tests around Cairo. In the Kirdasah detention center, Sayyid found himself sitting next to a trucker who had been busted for driving under the influence.

"I only took half a pill," the trucker said. "It wasn't even tramadol!"

He was an enormous dark-skinned Nubian from Aswan. He drove the long-distance route to Cairo, and like many drivers he took pills. But the Nubian used a knockoff version of Viagra—he claimed that this was a good way to stay alert. In Cairo, he was stopped at a police checkpoint, and apparently some chemical from the Viagra triggered his urine test. "I only took half a pill," he kept saying. He looked at Sayyid's dirty work clothes. "Tramadol?"

"No," Sayyid said. "Exchange of furniture."

Like the other detention rooms, the one at Kirdasah included a group of Islamists. Sayyid quickly learned that it was useful to be on good terms with the bearded men, who received better food than other detainees. The Brotherhood had a long tradition of supporting members who were in jail, and their prison networks had swung into motion since the Rabaa massacre. At Kirdasah, the Islamists shared steak, rice, and pasta with Sayyid. In return, he listened to the men talk about the Quran and the wickedness of Sisi. This was another Brotherhood tradition: for decades, they had preached in Egyptian prisons.

After four days, Sayyid was released. Aiman the Cat, who owned the rights to most of Sayyid's garbage route, proved his decency; he appeared at the Kirdasah station and helped Sayyid's sister negotiate with the police. Finally, Sayyid was given a court date. Before he was freed, some detainees were taken to be sentenced in a Giza courthouse. The poor Viagra-powered Nubian trucker got ten days in jail. *I only took half a pill!*

A couple of hours after Sayyid was released, he stopped by the spiderweb building. He was still dressed in the same clothes in which he had been arrested, but he looked much better than anybody deserved to look after spending three nights on the concrete floors of various Cairo detention rooms. When I opened the door, he gave me a smile and a big Egyptian hand slap. "*Hamdillah salema,*" I said, which is the traditional greeting for somebody who returns from a journey. I didn't know if there was a specific salutation for getting out of jail. Sayyid said he was hungry, so Leslie and I warmed up a plate of roast chicken. He ate the chicken happily.

"So what are you going to do now?" I asked.

"I have to pick up trash." He said that fortunately the detention had occurred over a weekend, when people didn't expect much service. But now the garbage was piling up, and he would be busy for a couple of days.

"No, I mean, what are you going to do about your wife?"

"Oh, that," he said. "I guess I have to talk to my lawyer. I think he's no good."

Sayyid had taken to referring to his lawyer as "the Sheikh of the Scammers." He suspected that the lawyer had deliberately kept him in the dark about the furniture case. Perhaps he wanted more money, or maybe he was in league with Wahiba, a conspiracy theory that appealed to Sayyid. But this wasn't what he wanted to talk about right now.

"I have to ask you something about America," he said. He explained that in detention one of the tramadol dealers had told him about an American chemical product with special powers. If a man sprayed himself with this special American product, he became sexually irresistible.

"Sayyid, there's no such thing," I said.

"Are you sure? This guy said that women can't control themselves if they smell it."

"*Ya rait!*" Leslie said scornfully. "You wish!"

He talked a little about the detention. The police had found an unresolved complaint in his file, something about a fight that happened years ago, and it had complicated his release. This was the kind of thing that Manu worried about: nobody ever had any idea what might show up in his police file. Sayyid finished the chicken quickly and asked for more. I had never known anybody who could eat like him.

I asked again if he was going to see his wife and children. He looked up. "When you make your next trip to America," he said, "can you pick up some of that special spray?"

"Sayyid, stop talking about this stupid stuff!" Leslie exploded. "You just spent four days in jail, and you haven't paid anything for your kids in weeks—and this is what you're thinking about? What's in your head? You need to think about your problems! Do something!"

"I guess so." He seemed mildly chastened.

"So what are you going to do about your wife?"

"I don't know," he said. "Maybe I'll talk to her."

I feared that like so many things in Egypt it would circle around and around, with the same pattern repeated endlessly. For a while, Sayyid grumbled about the charge of "exchange of furniture," but he wasn't complaining about the flawed legal system or the corrupt police. Instead, he seemed annoyed that he wasn't the one who had come up with the idea to file a case like that. He blamed the Sheikh of the Scammers. That was the main lesson Sayyid seemed to take from the case: from now on, he wouldn't pay his lawyer's outstanding bills.

CHAPTER 20

THE PRESIDENTIAL ELECTION WAS SCHEDULED FOR THE END OF MAY 2014. During the campaign, the new protest law was being strictly enforced, and Rifaat prepared a telephone dialogue for class. It was titled "At Your Service," and it combined two of his favorite things—Arabic politeness and Egyptian sarcasm:

A: *Hello, is this the Ministry of the Interior, Branch of Protests?*

B: *Yes it is, sir. Is there something I can help you with?*

A: *With your permission, I want to reserve a protest for tomorrow from two o'clock until six o'clock.*

B: *At your service, sir. Would you like Central Security Forces, ambulances, and emergency police with your protest?*

A: *Just the Central Security Forces, please. We are already full.*

B: *(Laughing.) It's sweet like honey, sir! Would you like water with your protest? Or do you want tear gas and nightsticks, because they are free?*

A: *May all be good with you, by God. But one likes to return home dry.*

B: *Do you want snipers, bird shot, and thugs with your order?*

A: *No, it's as sweet as jasmine this way. Thank you.*

Despite the repressive climate, Rifaat planned to vote for Sisi. It was another of his contradictions: he couldn't resist the appeal of a military man who seemed to combine strength with a softer side. Rifaat liked the way that Sisi spoke, the exaggerated gentleness of his voice, and he liked the clear allusions to Nasser. "Mubarak didn't care about the people," Rifaat said. "He wanted to deceive them. But the people love Sisi, and because the people love him, he'll do the right thing."

In class, we studied the lyrics of a popular song called "All of Us Love Sisi." It was sung by a man named Shabola, who had worked as a laundryman in an *ashwa'iyat* before finding fame as a performer:

You said you want orders, and here we are ordering you,
We order you to be the president and the people thank you.

The notion of a military leader responding to civilian orders had a long history in Egyptian politics. In 1967, after Egypt and its allies were routed by Israel in that year's Arab-Israeli War, Nasser announced his resignation. Citizens wept in the streets of Cairo, begging him to stay on, and soon the president agreed. He explained that he had no choice but to follow the will of the people.

Part of the dynamic was that it reversed the usual direction of gratitude in a democracy. The candidate didn't need to thank his supporters; instead, the supporters thanked the candidate for agreeing to run. And the responsibility for change was effectively theirs. Sisi often reminded Egyptians of their shortcomings: he said that people slept too late, and he criticized their work ethic. At a meeting of military officers that was recorded and released as part of the Sisileaks, the general complained that citizens expected *zabaleen* to pick up their trash but wouldn't pay for the service. They also spent too much time on their phones. "People are walking around all the time like this," Sisi said, holding an imaginary phone to his ear. "No, no, no, my son—countries like this will never grow and have a real will to work and fight."

He often sounded like a father hectoring a small child. "You are like the very older brother," he told a group of military officers in another leaked conversation, in which he described how the army should view the nation's citizens. "Or the very big father who has a son who is a bit of a failure, not paying attention." Strictness was essential to good parenting. "Are you going to endure my making you walk on your own two feet?" Sisi asked. "Are you going to endure waking up at five o'clock every day? Are you going to endure eating less, having less air-conditioning? Will you be able to stand my removing the subsidies altogether?" He continued, "This Sisi is torment and suffering."

Something about the allusions to family, and the Egyptians' tendency to criticize their own society, struck a chord. And it reversed another pattern of electoral politics: now it was the voters, and not the candidate, who made empty campaign promises. Shabola sang,

We will wake up at five o'clock, no laziness from now on,
If we eat only one meal, as long as it is with you it will be like honey,
A condiment with you is tastier than a kebab,
We'll live in peace and love, no more terrorism.

Sisi himself promised nothing. He had no real platform, and he didn't run as a member of a party. He never described the institution of any system or structure that would help to improve the flaws that he observed in Egyptian society. His campaign organized rallies in Cairo and other cities, but Sisi didn't bother to attend a single event. He was a naturally gifted speaker, but like many military men he seemed to dislike and distrust politics. He saw no need to tell his personal story, which remained somewhat mysterious. Even the campaign's official YouTube channel identified two conflicting birthplaces for the candidate.

Journalists weren't allowed to visit his central campaign headquarters, but a European diplomat told me about the experience. The rented building was located in the Fifth Settlement, one of Mubarak's desert cities. The headquarters were heavily secured, but after the diplomat passed through the metal detectors and was searched by soldiers, she found the place empty except for a pair of retired government officials. They were talking about how much they looked forward to getting back to their retirement after the election was finished.

"If you visit a campaign headquarters, it should be bustling with young people," she said. "He chose not to campaign. But that could have been an opportunity to build a connection with young people." She noted that in functioning democracies, the young play an important role in campaigns and in the offices of elected officials, where as aides they often have significant responsibilities. But in Egypt, where more than half the population was under the age of twenty-five, the lack of institutions meant that young people had no way of getting involved in politics, apart from protesting on the street.

For Sisi, dismissive attitudes toward the young seemed ingrained in his background. Within the hierarchical army, youths had little value other than as a raw resource—the hordes of conscripts who arrived every year. And Sisi's family followed strict traditions of paternalism. His grandfather had started a successful business making arabesques, wooden objects that are intricately patterned with inlaid mother-of-pearl. Over time, the extended Sisi clan came to dominate this trade in Khan al-Khalili, the premier tourist market in Cairo.

The family still owned nearly ten Khan al-Khalili shops, and one afternoon I stopped at a store that was being tended by Mossad Ali Hamama, the thirty-two-year-old son of one of Sisi's cousins. Hamama said that all teenage males in the clan—and only males—spent their summers apprenticed into some aspect of the business. As a boy, Sisi had trained as a *sadafgi:* he used a long-handled knife to carve out tiny pieces of mother-of-pearl.

"We don't have a situation where we say, 'This is the son of a business owner, and this is the son of a president,'" Hamama said. "The only rule is about the way the elders and the youngers interact. If we're talking about my father's cousin, if he's older than me, then I obey him." He continued, "If an elder comes into the shop, even if he's not in the business, he'll sit down here as if he owned the shop. Our family is not from Upper Egypt, but you can say we have this tradition of the Upper Egyptians."

An image came to mind: some uneducated geezer visiting from the ancestral village, sprawled out in a chair, barking for tea. I asked Hamama if, as a young person, this strict sense of hierarchy ever bothered him.

"No, it's the opposite," he replied. "Because just as I respect my elders, one day I will be old and somebody will respect me. It's a continuation. It's a feeling of safety to have this hierarchy."

During the period after the Rabaa massacre, Manu did some of his best research. By now, even the Egyptian private press no longer criticized the government. In the initial wake of the coup, journalists at such organizations had been so relieved at the defeat of the Brotherhood that they supported the military, and now fear contributed to their docility. For the most part, only foreign papers looked into the atrocities of the state. There was a notorious instance in which thirty-seven Egyptian prisoners died while being transported in a prison truck—the same kind of vehicle that had been used to move Sayyid around town during his detention. The authorities claimed that the prisoners had been Morsi supporters who rioted, leaving the cops with no choice but to fire tear gas at the vehicle, which resulted in the men dying by asphyxiation.

Working with Patrick Kingsley, a British correspondent for the *Guardian*, Manu interviewed former prisoners who had survived in the truck, policemen who had witnessed the event, and human rights activists who were also investigating. Kingsley's article revealed that the official story of the riot and the teargassing was almost certainly a fabrication. The deaths happened because of a combination of incompetence and cruelty: the van, which was designed to hold twenty-four people, had been packed with forty-five, and the vehicle was left in the August heat for hours. When prisoners begged for water and started to faint, they were taunted by cops. Most of the men who died were young, and some had been arrested at random; they had had nothing to do with Morsi or the protests.

After the prison-van deaths, I was struck by how sanguine Sayyid and his family were during his detention. But the real story of the deaths hadn't been told in the mainstream Egyptian press, and in any case people were desensitized. They knew that any contact with the police was dangerous and unpredictable, but this had been true for decades. And life was full of risks for people who worked hard jobs and lived in the *ashwa'iyat*.

Manu liked doing the research. It was one thing he truly had faith in—he said that even if most educated Egyptians ignored the abuses of the state, it was important for them to be documented. Of course, the work became riskier all the time, and so did being gay. At times, his attitude toward threats was almost nihilistic, as if there was nothing he could do to anticipate or avoid trouble. But this was also a kind of desensitization, because Manu often observed the randomness of danger in Cairo. A person could find himself in all kinds of threatening situations in the city, and survive unscathed, and then return home and have something terrible happen. It was like the spiderweb elevator outside my door.

Late one evening, Manu and a friend went to the gay hangout on the Qasr al-Nil Bridge. While they were there, they struck up a conversation with another man in his early twenties named Ahmed. The three of them talked for a while, and then they left in Manu's friend's car. They parked in another part of the city and drank some beers.

Ahmed was in his early twenties. He had a gentle manner, and he came from one of the *ashwa'iyat.* He chatted with Manu for hours, complaining about the things that young men often complained about: lack of job prospects, lack of money, lack of marriage possibilities. From what Manu could tell, Ahmed was straight—"at least by the standards of Egypt," which was Manu's usual qualifier. They had sex that evening.

Afterward, they drank beer and talked in Manu's living room. Manu was gazing out the window when Ahmed approached him from behind and shattered two beer bottles in rapid succession atop his head.

There had been no provocation. Later, Manu couldn't even recall what they had been talking about. He remembered that Ahmed came at him with a third, heavier bottle, and somehow Manu fought him off and pushed him out of the apartment. After locking the door, Manu collapsed, bleeding badly.

He called two foreign friends, who helped him get to the hospital. A doctor stitched his head and sent him home; over the next few days, Manu suffered from headaches and dizziness, so he returned to the hospital for a brain scan. The scan showed bleeding in the brain, and the doctor said that Manu had sustained a bad concussion. When the doctor asked how it had happened, Manu said he had fallen down.

Three days after the attack, Ahmed showed up outside the apartment, accompanied by another young man. Ahmed pleaded with Manu to talk with him, but Manu kept the heavy metal door to the apartment locked. He was shaking with fear when he shouted at Ahmed to leave. Manu didn't know why the young man had returned—it was one of many unanswerable questions. Why the sudden attack? Why hadn't he tried to steal anything? Why did he bring a friend when he came back?

I was out of the country when it happened, and Manu sent me a short note. He seemed different when I returned. The doctor told him not to drink alcohol for a month because of the concussion, and Manu was avoiding his usual downtown hangouts. His head was badly scarred. After recovering, he swore off the Qasr al-Nil Bridge. And soon he decided there was only one path forward: he would try to flee Egypt.

For much of the presidential campaign, I was traveling in the south. I took a couple of driving trips every month, searching for Chinese traders and visiting archaeological sites. In towns, I passed through heavily armed checkpoints, and I stopped at tourist destinations that used to be thronged before the Arab Spring. Since 2010, the year before the revolution, revenues from Egypt's ancient monuments had dropped by more than 95 percent. When I visited the famous tomb of Tutankhamun in Luxor, I was the only person there. A guard at a nobleman's crypt in Amarna said that his last visitor had left ten days earlier. He told me that once, on a hot day, he had fallen asleep inside the empty tomb, only to be awakened by an *'afrit* slapping him across the face. Guards in remote places often had stories about spirits—these seemed to be the only visitors nowadays.

Many archaeologists had worked steadily through the Arab Spring, and Abydos was particularly active. A team from the University of Pennsylvania was excavating what was believed to be the longest rock-cut tomb in Egypt. It had been built for Senwosret III, a powerful pharaoh who ruled during the Middle Kingdom, in the nineteenth century BC. Senwosret III was known for his military victories, especially in gold-rich Nubia, where he became the first pharaoh to establish a permanent military presence. He was also an effective propagandist. He commissioned hymns that, like Shabola's song about Sisi, addressed the pharaoh in the voice of the people:

How Egypt rejoices in your strong arm:
you have safeguarded its traditions.
How the common people rejoice in your counsel:
your power has won increase for them.

By the time of Senwosret III, the great age of pyramid building was long past, but the king wanted to connect himself to the glories of those early pharaohs. So he commissioned a massive tomb in Abydos, at the far edge of the Buried, beneath Mount Anubis. The natural form of the mountain recalled the shape of a pyramid, and the king's tomb was carved into the bedrock. Centuries later, the pharaohs of the New Kingdom would follow this pattern, constructing their own tombs beneath natural features in the Valley of the Kings.

The tomb of Senwosret III had been looted repeatedly in ancient times. Under the Romans, people used it as a quarry, hauling out beautifully carved pieces of red quartzite and other stones. They left a mess of rubble in their wake, and when modern archaeologists finally entered the tomb, in 1901, they soon determined that it was unlikely to contain artifacts of value. A number of Egyptologists believed that the chambers were actually a cenotaph—a symbolic tomb where the king wasn't buried. On the site, archaeologists made a cursory examination over a period of two years and then closed off the entrance, allowing it to be buried by the windblown sand.

A century later, in 2004, a University of Pennsylvania archaeologist named Josef Wegner returned to the site in order to conduct a thorough excavation. During Wegner's first season, a team of two hundred workers hauled sand for three months before they even reached the tomb's entrance. After that, they proceeded slowly into the tomb, room by room, carrying out rubble. Everything had to be moved by wheelbarrows and brigades of workers passing buckets by hand, because heavy machinery would damage the structure.

By the time I visited, Wegner had been excavating for nine years. His team had cleared out roughly half the length of the tomb, and they had arranged a generator that powered lights and fans for ventilation. From the entrance, we followed a string of bare electric bulbs down some steep ramps, and then we came to a long tunnel that ran into the bedrock. It passed two impressive side chambers.

"We dug this out last year," Wegner said, stopping in one of the chambers. He pointed at the roof, which was twenty feet high. "It was full to the ceiling with debris." The walls consisted of perfectly smooth hand-dressed limestone blocks that shined ghostly white in the electric light. "It's mind-boggling the work that went into this," Wegner said.

He hadn't figured out the original purpose of these rooms. Wegner believed that the tomb had been an actual burial place, and not a cenotaph, and he hoped that he could find evidence. He estimated that it would take another year or two to clear the tomb to its end point.

We continued to some wooden ramps and ladders that had been arranged by the excavators. The ramps descended into another long passageway where the team was currently working. Half a dozen young men chipped away at the debris with shovels and pickaxes. They were listening to Egyptian pop music on a speaker. This was where the line of electric lights and fans ended; up ahead, the tunnel continued, but it was mostly filled with rubble.

"If you want to keep going, you can," Wegner said, pointing to a gap in the debris. He had crawled through recently, along with some of his excavators. He estimated that it continued for at least three hundred more feet.

I took a headlamp out of my backpack. Wegner handed me a big battery-powered lantern. "I think you're going to want this," he said.

I clambered into the tunnel. For a short while, it was possible to crouch and walk, but then the debris forced me to crawl. The music echoed off the rock walls, growing steadily fainter, until it disappeared entirely. It was hard to imagine another setting in which a pop song felt so fleeting.

Soon the light of the excavation was also gone. My headlamp seemed as feeble as a candle, so I switched on the lantern. Above me, on the ceiling, I could see a red line that had been drawn more than thirty-eight centuries ago to guide the workers who carved this tunnel.

Ever so gradually, the red line curved to the right. The tunnel had been designed to bend a full 180 degrees, all the while descending into the bedrock. Wegner believed that the tunnel was a symbolic representation of the *amduat,* the path of the Egyptian sun god at night. According to tradition, each day ends with the god descending in the west, where he enters the earth and makes a full arc underground before reappearing in the east. That was my route—the tunnel tracked the nighttime sun.

Arthur Weigall, the first modern archaeologist who excavated this tomb, suffered from claustrophobia. Crawling through the passage, I felt a new appreciation for his love of the Sahara—"the breathing-space of the world," as he described it. Weigall started work on the Senwosret III tomb in 1901, but after experiencing the rubble-filled passage, he quickly passed the excavation off to Charles Currelly, a Canadian archaeologist. By 1903, Currelly had also had enough.

The intensity of the heat inside the passage surprised me. Most of my underground experience had been in natural caves, where running water and airflow create cool temperatures. But a long tomb, like a mine, is subject to the geothermal gradient: the deeper you go, the hotter it gets. Soon I was drenched in sweat. On the floor of the passage, I saw small pottery bowls with blackened centers, which served as simple torches in ancient times, when tomb thieves filled the bowls with flammable oil. Periodically I crawled past broken amphorae, the red vessels that Roman-era looters used to carry drinking water. They had worked in this place, quarrying the stone from the walls, during the third and fourth centuries AD. By then, the tomb was already ancient. I was closer in time to those Roman looters than they had been to the age of Senwosret III.

My breath came in gasps. It was impossible to imagine what it would have been like for the builders, whose tools consisted of nothing more sophisticated than bronze chisels and hard pounding stones. Wegner had told me that eventually I would reach what he believed to be the final chamber, where it was possible to stand upright. It took about ten minutes and felt like forever. After I was finally able to stand, I shone the light on my compass and saw that the tunnel's bend was complete. At the entrance, I had moved in a westward direction, but now I faced east. Directly ahead, beyond hundreds of feet of solid rock, lay the Nile's green valley.

I switched off the lantern. The darkness was total: it made no difference whether my eyes were open or closed. Intense heat radiated in from all directions—the floor, the ceiling, the walls. The only sound in this place was the pounding of my heart.

It's impossible to know what the ancient laborers thought about building this tomb. Maybe they resented it, or maybe they obediently followed the spirit of the king's song: "*How the common people rejoice in your counsel!*" They left no physical traces. The bodies of laborers must have been laid to rest somewhere near Abydos, but it wouldn't have been in the elevated and privileged terrain of the Buried. Most likely their graves were in the valley, where they were washed away by millennia of Nile floods.

For archaeologists, the best hope for an intact burial ground of the non-elite was always Akhenaten's city. "A will-of-the-wisp, the dream of a rich unplundered cemetery of the middle classes at el-'Amarneh, full of choice vases and amulets, beckons to each successive explorer," Francis Llewellyn Griffith, a British Egyptologist, wrote after excavating in 1923. The city's brief history meant that any cemetery could be precisely dated. Griffith sent surveyors into the desert, but he ultimately declared the search hopeless: "There are square miles of sand wastes leveled by wind and rain where a cemetery might lie without indications on the surface."

Nearly eighty years later, in 2003, Barry Kemp commissioned a modern survey of the desert. The surveyor found human bones and pieces of pottery on the surface of several locations, and test digs confirmed the find: four separate cemeteries, all of them apparently dedicated to the average workers who built the king's new city.

Under the guidance of Anna Stevens, the assistant director of the Amarna Project, excavators started with the largest of the cemeteries. When I visited them in the spring of the presidential election, the project had been ongoing for nearly a decade. They had collected a sample of bones that belonged to at least 440 Amarna residents. Only two sets were found with names: a woman named Maya and a woman named Hesyenre. But the other skeletons were intact enough to be studied as individuals. For each person, the team recorded the age of death, the condition of the bones, the signs of disease or injury, and the presence of any grave goods.

One morning at the dig house, I watched a young American bioarchaeologist named Ashley Shidner arrange a set of delicate, sparrowlike bones atop a wooden table. "The clavicle is here, and the upper arm, the ribs, the lower legs," she said. "This one is about a year and a half to two years old."

The bones showed evidence of malnutrition, which was common in the cemetery's children. "The growth delay starts around seven and a half months," Shidner said. "That's when you start transition feeding from breast milk to solid food." She continued, "Possibly the mother is making the decision that there's not enough food."

Even for Amarna residents who survived childhood, the prospects were grim. Of the burials where age at death was known, 70 percent of individuals were younger than thirty-five. More than one-third were dead by the age of fifteen. Only a few individuals lived beyond fifty. Children's growth patterns were delayed by as much as two years, and many adults sustained spinal damage, probably as a result of overwork during the construction of the new city.

It's hard to put the results into context, because there's never been such a detailed survey of an ancient commoners' cemetery elsewhere in Egypt. But there are some scattered examples, and the evidence seems to indicate that life in Amarna was significantly harder than it was in most times and places. Certainly the story of the bones contradicts everything that was inscribed into the walls of the king's buildings and the noblemen's tombs that were located high in the cliffs above the desert. In tomb scenes that feature the Great Aten Temple, hundreds of offering tables are heaped with food.

"I started out with the hypothesis that we should see good health and good nutrition because the drawings on the tombs show Akhenaten's reign being a time of great bounty," Jerry Rose, a professor from the University of Arkansas who was directing the bioarchaeologists, told me. "And he says that nobody had used this land before him. Nobody had contaminated the site, so we shouldn't have as much disease and parasitism. But not only did we find more disease, and more evidence of malnutrition, but we also found that we didn't get a teenage trough. Mortality was a straight line. There were just as many dead teenagers as babies and adults. The evidence points to something fairly extreme."

The commoners' cemetery showed no signs of Akhenaten's revolution. In the nobles' tombs, there are many scenes of the royal family, the Aten, and the rituals of the new faith. But none of that appears in the graves of average people. "There's no Aten," Anna Stevens said. "There's no mention of Akhenaten or Nefertiti. It's like it's not their place."

After the team finished studying the first cemetery, they proceeded to a second burial ground to the north. Anna Stevens sensed something strange from the beginning of the excavation. "At the end of the day, we'd come together for lunch, and we'd ask, 'Did anybody get an adult?'" she said. "And everybody would say no."

Of the 135 bodies that they excavated, over 90 percent were twenty-five or younger. More than half died between the ages of seven and fifteen. All of them, even the smallest children, show evidence of hard labor. Many seem to have been buried hastily. There's no evidence of violent death, but family groupings apparently broke down; in many cases, it looks as if two or three unrelated people were tossed together into a pit.

"This is very clearly not a normal death curve," Stevens said. "It may be no coincidence that this area had the king's limestone quarries. Is this a group of workers who are being conscripted on the basis of their youth and effectively worked to death?" She also wondered if a plague had struck near the end of Akhenaten's reign.

Like Kemp, Stevens had always focused on the city site rather than on the royal family. She had little interest in Akhenaten and Nefertiti, and she believed that Amarna's houses and streets would reflect the way that average people lived. But after excavating the cemeteries, she realized that even the hard evidence of a city can be misleading. "I think we always want to see the best in quiet little mud-brick houses," she said. "Even as trained archaeologists, we have a tendency to see the best of the living environment. It's the human remains that communicate the realities of life."

The Arab Spring also changed her perspective on the ancient rulers. When I talked to Egyptians in Amarna and Minya, they sometimes made direct comparisons: Morsi was Akhenaten, and Sisi was Horemheb. For Stevens, the connections weren't so literal, but she found herself fascinated by the eternal nature of certain patterns. "Living through this time has made me think much more about Akhenaten, and the impact of revolutions, and the downfall of dictators," she said. "I'm struck by this interest in a strong male leader. It's the same back then; it's the same now. Everybody is running after Sisi because he's a strong man."

I was in Amarna for the election. Voting was scheduled for two days in late May, but the government extended it by another day, because turnout was so weak. Sisi's opponent, a Nasserite named Hamdeen Sabahi, had few resources behind his campaign, and some of his supporters had been arrested. All Islamist parties and candidates had been banned.

On one of the days of voting, I drove to Minya to visit polling stations. As always, the vote was orderly and peaceful, but I noticed that Islamists seemed to be staying home—I saw fewer beards and *niqabs* than usual. Near one voting station, I bought some water from a kiosk that was run by two middle-aged men with bushy beards, prayer bruises, and clean hands. That was another telltale marker: every voter had his finger stained with purple ink, to protect against repeat voting. I asked one of the bearded men why he hadn't gone to the polls.

"We voted five times already," he said. "And the results of those votes were thrown in the garbage. So why do it again?"

He said he was a former member of al-Gama'a al-Islamiyya, the Islamist organization that had engaged in terrorism in the past, including the assassination of Sadat. Salah Bayoumi, the former bagpiper whom I met outside Cairo, had also been a member of this group. The last I heard, Bayoumi was still living freely in the desert village, but I hadn't contacted him since the coup—it seemed too likely to cause him trouble.

The man at the kiosk said that he had spent a total of seventeen years in prison. "You know how they treated people," he said. "Look at this—" He lifted the hem of his galabiya. Each ankle was encircled by a band of white scar tissue.

"This was from being hung upside down," he said. He explained that guards used to put handcuffs around his ankles, hoist him to the ceiling, and pummel him. He pointed to his companion: "He's the same." Without a word, the other bearded man lifted his galabiya: more white rings.

I asked the first man how he had felt when Sadat was shot.

"I was young and enthusiastic, so I was happy," he said. "But I felt different later." He explained that Mubarak had turned out to be even more repressive than Sadat.

I asked if he thought that the Islamists would react violently to Sisi's becoming president.

"People are committed to peacefulness," he said. "Have you seen any violence?"

He was right: there had been surprisingly few incidents during the election period. The Brotherhood had been banned as a terrorist organization, but there was no evidence that they were behind the scattered bombings and attacks that occasionally occurred. Most of the problems were in Sinai, where the most prominent terrorist group eventually pledged allegiance to ISIS, at the end of 2014. But there was virtually no unrest in Upper Egypt. During my travels, I sensed that the south was no longer a hotbed of radical Islamism, probably because people had already experienced it so intensely in the 1980s and 1990s. It was a kind of inoculation: citizens had seen firsthand that even the assassination of a president didn't change much.

I asked the bearded man whether he had done anything violent during his years with al-Gama'a al-Islamiyya.

"In terms of actually participating in violence, no," he said. "But maybe I helped arrange a situation, or hosted somebody who was going to do something."

"Was it wrong to use violence?"

"There's a difference between wrong and useless," he said, smiling. "The violence was simply useless."

I saw few young people at the polling stations. In the evening, there was a small pro-Sisi rally in one of the Minya parks, but the youths who showed up seemed halfhearted. Some of the young who did vote told me that they were doing so at the command of their fathers or clan elders. It was a tradition in many places for elders to instruct younger family members how to cast their ballots.

Across Egypt, men aged fifty-five or older represented only 5.7 percent of the population. I was often struck by how rare these older men were and yet how much power they wielded. Once, I mentioned this dynamic in an article about villages in the south, and Barry Kemp sent an email:

> As for the age profile of your population, it sounds very much like what we have found in the cemeteries of the people of Amarna. Very few reached their fifties and most had died before 25. But the reason was very different: high death rate amongst the young rather than a high birthrate. But the effect, for that time, would have been similar, privileging the few elders.

Before moving to Egypt, I had seen images of all the youths in Tahrir, and it seemed inevitable that sheer demographics would transform the country. Numbers meant power—to me, that seemed obvious. But now I realized that my assumption came from a perspective that was narrowly Western and democratic. Sometimes it was more useful to think in material terms, like an archaeologist. Real power comes from scarcity; abundance is something that one can afford to waste. In Egypt, youth was cheap.

Sisi won 96 percent of the vote. After taking office, the president formed an official youth commission, and as its director he appointed a man who was fifty-three years old. During Sisi's first year in power he announced that Egypt would build a brand-new capital city in the desert.

CHAPTER 21

MANU KNEW AS WELL AS ANYBODY THAT THIS WAS A TERRIBLE TIME TO be a refugee. Syrians came to Egypt from the east, and Libyans from the west; in both cases, they fled regimes that had collapsed or been weakened by the Arab Spring. The vast majority of these migrants hoped to continue to Europe, and they converged along Egypt's northern coast, searching for sea passage. As the crisis was building, Manu sometimes interviewed them for stories in the *Guardian*. In 2014, tens of thousands of migrants came to northern Egypt, and in one accident five hundred drowned while trying to sail to Malta. Manu met a Syrian in Alexandria who had made eleven attempts to cross the Mediterranean, and eleven times he had failed.

That was one of Manu's rules: no boats.

It was relatively rare for Egyptians to flee as refugees. The nation had suffered since 2011, but it had never been close to collapse, and it seemed even less likely that this would happen now. Other places in the region were much more vulnerable, because their borders had been stitched together by modern colonialists who cared little about tensions between tribes and sects. Despite all of the cultural incursions that Egypt had suffered over the centuries, its geography remained eternal: one river, one country. I almost never met Egyptians who talked about the place disintegrating. This was the faith that mattered most—not Islam, and not Christianity, but belief in the first place on earth to define itself as a nation.

Some Egyptian Muslim Brothers had fled after the Rabaa massacre, but otherwise most departures were people with money who found legal avenues like overseas degree programs. Manu decided that his best path was another version of the legal route. If he made a series of foreign trips abroad, as a tourist, then he could establish a pattern of travel that might persuade a European country to grant him a visa. His goal was to make it to Germany, which sometimes granted asylum to individuals who had suffered abuse or discrimination because of their sexuality.

Manu still had the police report from his arrest, and he met with a Cairo-based representative of the Office of the United Nations High Commissioner for Refugees to document his story. On his own, he arranged for a short tourist trip to Cyprus. He remembered what his father had said about the charge of attempted rape, and whether it would prevent him from leaving the country. *You'll know when you get to the airport.*

On the day of departure, Manu went to the passport control in the Cairo Airport. The official took his document and typed on a computer.

"Can you step aside?" he said.

Manu waited. The official took the passport to another computer. Time crawled: five minutes, ten minutes, fifteen. Manu felt a panic so intense that he wanted to run. But there was nothing he could do but wait. At last the official returned.

"Fine," he said.

In Cyprus, the first thing Manu did was buy a beer and sit down next to the sea.

In the months after Sayyid was released from detention, he once again tried to spend more time at home. On weekends, when he brought his sons to Zamalek, the boys looked happy and healthy. Sayyid rarely complained about Wahiba, who had dropped the charge of furniture theft. I kept waiting for the inevitable fight to flare up, but after a period of months I started to wonder if things had actually changed.

That year Ramadan came in June. One day, Sayyid invited Leslie and me to his home for the *iftar* meal, and we drove to Ard al-Liwa in the Honda. On the road, men walked between lanes of cars, handing out free plastic bags of fruit juice. This was Ramadan generosity—if a fasting driver happened to be stuck in traffic when the prayer call sounded, he could drink something to tide him over until he got home.

In Sayyid's neighborhood, the narrow streets had been decorated with silver streamers and traditional *fawanees* lanterns. Wahiba greeted us at the door. It was the first time I had seen her since the day she had brought her children to the Family Court Office, as part of the filing for divorce. Now she welcomed us into the home, her eyes smiling behind the *niqab*.

Most of the meal was already laid out on the floor of their upstairs sitting room: beef, chicken, potatoes cooked in tomato sauce, and peppers and vine leaves stuffed with rice. Sayyid and Zizou, the older son, sat on the floor, staring at the food and the cups of water that had been arranged around the plates. This was the second year that Zizou was fasting; he had just finished third grade. His brother, Yusuf, was still young enough that he wasn't expected to fast for the entire day. But he waited beside the food with everybody else. Even Lamis, who wasn't yet three, sat there without eating or drinking.

Sayyid was fasting this year. He had an exemption because of his labor, and in the past he had often eaten or at least drunk water during the hot days of hauling garbage. I sensed that now he was being strict about the fast almost as a form of penance. He looked exhausted, and he kept glancing at the television, which played the evening news. The program would be interrupted when the prayer call sounded.

Wahiba finished the last couple of dishes and joined us. Now the whole family was together, their eyes flickering back and forth between the food and the television. When I went to people's homes for *iftar,* there was always this final stretch of distracted waiting.

At last the news switched to the sound of the call, and everybody reached for water. Sayyid remarked that it was important not to drink too much at first. He ate steadily, pacing himself so as not to upset his empty stomach. With every bite, Wahiba had to tug at the bottom of her *niqab,* lifting it just enough so that she could get her fork into her mouth without revealing her face.

Before Leslie and I had come, we had wondered whether we would see Wahiba at all. But the couple seemed comfortable together, and after the meal we remained on the floor, chatting. The topic of marriage came up, and I asked how they first met. Sayyid told the story of catching a glimpse of Wahiba on her brother's balcony.

She went into another room and returned with a photo album from their wedding ceremony. She sat between Leslie and me, flipping through the pages. In the photographs, the bride and groom sat next to each other atop a raised platform. Sayyid wore a dark suit and tie, and he was thinner, with an unlined face—suddenly I saw how much the work as a *zabal* had aged him. Wahiba wore a white dress and her face was heavily made up. She was not smiling. Her expression seemed nervous, almost fearful. Only a month before Wahiba's wedding, she had turned eighteen. In the photographs she looked even younger.

She flipped through the album's pages, naming the various relatives and guests and laughing at the way that she and Sayyid had looked. I had never grown accustomed to interacting with women who wore the *niqab,* which of course was the reason they wore the garment in the first place. But now it seemed particularly absurd: a veiled woman showing me photographs of her face. What was the point? And perhaps the same thought occurred to Wahiba, because after a while she set the album down and went into the side room. When she returned her face was uncovered.

The only other time I had seen her unveiled was nearly three years earlier, at Lamis's *sebou* celebration. That glimpse had been so fleeting, and there had been so much conflict in the intervening period, that I had long ago forgotten what she looked like. But now I recognized her immediately—the fair skin, the strong features. She was sweating from having worn the *niqab* in the heat, and she wiped her face with a cloth.

And from the moment she removed the face covering, the tone of our interaction changed. The conversation became more familiar, more personal; there was a new warmth. And it was much easier for Leslie and me to understand Wahiba. As moderate speakers of Arabic, we often relied on facial expressions to supplement our comprehension, but this process was so subtle and instinctive that we didn't realize its importance. Now for the first time I grasped how much I lost when speaking with somebody whose face was obscured.

Her questions also seemed bolder once the veil was gone. She asked how Leslie and I had met, and Leslie explained that both of us had been working as journalists in Beijing.

"Were you married in China?"

I said that actually we hadn't had a formal wedding ceremony. I didn't mention the last-minute Egyptian-visa marriage in Ouray County—it was hard enough to explain in English.

"So how did you know you were married?" she said.

"I guess it was just a personal agreement."

"But were you together before you were married?" She narrowed her eyes slightly, and I gathered that she was referring to sex. "Yes," I said.

Wahiba shook her head. "That's *mamnouh* in Egypt," she said. "Not allowed."

"It's common in America."

"What about after people are married? Can they be with others at the same time?"

"Usually not," I said. "But there's no law against it. Sometimes people do this. It's different for everybody."

"What about for the two of you?"

"No," I said. "For us it's *mamnouh*."

In the weeks that followed, Sayyid seemed happy and relaxed. On weekends, when he brought the boys to Zamalek, they always stopped by our apartment. I told Sayyid that we wanted to have the family over for dinner, and one night I drove to Ard al-Liwa and picked them up. The boys wore neat new shirts and trousers, and Sayyid had a nice pair of jeans that he had acquired when a foreigner on his route moved away. Lamis wore an outfit that we had given her after the twins outgrew it. Wahiba's face was covered, and her black dress had silver embroidery on the front.

Leslie and I had spent some time considering possible menus. We wanted to serve something that could be identified as American, but it had to appeal to the rural Egyptian palate. Ideally there would be plenty of meat. Fried was always good. And so, for the first time in our married lives, Leslie and I prepared a dinner party that consisted of Shake 'n Bake chicken, instant biscuits, potatoes, and no wine.

The children loved it, and Sayyid ate his usual enormous amount. Wahiba kept her *niqab* on until the food appeared, and then she quietly pinned the garment to the back of her head. And that became the usual pattern: whenever we were together in a private setting, she met us with her face uncovered. I had always considered the *niqab* to have religious connotations, but now I realized that for Wahiba it was basically pragmatic. Life was simpler in her community if she wore the face cover: there was less harassment on the street, and she could run errands and take her sons to school without attracting attention. But if she was in a private setting with people who weren't going to judge her for supposed immodesty, then she discarded the veil.

She was strict with her children. In our home, if we handed the boys a plate of cookies or some other treat, they immediately passed it to our daughters without touching anything. We had to offer it three or four times before the boys would accept. These were the social rules I remembered from the *Dardasha* text, but in my experience they were rarely applied to Egyptian children. At my daughters' private school, where most kids came from prosperous Zamalek families, I never saw kids who were as well behaved as Zizou and Yusuf.

Once, I asked Wahiba if such strictness was typical in their neighborhood, and she shook her head and made the Egyptian negative tongue click—*tsk tsk*. "I don't let them play outside," she said. She was wary of the influence of the *ashwa'iyat,* and she was determined that her children would be educated.

When Zizou started fourth grade, Sayyid decided to apprentice him to a neighborhood carpenter. On weekends and during vacations, the boy was going to work from eight o'clock in the morning until six at night, and he would be paid about two dollars per day. Wahiba resisted this adamantly—it was the most significant conflict since Sayyid's detention. He mentioned it to Leslie and me, and we told him bluntly that his wife was right. The family wasn't desperately poor; it made no sense for a child so young to work. After a short while, Sayyid backed down. He seemed to make such decisions more quickly now; he didn't let problems fester the way he had in the past. I had never expected it, but the detention seemed to have solved some fundamental problem.

The boys attended the local public school, which was called Al-Quds, the Arabic name for Jerusalem. The school was so overcrowded that children attended in shifts. Zizou went for four hours in the morning, and Yusuf attended in the afternoon. Even so, each classroom was packed with around one hundred students.

The World Economic Forum had recently ranked Egyptian primary schools 141st out of 144 countries. Political instability didn't help; during the first four years of the Arab Spring, Egypt churned through five ministers of education. In Zizou's government-issued social studies textbook, some sections were euphemistic ("*The weather in Egypt is moderate year-round*"), while other parts promoted outright falsehoods ("*One-third of the world's monuments are located in Luxor*"). Sprinkled throughout such material were moments of brutal Egyptian honesty. Arabic lessons described citizens lighting garbage on fire, polluting the Nile, and filling the air with toxic emissions. For children packed like sardines in an Ard al-Liwa public school, it must have been demoralizing to read their home described so bluntly: "Ashwa'iyat *are places that appeared without planning from the state, and they lack services.*"

The book's section on history included an assignment:

> *Discuss with your teacher the meaning of this phrase: Whoever has no history has no present.*

The text had been published four years after the start of the revolution. It described Akhenaten as making "the first religious revolution in history," but it didn't mention Tahrir, or the Arab Spring, or the fall of Mubarak. Even the revolution of 1952 was omitted, along with Nasser. On the eternal question of which Egyptian president was the best, the authors took a strong position:

> *Do you know that President Mohammed Anwar Sadat was named the hero of war and peace? He led the Egyptian Army to defeat the Israeli Army in the October War in 1973. And he brought back Egypt's dignity. After the victory, he signed a treaty with Israel so we could live in peace and security.*

Along with this bit of misinformation—the October War actually ended with the Egyptian Third Army surrounded by the Israelis—there wasn't a single map in the book that showed the state of Israel. Every time the country appeared, it was labeled simply "Palestine," in Arabic. When I asked Zizou where Israel was located, he had no idea. Manu had told me that one of the great shocks of his childhood was taking a family vacation to north Sinai and suddenly realizing that Israel, the fearsome enemy, was actually right next door.

What could a parent do with all this? Like many Egyptians, Wahiba and Sayyid paid a significant amount of money for private tutorials, and Wahiba monitored the boys' homework. Every term, she proudly showed me Zizou's report cards: all of his grades were always *momtez*, "excellent." He ranked at the top of his class. It seemed miraculous: the child's father was illiterate; he lived in the *ashwa'iyat;* he attended a school so crowded that kids arrived in shifts like factory workers. The political and historical environment was so incoherent that the school was named after Jerusalem, and the textbooks idolized Sadat for his peace treaty, but Israel wasn't allowed to appear on a map. And yet Zizou seemed to be learning something. He read well, and he often asked me bright questions about America and China. Like his younger siblings, he was clearly intelligent, and all of them were poised and well behaved around adults. When I asked Zizou what he hoped to be when he grew up, he said, "Not a *zabal*."

The kids must have been affected by their parents' past conflicts, but I didn't recognize signs of trauma. In the same way, Sayyid and Wahiba had apparently moved beyond their issues. Every now and then, Wahiba referred obliquely to past problems—once, she said something in my presence about Sayyid having behaved badly. But she didn't dwell on it, and Sayyid never seemed to hold a grudge about getting picked up by the police.

As a foreigner, I instinctively believed that things left unresolved were problems. I had always assumed that Sayyid's detention would be the last straw; I didn't see how a couple could recover from such an event. But as time passed, I realized that the series of conflicts and court cases were much less dramatic from their perspective. It was normal life: this was simply how people worked out their differences in a flawed environment, using whatever tools were available. And the legitimacy of Wahiba's legal strategy was proved by its functionality. Even Sayyid seemed to recognize this. He never again withdrew support for his children, and he stopped trying to dominate his wife in all disagreements. Everything that struck me as an outsider—that the law had been abused, that the police were called in to put pressure on a personal conflict—was irrelevant. For the people involved, only one thing mattered. It worked.

CHAPTER 22

NEAR MINYA, HIGH ABOVE THE NILE'S EASTERN BANK, WORKERS IN pharaonic times carved out the blocks for two colossal statues that were never finished. Neither of these sites is formally open for tourism, and I learned about them from James Harrell, an archaeological geologist who had retired from the University of Toledo. He spent his winters roaming the deserts of Egypt, studying old quarries and mines.

Harrell said that one unfinished statue was particularly easy to find, and he gave me the GPS coordinates. I drove my Honda into New Minya, which had been built by the Mubarak regime on the edge of the desert plateau. I parked on the settlement's last road, and then I continued on foot across a stretch of sand and limestone outcrops. After a short walk, I came to the limestone bluffs that overlooked the Nile valley, four hundred feet below.

From above, the landscape of the river was laid out in a series of neat lines. Below the bluffs, there was a strip of sand-colored desert, followed by a band of green fields. Then there was the dark brown streak of the Nile. On the other side of the water, the old city of Minya stretched out in a long row of low gray buildings.

There were many signs of ancient quarrying atop the bluffs. Some sections of limestone had been cut away, and a couple of couch-sized chunks of rock had been abandoned, their edges neatly squared off. I followed the GPS coordinates until I came to the block for the colossal statue. It had been commissioned by Amenhotep III, who ruled for more than thirty years in the fourteenth century BC, until he was succeeded by his son Akhenaten. This was a period of unprecedented prosperity, and Amenhotep III seems to have been able to do whatever he wanted. He hunted and killed 110 lions during the first decade of his reign. He commissioned carved statues of squatting baboons that were thirty feet tall. Across Egypt, he built more massive monuments than any of his predecessors, and two unbelievably large statues of the king are still standing on Luxor's West Bank. These statues are known as the Colossi of Memnon, and each Colossus is carved from a single piece of quartzite that weighs about 720 tons.

This limestone block at the edge of New Minya was even bigger. The statue would have been more than seventy feet tall, or roughly as high as a five-story building. The workers had sketched out the rough shape of the seated king, and around it they had carved out all four sides of the block. In one place, the gap was narrow, so I hopped over. Atop the unfinished statue, I walked from end to end, counting my steps: sixty. Then I lay down on my stomach and peered over the edge of the block. It was a long way down. The side was scarred with the marks that chisels had made more than thirty-three centuries ago.

It's unclear why the block was abandoned, although Harrell speculates that perhaps the king died before the project was completed. The other unfinished statue is bigger still, and it's also located atop the bluffs near Minya. Both statues were probably intended to be erected in Luxor, which is about 250 miles upstream. Nobody knows how the ancient Egyptians planned to move these things.

The *rayis* of New Minya was named Ahmed Ibrahim AlDesouqi, and he worked in a brand-new government building less than half a mile from the unfinished statue. When I stopped by, he was sitting at his desk with a music video playing on a flat-screen TV. There wasn't a computer on the desk. No nail on the wall—this building was too new for Mubarak's portrait to have ever hung here, and the Sisi pictures had yet to come in. Morsi was a nonstarter when it came to portraits. During the year that he was in power, I never saw his picture hanging in a government office.

The *rayis* told me that by 2050 New Minya would be home to 600,000 residents, which was more than double the current population of old Minya. I asked him what people would do for work in the new city, and he acknowledged that they still hadn't figured out that part of the equation. "There are some carpentry shops," he said vaguely. "We're planning to have an industrial area and a place for craftsmen."

I drove through the new city's dusty streets, where construction crews were building apartment blocks, but there weren't many signs of residents. At one intersection they had constructed a huge cement figure of Akhenaten, as a symbol of regional pride. Another roadway had a statue of Nefertiti.

During other southern journeys, I visited New Aswan, New Sohag, and New Asyut. None of these places appeared to be thriving, but Sisi was determined to accelerate the pace of the desert construction. The New Urban Communities Authority administered these places, and in Cairo I stopped by to see an assistant minister named Khaled Mahmoud Abbas. He said that his bureau, which was usually called NUCA, currently oversaw twenty-three new cities and two more were being planned. They hoped to have fifteen to twenty million people living in these places by 2027.

"We are unique because we are turning desert into life," Abbas said. "All the other new cities in the world are not starting from scratch. They're in places that already have water and electricity. Not us."

He believed that the brand-new cities would inspire people to leave the *ashwa'iyat,* and he emphasized the bureau's youth-friendly policies. In many of the new cities, the government was building apartments whose purchase would be restricted to people between the ages of twenty-one and forty-five. Abbas said this was important in a country that was getting younger all the time.

One side effect of the revolution seemed to have been an increase in the birthrate. After 1980, the rate had dropped steadily, but the trend suddenly reversed after the last government health survey, in 2008. By 2014, the average number of births per woman had increased by more than 15 percent, from three births per woman to three and a half. The increase was particularly dramatic among women in their early twenties. Experts believed there were several reasons: Mubarak-era programs for contraception had abruptly stopped after the revolution, and meanwhile female labor participation decreased. The economy was bad, and political instability made families even less inclined than usual to allow their women to work. As a result, more women stayed home, where they tended to have more babies.

Abbas told me that his bureau was ahead of such demographic changes. "We have a strategic plan for the next fifty years," he said. "We want to build another thirty to forty new cities, all of them in the desert. By 2052, our country's population will be 160 to 180 million."

That was nearly double the current population of ninety-plus million. I asked if there were any government programs to encourage birth control.

He paused. "For now, no," he said slowly. Then he brightened. "But I think so for the future. I hope, *insha'allah*."

Sisi's new capital city was going to be located in the desert thirty miles east of Cairo, between two highways that ran to the city of Suez and the Red Sea. Developers estimated that the capital would cost 300 billion dollars, and much of the funding would come from the Gulf states. A government spokesman announced that in addition to government buildings, apartments, and hotels the new capital would contain the tallest building in Africa. The Egyptians contracted with a Chinese state-owned firm to do a significant share of the city's construction.

Back when Mubarak was president, he had also asked the Chinese to come build something in this desert. At Ain Sokhna, not far from where the Red Sea meets the Suez Canal, a state-owned company called the Tianjin Economic-Technological Development Area, or TEDA, constructed a Chinese-style factory town. The China-Egypt Suez Economic and Trade Cooperation Zone had been established in 2008, and its official motto was "Cooperation Makes the World Better."

From Cairo, it took less than two hours to reach the zone, and I often drove there in the Honda. The factory town was small—two and a half square miles—and it had been laid out in a grid of straight, wide streets. There was a Tianjin Road, a Chongqing Road, and a Shanghai Road. There were some concrete workers' dormitories and a yard for empty shipping containers. The containers had been piled up six units high, and their bright colors were visible for miles across the featureless landscape. From a distance they looked like stacks of Legos melting in the sun.

The idea was that Chinese companies would establish manufacturing operations here. They could hire Egyptian workers, whose wages were significantly lower than those in China, and then they could transport finished goods on the canal. The TEDA zone offered subsidized rent and utilities, and about fifty Chinese companies had set up shop. A few had been started by former lingerie dealers. One woman named Zhang Binghua had formerly sold underwear in the Egyptian *m'arad* markets, and she used her profits to open a thread-manufacturing company in the factory zone. She sourced some of her raw materials from Chinese plastic recyclers like Lin Xianfei in Asyut. Within the zone, other Chinese companies made plastic bags, toilet paper, diapers, metal pipes, and fiberglass. An entrepreneur named Wang Weiqiang produced the white *ghotra* head coverings worn by men in Saudi Arabia and other Gulf countries.

When I met Wang, I asked how he had gotten started with this particular product. Twenty years ago in Tianjin, which is located in northeastern China, Wang had made underwear and sweatpants. One of his closest friends had a factory that produced *ghotras.* Then the friend did something that angered Wang, who retaliated by poaching the friend's manager. With the manager's expertise, Wang was able to start manufacturing his own *ghotras.* "It was like blood," Wang said. "I did it as revenge."

I wondered what the Gulf Arabs, with their traditions of honor and vengeance, would make of the Chinese: here were a people whose idea of retaliation involved manufacturing white pieces of cloth for export. I asked Wang if his friend had been mad.

"Of course!" he said. "He was furious!"

"Are you still enemies?"

"No, we're friends again," Wang said. "He makes *ghotras,* too, but they're lower quality. I make the higher-quality ones, and he makes the cheaper ones. So we're not in competition."

It was a happy ending: in the Chinese factory world, no conflict is so big that it can't be solved by market share. Wang named his company Yashima, and for a decade it was highly profitable. He could sell top-quality *ghotras* for nearly sixty dollars each in Saudi Arabia. Then he decided to start an operation in Egypt.

"I have very good-quality Egyptian cotton here," he said. "My machinery is very modern. My investment is more than a million dollars for the factory here. But during these two years, I've lost a lot. It's all the problem of labor—the mentality of the workers. Our factory needs to run twenty-four hours a day; it's not just for one shift. In order to do this in Egypt, we have to hire male workers, and the men are really lazy." He continued, "Now I reject 90 percent of the men who apply. I use only girls and women. They are very good workers. But the problem is that they will work only during the daytime."

In the TEDA zone, this was a common complaint. Another entrepreneur named Xu Xin, who had had a successful career with Motorola in China, came to TEDA with a plan to manufacture low-price phones for Egyptian consumers. He also preferred to hire women, but he soon realized that the only ones who were willing to work were unmarried. After they got engaged or married, they invariably quit, which led to high turnover. The workers also couldn't live in the dormitories, the way people did in China, because in Egypt it was considered inappropriate for a young woman to be away from her family at night. So Xu couldn't run multiple shifts on his production line, and he had to bus female workers to and from the city of Suez, which added more than three hours to the workday. After a year, he shut down his cell-phone plant. The TEDA dormitories were also a bust—they were as empty as the shipping containers.

Wang Weiqiang was still struggling with his *ghotra* business. He was forty-four years old, and he rarely saw his wife and teenage daughter, who lived in Tianjin. When I asked if he enjoyed visiting any places in Egypt, he answered flatly. "No," he said. "Most of the time I spend in the factory. I'm working ten to fourteen hours a day."

The zone made sense on paper. It followed basic principles that had helped China boom for the last thirty years: Location is everything. Labor is mobile. Construct factory towns near highways and ports, and offer preferential policies to investors. The money will come, followed by the workers, and then you will succeed. But Egyptians, and especially Egyptian women, turned out to be much less mobile than their Chinese counterparts.

Wang Weiqiang liked his Egyptian employees, but he had learned to be patient with them. In his opinion, it was impossible to change anything fundamental about the workers. "Maybe China and Egypt are opposites," he said. "I think that Egypt is good for life. It's more relaxed, and people enjoy life here. But it's not so good for business."

I never met Chinese in Egypt who expressed an interest in reforming the country. They often mentioned things that they perceived to be weaknesses—a lack of work ethic among the people, a lack of system in the government—but the tone was different from that of many Westerners. There was little frustration; the Chinese seemed to accept that this was simply the way things were. There was also no guilt, because China had no colonial history in the region, and its government engaged with both Israel and Palestine. Unlike Westerners, Chinese entrepreneurs were almost never disappointed by the outcome of the Egyptian revolution. This was not because they believed that the Arab Spring had turned out well but because they had never had any faith in it in the first place.

In 2012, after Morsi was elected president, his first state visit was to China. Nearly two years later, when Sisi was elected, he also quickly made a trip to China. There was no indication that the change in leadership made any difference to the Chinese. In Cairo, I knew a diplomat from another Asian country who had lived in China and frequently dealt with Chinese officials, and I told her about my experiences with the lingerie dealers and entrepreneurs. The diplomat said they reminded her of what she observed in her work.

"The Chinese will sell people anything they like," she said. "They don't ask any questions. They don't care what you do with what they sell you. They won't ask whether the Egyptians are going to hold elections, or repress people, or throw journalists into jail. They don't care." She went on, "The Americans think, 'If everybody is like me, they're less likely to attack me.' The Chinese don't think like that. They don't try to make the world be like them. Their strategy is to make economic linkages, so if you break these economic linkages it's going to hurt you as much as it hurts them."

It was estimated that perhaps a million Chinese had come to Africa, where their strategy of building links usually created opportunities for resource extraction. The Chinese constructed highways, hospitals, airports, and other infrastructure, and in return they gained access to African minerals and resources that were in short supply in China. But in Egypt the calculus was different. The country possessed few natural resources that China needed, but it had cheap labor, as well as significant strategic value. The Middle East provided China with half its oil, and much of the Chinese trade to Europe passed through the Suez Canal.

The Chinese also saw an opportunity to gain standing in a region where America's reputation had been badly damaged. After Sisi was elected, the Chinese decided to increase the number of staff at their Cairo embassy by one-third, and they were constructing a new building. They also announced plans to almost double the size of the development zone at Ain Sokhna. But it was hard to imagine what would fill all that space, because a number of factories had recently shut down after experiencing problems attracting labor.

In Egypt, I observed a range of Chinese commercial activities, from small entrepreneurs to big government-funded projects, and their outcome always seemed to hinge on the same social issue: the role of women. The lingerie dealers, with their grassroots instincts, had figured out a clever way to profit from Egyptian gender disparity and marriage traditions. Meanwhile, the state-owned factory zone, which clumsily tried to import a Chinese template for development, was bleeding money. When I visited TEDA, I stayed in the only hotel, which, in the spirit of this mixed-up place, was called the Swiss Inn. There were rarely many other guests. At night I walked across the deserted street and ordered halal dumplings at Joy Luck, the zone's single Chinese restaurant. In China, factory towns are usually lively after dark, but this place was dead—no hum of night-shift machinery, no packs of young workers in uniform. On one road I counted 232 streetlights that weren't working. A gardener told me that his crew had planted a thousand palm trees, most of which died because of lack of water. Egypt was full of grandiose and misguided desert projects, both ancient and modern, but TEDA was one of the strangest: a lost Chinese factory town in the Sahara, where Ozymandian dreams had been foiled by a simple failure to get women out of their homes.

In the TEDA zone, a young entrepreneur named Wu Zhicheng produced inexpensive plastic dishware. The dishware was packaged into sets, many of which were purchased by lower-income Egyptian women who were preparing their dowries. One product, the Melamine Tray Set, was inscribed with an ode to marriage, in English:

We share much together,
It's your loving and your caring,
And knowing that you're near,
That gentle touch you have,
Makes my troubles disappear.

Wu was in his early thirties, and like many rural Chinese of his generation, he had a modest formal education. But he was perceptive, and he had seen more of Egypt than any other Chinese I met. After Wu started manufacturing dishware, he realized that he couldn't rely on a few wholesalers, the way he would in China. In Egypt, it was necessary to visit individual shops, shake people's hands, and show off the products.

So Wu did this for three years. In the first year, he put more than a hundred thousand miles on his Renault sedan. He drove to nearly every city in Egypt, and he was struck by the unsystematic way in which merchants stocked their products. "The supplier sells them goods, and they pay 20 percent up front," he explained. "Every week, the supplier stops by on the same day, maybe a Thursday, and the shopkeeper pays whatever he can. There's no set payment plan. It just depends on how much money the shopkeeper has."

Wu explained to his customers that he couldn't do this as an outsider. But he offered an alternative: pay cash up front and receive a significant discount. "This is my advantage," he said. "It's cheaper, and it's less complicated."

He found that this appealed to many Egyptian shopkeepers, and now the relationships were stable enough that he didn't have to travel so much. Nevertheless, he thought that he would probably leave the TEDA zone because of the difficulty in attracting labor. He employed about twenty women on his assembly line, and like everybody else he experienced high turnover because of engagements and marriages.

Before coming to Egypt, Wu had managed small factories in southeastern China. He had observed that young rural Chinese women were often motivated to work in factory towns out of a vague desire to get away from their families and their villages. But the starting point for Egyptian women workers was completely different. "They aren't trying to escape something, like the girls in China," he said. "Here they're doing it just for the money."

In fact, Egyptian women usually worked in order to participate in the traditional social system, rather than disrupt it. They wanted money in order to buy the appliances, dishware, clothing, lingerie, and other goods that would allow them to enter a marriage. Soad Abdel Hamid, a twenty-two-year-old who operated a plastic press on Wu's assembly line, told me that these responsibilities weighed on her. "I'm supposed to get married this year," she said. "But it seems that I won't, because I haven't finished buying my stuff." She said that marriages were often delayed or broken off because somebody failed to acquire the proper goods that were laid out in the contracts. Hamid planned to quit work after she married, which was true of almost every employee I met in Wu's factory.

Only one married woman was on the assembly line. Her name was Fatma Mohammed Mahmoud, and she was in her fifties. She said that for years she had wanted to get divorced, but her husband wouldn't agree to end the marriage, and her extended family was also opposed. "My siblings tell me not to, because for our traditions it's considered bad," she said. "We're from Upper Egypt. The minds are closed." As a result, she and her husband still lived in the same apartment, where they avoided interacting with each other. She took the factory job because he refused to give her enough money for expenses.

Of her single colleagues, only a young woman named Esma said that she planned to continue working after marriage. Previously, Esma had held a good job handling inventory at a large factory in her home city of Suez. Her fiancé had worked in the same plant, but the engagement collapsed. After that, Esma's father forced her to quit the job because he believed it was inappropriate for a young woman to work in the same place as her ex-fiancé, even though there were hundreds of other employees. "As Egyptians, when your parents give you an order, you have to follow it," Esma explained. So now she rode a bus for three hours every day in order to work a job with less pay and worse prospects.

In the TEDA zone, I found it easy to talk with the young Egyptian women workers. Like Egyptian men, they tended to be charismatic, funny, and outgoing. Around their homes, they would have been much more circumspect with me as a male stranger, but here in the Chinese zone they were freer. They often took the initiative and approached me: they asked boldly where I was from, and what I was doing, and what I thought about this place. They teased and flirted with their male co-workers, and they talked back to their Chinese bosses. They laughingly told me the Chinese words they had learned: *"good," "bad," "I want to rest," "Ali Baba."* They were under the impression that the *Arabian Nights* name was common in Mandarin, because the Chinese entrepreneurs in Egypt used it so often. But nobody in mainland China would have had any idea that this meant "thief."

During my years in China, I had visited dozens of factories, and usually I found young women workers to be shy and retiring. They could be intimidated by an encounter with a foreign journalist, and often it took a couple of meetings before they seemed comfortable talking with me. If I were to compare first impressions, without any cultural or economic context, I would feel certain that the Egyptian women were much more likely to succeed than their Chinese counterparts.

But over the long run, environment and system matter much more than individual personality. The most revealing question was whether a worker thought about starting a factory or a business of her own someday. In China, those shy and retiring girls rarely hesitated—this was part of their dream, and in many cases it would be fulfilled. But the Egyptian women laughed at the question. *"Mish mumkin!"* one said. "It's not possible!"

Like many Chinese, Wu Zhicheng praised the generosity and friendliness of Egyptians. "If your car breaks down on the road, the first person who passes will stop to help," he said. "That would never happen in China." He also appreciated the intense Egyptian sense of place. "In China, everybody has migrated and moved around," he said. "If you're in a city, nobody knows who you are. Even if you're living in close quarters with your neighbor, you're not really close. It's not like that here."

But he recognized that there were also costs to maintaining the tight Egyptian bonds with home and tradition. Wu's conclusion about the future prospects of his workers was simple: as long as they lacked a basic desire to escape the familiar, it was unlikely that they would change their lives in any significant way. He saw Egyptian politics in similar terms. In his view, the revolution was halfhearted because deep inside most people wanted things to stay the same. "It would have been better if they hadn't removed Mubarak," he said.

Many Chinese entrepreneurs said such things, and to a Westerner they sounded cynical. But the Chinese perspective might have been clearer. Their country and culture had experienced truly revolutionary change throughout the span of the twentieth century, for better and for worse, and they believed that the Egyptians had never committed themselves to such a wrenching transformation. And the Chinese saw Egypt for what it was, not for what they hoped it might become. During the first phase of the Egyptian Arab Spring, Westerners usually believed that they were witnessing the rise of a powerful social movement, whereas the Chinese tended to see the collapse of a weak state.

And the contact for Chinese entrepreneurs was so local and so pragmatic that they weren't distracted by the idea of sweeping political movements. From their perspective, the fundamental issue had nothing to do with the Muslim Brotherhood, or the army, or the president—it was family. Husbands and wives, parents and children, elders and youths: in Egypt, those relationships hadn't been changed at all by the Arab Spring, and until that happened there was no point in talking about a revolution.

At the end of 2014, the Chinese decided to build four amusement parks in the factory zone. Across the street from the International Drilling Material Manufacturing Company, which made metal pipes, TEDA constructed something called Dinosaur World. It featured large electric-powered models of Tyrannosaurus rex, Allosaurus, and other creatures. The prehistoric park included some anachronisms: a pirate-ship ride, a spaceship ride, and a Skyride, which was decorated with happy frogs. Wu Zhicheng suspected that somebody in the Chinese government-owned amusement industry was dumping overproduced goods. It was easy to imagine some cadre thinking: Why not jettison this stuff into the desert?

No TEDA official would speak on the record, but one administrator told me candidly that they wanted to generate publicity for the zone. "This way, people will come for the park, and while they're here, they'll learn about the development zone," he said. He hoped it might help with the labor problem. Of course, in Chinese he didn't say the Arabic word, but I was thinking it: *insha'allah*.

One spring weekend, TEDA invited everybody in the zone to attend a free test run of the amusement parks, and I drove out from Cairo. The wind was strong, whipping sand through the air, and most people fled the pools at Water World, which had been built next to some empty worker dorms. Along with Dinosaur World, the other parks were Candy World and Auto World. Auto World was located in the two-story building that in the past was leased to Xu Xin, the former Motorola executive who had come to Egypt to manufacture cell phones.

The go-karts and bumper cars of Auto World were popular with the government cadres who had flown in from Tianjin for the event. They wore dark suits, and their knees were cramped against the steering wheels of the miniature vehicles. The cadres rammed each other in the bumper cars, and they spun around the go-kart track, and then they got back in line and did it again. The interior of Auto World had been remodeled so successfully that there was no sign that this place once housed the cell-phone factory that failed for lack of female workers. Across the street, the electric dinosaurs came to life. They moved their limbs spasmodically, and opened their jaws, and roared through tinny speakers, as if shocked to find themselves in the Sahara.

CHAPTER 23

When my daughters were small, they rarely traveled far from the spiderweb building. We took our neighborhood walks, and they attended the nearby nursery school, and on weekends they played at the Gezira Club, a private park on the southern end of Zamalek. Often they didn't leave the island for months at a time.

After we bought the Honda, and the girls were bigger, we started taking them to historical sites. Our first short trip was to the Red Pyramid and the Bent Pyramid, at Dahshur, and then we took them to the Egyptian Museum on Tahrir Square. The winter before they turned five, we made a long family road trip to Upper Egypt. I drove the Cairo-Asyut Desert Highway, and then we crossed the river, climbed another new road into the Western Desert, and continued south to Abydos. We spent a couple of days in town, visiting the Shuna and the Temple of Seti I, and then we continued to Luxor and the Valley of the Kings.

I wondered how these journeys would echo in the girls' memories. Even at the most imposing sites, there was something intimate about the experience, because these places had been abandoned by tourists. When we drove to the Red Pyramid, we parked at the base of the structure, as if we had pulled up at a friend's house. There wasn't another car in the lot; the guard at the entrance was so bored that he didn't bother to accompany us inside. We descended a steep stairway for two hundred feet and passed through an initial chamber, and then we came to the final burial place of King Sneferu, deep in the heart of the pyramid. The twins' voices echoed off the corbeled roof.

In the temples of Abydos and Luxor, they loved to play amid the great stone pillars. They were fascinated by the images of the pharaohs, especially the huge stone statues of Akhenaten that were on display in the museums in

Cairo and Luxor. After we returned home from the southern trip, the girls obsessively drew pictures of the king in his war helmet and Nefertiti with her distinctive blue crown. They role-played, and they liked the way the letters of the names lined up: Ariel was Akhenaten; Natasha was Nefertiti. For two years, they had insisted on dressing identically, but now they suddenly differentiated: Ariel wore pants, and Natasha wore dresses. For Leslie and me, it was a relief; we no longer had to worry about matching outfits. The Eighteenth Dynasty had convinced the girls in a way we never could have.

That spring, their school had a day when children dressed up as their favorite characters from books. We made costumes by committee: I designed the outfits, based on images from Amarna; Leslie found the materials around Zamalek; Atiyat sewed everything. When the girls marched down the street on their way to school, some of the neighboring doormen applauded. One parent of a classmate saw Natasha's high blue crown and said, "Oh, look at the princess!"

"I'm not a princess," Natasha said. "I'm a co-regent."

Something about the art and the ideas of ancient Egypt naturally connected with children. They understood it at a visceral level: the pairings, the animal-headed gods, the beauty of the hieroglyphs. Virtually every foreign Egyptologist I met had started his or her career with a childhood obsession. Barry Kemp's father had been stationed with the British army in Egypt during World War II, and he sent back postcards of relics that fascinated his son. As a girl in Oklahoma, Marsha Hill had loved a book about an Amarna princess; now she was a curator at the Metropolitan Museum of Art. On a lonely chicken farm in Maine, Raymond Johnson had been entranced by *National Geographic* articles about Egypt; now he directed the University of Chicago's research center in Luxor. When I visited Matthew Adams in the Buried, he told me that as a child in small-town West Virginia he had built a model of an Egyptian tomb out of bedsheets in his grandmother's garage.

This experience seemed less standard for Egyptians in the field. Zahi Hawass, who was the most prominent native Egyptologist and who had been minister of antiquities before the revolution, told me that originally he wanted to be a lawyer. He had also studied to be a diplomat but failed the oral exams. He entered the field of antiquities as essentially a last resort, but then he realized that he loved the work. Such a path was common: for Egyptian Egyptologists, the starting point was often pragmatism rather than pure passion. Mamdouh Eldamaty, an excellent scholar who became minister of antiquities in 2014, answered bluntly when I asked about his childhood interests. "I always hated history," he said. He had hoped to become a doctor but failed to gain admission to medical school; after that, he tried to study commerce, only to realize that he hated business even more than he hated history. Like Hawass, Eldamaty had entered Egyptology as a third option, and then he discovered that he had a gift for ancient languages.

At times, it seemed to be the Egyptians who had an outsider's perspective on the field. The nation's relationship to its ancient past, like so many other things, can be contradictory. Average Egyptians take pride in their pharaonic history, but there's also a disconnect, because the tradition of the Islamic past is stronger and more immediate. This is captured perfectly by the design of Egypt's currency. Every denomination follows the same pattern: On one side of a bill, words are in Arabic, and there's an image of some famous Egyptian mosque. The other side pairs English text with a pharaonic statue or monument. The implication is clear: the ancients belong to foreigners, and Islam belongs to us.

Even Egyptians who have dedicated their lives to Egyptology can be remarkably non-possessive. Once, I mentioned the legacy of colonialism to Eldamaty, and I asked him if it was a problem that so many foreigners excavate in Egypt. I contrasted it to China, where the government would never allow outsiders to play such a prominent role in curating the national past. Eldamaty adamantly rejected the idea. "This is human heritage," he said. "We can't talk about it as just Egyptian heritage." He continued, "Whoever is qualified should do the work. Foreigner or Egyptian, it's the same."

Foreign scholars often said similar things, and they pointed out that European and American institutions had done so much to study and preserve ancient sites. But younger Egyptologists tended to be less comfortable with the situation. Laurel Bestock, the scholar at Brown who had excavated the coins and statues at Abydos, even questioned the starting point of her avocation. Like so many others, she had been inspired as a child: after reading mystery novels about Egyptian archaeology, she dreamed of going to the Sahara. "I think this is part of our legacy of not confronting colonialism," she said. "Our own interest was started so young. It wasn't a considered, adult interest; it was a childhood fascination. The academic interest grew out of the fascination. It's very hard for us to justify our own interest because it's essentially childish in its conception."

Perhaps it also reflected the elemental nature of ancient Egypt. So much of that lost world felt familiar, and so many of its ideas were foundational to Western civilization, that it was hard to think about ownership. But Bestock became uncomfortable enough that she stopped working in Abydos. She believed that the site was too foreign controlled, and she was critical of Matthew Adams, who excavated thoroughly but rarely published, which meant that others, both foreign and Egyptian, couldn't see the details of what he had found in Abydos. "Matt is a superb field archaeologist, but you have to go all the way to publication," she said.

Nowadays, Bestock excavated Egyptian sites in the Sudan, and she said that while she intended to do further work in Egypt, the model would be different. "I don't know any scholars of my generation who aspire to dig in this big way where you're sitting on one site," she said. "There's a difference between having a foreigner in charge of an entire site and having projects that are smaller and more collaborative from the beginning."

I wasn't sure how to characterize my own daughters' relationship with Egypt. At some level, it seemed elemental, and I came to believe that small children must come closest to living the time of the ancients. For them, things are repeated in the manner of *neheh:* games, words, bedtime routines. And then there's *djet,* the eternal present. My daughters had no concept of our life before Egypt, and they had no sense that it would ever end. They never questioned whether we belonged there. Throughout the years of the revolution, I often felt the stress of wanting to protect them, but their sense of normalcy was also reassuring. In the journals that Natasha kept for her first-grade writing class, blackouts were simply part of *neheh:*

> *December 15—I was reading a book in night time when the electricity turned off.*
>
> *December 20—I went to the pyramids and we went inside. It was dark.*
>
> *December 27—I was done with breakfast when the lights went away.*

One year, when we made a trip back to the United States, an uncle asked Ariel about her pet cat. She talked about him for a while, and then she said, "There is another Morsi who is a man, not a cat. He was the president."

The uncle asked where Morsi was now.

"He is in prison."

"Why?"

"He sent some people to kill some other people," Ariel said, matter-of-factly. "There's another president now. I don't know if he is bad or good. But his name is Sisi."

After that, Leslie and I realized that we needed to stop discussing politics in front of the girls. But they seemed immune to the negative parts of the environment, and they took pride in the country where they lived. They often told people that they were Egyptian. When a friend visited from Germany, he thought it was hilarious that these tiny Chinese Americans kept saying, "We love Cairo!" They had acquired the body language of little Cairenes. For an emphatic no, they said *"la'a,"* with a brisk shake of the head and a wave of the hand, and they made the *tsk-tsk* sound that was so common among Egyptians. Whenever Sayyid came over, they greeted him warmly as *'amu,* "uncle." He always called them by their Arabic nicknames, Aro and Nush-nush. As far as the girls were concerned, the famous Egyptian phrase was accurate: the country was *um al-duniya,* the "mother of the world."

But I was surprised that as the twins grew older, the language drifted away. Leslie and I had imagined that the girls would become fluent in Arabic, and they picked up words quickly when they were babies. But once they reached school age, they entered institutions where the primary language was English. It wasn't possible to send foreigners to a local public school, so we wanted a private school that instructed children in Arabic. But such places didn't exist, at least not near Zamalek.

There was a long history of upper-class Cairenes having their children instructed primarily in French or English. This dated to the colonial era, but as time passed, and as the Egyptian education system deteriorated, even the middle and lower-middle classes started sending their children to foreign-language schools. The man who ran the H Freedom kiosk wasn't well educated, and he lived in an *ashwa'iyat,* but he sent his children to an English-speaking school. Sometimes I met a cabbie whose kid was at a lycée.

At one point, Sayyid considered an English school for his children, but he decided it was too expensive.

At lower-quality private institutions, teachers often spoke the foreign language poorly, and children picked up strange accents and grammatical patterns. It was common for them to finish high school without being fully comfortable writing either Arabic or the foreign language. Even good private schools felt somewhat placeless. For kindergarten, we sent the twins to the Cairo British School, where they wore little British-style uniforms with an insignia on the left breast. In class, they kept a daily weather chart, the way kids do in England. There was a space for them to classify each day: sunny, rainy, cloudy, or snowy. Sunny yesterday, sunny today, sunny tomorrow—the chart never changed.

After that year, the Cairo British School relocated to one of the desert cities, so for first grade we sent the girls to the Irish School Cairo, on the Giza side of the river. British, Irish—what difference did it make? In the British school, they had had no British classmates; now at the Irish school there wasn't a single Irish student. Every morning, I drove the Honda across the river, parked in front of a building decorated with shamrocks, and sent my half-Chinese Egyptian-patriot kids off to study happily with their classmates Sharifa, Hussain, Hamza, Mohamed, and Abdulwassa.

The twins' Arabic comprehension was good, but they preferred not to speak much of the language. When Atiyat addressed them in Egyptian, they usually answered in English. Sometimes they tried the same thing with Uncle Sayyid. Leslie and I were horrified; after all, an interest in Arabic was one of the reasons we had come to Egypt in the first place. But small children have a powerful instinct for what is valued. Sometimes, when the twins played in our garden, they pretended they were speaking French.

One morning, while Sayyid was sorting the garbage of the spiderweb building, he found a bag that contained some women's clothing, a stack of notebooks, and an iPhone. He brought the phone to my apartment, along with a half-used sheet of Durjoy, the Bangladeshi Viagra knockoff. The Durjoy had turned up in the trash of another building on the street. It was Sayyid's best day of scavenging in a long while.

I plugged the iPhone into my charger. When I opened the home page, I saw that it belonged to a friend. She was an American who had worked as a reporter in Cairo, and recently she had left for a new job in London. She didn't live on our street, but before flying out, she had stayed for a couple of nights in an apartment upstairs. I sent her an email—by now, it was well established that this was part of my job as garbage consultant. I was often calling or stopping by some embassy with a passport that had ended up in the trash.

My friend responded quickly. She confirmed that it was her old phone; she had thrown it away because she was in such a rush ("Never again will I be so nonchalant about tossing out electronics"). She said that Sayyid was welcome to keep the phone.

"*Al-hamdulillah,* all of this is because I helped somebody," Sayyid said. He explained that a local doorman's son had recently suffered a bad accident, and Sayyid and others donated money for his medical care. Sayyid gave five hundred pounds, which represented most of a typical week's earnings.

"In Islam, if you help somebody, then it comes back to you," he said. He believed that this was why he had found the phone. He asked me to keep it for him temporarily; he didn't want to carry around something so valuable. And he wanted time to think about how he should go about selling it. "If people find out, they'll be jealous and give me the evil eye," he said. "Please don't tell anybody that you have it."

I put the phone in a desk drawer, and I promised not to say a word.

Within a day, the man who delivered tea around the neighborhood was asking me about the iPhone. "Abu Ismail!" he said, using the nickname that Sayyid had given me in honor of the maniac Salafi preacher who was now in prison. "How new is the phone, Abu Ismail? I want to see the phone!" I told the tea man awkwardly that I didn't have the phone with me.

Next, one of the old guys who hung out at H Freedom mentioned the iPhone, and then I started hearing about it from the parking attendants who worked down the street. Soon a couple of doormen on Ahmed Heshmat Street were bringing it up. These men knew me through Sayyid, because sometimes on Thursday nights I gave him bottles of beer in a black bag so he could share with his friends. Now they called out, "Abu Ismail! Abu Ismail!" and held imaginary phones to their ears.

After a few days, visitors began to arrive at the apartment for iPhone viewings. Sayyid would escort them in during the evening, after the twins had gone to bed. Most of the visitors were doormen and parking attendants, and they sat in a solemn ring in our living room. I felt obligated to offer tea. They handled the phone respectfully, each man studying it before passing it on to the next. Occasionally somebody mentioned a price. When they were gone I put the phone back in the drawer.

"How much longer will this go on?" Leslie asked one night, after a group left.

I said I didn't know, but I had a feeling it wasn't going to end well.

During the viewings, Sayyid chewed nervously at his mouth, the same way he had during the court battles. He worried constantly that somebody was going to cheat him. But he couldn't stop himself from talking about the phone, which only increased the risk of the evil eye, and that made him worry even more. He came to the apartment so often to look at the phone that I also found myself thinking obsessively about it. Every time I opened the desk drawer, I wished the damned thing would disappear.

Finally, Sayyid negotiated a price of five hundred pounds with a young parking attendant named Ahmed. It was the same amount of money that Sayyid had donated to the doorman with the injured son. This seemed to put him at ease—the number represented divine justice.

After the deal was made, Sayyid handed over the phone. Ahmed gave him two hundred pounds.

"Where's the other three hundred?" Sayyid asked.

"I don't have it," Ahmed said. "Maybe I'll have it later." But it was clear from the way he said it that he had no intention of paying the rest.

In Arabic class, I sometimes talked about Sayyid with Rifaat, and one week he prepared a lesson about the *zabaleen*. We discussed the lack of government services in many parts of Cairo, and the way that garbage had accumulated since the pig massacre, and he complained bitterly. "I don't blame the government only," he said. "I blame the people. But the leaders are better educated. If you treat people like animals, then they act like animals. And everything is so ugly!"

Nowadays, he often embarked on such mini-rants. The Egyptian medical system was a frequent target, because he was having trouble with a sore on his foot. It was slow healing, and the thing only worsened when he used an ointment that a doctor prescribed. So Rifaat went to a second physician, who said the first one had misdiagnosed. A third doctor disagreed with both of them. Maybe it was an ulcer, or skin cancer, or nothing at all; nobody seemed capable of giving a clear diagnosis. When Rifaat first showed it to Leslie and me, it was about the size of a nickel, but it hurt enough to give him trouble sleeping. In the dialogues that he prepared for class, characters seemed even unhappier than usual, and young people had no patience for their passive-aggressive and marriage-obsessed parents:

> ***Mother:*** *Your sister came today with her children. I hope to see your children,* insha'allah.
>
> ***Qasem:*** *Mom, aren't you getting bored of this topic?*

During class, Rifaat liked having friends or neighbors stop by, to give us a chance to hear different accents and vocabularies. And I could tell he enjoyed showing us off. Neither Leslie nor I could speak Egyptian fluently, but we had reached a level of comfort with the language, which wasn't easy for students our age. By now I was onto my seventh language notebook. Even as Rifaat's lists grew darker, it was satisfying to watch them pile up:

trade of white slavery	تجارة الرقيق الأبيض
wallet	محفظة
to promise	يوعد
virgin	عذراء
to defend	يدافع
honor of the family	شرف العيلة

One morning, Rifaat introduced us to a middle-aged woman who lived in the same building as the Kalimat school. She was dressed in expensive clothes, and we talked about politics. After a while, she started complaining about the young people who protested against Sisi. "They should give him a chance to fix things," she said, noting that Sisi had been in office for less than a year. Rifaat nodded in agreement, but then she started griping about the poor.

"These people expect everything for free," she said. "Free food, free electricity. This is why the country is so backward."

Rifaat's face started to change—his mouth grew tight and his eyes narrowed. But the woman didn't seem to notice. "We always worked, and we didn't cause these problems," she said. "They just want things to be given to them. We built this country, and now they're destroying it."

Every time she said the word *ehna*—"we"—Rifaat's face darkened. After she left, he exploded.

"*Ehna, ehna, ehna!*" he shouted. "We, we, we! That's what she thinks—it's us versus them. But these are the people who ruined everything! It's not the poor who demand things; it's the rich. They grabbed everything under Sadat and Mubarak!" He fumed about her lack of sympathy for the poor and the young who had gone to Tahrir. "When I was young, we were never like these rich people," he said. "We wanted to be educated, and we wanted to live comfortably, but we didn't expect to have everything for ourselves."

Leslie and I often teased Rifaat about his nostalgia, but that morning he seemed too upset. And although I disagreed with his adulation of Nasser, he was right about Egypt's social divides. And that vast gap—the countless poor on one side, the few rich on the other—was demoralizing for anybody in between. Egypt had become a lonely place for a man who saw himself as educated, secular, and staunchly middle class.

During Sisi's first year as president, his main project was an expansion of the Suez Canal. The project cost more than eight billion dollars, and it was funded by bank certificates of deposit that were sold to Egyptian citizens, with a high rate of interest. Few economists believed that the project should have been a top priority for a country in crisis. The currency was under intense pressure because of lack of exports, and if Egypt had devalued the pound and instituted policies that boosted manufacturing, perhaps the country could have attracted significant foreign investment that created jobs. But Sisi and the other military minds seemed fascinated by megaprojects—a widened canal, a brand-new capital.

Meanwhile, the political crackdown was harsher than anything that had happened under Mubarak. One of the terms we studied in class was "deep state," which people used to describe the way the Egyptian security forces had returned stronger than ever. Rifaat wouldn't say that he regretted voting for Sisi, but he was disappointed. In his opinion, Nasser might have been authoritarian, but at least he had a vision. "If you're a dictator, and things still don't work, then what's the point?" he said.

For class, he sometimes prepared recordings of Sisi's speeches and interviews, and one day we listened to the president talk about the revolution. He described a meeting with the leadership of the Brotherhood that had taken place on June 21, 2013, shortly before the coup. Sisi claimed that during this meeting the Brothers threatened to destabilize Egypt. They warned him that if Tamarrod and other activist groups were allowed to attack Morsi, then the Brotherhood would respond by bringing in supporters from Pakistan, Afghanistan, Libya, Palestine, and Syria.

By now, such conspiracy theories about outside interference were standard. The show trials of Morsi and others pushed the same idea, which served to justify Sisi's crackdown. Most of his speech was vague—he didn't even name the Brothers with whom he had supposedly met. But he kept repeating the date: June 21, 2013.

"He's doing that so it sounds like a fact," I said in class. "If he says the date enough times, then people believe it's an actual historical event."

"One of the television anchors said that they have a recording of the meeting," Rifaat said.

"So why didn't they play it?"

"That's true," he said.

He played the speech again, and we discussed Sisi's style of using Egyptian rather than *fusha*. "He's not eloquent," Rifaat said. "His language is very simple. But he's good at communicating. The way he speaks feels very familiar to the average Egyptian."

Rifaat liked to use speeches and radio transcripts because it was hard to find newspaper accounts that quoted political figures the way they actually talked, in Egyptian Arabic. Once, he brought us a newspaper interview of Suzanne Mubarak that had appeared before the revolution. She was asked what she ate for lunch (*"In fact, I don't have lunch, but if I do I just eat a small plate of fruit"*) and for dinner (*"I usually don't have dinner at all, but if it happens, it's just a cup of fruit juice"*). For Rifaat, the point of the lesson was political, and he worked himself into a frenzy: "These people stole millions of dollars, but all she eats is fruit!"

But it was also interesting to see who could be quoted in Egyptian. Probably Suzanne Mubarak's publicist had thought that it would make her seem down-to-earth, and her status as First Lady also allowed for the less formal language. Niloofar Haeri, an Iranian-American linguist at Johns Hopkins, once reviewed Egyptian newspapers in order to analyze this dynamic. She gave examples: the words of a comedian named Ade Imam were printed entirely in Egyptian, whereas the actor Omar Sharif, with his higher status, was given a mixture of direct quotations and other comments that had been translated into *fusha*. Meanwhile, a speech by Mubarak was delivered in Egyptian, but the following day it appeared in the state-run *Al-Ahram* newspaper entirely as *fusha*.

These translations often cleaned up a politician's words. Early in Sisi's presidency, he participated in a roundtable conversation in which he was asked about the possibility of political reform. Speaking Egyptian, he stumbled:

> *The ideal shape that you are calling for, that idealism is in books, but we cannot take everything you think about with paper and pen and then ask the state for it, no, it won't happen . . . but we are on a pathway in which we're succeeding each day more than the day before.*

In *Al-Ahram,* the quotation became, in *fusha,*

> *Idealism exists in books, but we're walking the pathway of success, and we will succeed day by day.*

To some degree, Egyptians take pride in their colloquial Arabic, and politicians from Nasser to Sisi have used it effectively in speeches. But there has always been a reluctance to see such words in print. Naguib Mahfouz was the first Arabic writer to win the Nobel Prize in Literature, and he was famous for portraying everyday life in Cairo. But Mahfouz never attempted to capture the slang and grammatical forms of actual Egyptian speech. He once compared Egyptian Arabic to "poverty and disease," and the dialogue of his novels consists of *fusha* phrasings that would never be uttered by real Cairenes. Even the most basic Egyptian terms—*yes, I want, how are you?*—don't appear in Mahfouz's *Palace Walk*. There's not even a standardized orthography for Egyptian Arabic, because nobody has taken it seriously enough as a literary language.

Niloofar Haeri pointed out such issues in her book *Sacred Language, Ordinary People*. When I talked with Haeri, she noted that there are other places in the world, such as German Switzerland, that also practice diglossia, in which one language is spoken in daily life and another is used for writing and education. But the difference is that both Swiss German and High German are living, spoken languages. *Fusha,* on the other hand, has not been used in daily life for at least a thousand years, and in fact it might never have been anybody's mother tongue. Even scholars of Arabic can't speak the language spontaneously without making mistakes, because its grammar is so demanding.

"The majority of Arab children are put into a position that I cannot think of an equivalent for any other group of children in the world," Haeri said. She explained that when a language is never used for daily life, its grammar remains needlessly complex, and it tends to be less flexible in terms of importing new terms and ideas. During years of research in Egypt, she noticed that most people have a passive relationship with *fusha:* they understand it well, but they struggle to speak it.

Haeri believed that this probably has an impact on literary expression and political life. While researching during the days of the Mubarak regime, she met a factory worker who became an activist. The worker wanted to contribute articles about labor issues to newspapers and political journals, but he couldn't simply write the way he spoke and thought. So first he enrolled in a course in *fusha*. "You are translating yourself into a medium over which you have far less mastery," Haeri said.

Over the years, a number of Egyptians have made similar points. Leila Ahmed, a professor at Harvard Divinity School, wrote a memoir, *A Border Passage,* in which she described her hatred of *fusha* as a Cairo schoolgirl in the 1950s. "In all of Egypt there was no school that I could have attended where I could have read books and learned to write in my mother tongue," she writes. "There is no linguistic reason why Egyptian Arabic could not be a written language, only political reasons." In the book, Ahmed recalls a Nasserite Arabic teacher criticizing her for speaking *fusha* poorly. "You're an Arab!" the teacher shouted. "And you don't know your own language!" Ahmed shouted back, "I am not an Arab! I am Egyptian! And anyway we don't speak like this!" In response, the teacher slapped her across the face.

Ahmed's book was attacked harshly by the critic Edward Said, who saw it as part of the Orientalist perception of Arabic. In an essay that was published posthumously, Said effectively gave Ahmed another slap: "Reading Ahmed's pathetic tirade makes one feel sorry that she never bothered to learn her own language."

The issue is sensitive in Western academia, where any criticism of *fusha* tends to be viewed as colonialist. But even Said's cutting remark—"her own language"—raises the issue of whom the language belongs to. I noticed that scholars who advocated for greater use of the colloquial were often women. There's evidence that women are less likely than men to incorporate elements of *fusha* into their everyday speech, which isn't surprising, given that the language tends to be used in predominately male environments. And men might have been more likely than women to feel a connection to the pan-Arab ideas of Nasser and others. Madiha Doss, a scholar of Arabic linguistics at Cairo University, told me that men in her department criticized her when she started researching Egyptian Arabic in the 1970s. "They said, 'You should not be studying something that separates Arabs,'" she remembered.

In Doss's opinion, the tragedy was that this attempt to protect Arab culture had only served to push Egyptians toward other languages. Now the country had reached a point where an education in Arabic was effectively a sign of low class. "It's as if you're imprisoning people with Arabic," she said.

And the difficulty of *fusha,* combined with the low quality of instruction, stunted written expression. "People don't write, because there is linguistic insecurity," she said.

She wondered if things might have developed differently if Egyptian Arabic had been accepted earlier as a written language. Certainly it seemed likely that literacy rates would have been higher. Because of the informal communication that dominates texting and the internet, Egyptians have recently started writing more in the colloquial. Doss noticed that the middle-aged doorman in her building, who had always been illiterate, was now able to text family and friends. He even left comments in Egyptian Arabic on Doss's Facebook page. In Doss's opinion, this was a positive step, but it was effectively too late, because so many Egyptian families and educational institutions had long ago shifted over to foreign-language instruction.

I noticed a similar transformation in Sayyid's literary abilities. When I first knew him, he had just started to use phones with texting features, and he needed help understanding the messages that his wife and others sent. But over time he improved, and now he could read most things that showed up on his phone. It wasn't because he had made a concerted effort, or studied formally, or enrolled in a literacy program. The only difference was that he picked up reading more easily when it followed the form of his everyday speech.

After Sayyid was cheated of the iPhone, the injustice bothered him, and he stopped by several times to talk about it. "Maybe you can tell Ahmed that your friend needs the phone back," he said one evening. I told him I'd try, and I thought about some of the things I had learned in Arabic class: the deep state, the conspiracy theories, the foreign meddling.

We walked to the building where Ahmed worked. He was sitting in front of the entrance, along with two doormen. Ahmed was in his twenties, a handsome man with curly hair. Most of the doormen and parking attendants on our street were Upper Egyptians who wore galabiyas, but Ahmed dressed in jeans and a polo shirt. He was a Cairo native, which was part of the disrespect—he came from a higher social class than Sayyid.

Ahmed greeted us and we exchanged the usual niceties. Then I said that Sayyid was hardworking and honest, and it would be a shame if he didn't receive the proper amount for his phone.

"I paid two hundred," Ahmed said. "That's what it's worth."

Now I explained that the phone once belonged to my friend, and she needed it back. I took two hundred pounds out of my pocket.

Ahmed looked at the money. "I can't do that," he said. "Anyway, I don't have the phone. My friend has it."

This was smart: my friend, your friend. There was only one more card left to play.

"My friend is a journalist," I said slowly. "She did a lot of interviews with the American embassy. Some of that information is on the phone, and the people at the American embassy need it. So the American embassy will be very concerned if we don't get the phone back."

This was Sisi rhetoric: if "American embassy" was repeated enough times, maybe it would start to sound like the truth. But still Ahmed said no.

"I'm afraid I'll have to tell the American embassy," I said. "I'll give them this address, and the American embassy will do something about it. They will talk with the Egyptian police."

A wave of nervousness flickered across his face, and then he recovered. He drew himself erect in the chair. The two doormen and Sayyid were watching.

"*W'allahy!*" Ahmed said loudly. "By God! I'm not afraid of anybody. I'm not afraid of the American embassy. I'm not afraid of the Egyptian government. I'm not afraid of the American government. I'm not afraid of Obama! I'm not afraid of Sisi!"

He looked at me sternly. "There's only one thing that I fear," he said. He pointed up at the nighttime sky. "*Allah!*" he said. "The only thing I fear is God! *W'allahy, w'allahy, w'allahy!*"

Then he sat down and said quietly that his friend would bring the phone tomorrow evening.

I thanked him and we shook hands. Sayyid and I stood up to go.

"There's one more thing," Ahmed said.

I asked him what it was.

"Could you bring us three beers?"

The phone went back in the drawer. I told Sayyid that he had a week. This time, there were no more iPhone viewing parties in my living room. He negotiated quietly, and he found a buyer for five hundred pounds–the same amount as the donation to the injured man. Justice was served; the money was paid; the phone disappeared. *W'allahy, w'allahy, w'allahy.*

CHAPTER 24

BY THE TIME THE EMPTY NAIL ON THE WALL IN ABYDOS WAS FINALLY COVered, the former *rayis* had been reassigned. There had been a long period, beginning with the fall of Mubarak, and continuing through the year of Morsi's presidency, and then into the early phase of the postcoup era, when the process of local promotions was frozen. Then, after Sisi took office, the bureaucracy began to move again. The Abydos *rayis* was promoted to a larger settlement, and a new *rayis* came to Abydos. A portrait of Sisi, smiling and wearing a dark suit, materialized atop the nail. And now that Egypt had almost everything in place—the constitution, the president, the cabinet, the local officials—it was time to elect a new parliament.

In recent history, the most successful candidate for parliament in the Abydos region was a man named Yusuf Hasan Yusuf. Before the revolution, when Mubarak's NDP was still in power, Yusuf had defeated the NDP candidate for a local seat. After the revolution, when the Muslim Brotherhood was ascendant, Yusuf had defeated the Brotherhood's candidate. For both campaigns, he took on the favorite without joining a party. He had no platform, and he didn't talk about issues or legislation. He never made a single campaign promise. He refused to hold rallies—in his opinion, such events were "fake." And yet he won both times, and now, for the elections that were scheduled for the end of 2015, Yusuf was running again. Once, I asked a rival candidate about the secret to Yusuf's strength.

"Yusuf is lucky," the candidate said, somewhat grudgingly. "Yusuf is a simple, kind man, and he's lucky."

Yusuf's trademark was a snow-white galabiya. He was a tall, handsome man in his mid-forties, and the white gowns contrasted nicely against his dark skin. His police-issue mustache was disarmed by the friendliness of his eyes. He ran a jewelry shop in downtown Balyana, the district seat, and he had a farm near Abydos, where he grew wheat, corn, and sugarcane. He had nine children and hoped for two more, *insha'allah*. When I asked what his kids were like, he laughed and said, "How much time do you have?"

He had been lucky in winning but not so lucky in serving. In December 2010, when Yusuf won his first parliamentary seat, he traveled to Cairo to join the new legislature. But the following month, the Tahrir movement began, and soon the parliament was disbanded. Then, after Yusuf won in the first post-Mubarak election, he once again traveled to Cairo, and once again the parliament was canceled. "I was confused," he said later. "But I just let it be. I felt like I didn't know what happened, whether it was a legitimate court order or something else."

And so he quietly returned to Upper Egypt, where he immediately began campaigning for the next parliamentary vote, even though nothing had been scheduled. "I'm always campaigning—it never stops," he said. "I don't do rallies. I do personal visits." The district, centered on the city of Balyana, covered a large area: two small cities and thirty-three villages, with a population of around 600,000. But Yusuf believed that he could win village by village, house by house, voter by voter. He visited people's homes, and he attended funerals. Such duties—*wegebat*—were expected of any high-ranking clan elder, so Yusuf merged them seamlessly into his political life. "I average more than fifty funerals per month," he said. "It can be three of them in a day. The grim reaper is keeping on, and we keep up with him. And if there are problems with the tribes, then I try to fix them. If somebody has an accident, or if somebody has a problem with his electricity or water, or if somebody wants to send his son to a certain school, then they talk with me. They see me as their representative."

People still used that word—*ne'ib*, "representative"—as a form of address for Yusuf and the other locals who had served in various Egyptian parliaments, even though those parliaments hadn't lasted more than a few months, and men like Yusuf had hardly had time to function as formal representatives. Nevertheless, they kept the titles, and they kept campaigning, even during the chaotic year of the Morsi presidency, when a parliamentary vote was never announced.

After the new campaign began, each of the four strongest candidates in

Balyana district spoke about his prospects with complete certainty. One was a high-ranking police officer who had recently retired, and he believed that nowadays, after all the instability, people wanted a representative from the security state. Two other local favorites had won seats in the first post-Tahrir election, along with Yusuf, so they also expected another victory. In 2012, the district had sent three representatives to Cairo, but for the new election the number had been reduced to two. Two seats, four favorites: somebody was going to lose. Lucky Yusuf swore it wouldn't be him.

Throughout the years of the Arab Spring, Josef Wegner and his University of Pennsylvania crew usually spent December and January excavating the massive tomb of Senwosret III. They also dug in the desert near the tomb's entrance. Various minor kings and nobles had built graves and other mortuary structures here, and the area had never been well studied.

One year, Wegner's team excavated a long narrow building that was believed to have housed the funeral barge of Senwosret III. A team of fifty made up a bucket brigade, passing sand down the line, and every day another three to five feet of the buried structure were revealed. First the roof appeared, then the walls. As the sand was hauled away, it became apparent that somebody had inscribed dozens of images of Nile boats onto the plaster walls: big boats and little boats, boats with sails and boats with oars. There were also animals: cattle, gazelles, ducks.

The scratchings were crude; this wasn't royal art. It seemed that the common people who worked here had made these pictures. "It's pretty unique," Wegner said one morning, when he took me inside the building, which was half-excavated. "There aren't really any parallels from this time period. It seems that workers were coming into this building, but why they would draw a boat on the wall is unclear."

The building's entrance faced north, and during the ancient past it had been filled with sand by the wind that runs upriver from the Mediterranean. "It's one of the wonders of Abydos," Wegner said. "All the sand coming and going. The sand tends to fill in things, to hide things."

Every day, as the bucket brigade worked, more pictures of ships appeared in this waterless place. Finally, the crew reached the floor of the building: no boat. Most likely it had been looted in ancient times. Wegner photographed and measured the walls, and later he published his findings in the *International Journal of Nautical Archaeology*. This was another Abydos wonder—you can dig deep in the desert and discover something that qualifies as nautical.

During the season that I visited, after the boat building had been photographed, the bucket brigade began its work once more. But now the chain of workers moved in the opposite direction, dumping sand atop the building, reburying it for the sake of preservation. When I returned the following year, there was no sign that anything lay beneath the surface.

One of Yusuf's main rivals for parliament, and his opposite in almost every respect, was Rafat Mohamed Mahmoud. Whereas Yusuf was friendly and talkative, Rafat was distant and silent. He had wealth instead of luck, and a stiff dignity instead of easy humor. Also unlike Yusuf, Rafat was a joiner. Before the revolution, he had belonged to the NDP, and after the party was disbanded, Rafat ran as an independent and won the second of the local seats, behind Yusuf. For the new election Rafat had changed affiliation yet again. He joined the Free Egyptians Party, which had been founded by a businessman from the richest family in the country.

Rafat himself came from what was reported to be the wealthiest clan in the Balyana district. They were known as the Abu'l Khair, and their rise had been relatively recent. In the 1980s and 1990s, some Abu'l Khair men became rich in the construction industry in Kuwait, and they invested in real estate back home. Rafat's older brother, Hishmat, had been the first Abu'l Khair to win a parliamentary seat. He had died relatively young, shortly before the revolution, and now Rafat sought to inherit his status.

One evening, I accompanied Rafat while he campaigned in the countryside near Abydos. His entourage of more than a dozen men traveled in a Mercedes sedan, a Jeep SUV, and two other vehicles. We started in late afternoon, following narrow dirt roads bordered by fields of clover and wheat. At every stop, the group was escorted into the *dawar*, the traditional reception area in a rural Egyptian home.

For prosperous families, these reception areas consisted of large open-air courtyards, and the young men of the clan were always lined up before Rafat and his entourage arrived. We were seated, and then the line of young men passed by, shaking our hands and offering cigarettes. Sometimes I was presented with twenty cigarettes, one after another, and I declined each one with the same phrase: "Thank you, I don't smoke." After the greeting, the young men served tea and other drinks. They remained standing throughout the meeting. The clan's elders, along with Rafat's entourage, were seated on soft couches.

Members of the entourage had specific campaign jobs. Four men drove the vehicles, another man kept track of the schedule, and an old sheikh recited prayers at every stop. A relative of Rafat's named Abu Steit was in charge of terminating the visits. Abu Steit was a short, pudgy man with a toothbrush mustache, and he carried a wooden cane and wore a turban. When the young men appeared with trays of drinks, Abu Steit always waved them off imperiously and shouted, "*Halawa!*"—"Sweets!" After that, some youth would scurry off to retrieve chocolate or cookies.

In Upper Egypt, politics is a late-evening endeavor, and by midnight I had lost track of how many sweets Abu Steit had consumed. As his blood sugar rose, so did my fascination: there was something mesmerizing about a little man with a Hitler mustache who, after tossing an empty chocolate wrapper at his feet, would suddenly pound his cane on the ground and yell, "*Al-Fatiha! Al-Fatiha!*" The Fatiha is the first sura of the Quran, and it was recited to bless Rafat's departure. This blessing might happen a minute after we arrived, or it could take half an hour; the timing depended entirely on Abu Steit's judgment.

Many visits were characterized by stretches of uncomfortable silence. There was no stump speech or formal introduction, and Rafat rarely spoke. He was a tall man in an expensive pin-striped galabiya, and usually he sat in the place of honor, staring into space, until Abu Steit mercifully called for the Fatiha. Nobody ever mentioned Rafat's NDP past or his current political affiliation. The Cairo-based Free Egyptians Party was essentially meaningless here; it paid for Rafat's posters and some other campaign expenses, but the party didn't have a local office. There was no functioning regional press that allowed a candidate to promote issues or policies.

Abu Steit seemed to determine the length of each visit according to the importance of the family. Visits were briefer at homes that appeared less prosperous, and these families rarely requested anything. Wealthier clans were far more likely to ask for help or services. But even these requests tended to be small, and usually they concerned utilities. This was a strength of Rafat's candidacy: until recently, he had been employed in the local electricity bureau. I had the impression that like many government workers he hadn't done much in this job, but it gave him connections. The subject often came up in *dawar* conversations.

"We still need permission here for electricity for three houses and for nine streetlamps. You saw it on your way here—there's no light in the street."

"We will try to help."

"We always received help from your brother, *allah yerhamoh,* may God bless his soul. When he was the representative, we used to tell him that we needed something and the next day we would have it."

"Yes, he was a legend, *allah yerhamoh.*"

"*Allah yerhamoh.* May you win, *insha'allah.*"

"We will bring four or five streetlamps now, and then later we'll get the rest."

"We also need bulbs for the lights on the bridge."

"*Insha'allah.*"

Dawar meetings often touched on the issue of tribes. There were two main groups in the area: the Hawwara, to which Yusuf belonged, and the Arabs, a tribe that included Rafat. When I first visited Abydos, this aspect of local culture confused me, because I had never thought of Egypt as truly tribal. Such groups were important in desert regions, especially in the Gulf states, whereas Egypt had more agricultural traditions. And the tribes in Abydos seemed indistinguishable. They spoke the same Egyptian Arabic; they dressed the same way; they looked like members of the same ethnic group. All of them were Muslim; most of them were farmers. But they claimed to be the descendants of warriors who had arrived from Saudi Arabia in the seventh century.

The archaeologists generally dismissed these ideas. Matthew Adams pointed out that the number of Arabs who conquered Egypt was tiny—four thousand soldiers—and it seemed unlikely that they had had much contact with the south. "My impression has always been that the villages are endogamous," Adams said. "They marry within the village. It's probably been like this forever." He laughed and said, "When you look at the figures on the tomb walls, you can recognize our workers!"

In fact, a small Bedouin group called the Hawwara had migrated to Upper Egypt, but they came from northwestern Africa, not the Gulf. They didn't arrive until medieval times, when they intermarried with natives. The Hawwara never maintained the kind of separation that would have resulted in distinctive cultural features, and they also couldn't have spread as widely as people now claimed. It was obvious that many locals who had no historical connection to this tribe now considered themselves members.

The group they called "the Arabs" was an even more recent creation. The phrase was popularized in the 1950s, as part of Nasser's Pan-Arabism. It replaced *fellaheen,* "farmers" or "peasants," which had negative connotations. People around Abydos had co-opted this pan-Arab term as a way of describing those who didn't identify as Hawwara.

Over time, the idea of two distinct groups became stronger, because it matched perfectly with the election system. Mubarak had emphasized the parliamentary campaigns, largely in order to claim that Egypt was democratic. In Cairo and other major cities, the vote was usually rigged, but officials didn't bother to interfere in remote places like Abydos. The NDP could generally recruit whoever happened to win, because candidates weren't coming from opposition parties with real principles or ideology.

In this environment, where elections were competitive but unstructured, locals developed their own proxies for parties. "They had an electoral system that needed some group, and the tribes came in handy," Hans Christian Korsholm Nielsen, a Danish anthropologist who had observed campaigns in the south, told me. He noted that even as recently as the 1960s and 1970s most people didn't identify with tribes. But as the ritual of elections became entrenched, people created new stories about their origins. Nielsen had observed one candidate near Aswan who campaigned with a local historian so that he could lecture voters on their supposed tribal past. They preferred a connection to Saudi Muslim ancestors over pharaonic people, who were seen as infidels.

In a sense, it was the political equivalent of the *ashwa'iyat.* Without any structure or institution shaping the elections, people figured out their own system, and for a foundation they turned to the organization they knew best:

the family. They used whatever history or media seemed helpful. Rafat's campaign entourage included a cousin named Souleiman Abu'l Khair, who worked as an actor in Cairo. He had a strong, sharp-featured face, and he often played Upper Egyptian cops and criminals on soap operas and Ramadan television specials.

Late in the evening, we stopped at the *dawar* of a wealthy landowner named Zabit Gebr. He told Souleiman that they should find a good screenwriter who could create a script about their tribe.

"We want a serious soap opera that represents the Arabs," Zabit said. "With the permission of the *ne'ib,* the representative, we should do this."

"There was a series called *The Judging of the Days,*" Souleiman said. "It talked about the conflicts within the Arabs."

"We don't need this!" Zabit said, and the elders laughed. "We want the guy who wrote the series *Sheikh al-Arab Hamam.* But there was a problem: he described somebody from the Hawwara as if he were Arab."

Zabit embarked on a long analysis of various television serials that featured Upper Egyptians. In his opinion, the shows often conflated tribes, and he believed that the Arabs needed to establish a clear identity in the entertainment industry. He thanked Souleiman for representing them as an actor. "Keep raising our heads for all of Egypt, *insha'allah,*" Zabit said.

"Have you watched *Khalaf Allah*?" Souleiman asked.

"I just watched two episodes."

"You have to watch it, because I play a good role."

Zabit complained that all of the time he spent staring at social media on his phone made it hard for him to watch television. "Facebook ruined our eyesight," he said. "It has weakened my eyes, man."

After the fall of Mubarak, when officials suddenly feared the vast numbers of disillusioned youths, they searched for ways in which young people could get involved in politics without protesting. If the officials had had true vision, they would have encouraged the development of parties and other institutions that could enlist the young. But instead they settled on a fairly simple quota system. For the first post-Tahrir parliamentary election, a number of seats were reserved for "list candidates," who competed as groups of allied individuals. These lists had to include traditionally underrepresented groups: women, Christians, and people under the age of thirty-five.

That year, the youngest person in all of Egypt to win a list seat in parliament came from Balyana district. He was a twenty-six-year-old named Mahmoud Hamdy Ahmed, and he also belonged to the Abu'l Khair clan. He and Rafat were cousins, but unlike Rafat, Mahmoud rose with the Islamist movement. He joined the Salafis' Nour Party, which won about a quarter of the seats in that first parliament.

Now that Sisi was in power, the election rules had been revised so that the number of list seats was drastically reduced. This was a way of defusing the Islamist movement, and it also meant fewer quotas for women and young people. In Balyana, Mahmoud responded by renouncing his membership in the Nour Party, which had been badly weakened, and he became an independent. But he kept his beard. No other candidate in the race appeared on posters with Salafi-style facial hair.

People interpreted the beard in different ways. Some said that Mahmoud was a true Islamist, while others claimed that he was nothing but an opportunist who had used the religious movement when it happened to be convenient. Local conspiracy theories, which were just as robust as the national versions, claimed that the beard was part of an elaborate family plot. Supposedly, Mahmoud and Rafat didn't get along, and Rafat told me that he and his cousin were "enemies." But some claimed this was just an act. In their opinion, the cousins had established themselves on opposite ends of the political spectrum—one with a history in the NDP, the other with an Islamist past—in order to distract locals from the fact that they were both Abu'l Khair.

Like many powerful clans in the south, the Abu'l Khair followed patterns that sometimes seemed premodern. They disliked living in small cities like Balyana; instead, individual family members built massive walled compounds in the remote countryside. As a clan became wealthier, it removed itself from society, and it restricted its women to a higher degree. The pattern of intermarriage also intensified. It was basically the same strategy that had been followed by ancient dynasties like the Eighteenth, when family marriages consolidated wealth and authority.

Around Balyana, the Hawwara were known for refusing to allow their daughters to marry anybody who wasn't considered part of the tribe. And for a wealthy family like the Abu'l Khair, the family tree was more like a family thicket. Rafat and the actor Souleiman were cousins in the local sense, with shared blood on both sides: their mothers were sisters, and their fathers were cousins. Rafat's and Mahmoud's connections were similarly entangled. When I talked to another cousin named Adl, I asked him to explain how everybody was related, and he ended up drawing detailed diagrams in my notebook. I learned that Adl and Mahmoud were connected all the way to their great-great-great-grandfather, who was also the great-great-grandfather of Rafat. Their shared direct ancestors included five Ahmeds, two Mohammeds, and two Mahmouds. Three women in Adl's family—two sisters and an aunt—were married to Rafat and his brothers. Adl planned to vote for his cousin Rafat over his cousin Mahmoud, because the family thicket was denser on Rafat's side.

When I visited Mahmoud's *dawar,* I found a tall, thin, bearded man whose eyes reflected shrewdness and suspicion in equal measure. He had been trained as a pharmacist, a career that attracts bright students in rural Egypt. His *dawar* was impossible to characterize. About a dozen men were hanging out, and some had Islamist beards while others were smoking water pipes, which should have been *haraam* to a real Salafi. There were also a couple of big, unsmiling men in sunglasses who looked like agents from the Amn al-Dawla, the State Security Investigations Service.

Mahmoud was cagey in conversation. He wouldn't explain why he had left the Nour Party, and he insisted that he was neither a Salafi nor an Islamist. "Here it's a tribal system," he said. "There's the Hawwara and the Arabs, and that's it. Nothing else. No Islamists or non-Islamists."

For the campaign, Mahmoud rode around the district in a chauffeured Mercedes 200 sedan. The vehicle still retained the special license plates that the government had issued to parliamentarians, although it had been more than three years since that legislature was disbanded. The car's back window was decorated with the campaign slogan: "Your Hand in My Hand . . . We Build for Your Children and for Mine." This sunny phrase was paired with the official campaign symbol, which was a cannon. In Balyana, Mahmoud's supporters had positioned wooden cannons at busy intersections, and they attached them to the roofs of three-wheeled *tuk-tuk* scooter-cabs, which cruised around town like an undersized cavalry.

Campaign symbols were mandatory across Egypt, because so many voters were illiterate. In each district, the selection of symbols was like a fantasy draft, with candidates choosing from 160 government-approved icons. The top draft pick in Balyana was wasted on a chandelier, which was like taking Sam Bowie over Michael Jordan. Yusuf was a red car. Rafat was an eagle. Other symbols had dubious connotations: a knife, a rifle, an ambulance. Would you elect a scorpion? "I voted for the lamp and the helicopter," one man told me outside a polling station. Another said he had voted for the boat. Often they forgot the names because their clan elders had simply told them which symbol to choose.

Mahmoud claimed that he had selected the cannon because "the others had already been taken." This made no sense—he picked fourth overall. Still, I had to admit that it took guts to show up for the first postcoup election wearing a Salafi beard and using a cannon for a symbol. Others were even more shameless. Elders from two different clans campaigned on the strength of their supposed connection to the young, and one of them—official slogan: "The Candidate of the Youth"—was sixty-five years old. Many aspiring parliamentarians used campaign photographs that had been taken at least twenty years earlier. Some of Rafat's banners featured a picture of his dead brother Hishmat, *allah yerhamoh,* probably because people seem to have liked Hishmat more than they liked Rafat.

During one of the winter archaeological campaigns, Josef Wegner and his team discovered a previously unknown pharaoh named Senebkay. The tomb was located near the entrance to the burial place of Senwosret III. And while Senwosret III's tomb was believed to be the longest in all of Egypt, Senebkay's was about the size of a walk-in closet. "It might officially be the smallest pharaoh's tomb in existence," Wegner said, when he showed me the cramped space. "My wife calls it the cutest little pharaoh's tomb ever found."

Senebkay ruled during the middle of the seventeenth century BC, about two hundred years after Senwosret III. By then, the Egyptian state had entered a period of sharp decline, now known as the Second Intermediate Period. In the past, historians generally believed that the country was split in two, with the foreign group known as the Hyksos ruling in the north while an Egyptian dynasty controlled the south from Thebes. But the records had never been clear. One of the most important king lists, a tattered papyrus now held in a museum in Turin, has a gaping hole in the section that covers this era.

Wegner's discovery filled in the blank. He realized that Senebkay was part of a third group that fought for control in the middle of the country, with Abydos as their base. Wegner named this group "the Abydos Dynasty," and they seemed to have responded to the collapse of central authority by creating their own version of the state. They gave pharaonic titles to their leaders, who declared themselves rulers of all of Egypt, although in truth their authority must have been much smaller. When they built tombs, they grabbed blocks and stones from the burials of more prosperous periods. Inside Senebkay's burial chamber, Wegner pointed out a large stone that had originally been inscribed by a Nubian chief as a stele that commemorated his pilgrimage to Abydos.

"It seems like they didn't have much access to materials," Wegner said. "It's a sign of economic decline."

He thought that perhaps the Hyksos had cut off trade routes to the north. Possibly for this reason, the Abydos Dynasty found itself at war, which appears to have gone badly for Senebkay. The king's mummified corpse contained between eighteen and twenty wounds from at least three different types of weapons. Hacking marks on Senebkay's hands, knees, and ankles probably came from short swords. There were arrow wounds in his back; perhaps the king tried to flee. If that was the case, he didn't get far. Three large battle-ax blows had shattered his cranium. In all of Egyptian history, this was the earliest confirmed instance of a pharaoh who died in battle.

At the end of the season, the king's remains were placed in a wooden box in the dig house. The next year, the team planned to excavate the tomb again and continue their research, but in the meantime they had to protect the site. A short bucket brigade went to work. It didn't take long to rebury the smallest pharaoh's tomb in Egypt.

During Morsi's year in office, I had gotten to know a couple of the Muslim Brothers who lived in Balyana district. Mohamed Wajih was the most dynamic, a young pharmacist who had served as the Brotherhood's district head of media relations. He was unmarried, and he lived with his parents and his younger brothers, not far from Abydos. Wajih decorated the family *dawar* with Brotherhood stickers and slogans, including a poster of the Dome of the Rock that said, in Arabic, "*Say No to Making Jerusalem Jewish.*"

After the Rabaa massacre, Wajih fled to Kuwait, where he found work as a pharmacist. His family remained in their home near Abydos. For a while, his younger brothers talked about joining the Brotherhood, but as the crackdown intensified, they gave up on this idea. After Sisi took office, their father removed all the posters and slogans from the *dawar*. He repainted the walls and inscribed a single Quranic phrase: "*Nothing will happen except for what God has written for us.*"

At the start of the parliamentary campaign, Wajih made his first visit home since the massacre, in order to get married. His relatives had quietly negotiated with local authorities, to make sure that Wajih wouldn't get arrested. I stopped in the *dawar* while Wajih was in town, and he talked about what had gone wrong in 2012 and 2013.

"The Brotherhood thought they could contain the deep state," he said. But he also believed that the group had made tactical errors. "For them to announce that they weren't running for president, and then to run—that was a mistake," he said. "I'm angry at the Brotherhood's leaders. If they had heard the voice of the people, and if they had responded, there wouldn't have been a coup. But it happened because of their way of thinking. They suffered extreme repression under Mubarak, and it shaped them. That's why they were so secretive."

He said he was finished with Egyptian politics. He was going back to Kuwait, and his wife would join him there. He didn't expect to return to Abydos.

In Cairo, it was no longer possible to meet with anybody associated with the Brotherhood, but the crackdown around Abydos had been lighter. I visited Ayman Abdel Hamid, a physician who had been the highest-ranking Brother in the district. He said that only two Brothers had been imprisoned, and he and others were left alone because they weren't active anymore and their families protected them. And local poverty made police more willing to let things slide. "Since life is already hard, they don't want to make it harder," he said. He still ran his private medical clinic, which served many lower-income residents.

I reminded him that in the spring of 2013, he had said there were only 150 Brothers in the district. At the time, the number seemed surprisingly low for a region with a population of 600,000. Now I asked again if that figure was accurate.

"That was the crowd around the Brotherhood, not the real members," Ayman said. "We were trying to exaggerate the numbers to scare other parties. It was just election tactics."

I asked what the real number had been.

"Ten members," he said, and smiled sadly. "Those were two of our mistakes. We exaggerated the numbers of our members to scare others. And we allowed some people to act like they were with us, but in truth they weren't."

The Brotherhood had a long history of bouncing back from crackdowns, but I sensed that something had changed. For the first time, the Brothers had actually held power, and their abysmal performance seemed to have convinced most Egyptians that the organization had no place in politics. And many of the Brotherhood's illusions had been exposed. If they had truly provided significant social services and charity, then the loss of these benefits should have been apparent after the crackdown. But I never met anybody who complained about such things disappearing, because in truth they had hardly existed.

When I talked with Ayman, I asked if he still met with his *'usra,* the Brotherhood "family" cell, and he shook his head. "I don't have anybody above me anymore," he said. "And there's nobody below me. I'm like the others—we're all just separate individuals now." These days, his only *'usra* was the clan.

In Cairo, I knew few people who cared about the parliamentary election. Neither Sayyid nor Manu bothered to vote, and most city people seem to have returned to the political disengagement of the Mubarak years. But in Balyana the locals took the election seriously. The winning candidates might be able to direct some government projects and funds to their supporters, but such benefits were likely to be small in such a poor region. The main incentive seemed to be pride—people cared about how their clans competed.

Four candidates were clearly the strongest, but fifteen others also campaigned. One of the youngest was a lawyer named Mahmoud Abu Mohasseb, and I accompanied him on some of his *dawar* visits. He had performed respectably in past elections, but this time, in the first round of voting, he finished seventeenth out of nineteen. Afterward, he stopped picking up my calls. When I knocked on his apartment door, I heard his son's muffled voice: "Daddy's not coming."

Close relatives in his village also hadn't seen him. "Others are mocking us," Khaled Abu Mohasseb, the candidate's cousin, said. "These results are shameful. It doesn't suit the name of the family."

Khaled had campaigned with his cousin, but now he blamed Mahmoud for a lack of effort. It seemed unfair; even months before the vote, the candidate had spent his evenings making home visits. But when I asked Khaled if he felt any sympathy for his cousin, he shook his head. "I feel more sorry for myself and for the family," he said.

It seemed very difficult to lose gracefully in Balyana. After the first round whittled the field down to four, there were endless recriminations and accusations by the others. One bitter man told me that he would have won, but his own relatives were bribed by opponents. Another failed candidate announced on Facebook that he was moving to Cairo because of "the stink of politics." Mohammed Abu Hilely, an eliminated candidate from the Arab tribe, claimed that his fellow tribesmen Rafat and Mahmoud had paid off voters.

Like others, Hilely conducted his tribal politics on social media. There had been a time when analysts talked about the "Facebook Revolution," and they believed that social media was driving the Arab Spring toward democracy. But now it was obvious that these same social media tools were just as useful for maintaining patriarchal structures like the tribes. After Hilely lost the Balyana election, he posted an angry YouTube video in which he called upon all Arabs to cross lines and vote for Yusuf in the final round.

There was an open-air coffee shop at the edge of the Buried, and men liked to hang out there and discuss local politics. One evening, I met Ahmed Diyab, a child psychologist who worked at the elementary school in Abydos. He predicted that the final outcome of Hilely's YouTube video would be a classic example of reverse psychology. By asking his tribesmen to support Yusuf and the Hawwara, Hilely had all but guaranteed they would do the opposite.

According to Diyab, his psychology background qualified him to analyze local political behavior, because candidates often acted like the children he worked with. "It's the same thing," he said. "Maybe a kid is peeing on himself as a way of attracting attention. Maybe I have a problem, but I can't express myself, so I use violence."

In Cairo, educated people often talked about the "deep state," the tentacles of the military, and the various conspiracy theories that supposedly connected the United States, Israel, Qatar, and the Brotherhood. Politics was distant and theoretical, but the Abydos version was simpler—this was basic human behavior. In some ways, I was impressed: without any guidance, locals had developed their own election traditions, which functioned remarkably well. After the first round, the finalists were perfectly split between two Hawwara and two Arabs, and fewer than thirty-eight hundred votes separated first from fourth. It was impossible to predict who would win the final round. I had never covered a more competitive democratic election.

But the underlying emptiness was tragic. What might have been accomplished if all this energy and effort had been harnessed by some coherent system? In Egypt, whether I looked at elections, or *ashwa'iyat,* or manufacturing, or garbage collection, the feeling was often the same: so much talent, so little structure. An election in Balyana revealed human behavior at its most basic, because nothing moderated the urges or redirected the instincts. It was a competition of bed wetters and tantrum throwers; losers lashed out, and anger was a common emotion, as was pride. The old controlled the young; the men controlled the women. The only real structure was the same one that had shaped local life since long before the first royal tombs were dug into the Buried. It had nothing to do with the Brotherhood, or the NDP, or Sisi, or any other political figure or group. For Egyptians, the family was the deep state.

I never witnessed a candidate interacting with a woman. The *dawar* meetings were male only, and they focused on elders, who generally decided how the extended family would vote. The wealthier and more powerful a person was, the more votes he controlled; Zabit Gebr, the man whom I visited with Rafat's entourage, told me proudly that he directed six hundred people of voting age. "When I give them the order on the day of the election, then the people have to go to the polling station," he said. "It's not their business whether it's wrong or right." This was one reason why elders participated so enthusiastically in the election. It allowed them to assert authority over the clan, and they clearly enjoyed the ritual of the meetings, where they could bark at young men in their prime, forcing them to fetch drinks or sweets.

The elders also decided whether to allow the women in the family to vote. This was one of the key uses of campaign funds: wealthy candidates hired cars and buses to take women back and forth to the polls without any risk of inappropriate contact with men. Zabit Gebr told me that he would tell his people to vote for the eagle, Rafat's symbol, but he wasn't going to allow the women out. "In our family, females die inside the house," he said. "They can go out to see a doctor, or go to the cemetery. That's it." He made one of those expressive Egyptian gestures—he turned his wrist as if locking a door.

The only way to interview a local woman was to go through connections. A friend arranged a meeting between me and Nora Abdel Mohammed, who was one of the few village women near Abydos who had a job. She was a clerk in a government office in Balyana, and she said she was able to do this because her husband was unusually enlightened. The election routine frustrated her. "I'd like to meet the candidate personally and hear what he has to say," she said. In her opinion, the Arab Spring had only made things worse, because people feared instability, and these rituals of democracy became just another opportunity for elders to boss around women and young people. Most of the women Nora knew were completely isolated in their family compounds. "Women in the homes need somebody to reach them," she said.

Candidates rarely mentioned women at all, because it was considered inappropriate. During all the *dawar* visits that I observed, I heard women talked about only once. The night before the final vote, I stopped by the riverside *dawar* of Nour Abu Steit, the fourth finalist. He was a short, fierce-looking man who had recently retired from the police. He was Hawwara, and he began our conversation by claiming that the Abu'l Khair candidates were buying votes. Then he shifted his conspiracy theorizing to the United States. He believed that U.S. foreign policy was based on the evil eye, because Americans were jealous of Egypt. "We've had Egyptian sovereignty for seven thousand years," he said. "You feel angry with us because of our civilization!"

He sat with his back to the Nile, surrounded by two dozen elders. A ripple of laughter ran through the group. "America is creating entities that divide the Arab world," he said.

I asked which entities had been created by Americans.

"ISIS," he said.

"So America created ISIS?"

"Yes," he said. "I hope that God sends you earthquakes and volcanoes!"

Nour glared at me, and he told a story about an American woman diplomat who had supposedly used sex to manipulate Saddam Hussein. The men laughed again; now the *dawar* had a certain bullying, locker-room feel. I often wondered how much of Egypt's political dysfunction—the pride, the shame, the anger, the stubbornness, the violence—could be attributed to the unrelenting maleness of authority. And gender segregation made it even worse. If nothing else, a man like Nour seemed likely to benefit from occasionally hearing a female voice say, *Maybe you should stop talking.*

"A woman with beautiful legs!" Nour said. He was still describing the American diplomat. "When Saddam talked to her, she took off her skirt, and she gave him the green light!" The men laughed, and Nour ranted on about American intrigues. Finally I asked if he opposed Egypt's acceptance of the roughly 1.5 billion dollars of annual aid that came from the United States.

"That number is weak!" he said. "It's not suitable for Egypt."

I asked what a suitable figure might be.

"Not less than eight billion dollars," he said proudly.

For the election's final round, I made a couple of trips south with Manu. We hadn't worked together for years, and I knew that this would likely be our last time. He was making steady progress with his plans. He was in the process of selling the Port Said apartment that he had inherited from his father, and every now and then he made a short trip to some country where visas were easily obtained by Egyptians. After Cyprus, he traveled to Saudi Arabia, Turkey, and then South Africa.

In Saudi Arabia, he participated in the traditional *'umrah* pilgrimage to Mecca. This impressed me as perhaps the least likely act ever performed by a gay man hoping to flee an Islamic republic. But Manu wanted stamps in his passport, and he said he might as well take advantage of his birthright. After all, his legal name was Mohamed.

The *'umrah* pilgrimage can be made at any time during the year, unlike the more important hajj. Manu was surprised by how much he enjoyed going to the Great Mosque of Mecca. Twice he performed the *tawaf,* the traditional counterclockwise walk around the Kaaba, the cube-like building that represents the most sacred site in Islam. On another day, Manu returned and hung out in the courtyard inside the mosque from midnight until dawn. He liked how relaxed the place felt in the middle of the night, and the contrast to the daytime scenes of white-clothed pilgrims flowing in a mass around the black building. And he liked looking at the Kaaba—he had no particular interest in Islam, but he sensed some power in the ancient structure.

In Abydos, Manu and I stayed in the only hotel in town, and we attended *dawar* meetings in the evenings. It was still easy to travel around the region, but something seemed to be changing. When I visited the old Abydos *rayis* in his new posting, he greeted me warmly, but after we talked for a while, he told me that any future meeting would have to be approved by his superior. The days of showing up unannounced at a government office, at least as a foreign journalist, seemed to be coming to an end. And now there were many more plainclothes police hanging around outside the Abydos hotel.

It had never been easy to characterize the Egyptian security climate, but these days it became even harder. When Westerners hear the term "police state," they generally assume that everything is controlled or monitored by the police. But a police state is often just a state that contains a lot of police. What these police actually do is a separate issue.

In Abydos, the police drank tea, and they hung out at road blockades, and they slept in cars outside my hotel. Often they failed to awaken when I showed up. I always gave the cops my phone number upon arrival in town, because it put them at ease, and it allowed them to do investigative work while sitting down. During my drives back to Cairo, they called repeatedly.

"Where are you?"

"I'm on the desert highway."

"Where on the desert highway?"

"I don't know. There aren't any towns here. It's the *sahera*."

This seemed to qualify as police monitoring. Sometimes they called twenty or thirty times during my drive. Once, when I was in Abydos with Manu, they insisted on providing a police escort back to the capital. The cop tailgated so closely that after a few miles I pulled over and yelled at him to back off. Then, after I passed the Sohag Airport, he rolled his lights and pulled me over. He looked upset.

"I thought you were going to Cairo!" he said.

"I am."

"So why did you go past the airport?"

"I'm driving to Cairo," I said.

"You're driving?"

"Did you think I was going to put my car on the airplane?"

Sitting in the passenger's seat, Manu burst into laughter. The officer had no response; he followed the Honda for a couple more miles and then gave up. For the rest of the drive, my phone rang periodically, and I answered the usual inane questions about my current location in the Sahara.

Having worked in Communist China, I had had the experience of being monitored by professionals, so I had trouble taking Egyptian cops seriously. But I knew this was dangerous, because the essence of the Egyptian police state was unpredictability. Nowadays, with more cops around, and with the vast majority of them as poorly trained and undisciplined as ever, the odds increased that somebody would make a mistake, or get confused, or misinterpret something. I knew that the election would be the last political event I covered in Egypt—for me, the Arab Spring was coming to an end.

I wanted Yusuf to win. It felt strange to feel so strongly about a candidate now, after the Egyptian democracy had collapsed. But Yusuf impressed me as a natural politician. His competition was hopelessly flawed: Nour was a blowhard xenophobe; Mahmoud was a crypto-Islamist opportunist; Rafat seemed to represent the essence of entitlement without talent. Each man projected an image of sternness, and they roared through the villages in entourages of expensive cars with air-conditioning. But Yusuf leaned out the open window of his beat-up Peugeot, waving and calling out to people. He had no platform—nobody did—but at least he loved being in public, shaking hands and talking to strangers. He had a reputation for generosity, and he often mediated in local disputes, serving as a calming influence. Virtually all the Copts I met planned to vote for Yusuf, because they believed in his decency. Copts represented around 10 percent of the local population, but most candidates ignored them, because they were outside the tribal system. None of the original nineteen candidates had been either Christian or female.

On the evening of the vote, after the polls closed, I waited in Yusuf's *dawar* in downtown Balyana. Some of the clan elders worked their phones, trying to track preliminary results. Outside, two or three hundred young men had gathered. A number of them carried guns, and most had big wooden staves that were used in a traditional dance called the *tahtib,* which would be performed if the candidate won. Given the long history of election fights in Upper Egypt, it seemed like a terrible idea to have mobs of young men standing around with sticks and guns.

All four candidates were at the election commission's headquarters, observing the count. Around midnight, somebody at Rafat's *dawar* called me to say that supporters were celebrating with gunfire. Soon after that, a young man burst into Yusuf's headquarters and shouted, "*Allahu akbar! Allahu akbar!*" Everybody ran outside. Manu and I found ourselves next to a cotton farmer in his sixties who reached into his galabiya, pulled out a 9-millimeter Helwan pistol, and shot four rounds into the sky. Other men fired rifles and shotguns. Manu and I drifted over to a doorway where we could stand with a roof over our heads.

After a few minutes, another mob of young men appeared on the street, firing guns and chanting Nour's name. The same thing was happening at Mahmoud's camp. At that moment, in different corners of the district, the supporters of all four candidates were claiming victory.

A Cairo television station called Al Hayah announced Yusuf and Nour as the winners, and the celebrations intensified. But soon there were rumors of a mistake, and then, at two o'clock in the morning, an official statement came: the television report had been completely wrong. The Abu'l Khair cousins had taken both seats.

At Yusuf's *dawar,* one of the elders stormed into the street, taking his anger out on the youths who had celebrated prematurely. "Have you heard the real results?" he shouted. "Who's celebrating now?" The mob of young men stood there, looking shocked, still clutching their sticks and guns.

Nationwide, the biggest victor was a coalition called For the Love of Egypt, which was led by a former army general named Sameh Seif El-Yazal. The coalition wasn't a formal party, although it seemed likely that Yazal would be able to build a majority in the parliament. After the election, I asked Yazal if he had any significant differences of opinion with Sisi, or if he had been bothered by the massacres and police killings in Cairo. Yazal said, "So far, for seventeen months now, I haven't seen a single mistake that he's made."

In Balyana, the overall winner was Mahmoud, and fewer than five hundred votes separated the other three candidates. After the winners were announced, Manu and I drove to Mahmoud's *dawar.* The sound of ululating rang out from the nearby house—on the upper floors, where the women were sequestered, a celebration was under way.

Mahmoud looked exhausted but happy. His shrewd, taciturn presence had always reminded me of the way that Naguib Mahfouz once described an Islamist character in a novel: "He had the ability, rare in Egyptians, to keep his secrets." I asked Mahmoud if there should be more space for political Islam, but he dodged the question. ("We have new matters now.") His response was similar when I mentioned the Muslim Brotherhood. ("I don't want to talk about old things.") I brought up Sisi, and he said nothing about the brutal crackdown. ("He's respectful.")

In Mahmoud's *dawar,* there was the usual strange assortment of characters: some bearded men sat nearby, along with a few thuggish individuals who looked like security agents. A well-built man with a shaved head asked if he could take a photograph with me. The clumsy way in which he made this request, as if out of friendship with the foreigner, only made it more ominous. Manu backed away; the last thing he wanted was to be documented. The man with the shaved head put his arm around me. When he handed his phone to a colleague, I saw that the home screen featured a picture of Sisi's face.

In the tradition of bad Balyana losers, Nour ranted about conspiracy theories after hearing the results, and he refused to meet with his supporters. I wondered if Yusuf was going to show up. Manu and I waited outside his *dawar* until well after two in the morning, and the crowd of young men still milled around the street, holding sticks and guns. At last Yusuf appeared. He had walked there alone from the election commission.

"You should go home," he said to the young men. "It's better than if a crime had happened."

A middle-aged man approached him, looking distraught.

"*W'allahy,* did you have an accident?" Yusuf said. He chuckled and kissed the man on both cheeks. "Go to sleep," he said. "Tomorrow we'll start a new life, *insha'allah*. God will compensate you with good things!"

For ten minutes he moved through the crowd. "Next time, next time," he said. His expression was calm, even happy, and he made no accusations or complaints about the other candidates. He greeted people and thanked them, and he gently warned the young men not to do anything rash. Slowly, the street cleared, and then Yusuf went inside and took a seat at the back of the *dawar*.

Once he was alone, his face suddenly transformed. The smile vanished, and his eyes sagged; he looked unspeakably sad. Manu and I sat nearby, and nobody said anything. All the elders had left. It was the emptiest *dawar* I'd ever seen.

After a while, I broke the silence. I said something about better luck next time.

"There's no next time," Yusuf said.

"You're not going to run again?"

"No," he said. "It's ended for me, politically."

He said he wanted to focus on farming and community projects. I asked why the election had gone the way it had.

"It wasn't about services or love," he said. "If it had been, I would have won." He believed that the Abu'l Khair cousins had had an overwhelming financial advantage.

While we were talking, a young boy came and sat nearby, his eyes full of tears. Yusuf stood up to go home, and he paused to comfort the boy. I asked if he was one of Yusuf's nine children.

"No," Yusuf said, and laughed lightly at this—his last act as a politician. He said, "I've never seen that boy before in my life."

CHAPTER 25

THROUGHOUT THE FALL, RIFAAT STRUGGLED WITH THE SORE ON HIS foot. Leslie gave him the phone number of a doctor we knew in Zamalek, and she offered to accompany him to an appointment, but Rifaat didn't take her up on it. We weren't having tutorials during this period because of work, and every now and then I called or sent Rifaat an email to say hello. Not long after the parliamentary elections, I telephoned and he became so upset when talking about his medical problems that he sounded close to tears. It didn't make sense that a small wound would be so upsetting, and I assumed he was just having a bad evening. Much of the news that fall was grim: at the end of October, the country suffered its worst terrorist attack since the beginning of the Arab Spring. An ISIS-affiliated group planted a bomb on a Metrojet plane that was departing from south Sinai, and more than two hundred died. Most educated Egyptians I knew were depressed about the way things were going in the country.

In January 2016, we took our last long family trip to Upper Egypt. We drove the length of the country to Abu Simbel, near the Sudanese border. The government had instituted a new requirement that south of Aswan any independent motorist had to be accompanied by a police escort, ostensibly because of concerns about terrorism. The escort left Aswan every morning at eleven o'clock from a site called the Unfinished Obelisk. This stone monument had probably been commissioned by Hatshepsut, the great female pharaoh of the Eighteenth Dynasty, and it was the largest obelisk ever carved in ancient Egypt. But the builders discovered some cracks in the granite and were forced to abandon it. The obelisk was still lying on its side in the quarry. If the thing had been hoisted up, it would have been taller than the Tower of London.

Only three private vehicles showed up for the convoy, and there weren't any other foreigners. A police car with a broken taillight took the lead, and some other cops rode in an old Chevrolet truck at the back. They were carrying Kalashnikovs. After a few miles, the police car turned around and headed back to Aswan. Not long after that, the Chevy with the Kalashnikovs roared past at a speed of about one hundred miles per hour. Probably they were bored; virtually all of the country's terrorist activity was happening in Sinai, and this part of Upper Egypt hadn't experienced any problems. It didn't take long for the Chevy to disappear into the horizon.

The small convoy of private vehicles soon broke apart, and for the next three hours we drove alone. The desert here was sandy and flatter than the landscapes around Abydos. To the east, I saw bright pools of blue, which I assumed were inlets of Lake Nasser. But then I realized the pools were mirages—they reappeared constantly, tracking our progress. I had never seen natural illusions that looked so real; some of the pools had rocks poking up in the center, like islands in a lake.

That afternoon we were the only visitors at Abu Simbel. The temple is a massive construction of Ramesses the Great, with four seated statues of the king carved into a cliff face. Originally, these figures sat near the banks of the Nile, but the site was flooded by the Aswan Dam that was constructed under the direction of Nasser. In the 1960s, teams of Egyptian and foreign conservators and engineers successfully moved the temple and the statues to higher ground, above the new lake.

When we arrived at the site, the twins started running toward the statues—this was always their response to these empty places. The girls were now five and a half years old, and over time I had photographed them at so many southern sites: at the Temple of Seti I, at the Great Aten Temple, at Kom Ombo, at Esna, at Karnak. In every photograph they were alone. I knew that someday these images would also feel mirage-like—twins in Abydos, twins in the Ramesseum, twins in the Valley of the Kings. Two tiny spots of pink on a plain, gazing up at the Colossi of Memnon.

After we returned to Cairo, I tried to call Rifaat but couldn't get through. I texted him—no response. A few days later, I sent an email:

> Hi, I have been trying to call you but the phone is always off. How are things? Are you feeling better? I hope that you've had a recovery. . . . I would like to schedule class for Tuesday morning, if you are free. Would that work for you? We have missed the classes terribly. I'm at the same number if you get a chance.

It was unusual for him not to respond, so finally I called his brother Raafat. There was a long silence after I greeted him.

"Rifaat," he said at last, "*itwaffa*."

The word hit me all the harder because Rifaat was the one who had taught me what it means.

Leslie and I drove to the Kalimat school. Raafat looked awful—he had lost weight, and his face was gaunt. He started to weep while we were talking. His brother's death had been one of many terrible events during the past half a year. A few months earlier, Raafat's wife had suddenly left him, and he had been bedridden for weeks with a slipped disk. He still had his home in the desert city outside Cairo, but it had become too painful for him to make the long drive into town. So for the time being, he lived in the language school. During this half year of disasters, there were hardly any students anyway. "Somebody must have given me the evil eye," he said.

He didn't know what had killed Rifaat. There had been so many contradictory diagnoses in Cairo, and at one point Rifaat even saw a physician overseas, during a short trip to London. The British doctor thought that it was simply a dermatological problem, and he referred him to a skin specialist.

"He gave him another cream to use, but it didn't get better," Raafat said. "And I was in and out of bed with my back. I wasn't able to check on him as much as I wanted to. And you know Rifaat—he liked being alone. He didn't want to bother anybody."

While Raafat was laid up with his bad back, he asked a Russian physician friend to check up on his brother. The physician was startled by what she saw. Rifaat, who had always been thin, now seemed dangerously underweight, and he suffered from shortness of breath. He was sweating constantly. In daytime, he often took showers to clean off the sweat. The physician told him the changes in temperature were weakening him, and she said he needed to go to a hospital. But Rifaat refused. He claimed he was starting to feel better.

Finally, Raafat and another brother went to the apartment. By now Rifaat could hardly breathe, but he still didn't want to go to the emergency room, because he feared that his foot would be amputated. His brothers insisted on transporting him to a nearby hospital, where the staff immediately put him into the intensive care unit. By the following morning he was dead.

The official cause was listed as tuberculosis, although Raafat doubted that this was accurate. Supposedly his brother had had a chest X-ray that showed nothing was wrong.

"I don't know who to believe," Raafat said. "All of them said different things. And at one point I used *wasta* and had a very famous doctor at Cairo University see him. He went to Rifaat's home. But he didn't say anything about chest problems or tuberculosis. I'm so angry at this idiot."

He believed that the Cairo University doctor, and some of the others who saw Rifaat near the end, had avoided proactive treatment because they feared being held liable. Raafat also blamed himself; if he hadn't been so wrapped up in his collapsing marriage and his back problems, then he would have been more attentive to his brother. Leslie and I felt terrible for not checking up on Rifaat more closely during the period when we weren't in class. But how could anybody have known it would end like this?

The funeral had already been held. I told Raafat that his brother had been a wonderful teacher and that we had missed seeing him in class during the past few months.

"He talked about your classes all the time," Raafat said. "And he had prepared a bunch of new lessons for you. He was ready for whenever you came back."

Rifaat had died four days before the fifth anniversary of the Egyptian Arab Spring. By now, nobody spoke hopefully about the political movement, and the government's crackdown on dissent had intensified. That was the first year I did nothing to cover the anniversary—it had become too dangerous to attend even the small, scattered protests that occasionally took place. In the spring, when I drove Ariel and Natasha to school, I listened to my vocabulary recordings. I felt nostalgic whenever I heard the lists from earlier and more optimistic phases of the revolution:

local elections	إنتخابات المحليات
People's Assembly	مجلس الشعب
Shura Council	مجلس الشورى
candidate	مرشح
potential	محتمل

The Cairo traffic was often stressful, but it was soothing to hear Rifaat reading the words. For me, his personality—prickly, contradictory, lovable—would always be connected to the language that Egyptians spoke. Every day I crossed the Nile to the sound of his voice:

I will never forgive you for what you did.

I will explain everything to you tomorrow.

Don't waste my time, please.

Are we going to spend the whole day talking about this stupid film?

On January 25, the day of the anniversary, a twenty-eight-year-old Italian graduate student named Giulio Regeni vanished. Regeni was studying at the University of Cambridge, and he was in Cairo to research a dissertation about labor activism. He hadn't participated in any political event that marked the anniversary, but his friends became increasingly frantic as they failed to find him. At last, nine days after Regeni disappeared, his body was discovered in a ditch beside the Cairo-Alexandria Desert Road.

At first, the police claimed that Regeni had died in a traffic accident, but the public prosecutor's office revealed that he had suffered bone fractures and bruises that couldn't have come from a car crash. His face was covered with cigarette burns and small stabbing wounds. An Egyptian forensics official estimated that he had been tortured for up to seven days.

In late March, the Ministry of the Interior claimed that four men who had been killed in a shoot-out with police were part of a criminal gang that had kidnapped Regeni. Officials displayed Regeni's passport and other possessions, which they said had been found with the gang members. But the story quickly collapsed under investigations by Egyptian and foreign journalists, until even government officials publicly acknowledged that there didn't seem to be a link to the supposed gang. Regeni's research was only mildly sensitive, and there was no logical reason why he would have been tortured. Italy recalled its ambassador to Egypt in protest.

While the story unfolded, Sisi delivered a nationally televised address. He claimed that Egypt was the victim of conspiracies, and he said, "Don't listen to anybody's words but mine." He criticized those who protested, and in a show of military math he blamed Egyptians for not contributing enough to a fund that had been established to help alleviate the country's ongoing financial crisis. "If only ten million of the ninety million mobile-phone owners in Egypt would donate one pound to Egypt every morning," he said, "then we would have ten million every day."

In Rifaat's classes, we had often watched clips from influential talk-show hosts, all of whom were adamantly pro-Sisi. But now a few openly criticized him. "I think the President no longer communicates with the people," Youssef Al-Hosiny, a host on the ONTV station, which was privately owned, said on air. In the past, Al-Hosiny had been so loyal that Sisi once offered him a job, but now the host turned to the camera and said, "Sir, are you annoyed by the chants, and not annoyed by the killing or the torture?"

I talked about the case with Anwar Sadat, a parliamentarian who had been named after his uncle, the late president. Sadat was highly respected by the international community, and his family's history allowed him to be more outspoken than most Egyptian public figures. He had just been named the head of the new parliament's human rights committee. "Every day, it's not only Regeni," Sadat told me, referring to the hundreds of disappearances of Egyptian citizens that had occurred since Sisi came to power. The country currently had more than forty thousand political prisoners.

Sadat said that under previous regimes it would have been unimaginable for a foreigner to be tortured to death. In his opinion, there must have been some terrible breakdown in command. "It could have happened because of young officers who are not professional," he said. "A mistake. It wasn't something intentional."

He had met Sisi a number of times. "To me, he is a military officer," he said. "He's not a politician." He continued, "He is sincere, yes, he is honest, and he wants to do something for the country. That I am sure about. But Nasser was sincere and honest, and he did terrible things. Being sincere and honest is not enough. My mother is sincere and honest; that doesn't mean she has to be president."

Sadat complained about the total lack of system in government. He was one of the few parliamentarians who had a real staff, and two of his aides had communicated with me before our interview. One aide was a lawyer, and the other an economist; they sat with us and contributed to the conversation, the way political aides do in the United States or Europe. Sadat acknowledged that he was able to run a professional staff because his family background had prepared him for politics, and he was capable of raising funds.

But whenever he returned to the district that he represented in the Delta, he was back in the real Egypt. At his office, people stood in line, asking for the same things they asked of local officials everywhere. "They think that the human rights committee is a committee that looks after *all* the rights," Sadat said. "I was in my constituency the day before yesterday, and somebody came who could not get married. He said, 'This is my right, to have a wife. What can you do to help me?'" Sadat shook his head. "This is how they see human rights."

Despite Sadat's criticism of Sisi, he didn't want to see the president overthrown. "I think whether Sisi is the perfect choice or not, we have no choice but to have him succeed," he said. "Egypt cannot afford any third revolution."

These days, I even heard similar comments from young activists. Few expressed a desire to overthrow the regime, and a number of people told me that their only hope was for what would come after Sisi. "He'll serve one term, maybe two terms, and that's it," Sadat said. "I'm not really much concerned about him. I'm more concerned about the structure of this country, the institutions in this country. This is where we have to try to see what can be done."

After Regeni's body was found, officials tried to plant various theories in the Egyptian press, and one of the first to appear in newspapers was that the Italian was gay. I often heard this explanation from Egyptian friends who wanted to apologize for the regime. Perhaps Regeni had gone to a pickup spot, they said, or maybe he had slept with a man who became enraged.

This theory didn't hold up for long. Regeni wasn't gay, and during his time in Egypt he had been in frequent contact with his girlfriend, who was in Ukraine. But it was telling that this was one of the first attempts to explain the death. It would have absolved the state, because people knew that such things happened to homosexuals. And it would have been partly Regeni's fault: any man who went to the Qasr al-Nil Bridge, or any other pickup spot, was taking a risk.

During this period, Manu began to suffer panic attacks. He told me that for a while he stopped reading about Regeni, because every time he did his heart beat as if it were out of control. But when an Italian journalist asked Manu to help with some research on Regeni's death, Manu agreed. He felt an obligation—he knew that what had happened to Regeni could also happen to him or many others. Throughout the project, he experienced moments of panic, but he finished the job. Afterward he decided not to accept any more risky assignments. His only goal now was to get out.

Not long before Regeni was murdered, he had attended a labor meeting and noticed somebody filming him in a suspicious manner. This disturbed him enough that he mentioned it to friends. When I read that detail, I remembered election night in Balyana, when the thuggish man insisted on taking a picture with me. Where had that photograph gone? How had it been interpreted? Most likely it disappeared into the chaos and the incompetence of the security state. After all, this was the same country where a police escort roared off at a hundred miles per hour, leaving a family with two five-year-olds to make their own way across the desert.

The police state could be brutal, or incompetent, or lazy, or even vaguely comic. But there wasn't a choice. You got whatever you happened to get, and Regeni, through no fault of his own, had met the worst possible end. As a registered foreign correspondent, I had more protections than a young graduate student would have, and there was no comparison with the threats experienced by average Egyptians. But even so, I felt a touch of Manu's panic. Leslie and I started updating each other frequently on our locations whenever we traveled for work. We had always planned to stay in Egypt for five or six years, and now we began to prepare for our own departure.

Over the course of the spring, I met with Raafat a few times to talk about his brother. The memory of the medical failure tortured him, as it did Leslie and me. For such a vibrant, intelligent person, the death seemed so senseless. Near the end of Rifaat's life, his brother had photographed the sore on his foot. In the picture, the foot is swollen to about twice its normal size, and the entire instep is missing. In its place—instead of that tender stretch of skin, where you might reach down and idly scratch—there is a hole the size of a golf ball. The hole is surrounded by dead tissue of black and brown and green.

I showed the photograph to a couple of doctors in the United States, in hopes of understanding what happened. They said that it could have been connected to the lymphoma that Rifaat had suffered a decade earlier. Even when a patient overcomes the cancer, his immune system may be permanently weakened. The doctors' best guess was that Rifaat had suffered an infection that spiraled out of control, culminating in fatal septic shock. But they couldn't say for sure, because they had never seen a sore that looked as bad as the one in the photograph.

One morning, I visited the apartment building that Raafat and Rifaat's father had constructed more than sixty years earlier, in the district of Shoubra. It was well built, with high ceilings and an open central stairway, but like our spiderweb building it was fading. More than half the units were leased out, but the income was negligible because of the rent-control laws that had been expanded under Nasser.

I met with Tariq and Wardiya, two of the siblings who still lived there. Wardiya had been the oldest of six, and the only girl. Over the years, I had met other members of the family, and Wardiya was the one who most resembled Rifaat. When I looked at her, I recognized the sharp eyes and the fine-boned face, although now it was strange to see these features surrounded by a conservative black *hijab*. She wore a long black dress. It was Ramadan, and the family was fasting; out of politeness, they offered me tea, which I declined for the same reason. That had been one of Rifaat's lessons—never eat or drink anything in front of somebody who is fasting, even if they insist.

Wardiya had been thirteen years older than Rifaat, and she had helped raise him. "But actually he was the one who taught me, who educated me," she said. Her formal schooling had ended at grade five, because her parents believed it was unnecessary to invest in a girl's education.

Wardiya and Tariq both said that as adults they had disagreed with many of Rifaat's ideas. "Some girls understood education in the wrong way," Tariq said. "We have our traditions. But some girls wanted to be like foreigners."

"I believe that things should be moderated," Wardiya said. "Not so open. Rifaat disagreed with this."

"He thought it was fine for women to go out, and to go abroad," Tariq said. "But we didn't."

"We didn't like his way," Wardiya said. "But he was better, actually. Recently we knew that everything he said was correct."

Rifaat had frequently advised her about raising her children. "He told me not to surround them so closely," Wardiya said. "Give them space to express their opinions. And don't beat them—he didn't like children to be beaten." Because of Rifaat's influence, she had sent her daughters to college, and now her son was a teacher of Arabic.

Wardiya was also a devotee of Umm Kulthum, although she hadn't been able to listen to the singer since Rifaat's death, because the sound of the great woman's voice made her too emotional. More than ever, she appreciated her brother's eccentricities—his refusal to eat meat, his refusal to go to mosque. His insistence that religion can be found in the way you treat people, rather than in the way you pray. "He had his own opinions, and I had my own opinions," she said. "His opinions were new and mine were old." Every now and then, after her brother's name was spoken, she mentioned God, and I murmured the response that Rifaat had taught me years earlier.

Allah yerhamoh, allah yerhamoh, allah yerhamoh.

CHAPTER 26

DURING OUR TIME IN THE SPIDERWEB BUILDING, I HAD LEARNED NOTHing more about its history. The landlady didn't know the significance of the web motif, and she said she had no record of the first owners. None of the other residents were old enough to remember when it was built. The upper stories had obviously been added onto an original structure, like the top layers of a wedding cake. In the 1980s and 1990s, Zamalek owners often did this as a way of generating income, because so many old apartments were under the rigid rent-control laws. Any new floors could be rented out at market rates.

In one story for the *New Yorker,* I described living in Cairo with my family, and I mentioned the spiderwebs, the balconies, and the ancient elevator. A reader sent a message:

> From your description of the building, it seems that it could be the one where I lived as a child until 1956. The address (at the time) is 2 Ahmed Hishmat Pasha. . . . The building used to belong to my grandparents. I could send you pictures of the building. I am very curious to know if it is the same building where I grew up.
>
> Thank you in advance,
>
> Dr. Albert Bivas
> Palo Alto, CA

I wrote back and told him the address was the same, and I attached some photographs. He responded with pictures of his own, in black and white. One image featured identical-twin toddler girls playing in front of a wrought-iron spiderweb. At the top of the photograph was a date: 1946.

The last time Manu and I had a drink together in Egypt was at the informal spot he called the Doormen's Bar. It was a pleasant evening, and we sat on the plastic lawn chairs in a narrow gap between two buildings. A black metal fire escape spiraled above us.

Manu was leaving in two days on a flight to Germany. A Berlin advocacy group that specialized in LGBT issues had invited him to participate in a roundtable discussion, and the embassy approved his visa. His recent pattern of overseas trips had convinced the Germans that he wasn't a risk to overstay. For the talk, he had researched the crackdown on Egyptian gay life that was currently happening under Sisi. "You can say three significant arrests per week," he said while we sat at the Doormen's Bar. "Often it's gay parties. Sometimes people are reported by their neighbors."

Recently he had had trouble with a resident of his building downtown. The neighbor was like so many others in Cairo: young, single, male, unemployed, undereducated, living with his parents. Manu often saw him drinking heavily in downtown bars. For a while, they were on friendly terms, and then somehow the young man figured out that Manu was gay.

The first thing he did was vandalize the bicycle that Manu locked near the building's entrance. He sliced up the seat and slit the tires with a knife. Then he bragged about the act to another neighbor, a high school student named Kareem who was friendly with Manu. The young man warned Kareem to stay away from the *khawwal*.

Manu never said a word to the young man; the last thing he wanted at such a time was a fight. He left the bike with its flat tires in the entrance.

Next, the young man began to talk about the police. "Don't go to this *khawwal*'s apartment," he said one day to Kareem. "The police are going to come soon. The guys in that apartment bring in women, and alcohol, and men, and they're going to get arrested."

At the Doormen's Bar, Manu had a shopping bag with a sweater that he was giving to Kareem as a going-away gift. They planned to meet in the neighborhood away from the building. "I don't see him there anymore," Manu said. "I told him not to stop by the apartment. I don't want the hassle."

Manu's roommate had planned a get-together in the apartment before his departure, but I persuaded him not to do it there. The risk seemed too high; after all his preparations, a single phone call could undo everything. So Manu and his friends met in a restaurant instead. It seemed awful that this was on his mind during his final days in Egypt—worrying about some adult male who was behaving like a middle school bully.

Manu's mood had seemed erratic lately. A few days earlier, we had been in another part of Cairo, and we had taken a cab together to Zamalek. On the way, we passed through an *ashwa'iyat,* and Manu suddenly became agitated. "It's so miserable," he said. "Even the things sold in the shop are miserable. Miserable cups, miserable food, miserable people doing miserable things. Look at the buildings—look how bad they are." For a moment, he reminded me of Rifaat ranting about the city's decline. But then Manu's tone changed abruptly and he talked about how much he would miss downtown Cairo. Despite the problems with the neighbor, the apartment had been home longer than any other place in Manu's adult life.

He had only a few friends in Germany, and he had never studied the language. There was no guarantee that he would receive asylum. Even if he applied successfully, conditions were likely to be difficult, because the country was currently flooded with refugees from the wars in Syria and Iraq. He said he was nervous about the initial days in Germany, and I tried to put him at ease. I said he was doing the right thing, because at least in Germany he'd be able to have a normal life, without worrying about the police or the neighbors.

"That's what depresses me," he said. "Why can't I live like that here?"

At the Cairo Airport passport control, the officer took Manu's document. He looked at the German visa. "Hey, Mohamed," he said. "Why are you going to Germany?"

Manu said he was giving a talk, and he handed over the NGO's invitation letter. In German, the letter explained that Manu would "give a lecture about LGBT people since the Egyptian revolution." The officer looked at the letter. Manu was certain that he wouldn't understand it.

"What are you talking about in Germany?" the officer finally asked.

"Human rights," Manu said.

The officer handed back the letter and waved him through.

In Berlin, Manu went to the roundtable discussion, and then he prepared materials for his declaration for asylum. He visited a lawyer who specialized in gay asylum seekers, and he went to Schwulenberatung, an organization that provides a range of services for the LGBT community. Since the start of the Arab Spring, Schwulenberatung had founded new programs for the refugees who were coming to Germany. A caseworker interviewed Manu and gave him a letter that identified him as a member of a vulnerable subgroup of the refugee population.

He didn't go to the Berlin Tegel Airport for his return flight to Cairo. Instead, he went to Tempelhof, the old airport that had been decommissioned in 2008. More than half a century earlier, Tempelhof had been the site of the Berlin airlift; now part of the complex had been converted into a camp and processing center for refugees. In 2016, the year that Manu arrived, more than 1.5 million foreigners were applying for protection status in Germany. More than half a million arrived that year.

Manu happened to show up at Tempelhof on a relatively slow day. There were only about forty others being processed at the same time as him. An official asked him why he was there. The Berlin lawyer had told Manu that he needed to declare two things.

"I'm applying for asylum," Manu said. "And I'm gay." It was the first time in his life that he had ever described himself in such a way to a government official.

The German government was trying to distribute newcomers as quickly as possible to camps around the country. After Manu was registered in the system, he was told to report immediately to a camp in Münster. An official gave him a train ticket for the five-hour journey.

The Münster camp was situated in an old air force base that had been constructed during the Hitler years. At the entrance, Manu was given a yellow wristband with an ID number, and his bag was searched by an immigrant from Morocco who worked in the camp. Manu had arrived from Cairo with only two pieces of luggage—the sum of his worldly possessions. He had left one bag with a friend in Berlin, and now the Moroccan searched the other one. He was furious to discover a wine opener.

"This is a sharp tool!" he shouted. "It's like a knife! Why are you bringing this thing?"

"It's just to open wine," Manu said.

"You can't have this here!"

The wine opener was confiscated. Manu was too stressed to think about the absurdity of this scene: a Moroccan, representing the German state, shouting at an Egyptian named Mohamed because he was in possession of a wine opener. But Manu had the presence of mind to show the letter that identified him as a member of a vulnerable population. Because of that, he was assigned a private room. That night he sent me a photograph of his arm:

> They put a yellow bracelet around my hand with my number on, looks like hitler left some of his legacy around. It's not a gay camp but they put me in a room alone, there are 600 other refugees in the camp but I haven't met any because I came late. Now I'm officially a refugee and it's not good.

The oldest photograph that Dr. Albert Bivas sent was dated June 11, 1933, when his grandparents held a ground-breaking ceremony for the spiderweb building. In the picture, Betty Bassan and Léon Bassan stand next to a foundation stone. Léon wears a double-breasted suit, and Betty wears a dark dress with a white collar. She is applying cement to the stone with a trowel. The couple is surrounded by a crowd of people in European-style clothes, and an Egyptian man in a white galabiya is helping with the cement.

The next photograph was from the inauguration of the finished building. A small group of men stand in front of the ground-floor balcony that, eight decades later, would lead to my office. There are signs for the various companies that contributed to the construction: the contracting firm, whose name is Italian, and the German agency that installed the elevator. The building itself is a magnificent example of late French Art Deco design. The facade is decorated with elegant vertical lines, and a ziggurat-shaped design has been incorporated into the balconies. These features are mixed with other styles: Greek-influenced columns, and stepped window frames with filigreed squares that are typical of Islamic architecture.

Albert and his family had resided in the same sprawling ground-floor apartment that we occupied. His maternal grandparents had lived directly upstairs. Albert was born in Cairo, in 1941, and then the family had four girls. The identical twins, Betty and Danièle, were born in September 1944, the year of the D-day invasion. In photographs, the baby twins are beautiful, with curly hair and enormous eyes, and they play on the balcony. The details of the scene—the metal spiderwebs, the intricate floor tiling—are exactly the same as they are in photographs of my own twins playing on the balcony.

Other features of the building, like the fire escape where Sayyid collected garbage, once had different uses:

> I suppose you also had a kitchen backdoor that took you to the service iron staircase. The people who used it (when we were not playing there) were the servants (one per pair of children, when we were small), the cook who helped my mother, the main servant who cleaned the apartment and directed the others, the people delivering milk or olive oil, etc.

Albert and I exchanged emails and photographs, and sometimes we talked on the telephone. We described the apartment's layout, comparing how each of our families had used the various rooms, and we discussed our different paths to Cairo. Albert's ancestors had drifted to Egypt, over the course of centuries, from the far side of the Mediterranean. They were Sephardic Jews who originally came from Spain or Portugal, having fled the Inquisition at the end of the fifteenth century. Eventually they settled in Constantinople, which was welcoming to Jews at that time.

In the late nineteenth century, a number of these Jewish families began relocating to Egypt. The Suez Canal had recently opened, creating new business opportunities in the country. Egypt was still part of the Ottoman Empire, so it was relatively easy to move there from Constantinople. And there was already a vibrant Jewish community in Cairo—some of these families had been there for centuries. They considered themselves Egyptians; a number of

Jewish activists had been prominent in the Egyptian nationalist movement of the early twentieth century. With all the newcomers, Egypt's Jewish population grew to around eighty thousand by the end of the 1940s.

For a child like Albert, identity was many-sided. Jews in the Middle East typically spoke multiple languages, and his maternal grandfather on the second floor loved to write poems in French, a language that he had taught in Egyptian schools. He and his wife also spoke Ladino, or Judeo-Spanish, a form of Old Spanish that incorporated words from Hebrew, Turkish, Arabic, and other languages. Albert's other grandfather lived in a different part of Cairo, and he spoke Arabic, Hebrew, Turkish, and Ladino. The regular newspaper that he read was printed in Aljamiado—it used the Arabic script to transcribe Ladino. On the ground floor of the spiderweb building, Albert's parents were also fluent in Ladino, but French was their everyday language. The father, a stockbroker and a factory owner, had been born in Egypt, and he spoke Arabic like a native.

Albert's legal name was Ibrahim, because at the time of his birth the Egyptian government required that even Jews be given Arabic names—a small indication of things to come. But the Cairo of his early childhood was mostly welcoming. The first time that Albert attended a Christmas party, it was hosted by a Muslim family that had prepared a beautifully decorated tree and invited friends who were Jewish, Christian, and Muslim. The Bivas family belonged to a private club on Zamalek, where Albert learned to swim and the twins took classes in acrobatic roller-skating. Across the street from the spiderweb building, Albert attended the Lycée Français, a private nonreligious school. In addition to French, students took English and *fusha,* although nobody learned much classical Arabic. Albert's strongest memory from *fusha* class was of the teacher yelling at kids to be quiet so that he could sleep at his desk.

The children picked up Egyptian Arabic on the street. Albert spoke it to shopkeepers, servants, and Mohammed, the building's doorman—"our guardian angel." In photographs, Mohammed has the dark skin of an Upper Egyptian, and he wears a white galabiya and turban. He stands proudly with the children, holding their hands.

"In school we took one class about the history of France, and another class about the history of Egypt," Albert remembered. "There were contradictions between these classes—sometimes we joked that we didn't know if our ancestors were the Gauls or the pharaohs!" He continued, "The same as when we were doing Passover in Cairo, and we would read the story about how we were slaves in Egypt. And now we were here! But how can we have servants here, if we were slaves? As children we were very amused by this."

This strange little world—the island in the Nile, the mixed languages, the building with its combination of Art Deco, classical, and Islamic architecture—began to seem increasingly fragile in the late 1940s. Even to a child it was clear that something was changing. Once, Albert went to the cinema with his father to see a French movie, and when a Jewish character appeared on-screen, people in the audience shouted, "Kill the Jew! Kill the Jew!" On November 29, 1947, after the United Nations passed a resolution calling for Palestine to be partitioned between Arabs and Jews, angry mobs gathered in downtown Cairo. Albert's family was out in its Citroën sedan, and the father yelled at the children to duck in their seats, in case people caught a glimpse of them in European dress. One year, on the first day of Egyptian history class, Albert's teacher instructed the students to open their brand-new books and tear out a certain number of pages, because he didn't want them to see anything negative about their country.

Albert's father ran a successful textile factory in the district of Shoubra. He had named it Albitex, after Albert, and his dream was that someday his only son would take over the business. Albert's father had studied law in Cairo, and he understood politics; in 1952, as protests against the monarchy intensified, he sensed that something was about to happen. He brought his wife and children to France that summer. In July, when the Free Officers carried out their revolution, the Bivas family was living in Paris.

Albert's mother was pregnant with their last child, and she wanted to return in order to give birth in the country that she considered her homeland. By December, Albert's father felt that things had stabilized, because the new president, Mohammed Naguib, was known to be friendly to Jews. So the family returned to the spiderweb building. But post-revolution presidencies have a way of ending abruptly, and Naguib was removed from office after a little more than a year. Albert's father knew that Nasser was different—his pan-Arab ideas had been hardened by the experience of the Arab-Israeli War. In 1956, Albert's father escorted the family to France again. This time they packed as much as they could in their luggage.

The father returned to Cairo to deal with his factory. That year, Nasser seized the Suez Canal, and the resulting war, in which Israel fought alongside the British and the French, represented the end for Egyptian Jews. Nasser's government arrested hundreds, and others began to panic; in the span of three months, at least ten thousand Jews fled the country. Nasser's government was advised by a number of former Nazi officials who had sought refuge after World War II, and they helped Egypt design anti-Semitic laws. It became possible to revoke Egyptian nationality from anybody who was declared to be a "Zionist," a term that was never defined. Soon, Jewish Egyptians were limited to a single piece of luggage on departure. Anybody caught carrying significant funds out of the country could be arrested.

Albert's elderly grandparents were allowed to leave on one-way passports, but they hadn't sold the spiderweb building. In France, the Egyptian passports of Albert, his mother, and his four siblings expired after six months, but the Egyptian embassy rejected their renewal. France classified them as officially stateless. In less than a year, they had gone from prosperous residents of a family-owned building to refugees.

In Cairo, Albert's father was trapped. The government refused to grant him the necessary documents to travel, and he was placed under house arrest. A guard was stationed outside the spiderweb building, and every morning he escorted Albert's father to the textile factory. For more than a year, the father ran the factory as a virtual prisoner, and he communicated with his family by letters. It was all but impossible for an Egyptian Jew to sell a significant asset, because buyers knew they could just wait for things to get even worse. Finally, the Egyptian foreman at the plant bought it at a steep discount, which presented Albert's father with a new problem. He couldn't carry cash out of Egypt, or convert it, or transfer it. But he had another idea. He bought two pairs of roller skates and mailed them to the twins.

Upon arrival in Berlin, Manu had felt an immediate euphoria—a new freedom, a new life. He loved the way the city looked, and he loved the clouded sky, which was so different from the Egyptian dome of blue. He wrote in an email:

> I like that grey light so much, makes things clearer and colours stronger to my eyes. It's relaxing if I compare it with the shiny Cairo.

But once the winter settled in, he often suffered from depression. He had never lived anywhere with such short, dark days. Sometimes the gloom reflected on the expressions of Germans. "When you look at the faces on the metro, on a working day, it's very sad," Manu told me once. "It's depressing. 'Why are you so sad? You're living in one of the best countries in the world!' It doesn't make any sense. Egyptians, they have all the disasters in the world, but they always make fun of the disasters. If something horrible happens, then one hour after they start making fun of it."

In Egypt, he had been exhausted by the unpredictability of so many people—the police, the neighbors, even lovers. But now German life was unpredictable in a different way. He didn't speak the language; he didn't know the system. The bureaucracy seemed capricious: as a refugee, he could be sent almost anywhere. While he was in the camp in Münster, he was interviewed by a government official, as part of his application for asylum. The official was accompanied by a Tunisian man who would serve as an Arabic translator.

But Manu refused to tell his story in Arabic, and he refused to tell it through a man. In Berlin, one of the people who worked at an NGO had told Manu that he had the right to choose the language and even the gender of the translator. Now at the interview Manu dismissed the Tunisian, and he insisted on having a woman who could translate from English to German. He believed that homophobic attitudes were too deeply ingrained in most Arab cultures, and even in the language itself. And he had always found it easier to talk about issues of sexuality with women.

He felt fortunate that the official representing the German government was also female. After the interview, Manu wrote me:

> It took around three and a half hours, but I was surprised she didn't ask me so many questions. At one occasion she told me in English, "I believe you!"

> I wanted to talk more about recent stuff because all that time I was just talking about old incidents but she said there is no need for this because she already made her decision.

She didn't say what this decision was. I told Manu that it must be positive or she wouldn't have spoken in such terms, but he was nervous. I had written a detailed letter in support of his application, testifying to what I knew about his life in Cairo, but now he returned to the Münster camp and stayed up late, describing experiences that hadn't been covered in the interview. He submitted this supplementary material the following morning. It was unclear when the decision would be announced, because the bureaucracy was struggling to process the flood of refugee and asylum applications.

After ten days in Münster, Manu was reassigned to another camp in a small city called Leverkusen, not far from Cologne. The Leverkusen camp consisted of a large main room that housed dozens of men. An official showed Manu his bed, but soon an argument broke out. The bed had formerly belonged to a Moroccan refugee who had disappeared from the camp three weeks earlier. Before leaving, he had asked a Moroccan friend to make sure that nobody took his spot.

Now this friend started arguing with the camp official, and it turned into a shouting match. Others in the room joined in. Finally Manu pulled the official aside.

"I can't stay here," he said. "It's against the law." He produced the letter that certified him as a member of a vulnerable group. The official agreed to let Manu stay outside the camp, and he found a temporary place in Cologne, sleeping in the apartment of a friend of a friend.

Because of the letter, Manu was able to initiate a transfer to another camp that supposedly included gay-friendly facilities. The camp was on the outskirts of Cologne, and it had recently been built in response to the refugee crisis. It consisted of ninety-six shipping containers that had been converted into a large dormitory for men. Of the ninety-six containers, three had been attached into a single block that was dedicated to gay refugees.

The gay shipping container, as Manu sometimes called it, was twenty feet long. There was a kitchen and two bedrooms. Manu shared this space with five Iraqis who had fled the war, and all but one of them came from rural areas. They were almost impossible to live with. They never cleaned the kitchen, and they stole Manu's food from the refrigerator. They talked constantly. Every weekend they invited over friends from other refugee camps in Germany; often there were seven or eight Iraqis staying in the shipping container. Once, when I telephoned Manu, he described what it was like.

"Remember when we were in Balyana?" he said. "And we would go into a *dawar,* and it was all men, and they're all talking about nothing? That's what it's like here, except it's gay. It's like a gay Balyana."

He spent a lot of time using the Wi-Fi at a nearby McDonald's. He never cooked; the Iraqis regularly trashed the kitchen, and in any case it was hard to figure out local supermarkets. Manu shopped with Google Translate, laboriously looking up words on packaged foods. That winter he ate sandwiches three times a day.

The only food that he could safely put in the communal refrigerator was pork. The Iraqis refused to touch it—*haraam,* they said. They didn't go to mosque, and they drank alcohol, but they did so with a great deal of guilt. All of them were applying for asylum as homosexuals, but they still believed that being gay was *haraam*. Once, while Manu was trying to sleep, he overheard a conversation.

"We have to stop this someday," one of the Iraqis said. "We can enjoy it now, but someday we have to stop."

Somebody else agreed—being attracted to men was a preventable condition. They talked about marriage, and how someday, after they had received asylum as homosexuals, they would hopefully find brides.

"At least we are Muslims, *al-hamdulillah,*" one said. "We know right from wrong. We can fix ourselves. But Germans live their lives without knowing right from wrong."

Manu lay silently in his bunk, and he never acknowledged hearing the discussion. "What can I say?" he remembered later. "It's not smart to get in this kind of conversation."

He thought about finding his own apartment in Cologne, but cheap housing was in short supply. He had some money from selling the apartment that he had inherited in Port Said, but the weakness of the Egyptian currency meant that it wasn't worth much.

One day at the entrance to the shipping-container camp, a Lebanese refugee threatened Manu. Manu and his roommates had never interacted much with others in the camp, because they feared what might happen if people found out they were gay. Their block of containers wasn't labeled in any way, but the other residents must have figured out why the six men kept to themselves.

"You *khawwal*!" the Lebanese said to Manu. "Don't look at me again! I've seen you looking at me. If you do it again, I'll kill you." He kept shouting: "Fuck your flag! Fuck you Egyptians!" This seemed bizarre to Manu: Was he supposed to be hurt by an insult to the flag of the country he had fled? At last, a guard persuaded the Lebanese to leave Manu alone. But he glared at Manu whenever he saw him around the camp.

Manu realized it was time to get out. And now he understood enough about the German bureaucracy to make it work for him. With the help of an NGO, he filed a report with the police, testifying to the homophobic attack in the camp. Then he traveled around Cologne, looking at apartments. He had been enrolled in a government-funded German course for a couple of months, and his command of language was already functional. He found a studio apartment and negotiated a monthly rent of less than seven hundred euros. He applied for rent assistance from the government, and the application included the documentation of the attack in the camp—it described his transfer as an emergency situation. Almost immediately, the paperwork was approved, and the government agreed to subsidize the apartment until Manu was able to find a job.

The building was located in a suburb of Cologne that was surrounded by forests and parks. The studio apartment was on the sixteenth floor, and it was small, but it had a large balcony. From the balcony Manu could see the spires of the famous Cologne Cathedral, the clustered buildings of downtown, and the long line of the Rhine River. The day he moved in was the happiest of that long winter.

At the end of the 1940s, Egypt was still home to around eighty thousand Jews, many of them prosperous and educated. Generally, they had to abandon much of their wealth, if not all of it. Albert Bivas's various Egyptian relatives scattered around the world, although most of them went to Israel or France. Albert lived with his mother and four sisters in a hotel near Paris.

It was there that they received the package with the roller skates, along with a letter. Albert's parents had arranged a code before they were separated, because they knew that outgoing mail would be searched in Cairo. His mother understood the message that was hidden in the words of the letter: Don't touch the skates.

Albert's father was separated from his family for fifteen months, and then he finally figured out a way to arrange an exit visa in secret. A friend brought him a plane ticket, and he exited the spiderweb building without alerting the guard. He carried nothing but a briefcase. In France, after the joyful reunion with his family, one of the first things he did was disassemble the wheels of a skate. There, in place of a ball bearing, was a diamond.

He had purchased the diamond in Cairo, with the money he made from the factory sale. Everything had required steep fees, and the diamond wasn't worth nearly the value of his business, but it was better than nothing. Albert's father sold the diamond and gave most of the proceeds to his brother, who had been an investor in the textile company. In France, it took Albert's father a long time to find work, and for years the family lived in near poverty. He eventually found a decent banking job in Strasbourg, where he was able to build a new career by working hard.

The family often talked about their old life in Cairo, but only in terms of reminiscence. There was no sense they might return. Albert's parents never regained the prosperity they had enjoyed in Egypt, but they didn't seem bitter. "I guess my parents drew a line," Albert said. "And we never crossed that line to think about what might have been." Undoubtedly, this perspective was shaped by recent history. Betty Kane, one of the twins, wrote in an email, "But we are still better off than the millions of Jews (including family members) living in Europe who were murdered in that era."

And while they couldn't take their wealth out of Cairo, the family's tradition of education proved more portable. All five children excelled at school and attended French universities. Both twins studied law, another sister studied political science and journalism, and the fourth became a doctor. Albert received a Ph.D. in physics, and he enjoyed a long career as a research physicist.

By the time I knew him, he was retired and working part-time as a high school tutor of French and physics, because he enjoyed the subjects. He had never gone back to Egypt.

The textile factory still exists, although now it's located in Sadat City. The company name was changed from Albitex. The former foreman who bought the factory later left it to his son, exactly as Albert's father had intended to do.

In 2016, the spiritual leader of the Egyptian Jewish community announced that there were six Jews left in the country. All were women older than sixty-five.

Manu was granted asylum at the beginning of the spring of 2017. Later, when I talked to some of the Germans who had consulted with him, they told me that his case had been unusually strong. Dirk Siegfried, a lawyer in Berlin, had worked with gay refugees since 1988, when Germany first began to accept homosexuality as a legitimate reason for asylum. Siegfried had received a grant to help Manu with his application and accompany him to his interview. But after Siegfried met with Manu and heard him talk, he advised Manu to handle the application on his own. They could save the grant money for another gay refugee who needed help.

"I seldom recommend that anyone start without a lawyer," Siegfried told me. But in certain cases, when a person is capable, he believed it's more empowering for him or her to stand alone. "You are kind of helpless in being an asylum seeker, but there are a lot of things you can decide," he said. And the narrative mattered—this was part of what distinguished Manu. "He was able to tell his story," Siegfried said. "He was self-aware."

Felix Coeln, a resident of Cologne who worked with a support group called the Rainbow Refugees, said that his clients from the Middle East had often been severely traumatized, both by war and by extreme prejudice against gays. "Manu also suffered trauma," he said. "But he managed to get things done." Coeln said that actually Manu had figured out the solutions to some problems, like getting transferred out of the Leverkusen camp, before Coeln had known what to do. "He always had a goal," he said. "Those refugees who succeed in settling themselves, in handling their own affairs, they tend to be the ones who have fewer problems." But Coeln said this was rare. He mentioned an Iraqi client who had twice suffered homophobic attacks in camps, by other Arabs. He had tried to move out on his own three times, but each time he had returned to the camps, because he was helpless on the outside. "He's like a fire without flames," Coeln said. "There's no life anymore. He's been here three years, and he hardly speaks any words in German."

After Manu settled into his new apartment, he avoided socializing with other Arabs. There was a Cologne group of gay Arabs that met regularly, but Manu went once and never returned. Sometimes he joked that he was going to join the Alternative für Deutschland, the far-right German group that was virulently anti-immigrant. "When an Arab is around, I don't feel free," Manu said. "It's a kind of trauma." He felt that he needed a period of separation, and he hoped that over time his feelings would stabilize.

But he worried about what would happen with all the newcomers. He remembered that evening in the shipping container, when he overheard the Iraqis talking about how someday they would stop being gay. "It was a horrible conversation," he said. "All I can hope is that years in Germany can change this behavior."

He wondered frankly why the country had opened itself to so many who were so different, himself included. Germans who worked with refugees often spoke of it as a national responsibility—sometimes, it almost seemed a form of penance. They certainly hadn't started the war that drove refugees out of Iraq, and they bore no special blame for the mess of the Arab Spring. But Germany had been guilty of other wars and other crimes, and perhaps people's memories were longer than those of the Americans. This was true of even the young. Marlen Vahle was a recent college graduate who worked with an NGO called Kölner Flüchtlingsrat, where she served refugees. She had assisted Manu with some of his applications. Once, I asked Vahle why she thought Germany was undertaking this endeavor.

"Because of history," she said. At various times in the past, she explained, terrible events had driven people from their homes, and sometimes nobody helped. "We had Hitler and the persecution of Jewish people," she said. "You can always make the comparison and say at that time it was the Jewish people and now it's the Islamic people."

There was one question about the building that Albert Bivas couldn't answer. When I asked about the spiderwebs, he contacted his sisters and other relatives, but nobody knew the significance of the motif. Art historians told me that the angular form of the webs was classic Art Deco style, but it wasn't some standardized symbol. The exact meaning of this particular web was lost with the generation that constructed the building.

Léon Bassan, Albert's grandfather, had been able to return to Cairo briefly, in 1959. He was allowed to sell the spiderweb building, and that May, as he prepared to leave Egypt for the last time, he wrote a farewell poem in French about the place he had built:

Adieu my old home, dear nest of my children.
Seeing their cradle, my poor heart is breaking.
I tremble as I carry away their childhood pictures,
My mind persists in remembering their games
Adieu the beautiful portico that decorated my living room
Adieu my golden dreams.

More than half a century later, Albert didn't know whom the building had been sold to, or what the price had been. But on other points his memory was still as clear as a child's. He remembered the *mekwegi,* the neighborhood ironing man, and how he kept some water in his mouth and sprayed it onto clothes while working his hot irons. He remembered going to outdoor movies in Zamalek, and how the children shrieked with joy whenever a lizard crawled across the face of a starlet in close-up. He remembered that the family Citroën had eleven horsepower, and he remembered riding in it to the pyramids. He remembered that a local child would ask tourists for a coin, and then he would climb the Great Pyramid, barefoot, hopping from stone to stone, following some secret route up the crumbling structure, until at last he waved triumphantly from the top.

Sometimes Albert still dreamed of the Egyptian Museum. "I was in love with it," he said. "I had books about it that I got later, after we left. I was disappointed when I went to the Louvre. I went to the British Museum in London, and I expected to see the same things. But to see the real thing in the right place—it was special. It left a very important mark in my memory."

His twin sisters lived in different cities on the American East Coast, and in photographs the women were still hard to tell apart. We marveled at the coincidences—the way the old black-and-white pictures of those baby girls lined up with images of Ariel and Natasha. In the dining room of that sprawling apartment, Albert's parents used to speak Ladino when they didn't want their children to understand, the same way Leslie and I used Chinese for private conversations. Albert's wife was named Natalie, but she went by Natasha; their only daughter was Arielle. What were the odds? But maybe that was the meaning of the spiderwebs. They connected it all: the revolutions and the refugees, the untimely events and the unlikely languages. There were webs around the building, and webs around the island; they continued the length of the great river and beyond. The webs ran everywhere from this place they called *um al-duniya,* the mother of the world.

CHAPTER 27

WHEN I TOLD SAYYID THAT WE WERE MOVING BACK TO THE UNITED States, he became very quiet. Then he said, softly, "I'm *z'alen.*" The word usually translates as "angry," but its meaning ranges to "upset." He asked why we had to leave, and I said my job was finished. But this wasn't accurate. Nobody had asked us to go to Egypt, and nobody was asking us to leave. The *New Yorker* wouldn't send anybody to replace me after I was gone.

It was impossible to tell Sayyid the truth: that I was leaving his country because there were limits to how long I could stay in a place where life was so difficult. I was concerned about the risks of my work, and for years I had had a nagging fear of what might happen if somebody—my wife, my children—needed urgent medical care. If I had answered him honestly, the simplest response would have been to say I was *t'aben.* It means "tired," but also "sick"; the word covers anything from a diagnosed illness to a general state of exhaustion. Some Arabic terms for feelings seem less specific than what a person would say in English. And perhaps this vagueness makes the words more useful—blurred meanings for blurred emotions. It's never easy to leave a place after five years, and those five years in Egypt had been unusually long.

We finally had some visitors during the last six months. That was part of the loneliness of living through a revolution—friends and family tended to stay away. It wasn't until the end that a string of guests came to Cairo, and Leslie and I escorted everybody to the Egyptian Museum and the pyramids.

Longtime foreign residents sometimes complained about how sick they were of taking people to the pyramids. *T'aben:* the hectic drive along the Ring Road, the heat and dust of the Giza Plateau, the hordes of souvenir vendors. But we had had so few visitors that it was still a thrill to show off these places. I took guests to the pyramids and the museum half a dozen times, and I traveled to Luxor. I drove two visiting friends to Amarna, where we spent a day visiting the ruined city and the abandoned tombs. And now I realized how much the ancient sites had helped me maintain some equilibrium during the revolution. They gave me a different perspective on the past and the present, and on the movement of time: the cycles of *neheh,* the permanence of *djet.* My years in Egypt were long, but they were also impossibly short; time could have both qualities at once. All the intensity of this period, from the Tahrir movement to its aftermath, was already starting to fade. Someday it would feel as distant as the cities and tombs beneath the sand.

In March 2016, my parents came to Egypt for the first time. We visited Luxor and Cairo, the pyramids and the museum, and one evening we had dinner at Sayyid and Wahiba's home. Before the meal, Sayyid and the boys took us on a walk through the *ashwa'iyat,* past the various recycling operations. Wahiba and her mother prepared a massive spread of roast chicken, beef, potatoes, and rice wrapped in vine leaves. It was the highlight of my parents' trip; they were amazed that they could enter this sprawling neighborhood and find themselves in a neat home with such well-behaved children. Zizou and Yusuf showed us their schoolbooks, and they asked curious questions about the places we had been. Nobody in Sayyid's family had ever gone to the pyramids or to the museum, although they lived less than five miles from each site.

After my parents visited, I told Sayyid that I wanted to take his family to the Egyptian Museum. Initially, he declined. "I don't think we're allowed to go there," he said.

I said they certainly were, like any other Egyptian or foreigner, and I offered to pick them up in the Honda. A couple of days later, he told me that he and the children could go, but not Wahiba. "She says a woman in a *niqab* isn't allowed in the museum," he said. "And she's afraid that if people see somebody in a *niqab* with an American, they'll think she's from the Muslim Brotherhood."

It was pointless to push against this conspiracy theory; virtually all Egyptians now believed that the Americans had spawned and supported the Brotherhood. But I assured Sayyid that a woman in a *niqab* could go to the museum, and I explained that I would bring my Egyptian press card, as a way of showing that the government approved of my presence in the country. This seemed to put him at ease, and early one Friday morning I drove out to Ard al-Liwa to pick them up.

The neighborhood had continued to change rapidly throughout the post-Tahrir years. After the first illegal entrance ramp was built, others followed suit, and now I counted eight different access points along a five-mile stretch of the Ring Road. A couple of the entrances were makeshift ramps of packed dirt, but the rest were well built out of concrete. And house construction was still booming in Ard al-Liwa. Like many of their neighbors, Sayyid and Wahiba were adding another story onto their house. Someday it would be an apartment for Zizou, after he married, and then they would build another floor for Yusuf. They were doing it slowly, as money came in, and in the meantime they raised chickens on the half-built rooftop.

Everybody in the family had dressed up for the trip to the museum. Zizou and Yusuf had new scarves that matched their shirts, and Wahiba wore a heavy, long dress embroidered with a bright pattern of beads. I drove the Honda across the 6th October Bridge to the entrance of the new public parking garage beneath Tahrir Square. The garage was mostly empty, and I parked near an attendant who was wearing a blue jumpsuit. Wahiba called out to him from the car: "Is it okay to be here in a *niqab*?"

The attendant seemed surprised by the question, but he said there was no problem. We took an elevator up to the square. As we approached the museum's front gate, where police and tour buses had congregated, Wahiba and Sayyid became tentative and slow moving. They stood back at the gate's metal detector, confused by this contraption. I helped Sayyid walk through, and Zizou showed his mother how to put her purse onto the conveyor belt. I directed them to wait inside the museum's yard while I purchased tickets. They glanced around nervously.

"Don't go anywhere," I said. "And if anybody asks to be your guide, tell them you already have one. I'll be back in five minutes."

The line for tickets wasn't long. But before I even made it to the window, I looked back and saw Sayyid being escorted away by some larger man. Wahiba and the children trailed behind. I ran after them and tapped the man on the shoulder.

"Thank you, but they're with me," I said. "They don't need a guide today."

"I'm not a guide," the man said. He shifted his jacket slightly to reveal something at his hip: a sidearm. My heart dropped. "Police," he said. He held Sayyid firmly by the arm. "I have to ask him some questions."

As part of my preparations for leaving, I had made a final trip to Abydos. Josef Wegner and his team were still working in the tomb of Senwosret III, which they had cleared to the point where I had crawled almost three years earlier. The line of electric lights and fans had been extended, and now we could walk upright through the long, curving tunnel. Wegner pointed out some places on the wall where a red hieroglyph had been painted: *nefr.*

"It means 'good,'" he said. He explained that supervisors in ancient times used to check the construction quality and leave the hieroglyph. Partway down the tunnel, other words had been written in candle soot on the ceiling. They had been inscribed by Charles Currelly, the Canadian excavator who had been sent here by the London-based Egypt Exploration Fund. After more than a century the soot was still clear:

C. T. CURRELLY

1902

E.E.F.

During my first visit, Wegner had thought that the place where I crawled to was probably the burial chamber. Now, after all the debris had been removed, it seemed that the passage continued even farther into the bedrock. But it was hard to say for certain, because Roman-era looters had dug so many side tunnels and test holes. "It would have taken years and years," Wegner said of the looting. "I would have loved to have seen what kind of scene this was. It must have been dozens and dozens of workers. They had oil lamps and no ventilation. I can't imagine what it was like—it's bad enough today with electric lights and fans."

The temperature was hot; both of us were sweating. Deep beneath the mountain, the scene looked slightly crazed. In some places, looters had burrowed ten or twenty feet into the bedrock, leaving behind piles of dirt and huge broken stones. What exactly had they been searching for? And how had that ancient investigation ended? "I think they were drowning in debris," Wegner said.

His team had found a broken stone sarcophagus halfway into the tunnel. It seemed that looters dragged it partway out and then gave up. Wegner thought it was unlikely that any human remains were still in the tomb. They were now six hundred feet into the mountain, and he wasn't sure how much farther he wanted to chase the looters. "I think another year or two," he said. But he had said the same thing a couple years earlier.

Out in the Buried, Ahmed still managed the dig house. He had recently opened a side business, a furniture store on the road to Balyana. That was the outcome of his carpentry hobby: he had gone from building the fake APC to making furniture to sourcing it from wholesalers. He said that business was good, because many locals had built illegally during the unregulated years of the Arab Spring, and now they needed to furnish these new homes.

One evening, I drove down the road to say good-bye to Yusuf, the parliamentary candidate who had lost the previous year's election. He greeted me in front of his building in downtown Balyana, wearing his trademark white galabiya. We had dinner in his home, and Yusuf was still adamant that he would never again run for office. He had instructed his nine children to do the same.

"I told them it's *mamnouh*," he said. "Banned. They can be doctors or lawyers or pharmacists, but nothing in politics. It's no good here. The way that people judge each other by tribes—this isn't real politics. It should be based on the individual."

He had enrolled in a law course at Cairo University. As a young man, he hadn't been able to attend college, but now he wanted to improve his education. He showed me a stack of textbooks in his office; the next month he would drive to Cairo for exams. He wasn't sure how he would use his law degree, but he hoped to apply it to some kind of public service.

I asked about the two Abu'l Khair cousins who had been elected as local representatives, and Yusuf laughed and shook his head. Mahmoud, the bearded Islamist who once joined the Salafis' party, now hosted rallies in support of Sisi. The new parliament was even more toothless than the assemblies of the Mubarak years.

Rifaat Mohammed Ahmed, the old shoe-shine man who had worked in the parliament building since the days of Nasser, was still there. Four years ago, I had listened to him criticize the previous legislature while preparing to shine the shoes of Sobhi Saleh, one of the Brotherhood leaders. Nowadays, Saleh was in prison, and Rifaat, like a kind of polishing historian, was remembering yet another ousted parliament. "The Brotherhood experience was a very hard and bitter one," he told *Al-Masry al-Youm*, when the newspaper asked him for his insights. "They were doubting everyone around them because they had just come out of prison." Nevertheless, he had kind words for the man whose shoes he once shined. "Saad el-Katatni and Sobhi Saleh were respectful," said Rifaat. "But I see that they have suffered because of the faults of others."

At the Egyptian Museum, the plainclothes cop interrogated Sayyid near the entrance. I waited nearby with Wahiba and the children. I felt terrible, although neither Wahiba nor Sayyid seemed surprised. After all, any Egyptian could tell that they came from a social class that rarely visited the museum.

Finally, the cop motioned to me. I held up my passport and Egyptian press card. "They're friends of mine, and they're just going to the museum, like anybody else," I said. "I'm going to buy their tickets now. There's nothing to worry about."

But the officer waved off my documents. "He works in *nadafa,*" he said, pointing to Sayyid. "Hygiene. That's a service for the city. He should be allowed in for free!"

I was speechless. For the first time, I looked at the officer's face—he had a friendly smile behind the regulation mustache. Even in a police state there were bound to be some good ones. The cop escorted Sayyid and his family to the museum door, where the guards let all five members of the family enter without paying. The officer called after Sayyid, "Thank you for your service!"

I had no idea what the family would make of the museum. Over the years, it had become one of my favorite places in the city, and I probably visited forty or fifty times. My press card gave me free admission, and if I had an interview or an appointment near Tahrir, I often stopped by the museum for half an hour.

It was no surprise that the exhibits still loomed so vividly in the memory of a former resident like Albert Bivas. Opened in 1902, the museum looked like a sprawling palace, with big windows and skylights. Security was stunningly lax. Most statues weren't surrounded by barriers, and there were few guards; sometimes tourists touched the objects. When I visited with a friend who lived in China, he remarked that you could never have such an exhibit in Beijing or Shanghai, where people put their hands all over things unless they were physically prevented from doing so.

In the Egyptian Museum, some of the more valuable objects were housed in handmade wooden cases so old that they themselves were basically artifacts. Even many of the priceless burial goods of Tutankhamun were displayed in glass boxes secured with tiny old-fashioned locks made by a Chinese company called Tri-Circle. I looked up the Tri-Circle locks online—they cost two dollars each. I had no idea what these locks had been designed for, but it wasn't four-thousand-year-old treasures; I wouldn't secure Natasha's bicycle with such a thing. In the museum, many artifacts were unlabeled. The labels that did exist often conveyed nothing:

> *A group of amulets, the meaning of which is not yet clear for the scholars.*

But somehow it all contributed to the mood. The old building conveyed the fantasy sensation of an overstuffed attic, and it inspired none of the guilt and OCD behavioral patterns endemic to great museums worldwide. It was impossible to get lost in texts, because texts hardly existed; and nobody felt compelled to approach this place in a systematic fashion, because there was no system. I rarely brought a guidebook. Often I just walked through a few rooms and let my mind wander.

The government was in the process of building a new complex, which would house many of the most important artifacts. It was located out near the pyramids and would cost around a billion dollars. Perhaps this would be an improvement; certainly, it would be nice to view the artifacts under proper lighting. But I was glad to have lived in Cairo during an era when the old quirky museum still contained everything. It was like a neighborhood park that I often passed through on my way somewhere else.

I was concerned that Sayyid and his family might feel overwhelmed or bored. Zizou, the older son, was about to finish the fourth grade at the *ashwa'iyat* school that was named after Jerusalem, and I had always wondered about the quality of education there. But Zizou read well, and he often referred to Mr. Ali, the teacher who instructed his overcrowded class. During the evenings, Wahiba paid Mr. Ali to give her son private tutorials.

In the museum's Amarna room, there was a larger-than-life statue that portrayed Akhenaten with what appeared to be a pregnant woman's belly. It was an amazing figure—scholars thought that perhaps it dated to a phase when the king was trying to reconcile the duality of male and female. Later, he seemed to accomplish this by elevating Nefertiti, and the statue's unusual manner of portrayal was abandoned, like so much else during this period. Archaeologists had discovered it beneath the ruins of Akhenaten's own temple at Karnak. Essentially the king had buried this version of himself.

Now Zizou recognized the figure immediately. "Akhenaten started a revolution of religion," he said. "He was the first person to believe in a single god. And he worshipped the sun." At a display of material from the Giza pyramids, the boy mentioned that some experts believe that ancient Egyptians poured oil onto the ground, to make it easier to slide the massive stone blocks. When we came across the name of Senwosret III, I asked Zizou if he had heard of the king. "He built the canal between the Red Sea and the Nile," the boy said. "He was king during the Middle Kingdom."

"Where did you learn that?" I asked.

"From Mr. Ali."

I thought, *God bless Mr. Ali.*

I took them into the room of royal mummies on the second floor. It required an extra ticket, and the presence of a female security attendant made Sayyid and Wahiba nervous.

"Is it okay if I'm here in a *niqab*?" Wahiba asked the security attendant.

"Of course!" the woman said. "As long as you have a ticket, you're fine."

"I wasn't sure," Wahiba said.

"You look very *chic,*" the attendant said kindly, using the French term that's common in Egyptian Arabic. "You're wearing a nice dress, not one of those huge black things. We don't like it when women wear those, because they could be hiding something underneath."

Wahiba thanked her, her eyes smiling behind the veil. Sayyid stood near the entrance of the room with a thoughtful expression.

"I can smell them," he said.

He pointed to the line of mummies in display cases. I said I didn't think they had any scent after thousands of years, but he shook his head. "They smell bad," he said. I would have thought that working with garbage would desensitize a person, but the opposite seemed to be true—I had never known anybody with a stronger sense of smell. Sometimes Sayyid knocked on my apartment door and told me what we had cooked for dinner that evening, because the fragrance still lingered on the metal staircase outside.

He covered his nose while examining the mummies. One by one, he passed the god-kings: Thutmose II, Amenhotep II, Seti I, Ramesses the Great. Once upon a time, each pharaoh would have been called by the series of royal titles: Horus, Horus of Gold, He of the Two Ladies, He of the Sedge and the Bee. *Look on my works, ye Mighty, and despair!* Now their faces were black and withered, with yellowed teeth that jutted out from open mouths, as if in pain. They lay beneath smudged glass, where the scent of their bodies offended the garbageman. The labels here, unlike those in other parts of the museum, were worth reading:

> *Now known to be Hatshepsut, great female pharaoh of the 18th Dynasty, this mummy is of an obese female with bad teeth who died between the ages of 45 and 60.*

> *Ramesses the Great ruled Egypt for about 67 years. He suffered many health problems in his old age: he had many dental abscesses, severe arthritis in his hip joints, and arteriosclerosis. His silky white hair may have been yellowed by mummification chemicals.*

Most visitors to the museum were Chinese. That was also true at many sites in Luxor; from 2014 to 2016, the number of Chinese tourists to Egypt had more than tripled. The Chinese came from a country full of overcrowded sites of antiquity, and they recognized a bargain when they saw it. Whenever I went to Luxor's West Bank, I thought, *Valley of the Chinese.*

Meanwhile, many of the Chinese lingerie dealers whom I had met were leaving the country. The ones in Minya returned to Zhejiang, along with a number who were based in Cairo, and then Kiki and John decided to go. Kiki's parents continued to run the recycling plant in Asyut, but they saw no point in maintaining the retail lingerie business, because the Egyptian currency was under so much pressure. Profits were falling, and it was becoming difficult to exchange and repatriate money. In Cairo, I no longer used ATMs or credit cards; everything had to be in cash, and most people changed dollars with black-market dealers, who paid almost double the official rate. Near the end of 2016, the government finally abandoned its attempts to shore up the currency, and the pound was devalued. When we first moved to Egypt, the rate was less than six pounds to the dollar; now it was more than eighteen.

All of this made tourism cheaper, and Mandarin became the main language I heard in the museum. Invariably, the Chinese tour groups were led by an Egyptian guide with the national gift for language. It was the only country I had ever been where Chinese were routinely guided by natives who spoke Mandarin well. Many of these guides had never even traveled to China.

This scene fascinated Sayyid and his family, and they tagged along at the back of one group just to hear the Egyptian speak the strange language. Later, when we were leaving the Amarna room, Wahiba asked me, "Are those Chinese people supposed to be doing that?"

Across the room, at the famous statue of the pregnant-bellied Akhenaten, half a dozen Chinese had formed a ring. They clasped hands, and the person at each end of the ring touched the red quartzite statue, as if the pharaoh were a missing link. The Chinese were young, and they looked like upper-middle-class urbanites.

I approached them, and a man introduced himself as the leader of the group. They were there for some kind of spiritual reasons; the leader taught at a Daoist institute in Xi'an. He had no idea who Akhenaten was, and he knew nothing about Egyptian history; there weren't any Chinese labels at the museum. "This statue gives me a different feeling, so we want to be close to it," he explained. "That's all we want, to be close to these things."

I told him not to touch the statues, but later I saw the group on the ground floor doing the same thing with a figure of Hatshepsut. This ritual seemed vaguely connected to the traditional Chinese concept of qi, the energy that flows through all living things. But mystical and vaguely New Age ideas were also becoming popular among Chinese yuppies. It seemed inevitable: now it was the Chinese's turn to come to Egypt, and look at figures like Akhenaten, and see whatever they wanted to see. Two years later, in the fall of 2018, Chinese-funded archaeologists began to excavate in Egypt for the first time in history.

As I exited the museum with Sayyid and his family, we stopped in the gift shop. The children had loved the exhibits, and I wanted to find something for them, but the museum had only one book for children. It was titled *Here Is Egypt: 7000 Years of Civilization*. There were multiple language versions: English, French, German, Spanish, Italian—but no Arabic.

In Cologne, Manu kept a notebook of German vocabulary:

I want (in a polite way)	*Ich möchte*
I would like to have please	*Ich möchte gerne*
to miss someone	*Ich vermisse*

He posted German phrases on the walls of his apartment:

During the school year the students do an internship.

Most students begin applying to jobs the moment school is finished.

at the same time

after the event

before the event

I visited him in the summer of 2018, after he had been settled there for more than a year. Germany has a system of language examinations that qualify newcomers for jobs, and Manu had passed the first one with a score of

164 out of 165. Now another course met for four hours a day, to prepare him for the next exam.

party	*Partei*
voting program	*Wahl Programme*
private/secret	*Geheime*
the dictatorial regime	*Die Diktatur*
the dictator	*Die Dictator*

He had been much happier since moving into the apartment, but some days he longed for Egypt. "I miss knowing everything," he said. "Knowing the place. Being confident in the place. I don't have that here. I'm hesitant, uncertain." He was surprised by the depth of this feeling—whatever it meant to be Egyptian went far beyond logic or reason. That connection had always been the great strength of the country, and also its weakness, because it was hard for people to change something that felt so elemental. And even now, after Manu had fled his homeland, he felt the pull. "You forget the bad things, and you remember the good things," he said. "And you miss Cairo."

But for the most part he was happy in his new home. His appearance had changed in small, subtle ways, but these things added up to something more significant. He wore hoop earrings, and he was strikingly fit; he went to a gym compulsively. And his mannerisms had changed. He said that a gay friend from Cairo recently visited and declared, "Manu, you're more gay!" When we first met in 2011, while reporting at the mosque on Tahrir, I had been struck by how careful he seemed. Now that wariness was gone— something inside him had relaxed.

One night, we walked around downtown Cologne, and he pointed out some Germans who were waiting at a red pedestrian light, even though there weren't any cars. "I love that," he said. "Always in Egypt one of the things that made me crazy is that there's no system. I always wanted a system. But it was just chaos. Here when you cross the street, you don't have to look for the cars. Just look at the light."

As an asylee, he still qualified for significant support from the government. There was a subsidy for his apartment, and his German course was covered, and he received more than four hundred euros per month for living expenses. But he had recently applied for a position to work at a Jobcenter bureau in Berlin, and he would begin training in October. He would speak Arabic as well as German, because the Jobcenter handled many refugees. "I want to do something useful," he said. "This is really the first time I'm looking to the future."

After he started a job, the subsidies would diminish, which explained some of the sentences on the apartment wall: *"Most students begin applying to jobs the moment school is finished."* Manu said class materials always pushed these ideas: how to search for a job, how to handle an interview, how to settle into work.

"There are hidden messages in every text," he said. "I like this way of learning." He showed me his government-issued textbook. One section had a photograph of two men smiling:

> *Mr. Kästner has recently moved into a shared apartment with his partner. So it has become known that he is gay. The board of the sports club, in which Mr. Kästner has been active for three years, would therefore like to exclude him.*

Manu enjoyed seeing how the various people in his class responded to the subtle propaganda of the German materials. When they talked about the gay couple, a Turkish man mocked the idea of two men being together. But other students pushed against his homophobia. On another occasion, there was a lesson about women's freedom, and a bearded Syrian said, in German, that he would never tolerate his wife removing her *hijab*. An Iranian woman argued with him fiercely. "This is Germany," she said. "If you don't like it, then you can leave."

One afternoon, I accompanied Manu to class. The teacher, a young energetic German with her blond hair tied up in a ponytail, led the students in a review of a one-page article. They were preparing for a test that required them to read an article and then discuss it with an examiner. Today's text was about *Müllsünder.*

"Do you know what *Sünder* means?" the teacher said in German.

A Syrian woman sitting next to Manu stumbled: *"Shu—Sünder?"*

"Muznib," Manu whispered in Arabic. "Sinner."

"Ahh," the Syrian woman said.

"It means *haraam*," the teacher said. After using the Arabic word, she returned to German. "This is about people who do bad stuff with garbage. The garbage sinner is somebody who throws garbage outside the bin." She read from the text:

> *Litterers in downtown Frankfurt can now expect drastic penalties. Whoever drops his cigarette butt on the street pays 20 euros. Whoever spits out his gum pays 35 euros. A pile from a dog costs 75 euros, and feeding a pigeon is 100 euros.*

"What could be an argument in favor of the fines?" the teacher asked.

One of the Syrian men read from the text: "Since the fine system was established, the city became cleaner."

"That means it works," the Iranian woman said.

The teacher wrote on the board, in big letters, "FINES WORK."

"What if there are no garbage bins?" a Russian woman asked.

"Use your pockets," said another Syrian.

"Do you think this could be an argument against this system?" the teacher asked.

"Yes, because there aren't enough bins," the Iranian woman said.

"I don't think this is correct," Manu said. "Compared with Egypt, there are garbage bins everywhere."

The class included people from around ten nationalities, and all of them participated animatedly in the discussion. It made me think that Sayyid had been right all along—in the end, everything in the world comes down to trash.

"Some of these fines are a little too expensive," the Iranian woman said.

"I think thirty-five for gum is not expensive," Manu said. "It stays on the street for many years."

"This is not good for the environment," a Frenchwoman agreed. "It takes a long time to—" She paused, searching for the word.

"A long time to integrate," the teacher said. She smiled to let them know that it was a joke, and all the students laughed.

Before I left Egypt, I took Sayyid and his family to the pyramids. While we were standing at the entrance to the Great Pyramid, a young American woman tried to climb the eastern face of the monument. She made it about fifty feet before a security guard noticed. He yelled, and other guards came running; they fanned out in a line below the woman. The woman would clamber up another block or two, and the men would yell and begin to chase, and then she would stop. Finally they persuaded her to come down. Throughout this standoff, Sayyid and his family watched intently.

I had never fully appreciated all the ridiculous things that tourists do in Egypt until I went to sites with Sayyid and his family. The foreigners occupied about half their attention; at the museum, they had been fascinated by the Chinese artifact touchers, and now at the pyramids they were entertained by inappropriate Westerners. At a famous lookout spot above the pyramids, we saw a tall American woman who was wearing the shortest shorts I had ever seen in Egypt. She was trailed by about a dozen Egyptian men, all of whom were trying to appear busy with their phones while they followed the American and her scandalous clothes. A couple of the men were camel tenders who had abandoned their animals, staked in the sand. When this little parade passed us, Wahiba took out her own phone and shot a picture of the woman. Wahiba's face was red from trying not to laugh.

On the car ride over, she and Sayyid had discussed whether she should wear the *niqab*. Wahiba was certain that the security people would mistake her for an ISIS terrorist who planned to blow up the pyramids, so she left the face covering in the Honda. As always, I was impressed by the amount of forethought and negotiation that went into the management of this garment. The *niqab* was never to be taken for granted: Wahiba constantly evaluated its significance, because it meant different things in different parts of the city.

And I imagined that being a woman in Egypt was similar. It required constant energy, thought, and adjustment; no woman could be comfortable with some essential identity that she had determined for herself. Instead, she had to accept the judgments of the men around her, shifting her dress and behavior according to whoever they might be: husband, close relative, distant relative, friend of husband, neighbor, man on the street. Of course, the cultures in America and Europe also placed unfair demands on women, but there was no comparison to Egypt. From my perspective, this was one of the greatest failures of the revolution. Despite all the turmoil, the vast majority of Egyptians had never been forced to reconsider the roles of women and young people in their society.

But at least they had the raw material for a better way—all that talent and force of personality. One reason I liked spending time with Sayyid and Wahiba was that they were the only Egyptian couple I knew who had changed. I never pretended that this represented a solution: the fights, the angry texts, the court cases. And I knew that while individuals can impress and inspire, systems and environments matter most of all.

Still, it was a small good thing—in the end, these people showed the possibility of transformation. After all the fighting, they shared their household in better ways, and their children clearly thrived. Wahiba often talked about how she'd like to get a job someday, after the kids were older, and now Sayyid agreed—*insha'allah.*

The last site we visited on the Giza Plateau was the Great Sphinx. There's a temple complex in front of the Sphinx, and within the temple there's a hole where archaeologists excavated a famous statue of King Khafre. The statue, which is beautifully made of black diorite, was given a place of honor in the Egyptian Museum, and the statue's face decorates the English-language side of the Egyptian ten-pound bill. On the Arabic side of the bill, there's an image of Cairo's Al-Rifa'i Mosque.

For some reason, it had become a tradition for tourists to throw money into the hole in front of the Sphinx. Of all the strange things that foreigners and rich Egyptians did at the ancient sites, this ritual most impressed Sayyid and his family. They stood there for nearly a quarter hour, watching people throw away money. A rainbow of currencies covered the bottom of the pit—pounds, euros, dollars, yen, renminbi.

Sayyid and Wahiba asked me why people did this, and I told them it was for good luck. But I could see they didn't quite understand. Finally, we left the hole and visited the Great Sphinx. We stood there for just a few minutes. Tourists usually leave via a side entrance, but Wahiba insisted we go back the way we had come. She wasn't finished with that hole yet.

She waited there until she saw a friendly-looking middle-class Egyptian couple. Wahiba approached them and asked why people threw their money away.

"For luck," the woman said.

"What kind of luck?"

"For example, if you want to get married. Are you married?"

Wahiba said she was.

"Do you have children?"

"Yes."

"Well," the woman said, "do you want to have more children?"

I had never heard Sayyid and Wahiba discuss this, and I certainly hadn't imagined what I would see more than a year later, on a return trip to Cairo: a beautiful month-old girl named Rimess, her ears pierced with tiny gold earrings in the shape of hands, to ward off the evil eye. The proud mother, the happy father. But from Wahiba's answer to the woman at the Sphinx, maybe she hadn't imagined this scene either.

"No," she said.

"Then it can be for something else," the woman said. "You can wish for anything you want."

Wahiba thanked her, and the middle-class couple continued to the Sphinx. Wahiba stood there for a while. Then, slowly, she reached into her purse, took out a one-pound coin, and tossed it into the hole.

ACKNOWLEDGMENTS

Even the first small step of this project—moving to Cairo—benefited from the assistance of many people. In 2011, after the Egyptian Arab Spring began, Leslie and I realized that it would be reckless to arrive without a serious introductory course in Arabic. We were fortunate to be supported by the Kathryn Davis Fellowships for Peace at Middlebury College's Intensive Arabic Summer Program. Dr. Mahmoud Abdalla, the director of the Arabic program, showed us great kindness and flexibility, making sure that our housing was appropriate for a family with one-year-old twins. The program's teachers and staff did a wonderful job of preparing us for the transition to Cairo.

During my five years in Egypt, I was supported by the MacArthur Foundation, whose generosity allowed me to continue studying Egyptian Arabic while also pursuing long-term research projects.

At the Kalimat Language and Cultural Centre, Leslie and I were blessed with wonderful teachers: Sherif El-Habibi, Sami Farag, Raafat Amin, and, of course, Rifaat Amin. All four instructors taught us so much about the language of the moment, and they did so with characteristic Egyptian humor and life.

I was also fortunate to work with a number of resourceful researchers and translators. During my first spring in Egypt, Magdy Samaan arranged interviews with a wide range of Muslim Brotherhood officials and parliamentarians. Heba Habib accompanied me to Brotherhood rallies in Suez, Ismailia, and Cairo. From the end of 2012 to 2015, I worked with Hassan ElNaggar, whose skills at simultaneous translation were remarkable. His skills on the Cairo roads were nearly as impressive, and he also helped prepare me for driving in the city. Hassan and I worked together during a period that was stressful and occasionally violent, and I'm grateful for his courage.

Near the end of my time in Egypt, I worked with Merna Thomas, whose research into Sisileaks and other aspects of the new regime was invaluable.

I am grateful to the many Egyptologists who were generous with their time and expertise. Matthew Adams, the Abydos field director for the Institute of Fine Arts at New York University, first welcomed me to the site, where I benefited from his lucid explanations of the digs and their history. Later, Josef Wegner allowed me to observe the University of Pennsylvania excavations in and around the tomb of Senwosret III. It was particularly useful to visit Wegner's projects during three successive years, which gave me some sense of the patience, care, and long-term planning that go into a first-rate excavation. During every visit to Abydos, I enjoyed meeting with Ibrahim Mohammed Ali, the Gufti *rayis,* whose dignity and stoicism helped me understand how such a site survives the periodic swings of Egyptian national politics.

Laurel Bestock provided detailed background of the Brown University dig that preceded the start of the Tahrir protests. I appreciated the openness of Ahmed Ragab, the manager of the Abydos dig house, who described the events of that harrowing period. Individuals like Ahmed, who did everything he could to protect Abydos's cultural heritage, are among the heroes of the Egyptian Arab Spring.

In Cairo and in Amarna, Barry Kemp and Anna Stevens were generous in their introductions to the work that was being carried out by the Amarna Project. I also learned a great deal from the project's team of bioarchaeologists, which was led first by Jerry Rose of the University of Arkansas–Fayetteville and then by Gretchen Dabbs of Southern Illinois University.

One of my favorite places in all of Upper Egypt was the Chicago House, in part because of the beautiful setting and the Art Deco architecture, but mostly because of the hospitality of Raymond Johnson and Jay Heidel. Ray's enthusiasm for the art and ideas of the Amarna period, and his dedication in piecing together broken artifacts, were inspiring. I also greatly appreciated his willingness to review sections of this manuscript.

Officials at the Ministry of Antiquities were under great pressures, both political and financial, but they remained diligent in answering my requests for interviews and for access to sites. Mamdouh Eldamaty was especially helpful during my visits to Luxor.

A number of threads of this narrative began as stories for the *New Yorker,* where I benefited from the guidance of David Remnick and my editor, Willing Davidson. I especially appreciated their interest in nontraditional stories. I'm grateful to the *New Yorker* staff, who fact-checked these projects, both in Arabic and in Chinese: Nana Asfour, Sameen Gauhar, Yasmine Al-Sayyad, and Jiayang Fan.

Much of my research into archaeology was supported by *National Geographic,* where my editors were Oliver Payne and Glenn Oeland. On long evenings of research in the tombs of the Valley of the Kings, I was fortunate to work with Terry Garcia and Fredrik Hiebert.

For twenty years, I've been represented by William Clark, and I much appreciate his work in finding the best home for this book. At Penguin Press, Scott Moyers had faith in the project from the beginning, and he offered key encouragement and criticism after reading the first draft. Mia Council helped us hold everything together during a very long process of editing and fact checking.

I'm grateful to Albert Bivas for reaching out when he recognized the spiderweb building from my description in an article. After years of living in the apartment, it was a thrill to finally learn about its original occupants. I'm also deeply grateful to Albert's sisters: Vicky Bivas-Devos, Betty Kane, Danièle Cohen Grossman, and Michèle Elkins. The Bivas siblings were diligent in their efforts to answer my questions about the building and their family history, and they tracked down old photographs and stray memories. I'm grateful that they allowed me to record a small glimpse of their lost world of Cairo.

Leslie and I probably would not have moved to Cairo without the encouragement of Elisabeth and Darryl Kennedy, and we much appreciated their friendship and support during our years in the city (as well as their hospitality at the Red Sea). I'm grateful to Darryl for many discussions about Egyptian culture and faith, and I appreciated his review of a draft of this book. The manuscript was also improved greatly by the suggestions of Ian Johnson and Michael Meyer, two China friends who have been faithful readers through five books.

My sister, Angela Hessler, had the brilliant idea to incorporate the spiderweb design into her historical timelines. The maps she drew were both meticulous and beautiful—thank you for capturing the wonder of the Egyptian landscape, that gift of the Nile.

For any nonfiction writer, so much comes down to chance. You might end up in China for ten years of a boom, or maybe you happen to go to Egypt during five years of political struggle. Either way, this brief instant in the history of a country becomes your world. Timing is everything, and so are chance encounters. But there's something more reliable about the relationships that deepen over time, and the individuals whose stories extend well beyond the moment.

My family's life in Zamalek wouldn't have been the same without Sayyid. Over the years, he enlivened our home with his visits, and I always enjoyed his openness, humor, and insight. Wahiba and her mother were generous hosts whenever

I went to Ard al-Liwa, and I especially appreciated their welcoming my parents. Together Sayyid and Wahiba reflected some of the best Egyptian qualities: resourcefulness, optimism, and pure force of character.

While writing this book, I often wished that I could ask Rifaat Amin a question about an Arabic word or some aspect of Egyptian society. Leslie and I have felt his loss for the last three years, and I've heard from other former students who feel the same way. I am grateful to Raafat, Wardiya, and Tariq for sharing their memories, and I hope they know how many people were touched by their brother's energy, dedication, and intelligence.

Manu was one of those chance meetings—I had no introduction to him when we first worked together. During my first year in the country, we were together in a few dangerous situations, and I was impressed by his calmness and courage. As time passed, I understood better where the courage came from. I hope that someday Egyptians like Manu will be able to live freely and fully in their homeland.

People tell you that your children grow up in a flash. But this is not true if you move to Cairo with two toddlers during year one of a revolution. In my memory, those years passed very slowly, because the challenge of keeping up with the political events was matched by the challenge of the little revolutionaries at home. Learning to run, learning to talk, learning to think. I'm grateful to have shared this experience, and all the hours of Arabic class, with Leslie. As Rifaat used to say: إيد لوحدها متصقفش

More than twenty years ago, when I completed a draft of *River Town,* the first person to read it was Doug Hunt at the University of Missouri. Since then he has been my most faithful and reliable reader, through times both good and bad. This book is dedicated to him.

Ridgway, Colorado
January 2019

NOTES

The events described in this book are of two main types: those I observed directly or spoke about directly with the principals, and events that I have cited from other sources. I have listed the sources below, along with references for the various facts and statistics that appear in the book. In cases in which I interviewed an official, scholar, or political figure, I have given the date of the meeting.

For Manu's personal history, I witnessed some events myself, and then we had a series of interviews and phone conversations from 2016 to 2018, both in Egypt and in Germany. I met with Sayyid regularly from late 2011 to the summer of 2016, when my family moved out of Cairo, and then again on return trips in 2017 and 2018. I usually met Sayyid and his family members alone, but periodically I scheduled more formal interviews with a translator, in order to clarify things that I didn't understand. I learned some of Rifaat's family history and personal background during our Arabic classes, but I also depended on interviews with his siblings Raafat, Tariq, and Wardiya, conducted after their brother's death, from 2016 to 2017.

I have not altered the sequence of any events, and I have used real names with a few exceptions. I have changed the name of Manu's friend "Tariq," because of the political sensitivity of his relationship with the Muslim Brotherhood. I also changed the name of Sayyid's sister "Leila," and the name of her daughter, at Leila's request. Finally, in chapter 8, when I describe accompanying Sayyid on his garbage route in Zamalek, I have changed the names of the residents of the apartments where we picked up trash.

Frontispiece: **"Akhenaten and Nefertiti distributing rewards":** This image is based on a drawing by Norman de Garis Davies, who worked at Amarna and other sites under the auspices of the Egypt Exploration Fund. See N. de G. Davies, *The Rock Tombs of El Amarna: Part III—The Tombs of Huya and Ahmes* (London: Gilbert & Rivington, Limited, 1905), plate XVI.

viii **Timeline of Egyptian History:** For the timeline dates of ancient periods, we used Ian Shaw, *The Oxford History of Ancient Egypt* (New York: Oxford University Press, 2003). For dates from the Byzantine period to modern times, we used Jason Thompson, *A History of Egypt: From Earliest Times to the Present* (New York: Anchor Books, 2009).

PART ONE: THE PRESIDENT

3 **"Worship the king within your bodies":** Toby Wilkinson, *The Rise and Fall of Ancient Egypt: The History of a Civilization from 3000 BC to Cleopatra* (London: Bloomsbury, 2011), 169.

Chapter 1

5 **archaeologists from Brown University:** I spoke and corresponded with Laurel Bestock in October and November 2018. For more details on the excavation, see Laurel Bestock, "Brown University Abydos Project: Preliminary Report on the First Two Seasons," *Journal of the American Research Center in Egypt* 48 (2012): 35–79.

6 **the Buried:** *Al-Madfuna* is a shortened form of *al-Araba al-Madfuna,* or "the Buried Araba," which is the full name of one of the nearby villages. The name may refer to ancient funeral corteges that were interred beneath the earth.

6 **the oldest standing mud-brick buildings:** Toby Wilkinson identifies the Shunet al-Zebib as one of the two oldest such buildings, both built by Khasekhemwy. Toby Wilkinson, *The Nile: Travelling Downriver Through Egypt's Past and Present* (New York: Vintage Books, 2015), 170.

6 **"sort of police station":** David O'Connor, *Abydos: Egypt's First Pharaohs and the Cult of Osiris* (Cairo: American University in Cairo Press, 2009), 160.

6 **On January 28, 2011:** David Batty and Alex Olorenshaw, "Egypt Protests—as They Happened," *Guardian,* Jan. 29, 2011, www.theguardian.com/world/2011/jan/29/egypt-protests-government-live-blog.

7 **attackers had freed hundreds of criminals:** The Wadi al-Natroun prison break occurred on January 30, 2011, and the escapees included Morsi and more than thirty Brotherhood leaders. Ben Hubbard, "Egypt Calls for New Look at Morsi Prison Escape in 2011," *New York Times,* July 11, 2013, www.nytimes.com/2013/07/12/world/middleeast/egypt-christians.html.

9 **The earliest known written words:** O'Connor, *Abydos,* 143.

9 **The Buried is the stage:** From my interview with Adams on March 24, 2015.

9 **Ahmed constructed a large rectangular wooden box:** Ragab described the construction of the APC, and his patrolling of the site, when we met on Feb. 27, 2013.

11 ***Neheh* is the time of cycles:** For material on *djet* and *neheh,* see W. Raymond Johnson, "The Setting: History, Religion, and Art," in *Pharaohs of the Sun: Akhenaten, Nefertiti, Tutankhamun,* ed. Rita E. Freed, Yvonne J. Markowitz, and Sue H. D'Auria (London: Thames & Hudson, 1999), 38–40.

11 **It's an island:** Erik Hornung, *Conceptions of God in Ancient Egypt: The One and the Many,* trans. John Baines (Ithaca, N.Y.: Cornell University Press, 1983), 183.

11 **"saw normal time as a circle":** Johnson, "Setting," 38.

11 **a natural response to the southern terrain:** Johnson discussed his ideas about the connection between the desert and *djet,* and the river valley and *neheh,* in a conversation with me on March 31, 2014.

11 **undertook an archaeology of the revolution:** I visited Adams and his team in February and March 2013, when they were excavating the pits that had been looted in 2011. See also Matthew Douglas Adams, "In the Footsteps of Looters: Assessing the Damage from the 2011 Looting in the North Cemetery at Abydos," *Journal of the American Research Center in Egypt* 51 (2015): 5–63.

Chapter 3

23 **Egyptian Third Army surrounded:** Charles Mohr, "Trapped Egyptian Force Seen at Root of Problem," *New York Times,* Oct. 26, 1973, www.nytimes.com/1973/10/26/archives/trapped-egyptian-force-seen-at-root-of-problem-egyptian-forge-held.html.

24 **I saw a thief:** I witnessed the theft at the Omar Makram Mosque on November 20, 2011.

26 **more than twenty people had been killed:** On November 21, 2011, the Egyptian

Health Ministry announced that at least twenty-three people had been killed. David D. Kirkpatrick and Liam Stack, "Egypt's Civilian Government Submits Offer to Resign," *New York Times,* Nov. 21, 2011.

28 **The funeral began:** I observed the funeral at the Omar Makram Mosque at 2:00 p.m. on November 22, 2011.

31 **walls of concrete and barbed wire:** There were several attempts by Al-Azhar clerics to negotiate a truce. See David D. Kirkpatrick and Anthony Shadid, "Military Moves to End Clashes in Egyptian Square," *New York Times,* Nov. 23, 2011.

The truce finally held on the morning of November 24, 2011, and the military began constructing barricades. See Heba Afify and Lindsey Parietti, "Protestors Evacuate Mohamed Mahmoud Street as Some Confront Military at Barricade," *Al-Masry al-Youm,* Nov. 24, 2011.

33 **"We want a civic democratic state":** For a fuller account of Sheikh Mazhar Shahin's comments, see David D. Kirkpatrick, "Egyptian Islamists Rally to Protest Military Rule," *New York Times,* Nov. 18, 2011.

33 **nowhere to be seen:** I referred to the imam's absence in my article about the protests. See Peter Hessler, "The Mosque on the Square," *New Yorker,* Dec. 19 & 26, 2011, 46–57. During the editing process, a fact-checker contacted an assistant to Sheikh Mazhar Shahin who claimed that in fact the imam had been in the mosque every day between sunset and evening prayers, as required by law. This contradicted what Manu and I had observed over the period of protests. After Sheikh Mazhar denied this, I told him that we could talk about it the following day, in the mosque, between the sunset and the evening prayers. Manu and I returned for this appointment, but once again the imam was not in attendance.

34 **more than half of eligible voters:** "Muslim Brotherhood Tops Egyptian Poll Results," *Al-Jazeera,* Jan. 22, 2012, www.aljazeera.com/news/middleeast/2012/01/201212125958580264.html.

34 **The Muslim Brotherhood won 47 percent:** David D. Kirkpatrick, "Islamists Win 70% of Seats in the Egyptian Parliament," *New York Times,* Jan. 21, 2012, www.nytimes.com/2012/01/22/world/middleeast/muslim-brotherhood-wins-47-of-egypt-assembly-seats.html.

34 **no left-leaning party won:** The best performance by any non-Islamist party in the 2011–2012 parliamentary election was by the Wafd Party, which won 8 percent of the seats. See Jeffrey Martini and Stephen M. Worman, "Voting Patterns in Post-Mubarak Egypt," Rand Corporation, 2013, 6.

35 **"I agree with the other Brotherhood leaders":** I met with Mohamed Beltagy on December 30, 2011.

37 **an estimated forty-seven people:** The most common figure for the number of deaths at the Mohammed Mahmoud protests was 47, although there was some uncertainty. The state-run *Al-Ahram* described it as "around 47." See "Police Warn Against 'Aggression' on Mohamed Mahmoud Clashes Anniversary," *Ahram Online,* Nov. 17, 2013, english.ahram.org.eg/NewsContent/1/64/86683/Egypt/Politics-/Police-warn-against-aggression-on-Mohamed-Mahmoud-.aspx.

38 **But Waleed's crime:** The theft in the mosque was confirmed by multiple volunteers at Omar Makram, as well as by the mother of one of the victims, a teenager whose phone and money were stolen.

Chapter 4

39 **a fleet of a dozen ships:** O'Connor, *Abydos,* 183–94.

40 **"The Fast One":** This translation of the dog's name is from Günter Dreyer, who described the dog burial to me in Abydos on March 14, 2013.

40 **forty-five hundred liters of wine:** O'Connor, *Abydos,* 143.

40 **amulets of lapis lazuli:** Matthew Adams described finding such amulets in an interview with me on Feb. 26, 2013.

40 **the British archaeologist could still smell the ointment:** O'Connor, *Abydos,* 148.

40 **people with a common identity:** Wilkinson, *Rise and Fall of Ancient Egypt,* 10.

41 **"He made a foreign expedition":** Barry J. Kemp, *Ancient Egypt: Anatomy of a Civilization* (London: Routledge, 1993), 46.

41 **more than forty retainers:** These figures include the burials at each king's royal tomb and the burials at his ritual enclosure. King Aha had 12 burials around his monument and 30 around his tomb; King Djer's monument had 260 and another 350 for his tomb. These figures are from my interview with Matthew Adams on Feb. 26, 2013.

41 **under the age of twenty-five:** From my interview with Günter Dreyer on March 13, 2013.

41 **used in some Mesopotamian buildings:** Wilkinson, *Rise and Fall of Ancient Egypt,* 44.

42 **vertical lines of the Art Deco style:** The connection between the vertical lines of ancient Middle Eastern architecture and the Art Deco style was confirmed in a September 2018 email exchange that I had with Martin Filler, an architectural critic, and his wife, Rosemarie Haag Bletter, an architectural historian who has written extensively about Art Deco.

43 **More than forty-three centuries:** According to Toby Wilkinson, author of *The Rise and Fall of Ancient Egypt,* the first building known with certainty to have surpassed the height of the Great Pyramid is the St. Nikolai Church in Hamburg, completed in 1874, and with a height two feet taller (483 feet to 481). The Lincoln Cathedral, completed in 1311, is reputed to have been taller, but the height was not independently verified and the central spire collapsed in 1539. This is from email correspondence with Wilkinson, November 2018.

43 **centuries before they used the wheel:** From my interview with Barry Kemp on April 6, 2014. Kemp noted that the wheel appears in Egyptian art in the late Old Kingdom, in a picture of wheels attached to a ladder used in a siege.

43 **hieroglyphs in remarkably stable forms:** Kemp, *Ancient Egypt,* 26.

44 **"They expected logic":** Barry Kemp, *The City of Akhenaten and Nefertiti: Amarna and Its People* (Cairo: American University in Cairo Press, 2012), 26.

44 **2.3 million carved stone blocks:** Wilkinson, *Rise and Fall of Ancient Egypt,* 72.

44 **wrote all fractions with a numerator of one:** Kemp, *Ancient Egypt,* 116–17.

44 **"They must have had abstract thinking":** I interviewed Hany El-Hosseiny at Cairo University on Dec. 1, 2016.

44 **"In recent years archaeologists":** Ibid., 235.

44 **"They exemplify a general characteristic":** Ibid., 117.

45 **invented the crown and the scepter:** Wilkinson, *Rise and Fall of Ancient Egypt,* 44–45.

46 **"One stormy night":** Wilkinson, *Nile,* 174.

46 **old-fashioned house key:** Josef Wegner described the discoveries of Charles Currelly's house key, the murdered girl, and the lightning strike during interviews on December 11, 2013.

Chapter 5

51 **approximately 40 percent of Egyptians:** "Keeping It in the Family," *Economist,* Feb. 27, 2016.

56 **a set dialogue that showed the proper way:** Mustafa Mughazy, *Dardasha Egyptian Arabic: Elementary Level* (Madison, Wis.: NALRC Press, 2004), 14.
57 ***"Tell us about the Yellow River":*** Helen T. Lin, *Speaking Chinese About China* (Beijing: Beijing Foreign Languages Printing House, 1995), 1.
57 **first vocabulary list:** Mughazy, *Dardasha Egyptian Arabic,* 12.
57 **"You might have noticed":** Ibid., 49.
57 ***"After a few times of being offered":*** Ibid., 92.
57 **Another chapter described the "evil eye":** Ibid., 71.
62 ***"He works very hard":*** Lin, *Speaking Chinese About China,* 88.
62 ***"Everyone is working very hard":*** Ibid., 145.
62 ***"We have realized":*** Ibid., 185.
62 ***"Do the Chinese leaders themselves":*** Ibid., 100.
62 **"Ya hag, *I'm an engineer*":** Mughazy, *Dardasha Egyptian Arabic,* 182.
62 **"Hello! Is Mr. Gumaa there?":** Ibid., 152.
67 **"What about your friends":** Ibid., 183.
67 **"As you might have noticed":** Ibid., 224.
68 **"What's for lunch today?":** Ibid., 135.
68 **"If only I knew who was calling":** Ibid., 162.
68 **"You Are Irritable":** Ibid., 152.

Chapter 6

70 **The new parliament had been in session:** I visited the parliament building and spoke with Sobhi Saleh on March 18, 2012.
73 **The last native to declare himself pharaoh:** Ankwennefer was the last Egyptian to declare himself pharaoh. See Wilkinson, *Nile,* 35.
74 **The British simply purchased the country's debt:** Zachary Karabell, *Parting the Desert: The Creation of the Suez Canal* (New York: Vintage Books, 2004), 264.
74 **"We are weary of this life":** Richard P. Mitchell, *The Society of the Muslim Brothers* (New York: Oxford University Press, 1993), 8.
74 **He often used the word *nizam*:** Ibid., 234–35.
74 **This word never appears in the Quran:** John Calvert, *Sayyid Qutb and the Origins of Radical Islamism* (New York: Columbia University Press, 2010), 130.
74 **Banna's use of the concept as anachronistic:** Wilfred Cantwell Smith, a professor of comparative religion at Harvard University, described this sense of Islam as a *nizam* as a "modern idea (and perhaps a rather questionable one)." See ibid.
75 **"neither Banna nor the movement":** Mitchell, *Society of the Muslim Brothers,* 327.
75 **between 300,000 and 600,000 members:** Ibid., 328.
75 **ranged from 400,000 to more than 2 million:** All of these figures were from my interviews with Brotherhood leaders or spokesmen in March 2012. On March 15, Yasser Ali Elsaid, a spokesman for the Freedom and Justice Party, told me there were more than 700,000 members of the Brotherhood. On March 26, Rashad al-Bayoumi, a member of the Guidance Bureau, said there might be as many as two million Brothers. Also on March 26, Nader Omran, another Freedom and Justice spokesman, told me there were only 400,000 Brothers in Egypt.
76 **"We sent this message":** Elsaid made these comments to me on March 15, 2012.
76 **"As we heard earlier":** From my observation of parliament on February 12, 2012.
76 **"A lot of people are talking":** From my observation of parliament on February 13, 2012.
77 **"There's a mafia involved":** From my observation of parliament on February 12, 2012.

77 **"We have eighty-five million people":** From my observation of parliament on February 19, 2012.

77 **Only 2 percent of the legislators were female:** "Egypt's New Parliament Holds First Session—in Pictures," *Guardian,* Jan. 23, 2012, www.theguardian.com/world/gallery/2012/jan/23/egypt-parliament-first-session-pictures.

77 **"Let's stop this broadcast":** From my observation of parliament on February 19, 2012.

77 **"Do you know what this government":** From my observation of parliament on April 24, 2012.

78 **In the 1860s, Frédéric-Auguste Bartholdi:** Karabell, *Parting the Desert,* 242–43.

79 **a *khawwal* was a cross-dressing male dancer:** Joseph A. Boone, *The Homoerotics of Orientalism* (New York: Columbia University Press, 2015), 188.

82 **celebration of three marriages:** From my observation of a rally for Morsi in Ismailia on the evening of May 11, 2012.

83 **only 3.6 percent of respondents:** "Poll: Moussa Leads Presidential Candidates with 41.1%, Morsy Last at 3.6%," *Egypt Independent,* April 30, 2012, www.egyptindependent.com/poll-moussa-leads-presidential-runners-411-news1hold/.

83 **In his words, he was an "exile":** Calvert, *Sayyid Qutb and the Origins of Radical Islamism,* 66.

83 **"A given society is a *nizam*":** Ibid., 90.

84 **probably a virgin for his entire life:** Ibid., 110.

84 **"I fear that when the wheel of life":** Ibid., 153.

84 **Mohammed Morsi admired Qutb's writing:** Eric Trager, *Arab Fall: How the Muslim Brotherhood Won and Lost Egypt in 891 Days* (Washington, D.C.: Georgetown University Press, 2016), 78.

85 **fifteen were engineers, doctors, or scientists:** Peter Hessler, "Brothers Keepers," *New Yorker,* Dec. 24 & 31, 2012.

85 **"Something happened from the inside":** For Morsi's conspiracy-theory comments about the 9/11 attacks, see Shadi Hamid, "Brother Number One," *Foreign Policy,* June 7, 2012, foreignpolicy.com/2012/06/07/brother-number-one/.

85 **"killers and vampires":** For Morsi's comments on Israel, and on restricting the Egyptian presidency to Muslim men, see David D. Kirkpatrick, "The New Islamists," *New York Times,* April 23, 2012.

87 **"This stems from belief":** Richard Stengel, Bobby Ghosh, and Karl Vick, "*Time*'s Interview with Egyptian President Mohamed Morsi," *Time,* Nov. 28, 2012, world.time.com/2012/11/28/transcript-times-interview-with-egyptian-president-mohamed-morsi/.

92 **"a role model":** David D. Kirkpatrick, "Egyptian Is Counting on Worries of Elites," *New York Times,* May 27, 2012, www.newyorktimes.com/2012/05/28/world/middleeast/ahmed-shafik-counting-on-egyptian-elites-fears.html.

95 **"We were worried":** I interviewed Dr. Nussaiba Ashraf on June 24, 2012.

PART TWO: THE COUP

99 **"To whom shall I speak today?":** This poem is also known as "Dialogue of a Man and His Ba." I have used the translation by Jan Assmann. See *Self, Soul, and Body in Religious Experience,* ed. Albert I. Baumgarten, Jan Assmann, and Guy G. Stroumsa (Boston: Brill, 1998), 395.

Chapter 7

101 **About a thousand people gathered:** Most material about the Abydos protests is from my interviews with residents and officials. There is also a short video on YouTube of the demonstration: www.youtube.com/watch?v=kOJE16hJIIs.

104 **"It's not our past":** From my interview with Adams on March 27, 2012.

106 **the Egyptian pharaonic state lasted:** Wilkinson, *Rise and Fall of Ancient Egypt,* 10.

106 **"But rational knowledge":** Kemp, *Ancient Egypt,* 5.

109 **"I gave bread to the hungry":** Shaw, *The Oxford History of Ancient Egypt,* 118.

110 **"The evidence suggests that local society":** From my conversation with Matthew Adams on Feb. 28, 2013.

111 **Arthur Weigall described villagers:** Arthur Weigall, *The Life and Times of Akhnaton: Pharaoh of Egypt* (London: Thornton Butterworth, 1922), 36–37.

Chapter 8

113 **"Madame Heba," he said:** I have changed the names of the residents whose garbage was discussed by Sayyid.

114 **migrants arrived from Dakhla:** Wael Fahmi and Keith Sutton, "Cairo's Contested Garbage: Sustainable Solid Waste Management and the Zabaleen's Right to the City," *Sustainability* 2, no. 6 (2010): 1767–68.

115 **In 1950, the population of Greater Cairo:** For the definition of Greater Cairo, I am following the work of David Sims, who in turn follows the study area that was defined by the Japan International Cooperation Agency. This definition includes Giza and Shoubra al-Khayma and the desert cities that surround the capital. For the 1950 population and subsequent growth, see David Sims, *Understanding Cairo: The Logic of a City out of Control* (Cairo: American University in Cairo Press, 2012), 45.

115 **"Over the course of five decades":** Wael Salah Fahmi and Keith Sutton, "Cairo's Zabaleen Garbage Recyclers: Multi-nationals' Takeover and State Relocation Plans," *Habitat International* 30, no. 4 (2006): 820.

115 **slaughter of all Egyptian pigs:** Fahmi and Sutton, "Cairo's Contested Garbage," 1773.

116 **"Cleanliness comes from faith":** Morsi made these comments about waste disposal in an interview with the radio station Al-Bernamag al-'Am, on July 23, 2012, https://www.youtube.com/watch?v=b1G-m80jF8A.

120 **five billion tramadol pills in Egypt:** Peter Schwartzstein, "Egypt's New Drug Addiction," *Daily Beast,* July 18, 2015, www.thedailybeast.com/egypts-new-drug-addiction.

121 **two-thirds of the people in Greater Cairo:** Sims, *Understanding Cairo,* 3.

121 **"a token exodus into the desert":** Ibid., 74–75.

121 **only 800,000 people had settled:** Ibid., 83.

122 **"Cairo provides better cheap housing":** I met with David Sims in Zamalek on Nov. 20, 2013.

122 **more than three-quarters of the residents:** Ibid., 228.

123 **"In a way it seems that government planners":** Ibid., 89.

Chapter 9

132 **"an authentically Egyptian woman":** Yasser Rizk, "Al-Sisi fi al-Goz' al-Thany min Hewaroh: Enfagart fi al-Shater 'Entom 'Ayzeen ya Tohkomuna ya Timawwituna," *Al-Masry al-Youm,* Oct. 8, 2013, www.almasryalyoum.com/news/details/326660.

132 **wife remove her *hijab*:** Shima' Galhoun, "Al-Watan fi Masqat Ra's al-Sisi . . . Hona al-Gamaleyyah Masna' al-Rigal," *Al-Watan,* Aug. 24, 2013, www.elwatannews.com/news/details/278834.

133 **"Democracy in the Middle East":** Brigadier General Abdelfattah Said ElSisi, "Democracy in the Middle East," U.S Army War College, March 15, 2006, www.documentcloud.org/documents/1173610-sisi.html.

136 **grandson of an African slave:** Lawrence Wright, *Thirteen Days in September* (London: Oneworld, 2014), 10.

136 **"I admire you":** Ibid., 13.

136 **the American intelligence community:** Ibid., 20.

136 **arrested many of Nasser's corrupt friends:** Ibid.

137 **sentenced to prison terms:** William E. Farrell, "5 in Sadat Trial Sentenced to Die; 17 Others Convicted and 2 Cleared," *New York Times,* March 7, 1982, www.nytimes.com/1982/03/07/world/5-in-sadat-trial-sentenced-to-die-17-other-convicted-and-2-cleared.html.

138 **helped supply working weapons:** Ahmed al-Khateeb, "Efrag Amni 'an awwal Kiyadi fi Tanzeem al-Gehad ba'd Eghlak Malaff al-Gama'ah al-Islamiyyah," *Al-Masry al-Youm,* Nov. 12, 2006, today.almasryalyoum.com/article2.aspx?ArticleID=40540.

139 **Another Egyptian journalist:** Abdou Monem, a journalist who was imprisoned in the Tora Prison, met Bayoumi there. On Monem's blog, he described Bayoumi and his planned postcoup role as a bicycle messenger. Abdou Monem, "Ba'd 25 Sana Sign . . . Al-Efrag 'an Abu Basira," Dec. 11, 2006, afkarmonem.blogspot.com/2006/12/25.html.

145 **at a rate of 73 percent or higher:** Morsi won by 882,751 votes. If the police and army had voted and opposed him at a rate of 73 percent, he would have lost by more than 37,000 votes. For the estimated number of officers at this time, see Peter Hessler, "Big Brothers," *New Yorker,* Jan. 14, 2013, 28.

146 **detained innocent bystanders:** David D. Kirkpatrick, "Morsi's Opponents Describe Abuse by President's Allies," *New York Times,* Dec. 11, 2012.

146 **Amr Darrag, a Brotherhood:** I spoke with Walid el-Bedry on December 9, 2012, and with Amr Darrag on December 31, 2012.

147 **I went to the Presidential Palace:** I observed these events on the evening of December 7, 2012.

150 **"The defense minister should be asked":** "Brotherhood Refused Meeting with Defense Minister, Sources Say," *Al-Masry al-Youm,* Dec. 14, 2012, www.egyptindependent.com/brotherhood-refused-meeting-defense-minister-sources-say/.

150 **"It gives a broad space":** I met with Gaber Gad Nassar on December 11, 2012.

Chapter 10

154 **"The Egyptians avoid following":** Ahmed Abdel-Hamid Youssef, *From Pharaoh's Lips: Ancient Egyptian Language in the Arabic of Today* (Cairo: American University in Cairo Press, 2003), 5.

155 **"language became a binding factor":** Kees Versteegh, *The Arabic Language* (Edinburgh: Edinburgh University Press, 2008), 93.

155 **language of administration switched to Arabic:** Thompson, *History of Egypt,* 169.

155 **a bishop named Severus:** Versteegh, *Arabic Language,* 95.

156 **called themselves *arabizantes*:** Ibid., 2.

156 **"retina" and "cornea":** Ibid., 228.

156 **The first Western analysis of Arabic:** Ibid., 2.

159 **They sought out Bedouins:** Ibid., 50.

159 **Some Bedouins even set up camps:** Marie Andrée Gouttenoire, "Représentations et écritures du voyage au désert des lexicographes et grammairiens en langue arabe de l'espace iraqien des II/VIIIe et III/IXe siècles" (Ph.D. diss., University of Aix-Marseille, 2010).

159 **"They speak according to their desert nature":** Versteegh, *Arabic Language,* 63.

160 **"side by side":** Charles A. Ferguson, "The Arabic Koine," *Language* 35, no. 4 (Oct.–Dec. 1959): 616.

160 **"It will not be long":** Niloofar Haeri, *Sacred Language, Ordinary People: Dilemmas of Culture and Politics in Egypt* (New York: Palgrave Macmillan, 2003), 83.

161 **New terms were coined:** Versteegh, *Arabic Language,* 180–83.

161 **When the president delivered public speeches:** Haeri, *Sacred Language, Ordinary People,* 93.

162 **he met secretly with leaders of the Muslim Brotherhood:** For Nasser's relationship with the Brotherhood, see Calvert, *Sayyid Qutb and the Origins of Radical Islamism,* 180–95.

165 **about 40 percent of occupied units:** For rent control in Greater Cairo proper, see Sims, *Understanding Cairo,* 147.

165 **Nasser strengthened this policy:** Ibid., 146.

Chapter 11

168 **It was the end of April:** My observation of the Balyana district office was on April 23, 2013.

172 **"the most troublesome people":** For Petrie's comments on the Quftis, see Wilkinson, *Nile,* 147–48.

173 **Yehia Abdel-Azim Mukhaimer:** I met with the Morsi-appointed governor of Sohag on April 22, 2013.

174 **"We have a presence":** I interviewed Youssef el-Sharif in the Sohag office of the Freedom and Justice Party on April 22, 2013.

174 **Ayman Abdel Hamid:** I visited the Balyana office of the Muslim Brotherhood, and spoke with Hamid about membership figures for the Brotherhood, on April 22, 2013. On that day, Hamid said the district had 150 Brothers. Seven hundred people had joined the Freedom and Justice Party (which did not involve joining the Brotherhood).

175 **Chief Mouth of the Country:** Christina Hanus, "Before and After Amarna: The Beginnings and Consequences of the Cult of the Aten," in *In the Light of Amarna: 100 Years of the Nefertiti Discovery,* ed. Friederike Seyfried (Berlin: Staatliche Museen zu Berlin, 2012), 37.

175 **Royal Seal-Bearer:** Wilkinson, *Rise and Fall of Ancient Egypt,* 112.

175 **a vizier named Khentika:** Ibid., 99.

175 **more than eighty titles:** This official was Qenamun, who served under Amenhotep II, during the Eighteenth Dynasty. See ibid., 251.

176 **"As you desire to see me":** All quotations are from Vincent A. Tobin, "The Tale of the Eloquent Peasant," in *The Literature of Ancient Egypt: An Anthology of Stories, Instructions, Stelae, Autobiographies, and Poetry,* ed. William Kelly Simpson (Cairo: American University in Cairo Press, 2003), 25–44.

177 **together we visited Michael Jones:** I met with Adams and Jones in Cairo on March 19, 2013.

Chapter 12

181 **liquor store on 26th July Street:** I observed the scene at Drinkies on the evening of December 9, 2012.

184 **"Due to the heavy smell":** The school sent out the email on January 28, 2013.

184 **dimming the lights:** "Cairo Airport Turns Lights Down, Airlines Change Schedules," *Egypt Independent,* April 3, 2013, www.egyptindependent.com/cairo-airport-turns-lights-down-airlines-change-schedules/.

185 **Tamarrod national headquarters:** I visited the headquarters on June 24, 2013.

187 **Morsi gave a televised speech:** All quotations are from the Atlantic Council's translation of Morsi's June 26, 2013, address to the nation: www.atlanticcouncil.org/blogs/menasource/translation-president-mohamed-morsi-s-address-to-the-nation.

188 **"We all agree, brothers":** David D. Kirkpatrick, "Egypt, Its Streets a Tinderbox, Braces for a Spark," *New York Times,* June 29, 2013, www.nytimes.com/2013/06/30/world/middleeast/egypt-its-streets-a-tinderbox-braces-for-a-spark.html.

191 **"participation in politics":** Samuel P. Huntington, *Political Order in Changing Societies* (New Haven, Conn.: Yale University Press, 2006), 2.

192 **"Each social force":** Ibid., 88.

192 **Mohamed Kadry Said:** I met with the retired major general on July 2, 2013.

192 **military agents had infiltrated:** For background on outside support of Tamarrod, see Neil Ketchley, "How Egypt's Generals Used Street Protests to Stage a Coup," *Washington Post,* July 3, 2017, www.washingtonpost.com/news/monkey-cage/wp/2017/07/03/how-egypts-generals-used-street-protests-to-stage-a-coup/?utm_term=.96e17643c64b.

194 **"The people empowered me":** David D. Kirkpatrick and Ben Hubbard, "Morsi Defies Egypt Army's Ultimatum to Bend to Protest," *New York Times,* July 2, 2013.

195 **terrorist dummy bomb:** "Improvised Bomb Defused in Cairo's Zamalek," *Ahram Online,* Jan. 21, 2014.

196 **"Our chemistry was very good":** I interviewed Chuck Hagel on Dec. 15, 2015.

196 **"I can't tell you that I recall":** I spoke with Panetta by telephone on March 8, 2016.

196 **"The term 'Muslim Brotherhood'":** Kessler, "Truth About Egypt's Revolution."

198 **"The degree of tribal division":** Jeffrey Goldberg, "The Obama Doctrine," *Atlantic Monthly,* April 2016, www.theatlantic.com/magazine/archive/2016/04/the-obama-doctrine/471525/.

Chapter 13

204 **Sayyid's sister Leila:** Sayyid's sister asked me not to use her real name. I also changed the name of her daughter.

214 **90 percent of Egyptian women:** Ministry of Health and Population, "Egypt Health Issues Survey 2015," Oct. 2015, dhsprogram.com/pubs/pdf/FR313/FR313.pdf.

216 **an African tribal custom:** Geneive Abdo, *No God but God: Egypt and the Triumph of Islam* (London: Oxford University Press, 2000), 55–59.

216 **more than two-thirds of the population:** Sims, *Understanding Cairo,* 29.

217 **between 25 and 40 percent of all workers:** Ibid., 218.

Chapter 14

219 **more than a thousand people died:** "All According to Plan: The Rab'a Massacre and Mass Killings of Protesters in Egypt," Human Rights Watch, Aug. 12, 2014, www.hrw

.org/report/2014/08/12/all-according-plan/raba-massacre-and-mass-killings -protesters-egypt.

220 **police panicked and opened fire:** The Delta shooting of the journalists occurred in Beheira on August 19, 2013. See Aya Batrawy, "Egyptian Reporter Killed at Checkpoint," Associated Press, Aug. 20, 2013, www.apnews.com/b72146ca863344808fe5d3270a07676b.

222 **he had warned Sisi to control:** I met with Hagel on December 15, 2015.

224 **alleging that the United States had conspired:** Jonathan S. Landay, "In Egypt, the Press Turns Yellow as It Takes on Opponents of Military Takeover," McClatchy, Aug. 30, 2013, www.mcclatchydc.com/news/nation-world/national/article24755116.html.

225 **"It was Obama":** I met with Governor Zeyada on April 10, 2014.

228 **small city of Mallawi:** I made my first trip to the Mallawi Museum on March 20, 2014.

PART THREE: THE PRESIDENT

237 **"The words that men say":** Hornung, *Conceptions of God in Ancient Egypt,* 211.

Chapter 15

240 **"Monday—Walked six hours":** Sahar Abdel-Hakim and Deborah Manley, eds., *Traveling Through the Deserts of Egypt: From 450 BC to the Twentieth Century* (Cairo: American University in Cairo Press, 2009), 10.

240 **"It is not the heat":** Ibid.

240 **"There is something grand":** Ibid., 1.

240 **"the cleanliness of a country":** Ibid., 18.

241 **"The desert is the breathing-space":** Ibid., 212.

241 **Paul became the first Christian hermit:** Shaw, *Oxford History of Ancient Egypt,* 431.

241 **"Behold, it is a pharaoh":** Dominic Montserrat, *Akhenaten: History, Fantasy, and Ancient Egypt* (London: Routledge, 2003), 19.

241 **"It says much about":** Wilkinson, *Nile,* 197.

242 **"The entire land performs":** All quotations from the Hymn to the Aten are from William Kelly Simpson, "The Hymn to the Aten," in Simpson, *Literature of Ancient Egypt,* 278–83.

242 **"It is an overwhelming site":** Montserrat, *Akhenaten,* 68.

242 **"The danger of being":** Kemp, *City of Akhenaten and Nefertiti,* 121.

243 **Barry Kemp had found a piece:** Kemp found the statue fragment on April 6, 2014.

245 **"*individual* in human history":** Montserrat, *Akhenaten,* 3. All the references to interpretations of Akhenaten in this paragraph come from Montserrat's book.

245 **"If I were a millionaire":** Ibid., 94.

245 **"a sign rather than a person":** Ibid., 1.

245 **adopt key innovations:** Peter Hessler, "Meet King Tut's Father, Egypt's First Revolutionary," *National Geographic,* May 2017, www.nationalgeographic.com/magazine/2017/05/akhenaten-revolutionary-egypt-king/.

246 **three successive generations:** Wilkinson, *Rise and Fall of Ancient Egypt,* 222.

246 **"I shall give to you":** Shaw, *Oxford History of Ancient Egypt,* 247.

247 **"Why should my messengers":** Wilkinson, *Rise and Fall of Ancient Egypt,* 297.

247 **"He tried to be as ancient":** I met with Bayer in Hildesheim, Germany, on June 10, 2014.

247 **"Akhenaten appears to represent":** Kemp, *City of Akhenaten and Nefertiti,* 17.

248 **"Akhenaten's kingship provides":** Kemp, *Ancient Egypt,* 217.

249 **groups that felt marginalized:** Montserrat, *Akhenaten,* 2.
250 **"They're four thousand miles apart":** From my interview with Johnson on April 2, 2014.
250 **"sometimes painful truthfulness":** W. Raymond Johnson, "Amenhotep III and Amarna: Some New Considerations," *Journal of Egyptian Archaeology* 82 (1996): 78.
250 **"This preoccupation with the present":** Johnson, "Setting," 47.
251 **"Everybody likes revolutionaries":** I met Marsha Hill at Amarna on April 6, 2014.
252 **"a chance bivouac":** Montserrat, *Akhenaten,* 49.
253 **"Amarna seems like the antithesis":** Kemp, *City of Akhenaten and Nefertiti,* 161.
253 **an "urban village":** Ibid., 299.
253 **"This kind of plan":** Ibid., 168.
253 **"What you see in the modern slum":** I spoke with Erickson by telephone on October 17, 2014.
256 **"The building itself":** My conversation with Seyfried was on June 10, 2014.

Chapter 16

258 **"I'm one of the people":** The audio recording of Sisi speaking with Yasser Rizk was posted on December 11, 2013, and can be found here: www.youtube.com/watch?v=ryTnDOGWEbQ.
259 **Exactly four months and a day:** I attended the first day of Morsi's trial on November 4, 2013. See Peter Hessler, "Morsi's Chaotic Day in Court," *New Yorker,* Nov. 6, 2013, www.newyorker.com/news/news-desk/morsis-chaotic-day-in-court.
264 **"If I run, then it must be":** David D. Kirkpatrick, "Presidential Run Likely for Egypt's Top General," *New York Times,* Jan. 11, 2014, www.nytimes.com/2014/01/12/world/middleeast/egypt.html.
264 **"Egypt is the gift of the Nile":** For the 2014 constitution, see www.sis.gov.eg/Newvr/Dustor-en001.pdf.
264 **"the timeless Nile":** For the 2012 constitution, see www.ilo.org/dyn/natlex/docs/ELECTRONIC/91655/106411/F-196699313/Egypt.pdf.
265 **98 percent of the voters:** Peter Hessler, "If Everyone Votes Yes, Is It Democracy?," *New Yorker,* Jan. 17, 2014, www.newyorker.com/news/news-desk/if-everyone-votes-yes-is-it-democracy.
271 **more than sixty people died:** Sarah Saleeb, "January 25, 2014: A Recap," Atlantic Council, Jan. 27, 2014, www.atlanticcouncil.org/blogs/menasource/january-25-2014-a-recap.
272 **Morsi's second court appearance:** I attended Morsi's second court appearance on January 28, 2014.
272 **"Any attempt to turn":** I met with Beltagy on December 30, 2011.
273 **Like many tragic public events:** For video of the shooting of Asmaa el-Beltagy, see www.youtube.com/watch?v=r8ZHxy7kfs8.
273 **Asmaa died on an operating table:** Peter Hessler, "The Revolution on Trial," *New Yorker,* March 10, 2014, 28.
274 **"We have been underground":** I interviewed Mansour on Nov. 27, 2011.
274 **I had met Saleh:** I interviewed Saleh on March 18, 2012.
274 **I had trouble recognizing:** I interviewed Bayoumi on March 26, 2012.
274 **"Yes, we do want":** I observed Hegazy at a rally for Morsi's presidential campaign, in Ismailia, on the evening of May 11, 2012.
274 **eight hundred members:** For details on the charges regarding the prison break, and Beltagy's comments in court, see Hessler, "Revolution on Trial," 29.

Chapter 17

285 **unorthodox applications of the law:** Christine Hegel-Cantarella, "Kin-to-Be: Betrothals, Legal Documents, and Reconfiguring Relational Obligations in Egypt," *Law, Culture, and the Humanities* 7, no. 3 (2011): 1–17.

Chapter 18

289 **China-Egypt Trade Association:** I met with Chen at the trade association on March 22, 2015.

290 **Valentine's Day at the store:** I observed sales in the Asyut shop on February 14, 2015.

300 **"They were husband and wife":** Peter Hessler, *River Town: Two Years on the Yangtze* (New York: HarperCollins, 2001), 152.

Chapter 20

310 **"You said you want orders":** For Shabola's song, see www.youtube.com/watch?v=TRXQvxa6UBs.

310 **"People are walking around":** The video recording of Sisi's comments about mobile phone use appeared on October 2, 2013. See www.youtube.com/watch?v=mrZuGj2KySY.

310 **"You are like the very older brother":** From an audio recording that was leaked on November 29, 2013: www.youtube.com/watch?v=snbNniTSqrQ.

310 **"Are you going to endure":** From an audio recording leaked on January 27, 2014: www.youtube.com/watch?v=0uVKra-pzxU.

312 **"We don't have a situation":** I visited Hamama and the Sisi family shops in Khan al-Khalili on June 16, 2016.

313 **Kingsley's article revealed:** Patrick Kingsley, "How Did 37 Prisoners Come to Die at Cairo Prison Abu Zaabal?," *Guardian,* Feb. 22, 2014, www.theguardian.com/world/2014/feb/22/cairo-prison-abu-zabaal-deaths-37-prisoners.

315 **more than 95 percent:** Patrick Kingsley, "Egypt's Tourism Revenues Fall After Political Upheavals," *Guardian,* Aug. 29, 2014, www.theguardian.com/world/2014/aug/29/egypt-tourism-revenue-falls-95-percent.

315 **"How Egypt rejoices":** Wilkinson, *Rise and Fall of Ancient Egypt,* 174.

316 **Wegner had been excavating:** My first visit to Wegner's excavation was December 11, 2013.

318 **"A will-of-the-wisp":** "Background: South Tombs Cemetery," Amarna Project website, amarnaproject.com/pages/recent_projects/excavation/south_tombs_cemetery/.

319 **the spring of the presidential election:** I visited the excavating and analysis teams at Amarna in March, April, and May 2014.

319 **at least 440 Amarna residents:** Hessler, "Meet King Tut's Father." These statistics were updated in an email exchange with Kemp in November 2018.

320 **Of the 135 bodies:** Ibid.

321 **to visit polling stations:** I visited Minya polling stations on May 26, 2014.

323 **only 5.7 percent of the population:** Peter Hessler, "Living-Room Democracy," *New Yorker,* March 7, 2016, 32.

323 **"As for the age profile":** Kemp emailed me these comments on March 5, 2016.

Chapter 21

325 **eleven attempts to cross:** Patrick Kingsley, "Desperate Syrian Refugees Risk All in Bid to Reach Europe," *Guardian,* Sept. 18, 2014, www.theguardian.com/global-development/2014/sep/18/desperate-syrian-refugees-europe-mediterranean.

330 **Egyptian primary schools 141st:** Klaus Schwab, "The Global Competitiveness Report 2014–2015," World Economic Forum, 452.

331 ***"The weather in Egypt":*** The Egyptian social studies textbook was published by the Ministry of Education, and appears in two parts. These initial references are all from part 1. Yehya Teyyah Soleiman, Magdy Abdel Hamid al-Sersy, Salah al-Din Arafa Mahmoud, and Samier Mostafa Soleiman, *Balady Masr: al-darasat al-igtma'yah,* 1 (Cairo: Wizarat al-Tarbiyah w' al-Ta'lim, 2015–2016), 11.

331 ***"One-third of the world's monuments":*** Ibid., 12.

331 **"Ashwa'iyat *are places":*** Ibid., 27.

331 **"Whoever has no history":** Ibid., 5.

331 **"Sadat was named the hero":** This reference is from part 2. Yehya Teyyah Soleiman, Magdy Abdel Hamid al-Sersy, Salah al-Din Arafa Mahmoud, and Samier Mostafa Soleiman, *Balady Masr: al-darasat al-igtma'yah,* 2 (Cairo: Wizarat al-Tarbiyah w' al-Ta'lim, 2015–2016), 32.

Chapter 22

334 **The *rayis* of New Minya:** I visited New Minya on May 24, 2014.

335 **The New Urban Communities Authority:** I visited NUCA and Khaled Mahmoud Abbas on May 22, 2014.

335 **increased by more than 15 percent:** *Egypt Demographic and Health Survey 2014,* Ministry of Health and Population, 43–45, egypt.unfpa.org/sites/default/files/pub-pdf/0e0409a0-7af6-46d5-a346-7a7d9aeb12c6.pdf.

336 **Sisi's new capital city:** Shady Bushra and Yara Bayoumy, "Egypt's New Capital: President al-Sisi's $300 Billion Plan to Beat Cairo Traffic," *Independent,* March 19, 2015, www.independent.co.uk/news/world/middle-east/egypts-new-capital-president-al-sisis-300-billion-plan-to-beat-cairo-traffic-10120211.html.

336 **China-Egypt Suez Economic and Trade Cooperation Zone:** I visited the Chinese development zone repeatedly from 2013 to 2016. See Peter Hessler, "Learning to Speak Lingerie," *New Yorker,* Aug. 10 & 17, 2015, 56–65.

339 **perhaps a million Chinese:** Howard W. French, *China's Second Continent: How a Million Migrants Are Building a New Empire in Africa* (New York: Vintage Books, 2015), 13.

345 **One spring weekend:** I attended the test run of the TEDA amusement parks on March 27, 2015.

Chapter 23

348 **"This is human heritage":** I interviewed Eldamaty in Luxor on Feb. 3, 2018.

348 **"I think this is part of our legacy":** I spoke with Bestock by telephone on Nov. 7, 2018.

357 **a comedian named Ade Imam:** For Haeri's analysis of who can say things in Egyptian Arabic in print, see her *Sacred Language, Ordinary People,* 99–103.

357 **"The ideal shape":** Sisi spoke at a roundtable discussion at the Presidential Palace on April 13, 2016. See www.youtube.com/watch?v=V-zbojIGRc8&t=1s.

357 **"Idealism exists in books":** Ahmed Samy Metwally and Shady Abdallah Zalatah, "Fi Liqa' ma' Momatheleyy mokhtalaf Fe'at al-Mogtama'a," *Al-Ahram,* April 14, 2016, http://www.ahram.org.eg/News/151874/136/497857/متابعات/فى-لقاء-مع-ممثلى-مختلف-فئات-المجتمعالسيسى-لم-أخذلك.aspx.

358 **"The majority of Arab children":** I interviewed Haeri by telephone on Feb. 6, 2017.

359 **"In all of Egypt":** Leila Ahmed, *A Border Passage: From Cairo to America—a Woman's Journey* (New York: Penguin, 2000), 282–83.

359 **"You're an Arab!":** Ibid., 243.

359 **"Reading Ahmed's pathetic tirade":** Edward Said, "Living in Arabic," *Al-Ahram Weekly,* Feb. 12–18, 2004.

359 **women are less likely than men:** For a discussion of the tendency of women Arabic speakers to use *fusha* less than men do, see Reem Bassiouney, "Identity and Code-Choice in the Speech of Educated Women and Men in Egypt: Evidence from Talk Shows," in *Arabic and the Media: Linguistic Analyses and Applications,* ed. Reem Bassiouney (Leiden: Koninklijke Brill NV, 2010), 97–99.

359 **"They said, 'You should not be studying'":** I interviewed Doss in Zamalek on Nov. 28, 2016.

Chapter 24

364 **"How much time do you have?":** From my conversation with Yusuf on June 2, 2014.

365 **Wegner's team excavated:** I observed Wegner's team excavating on May 31, June 1, and June 4, 2014.

365 **images of Nile boats:** For information about Wegner's excavation, see Josef Wegner, "A Royal Boat Burial and Watercraft Tableau of Egypt's 12th Dynasty (c. 1850 BCE) at South Abydos," *International Journal of Nautical Archaeology* 46, no. 1 (2017): 5–30.

366 **while he campaigned:** I observed Rafat's campaign on the evening of October 3, 2015.

369 **"They had an electoral system":** I met with Nielsen on November 21, 2015. For background on Nielsen's research in Aswan, see Hans Christian Korsholm Nielsen, "Adapting to Change: Tribal Influence on the 2011–2012 Parliamentary Elections in Aswan Governorate," in *The Political Economy of the New Egyptian Republic,* ed. Nicholas S. Hopkins (Cairo: American University in Cairo Press, 2015), 112–33.

372 **When I visited Mahmoud's *dawar*:** My first visit to Mahmoud's *dawar* was on October 4, 2015.

373 **pharaoh named Senebkay:** Wegner's team discovered Senebkay in January 2014. See Nick Romeo, "Pharaoh of 'Lost Dynasty' Died Brutal Death, Forensic Study Reveals," *National Geographic,* March 3, 2015, news.nationalgeographic.com/news/2015/03/150303-pharaoh-senebkay-forensic-skeleton-abydos-egypt-archaeology/.

373 **"It might officially be":** I visited Senebkay's tomb with Wegner on January 4, 2016.

375 **"The Brotherhood thought they could":** I met with Wajih on September 27, 2015.

376 **"That was the crowd":** Hamid spoke with me, and gave more accurate figures of local Brotherhood members, on June 25, 2015.

378 **their own election traditions:** Hessler, "Living-Room Democracy," 30–35.

379 **"I'd like to meet the candidate":** I interviewed Nora Abdel Mohammed on Oct. 26, 2015.

379 **"We've had Egyptian sovereignty":** I met Steit in his *dawar* on October 26, 2015.

383 **after the polls closed:** The voting in Balyana took place on October 27–28, 2015. I observed Yusuf's *dawar* on the evening of the twenty-eighth.

384 **"So far, for seventeen months":** I met Yazal on November 4, 2015.

384 **"He had the ability":** Calvert, *Sayyid Qutb and the Origins of Radical Islamism,* 115.

Chapter 25

390 **his body was discovered:** For a detailed account of the death of Regeni, see Alexander Stille, "Who Murdered Giulio Regeni?," *Guardian,* Oct. 4, 2016, www.theguardian.com/world/2016/oct/04/egypt-murder-giulio-regeni.

391 **"Don't listen to anybody's words":** Sisi's speech was delivered on February 24, 2016. See Peter Hessler, "The Shadow General," *New Yorker,* Jan. 2, 2017, 52.

391 **"I think the President no longer communicates":** Ibid.

391 **"Every day, it's not only Regeni":** I met with Sadat on May 3, 2016. In August of that year, Sadat resigned from the parliament's human rights committee, citing a lack of cooperation by the government.

393 **the Italian was gay:** For the false theories that Regeni was gay, see Stille, "Who Murdered Giulio Regeni?"

Chapter 26

396 **"From your description":** I received an initial email from Bivas on May 6, 2018. We corresponded with multiple emails and phone calls through the rest of 2018.

399 **more than 1.5 million:** From German government statistics, see www.destatis.de/EN/FactsFigures/SocietyState/Population/MigrationIntegration/Tables_ProtectionSeekers/TablesMigrationStructureDemographicDataPersonsSeekingProtectionYear.html;jsessionid=01FAC3B96BD23B0D07693896FFAF4A1D.InternetLive1.

404 **advised by a number of former Nazi officials:** "The Plight of the Jews in Egypt," American Jewish Committee, March 1957, 6–12.

410 **six Jews left:** "Egypt's Jewish Community Diminished to 6 Women After Death of Lucy Saul," *Egypt Independent,* July 30, 2016.

410 **Manu was granted asylum:** Manu received asylum on March 7, 2017.

410 **Dirk Siegfried, a lawyer in Berlin:** I met with Siegfried on August 22, 2018.

410 **Felix Coeln, a resident of Cologne:** I met with Coeln on August 25, 2018.

411 **Marlen Vahle was a recent college graduate:** I met with Vahle on August 27, 2018.

412 **"Adieu my old home":** Léon Bassan's unpublished poem was written in Zamalek on May 14, 1959. Albert Bivas has translated it from the original French.

Chapter 27

417 **tomb of Senwosret III:** My final visit to Wegner's project was June 12–14, 2016.

419 **"The Brotherhood experience":** Rifaat Mohammed Ahmed, the parliament's shoeshine man, was featured in an article about the new assembly. See Ahmed Ahly, "'Am Rifaat' maseh ahdhyat al-Barlaman: Atef Sedky bayan al-Hokumah hafyan bsaby," *Al-Masry al-Youm,* Oct. 4, 2016, www.masrawy.com/news/news_reports/details/2016/10/4/947545/-ع-م-رفعت-ماسح-أحذية-البرلمان-عاطف-صدقي-ألقى-بيان-الحكومة-حافي-ا-بسببي-حوار-.

422 **the number of Chinese tourists:** "Tourism Revives as More Chinese Tourists Flock to Egypt," *Xinhua,* April 19, 2016, www.chinadaily.com.cn/business/2016-04/19/content_24659851.htm.

424 **Chinese-funded archaeologists began to excavate:** Nevine El-Aref, "China Signs Its First MoU with Egypt in the Archaeology Field," *Al-Ahram,* Oct. 28, 2018, english.ahram.org.eg/NewsContent/9/40/315261/Heritage/Ancient-Egypt/China-signs-its-first-MoU-with-Egypt-in-the-archae.aspx.

426 **"Mr. Kästner has recently":** Joachim Becker, ed., *Orientierungskurs: Grundwissen Politik, Geschichte und Gesellschaft in Deutschland* (Berlin: Cornelsen, 2017), 13.

INDEX